Genealogist's Handbook for New England Research

Genealogist's Handbook for New England Research

5th edition

edited by
Michael J. Leclerc

New England Historic
Genealogical Society

ISBN-13: 978-0-88082-260-2
Library of Congress Control Number: 2011938218

Cover design by Carolyn Sheppard Oakley.
Cover image of Cape Neddick ("Nubble") Light, near York, Maine. Photo by Jeremy D'Entremont, *lighthouse.cc*.
Maps by Mapping Specialists, Inc., Fitchburg, Wisconsin.

Second printing June 2012 by Yurchak Printing, Landisville, Pennsylvania.

NEW ENGLAND HISTORIC GENEALOGICAL SOCIETY®
99–101 Newbury Street
Boston, Massachusetts 02116-3007

Contents

Preface

For more than three decades, the *Genealogist's Handbook for New England Research* has been the principal research guide for this area of the country. The first edition was published in 1980 by the New England Library Association. Marcia Wiswall Lindberg chaired the NELA Bibliography Committee, which put the book together. Members of the committee were Laura P. Abbott, Robert Charles Anderson, Duane E. Crabtree, David C. Dearborn, Joan S. Hayden, Thomas J. Kemp, Karen M. Light, and Denis J. Lesieur.

That first edition sold through six printings in four years. In 1984, NELA transferred the book's copyright to NEHGS. Marcia Wiswall Lindberg continued to work on the *Handbook*, editing the second edition in 1985, and the third edition in 1993. Marcia Melnyk, then an NEHGS staff member, took over as editor for the fourth edition in 1999.

The longevity of this book is a testament to its importance as a research tool. From the beginning, the *Handbook* was conceived as a guide to assist individuals researching their family history, not as a "how-to" book. For this edition, we started from the very foundation to create a new version. All information has been researched anew.

The world of genealogy has changed a great deal since the last edition of this book was published more than a decade ago. Information technology has vastly changed the way we research (and produce books), and this edition reflects many of those changes. Past editions of the book were updated by sending letters through the U.S. Postal Service and following up with hundreds of telephone calls. For this edition we conducted a great amount of research on websites, and sent emails instead of postal mail.

Among the key features of this edition:

- **An essay on each state** introduces each state chapter, giving information specific to researching that locality

- **Standardized information** in town tables across all states

- **Statewide maps showing county boundaries**

- **County maps showing town boundaries,** as well as towns in bordering counties. County seats are in boldface.

- **Illustrations** from the NEHGS collections

- **Lists of major repositories with significant regional or statewide collections.** Because descriptive information about these repositories and collections is readily available online, we have not included that information here. We also have not included information about local public libraries, for the same reason.

- **"Tabs" in the margin** to facilitate location of a particular section of the book

Read "Using This Book" on the following pages for a complete understanding of the new layout and information.

Acknowledgments

The fifth edition of the *Handbook* is the result of the work of many individuals over several years. Their experience and knowledge have contributed to another in a long line of valuable NEHGS guidebooks. From the very start, and throughout the process of creating this edition, genealogists on the NEHGS staff offered a great number of suggestions for updating the book, including Valerie Beaudrault; Sally Benny; Christopher Carter; Marie E. Daly; Mary Blauss Edwards; Henry B. Hoff, CG, FASG; Kyle Hurst; David Allen Lambert; Judith Lucey; Rhonda R. McClure; Julie Helen Otto; Natyra Pancsofar; and Timothy G.X. Salls.

Helen Herzer and Virginia Siggia helped to review and format the data. It is impossible for me to express the debt of gratitude I feel toward Jean Perkinson. She has worked diligently for more than a year, collecting and verifying contact information for land and probate repositories, and assisting with numerous lookups.

Much gratitude also is due to Scott Andrew Bartley; Christopher Child; David Curtis Dearborn, FASG; and Maureen Taylor for authoring introductory essays on researching in the states. Special thanks to Cherry Fletcher Bamberg, FASG, editor of *Rhode Island Roots,* and Nicholas Noyes of the Maine Historical Society for reviewing essays and providing valuable feedback. Jerome Anderson and Rhonda R. McClure provided important proofreading assistance.

The publications staff worked to create the new format and layout for this edition, identified and formatted images, proofed many versions of the text, and more. Many thanks to Lynn Betlock, Ginevra Morse, Jean Powers, Scott C. Steward, and Penny Stratton. A very special thanks to Carolyn Sheppard Oakley, who did such a wonderful job creating the layout for the book as well as designing the cover.

Michael J. Leclerc
Boston, February 2012

Using This Book

This edition of the *Genealogist's Handbook for New England Research* is different from earlier editions. We have standardized the information available for towns and counties so it is the same for every state. We have removed smaller libraries and repositories with limited collections. It is wise to check websites for the most up-to-date information about a repository. Contact the staff with any questions prior to visiting in person, and ask about closures for state or local holidays.

The first chapter of this book includes general information about researching and recordkeeping in New England. There is also a discussion of researching colonial-era ancestors. A list of major repositories that cover all of New England rounds out this section. Chapters follow on all six New England states. They each include the following elements:

Introductory Essay

Each profile starts with an introductory essay outlining research in that state. The profile provides general information about the state, followed by specific information concerning essential genealogical resources:

- Vital Records
- Church Records
- Probate Records
- Land Records
- Court Records
- Military Records

The essay concludes with information about other resources specific to that state, such as state censuses, state immigration records (as opposed to federal records), etc.

Statewide Information

Each introductory essay is followed by a map of the entire state with county boundaries marked and the shire towns for each county. Next, you will find a list of major repositories and organizations in the state, with contact information and a brief description. Among the types of repositories you will find, where available:

- State archives

- State library

- State judicial archives

- State historical society

- State genealogical society

- Major repositories with extensive collections of interest to genealogists

County Information

There follows a list of the counties for the state, with the date of county formation, parent counties, probate and deed districts, and any other particularly noteworthy information for the county. One example from Vermont is Washington County:

Name	Inc.	Parent(s)	Probate District(s)	Deed District(s)	Note
Washington	1810	Addison, Caledonia, Chittenden, and Orange	Washington	Towns	Called Jefferson to 1814.

After this table, the counties appear in alphabetical order with:

- A map of the county, with towns named, including towns in bordering counties

- The date of county formation

- Parent county/counties

- Daughter county/counties

- County seat

- List of towns in the county

Probate and Land

The next section lists all government agencies responsible for registration of probate and deeds. This varies from state to state. Some states register this information on the county level, some in districts, and some at the town level.

Cities, Towns, and Plantations

The final section contains information about cities and towns (and plantations in the state of Maine). For each state there is a table with:

- Current city/town/plantation name

- Date of grant/incorporation as a town

- Current county in which the town is located

- Parent town(s)

- Daughter town(s)

- Special notes for the town, such as date of settlement, date of original grant, name changes, etc.

- Information on vital records and church records available in published form, manuscript, typescript, or on *AmericanAncestors.org*.

Names bolded in the Parent column are the original parent towns. Names not bolded are towns from which land was later annexed. One example from Maine is the town of Alfred:

Town	Inc.	County	Parent	Daughter	Note	VR	CR
Alfred	1808	York	**Sanford,** Waterboro	Sanford	Created as district 1794.	D, P	

From this entry, you can see that Alfred was created as a district from the town of Sanford in 1794. It is located in York County. In 1808 it was ceded as a separate town. Part of the town of Waterboro was later annexed to Alfred, and a part of Alfred was later ceded back to Sanford. Using the key provided, users will see that the D in the vital records column indicates that Alfred was one of the towns to file pre-1892 delayed returns of birth, marriage, and death with the state, and the P indicates that a volume of vital records transcribed from the original town records has been published. No transcriptions of church records for Alfred are known to exist in published or manuscript form. A note about vital record and church record column information: the non-published material includes only the NEHGS collections. You might also find it helpful to consult the catalogs of state and local historical societies and the National Union Catalog of Manuscript Collections at *www.loc.gov*.

After the town table you will find special tables listing extinct towns, unincorporated (and most likely uninhabited) towns, and towns ceded to other states.

Maps

The maps in this book depict town, county, state, and, in some cases, country boundaries. They do not include inland waterways, and coastal regions in particular are roughly detailed.

About the Contributors

Scott Andrew Bartley is a genealogist, archivist, librarian, and editor specializing in Vermont, *Mayflower* lineages, and colonial New England. He was formerly manuscripts curator at the New England Historic Genealogical Society, and later librarian/archivist for the Massachusetts Society of *Mayflower* Descendants and editor of their journal, *Mayflower Descendant*. He now edits *Vermont Genealogy* (the journal of the Genealogical Society of Vermont), edits and researches for the Newbury Street Press, and is the editor/researcher of the forthcoming Isaac Allerton six-generation genealogy for the General Society of *Mayflower* Descendants. He also performs client research and is a content specialist for *FamilySearch.org*'s wiki for New England.

Lynn Betlock joined the NEHGS staff in 1995. Since 2003 she has been managing editor of *American Ancestors* (formerly *New England Ancestors*) magazine. She is also editor of the NEHGS enewsletter *The Weekly Genealogist*, and contributes to Society books and the Great Migration Study Project.

Christopher Challender Child joined the NEHGS staff in 1997 and currently serves as Genealogist of the Newbury Street Press (a publishing imprint of NEHGS). He has written for the *The New England Historical and Genealogical Register*, *American Ancestors* magazine, and *The Mayflower Descendant*, and lectures on a variety of genealogical topics, with a special focus on New England and New York research. He is co-editor of *The Ancestry of Catherine Middleton* (NEHGS, 2011) and co-compiler of *The Descendants of Judge John Lowell of Newburyport, Massachusetts* (Newbury Street Press, 2011).

David Curtis Dearborn joined the NEHGS staff in 1976 and serves as reference librarian. He is a consulting editor for the *Register* and a contributing editor of *The American Genealogist*, and has published articles in the *Register* and *American Ancestors* magazine, as well as other local and national genealogical publications. He is a fellow of the American Society of Genealogists and former president of the Massachusetts Genealogical Council. He is a frequent speaker at NEHGS educational programs, and at genealogical conferences around the country.

Michael J. Leclerc, an internationally recognized genealogist specializing in New England research, is Chief Genealogist at Mocavo. He was previously Director of Special Projects and editor of *The Weekly Genealogist* at NEHGS. He is a board member of the Association of Professional Genealogists, and was a board member and Vice-President of Administration for the Federation of Genealogical Societies. He has been featured in the *Boston Globe*, *New York Times*, and *Time* magazine, and has published articles in numerous scholarly journals and popular magazines. He has appeared on television shows and delivered educational presentations throughout North America and Europe.

Maureen Taylor is an expert on photo identification and photo preservation. Formerly Director of Library User Services at NEHGS, this Ocean State native also specializes in Rhode Island history and genealogy, and was director of the Rhode Island Historical Society library and president of the Rhode Island Genealogical Society. She is the author of several books on Rhode Island, including *Picturing Rhode Island* and *Runaways, Deserters, And Notorious Villains From Rhode Island Newspapers*. Her recent works include *Preserving Your Family Photographs, Fashionable Folks: Bonnets and Hats, 1840–1900,* and *The Last Muster: Images of the Revolutionary War Generation.*

New England

Lynn Betlock

New England—Connecticut, Maine, Massachusetts, New Hampshire, Rhode Island, and Vermont—provides special opportunities and challenges for those researching their ancestry. In many ways, New England is unique in the quantity and quality of records dating back to the earliest settlements.

Sources for Great Migration-Era Research

The Great Migration—the movement of about 20,000 men, women, and children from England to New England—occurred from 1620 to about 1643, beginning with the arrival of the *Mayflower* and ending with the English Civil War. When genealogical research began in earnest in the nineteenth century, these earliest settlers attracted a great deal of attention.

Several major comprehensive surveys of immigrants to New England were published in the late-nineteenth and early-twentieth centuries: Savage's *Genealogical Dictionary of the First Settlers of New England* (1860-1862); Austin's *Genealogical Dictionary of Rhode Island* (1887); Pope's *Pioneers of Massachusetts* (1900); and Noyes, Libby, and Davis's *Genealogical Dictionary of Maine and New Hampshire* (1928-1939). While these works continue to be valuable resources, more recent research had superseded much of their information by the end of the twentieth century.

In 1988, Robert Charles Anderson conceived the idea of the Great Migration Study Project, which would focus on creating comprehensive biographical and genealogical accounts of all early immigrants to New England. He sent a proposal to the New England Historic Genealogical Society, and an agreement was quickly reached. Two series of books have been published: *The Great Migration Begins: Immigrants to New England, 1620–1633* (3 vols.; 1995) and *The Great Migration: Immigrants to New England, 1634–1635* (7 vols.; 1999–2011), as well as the quarterly *Great Migration Newsletter* (20 vols. to date). These volumes, comprising approximately 2,200 individual sketches, should be the first source researchers consult for this time period.

Hundreds of primary and secondary sources were used to compile the *Great Migration* series, and citations are embedded within the sketches. In addition, Anderson's discussion of the sources themselves is extremely useful; see the first volume of the first series and each of the volumes in the second series for a sixteen-page section in the front matter (in print or online at *AmericanAncestors.org*) entitled "Sources." Anderson's discussion of the most important sources for the time period should be required reading for Great Migration-era researchers.

Another helpful essay by Robert Charles Anderson is "Colonial English Research,"

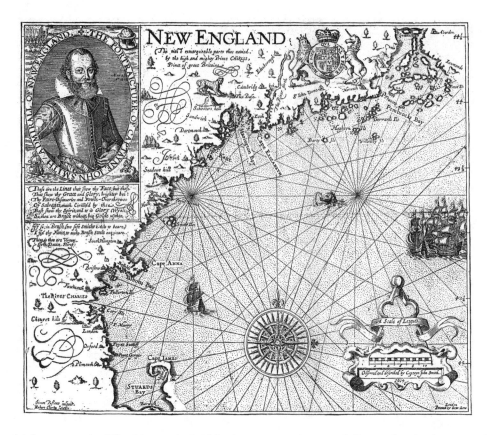

which appears in *The Source: A Guidebook to American Genealogy*, 3rd ed., edited by Loretto Dennis Szucs and Sandra Hargreaves Luebking (Provo, Utah: Ancestry, 2006), 679–97. The essay covers the New England colonies that existed independently prior to nationhood (Connecticut, Massachusetts, New Hampshire, and Rhode Island), as well as the other nine American colonies belonging to England. Anderson reminds genealogists researching the colonial period that "the process of building new institutions had a certain trial-and-error element to it. As a result, almost without exception, the earliest record books, whether generated by town, county, or colony, were an amalgamation of many different types of records entered together in the same volume, sometimes in no particular order. Researchers accustomed to records neatly separated into different books by record type need to be prepared to look for records in unlikely places."[1]

The following selection and description of early New England sources has been adapted primarily from Anderson's Sources section from the *Great Migration* series.

Passenger lists: Passenger lists generated in the seventeenth century are quite different from the more revealing documents created in the nineteenth century. No lists were created upon a ship's arrival in New England. The records that do survive are those created in England prior to a ship's departure, in Port Books and in Licenses to Pass Overseas. Unfortunately, relatively few of these records survive from the time of the Great

---

[1] Anderson, in *The Source,* 679.

Above: "Smith's Map of New England, 1614." John Fiske, *The Beginnings of New England* (1889), p. 83.

Migration. The best years for passenger lists are 1634 and 1635; even so, less than half of 1634 immigrants can be found on a passenger list. For 1635, the percentage is higher; an estimated two-thirds to three-quarters of immigrants are covered. The two most important and readily available volumes of existing passenger list compilations are John Camden Hotten, *The Original Lists of Persons of Quality* . . . (New York: 1880; rpt. Baltimore: Genealogical Publishing Company, 1962, 1968) and Peter Wilson Coldham, *The Complete Book of Emigrants: 1607–1660* (Baltimore: Genealogical Publishing Company, 1987).

Lists of Freemen: New England freemanship was primarily political in nature: freemen were allowed to vote for colony officers. In the most Puritan of the colonies—Massachusetts Bay and New Haven—church membership was a prerequisite for freemanship. Finding a person's name on a freeman list can establish residence at a date and place and, in the case of Massachusetts Bay and New Haven, determine prior church membership. The Sources section in the *Great Migration* volumes explains freemanship and freemen lists in more detail for each colony (Massachusetts Bay, Plymouth, Rhode Island, Connecticut, and New Haven).

Colony and Court Records: The separation of executive, legislative, and judicial powers had not yet occurred in early New England, and a colony's General Court could address a wide range of business. Some early colony records include lower-level court records. The lower court records for Essex County in Massachusetts Bay are particularly detailed and offer rich biographical information that cannot be found in other areas of New England.

Below is the bibliographic information for the printed volumes of records for Essex County and each of the New England colonies. Although Maine and New Hampshire were not separate jurisdictions during the Great Migration years and did not have colony status, some court records and official documents for those specific regions have been published and are included here.

Connecticut Colony: *The Public Records of the Colony of Connecticut, 1636–1776*, 15 vols. (Hartford: Case, Lockwood & Brainard, 1850–90). Also Helen Schatvet Ullmann, trans., *Colony of Connecticut Minutes of the Court of Assistants, 1669–1711* (Boston: NEHGS, 2009).

Essex County, Massachusetts Bay: *Records and Files of the Quarterly Courts of Essex County, Massachusetts, 1636–1686*, 9 vols. (Salem: Essex Institute, 1911–75).

Maine: *Province and Court Records of Maine*, 6 vols. (Portland: Maine Historical Society, 1928–75; rpt. vols. 1–3, Newburyport, Mass., 1991).

Massachusetts Bay Colony: Nathaniel B. Shurtleff, ed., *Records of the Governor and Company of the Massachusetts Bay in New England* (1628–86), 5 vols. in 6 (Boston: W. White, 1853–54).

New Hampshire: Nathaniel Boulton, ed., *Provincial Papers, Documents and Records Relating to the Province of New Hampshire from 1686 to 1722*, 40 vols. (Manchester, N.H., 1867–1943).

New Haven Colony: Charles J. Hoadly, ed., *Records of the Colony and Plantation of New Haven, 1638–1649, 1653–1664*, 2 vols. (Hartford: Case, Tiffany, 1857–58).

Plymouth Colony: Nathaniel B. Shurtleff and David Pulsifer, eds., *Records of the Colony of New Plymouth in New England*, 12 vols. in 10 (Boston: W. White, 1855–61).

Rhode Island Colony: John Russell Bartlett, ed., *Records of the Colony of Rhode Island and Providence Plantations 1632–1692*, 10 vols. (Providence: A. C. Greene, 1856–65).

Notarial Records: Two notaries in Boston, William Aspinwall and Thomas Lechford, left valuable records of their transactions

during the first two decades of settlement. Their notarial duties included drafting powers of attorney, which were needed for tending to official business in England. The records relating to powers of attorney offer valuable clues for determining English origins and connections. Both sets of records have been published.

A Volume Relating to the Early History of Boston Containing the Aspinwall Notarial Records from 1644 to 1651 (Boston, 1903).

Thomas Lechford, *Note-Book Kept by Thomas Lechford, Esq., Lawyer, in Boston, Massachusetts Bay, from June 27, 1638, to July 29, 1641* (Cambridge, 1885; rpt. Camden, Maine, 1988).

Town Records: In her book *Digging for Genealogical Treasure in New England Town Records*[2] Ann Smith Lainhart writes, "Any historian or genealogist who neglects to study town records in the colonial period is running the risk of missing some of the most intimate detail about New Englanders that he is likely to find anywhere. . . . For people who owned property and left wills, one can often trace movements and progeny reasonably well using

probate and land records, but for the poor, town records are often the only source of information." The records kept vary by town but, as Lainhart details, could include: selectmen or council minutes, lists of town officers, treasurer's records, tax and assessor records, land records, licenses, ear or cattle marks, military records, poor records, and more.

Generally, the town records for the earliest New England settlements begin in 1633 or 1634. Most of these have been published and key Massachusetts towns are listed below. The citation information for other towns of this period is listed in the Sources section of the *Great Migration* series. Note that the early Lynn records are lost, the first two leaves of the Dorchester records are lost, and use of the (unpublished) Charlestown records requires caution, as a 1660s copyist omitted some records and misread many names.

Boston: "Boston Town Records," in *Second Report of the Record Commissioners of the City of Boston; containing the Boston Records, 1634–1660, and the Book of Possessions,* 2nd ed. (Boston: Rockwell and Churchill, 1881).

Cambridge: *The Records of the Town of Cambridge (Formerly Newtowne) Massachusetts, 1630–1703* (Cambridge: University Press, 1901).

---

[2] Ann S. Lainhart, *Digging for Genealogical Treasure in New England Town Records* (Boston: NEHGS, 1996), p. 3.

Above: "The Return of the *Mayflower*." Leonard Bacon, *The Genesis of the New England Churches* (1874), p. 337.

Dorchester: *Fourth Report of the Record Commissioners of the City of Boston. 1880. Dorchester Town Records* (Boston: Rockwell and Churchill, 1883).

Plymouth: *Records of the Town of Plymouth,* Volume 1, 1636 to 1705 (Plymouth: Avery & Doten, 1889).

Roxbury: Robert J. Dunkle and Ann S. Lainhart, *The Town Records of Roxbury, Massachusetts, 1647 to 1730, Being Volume One of the Original* (Boston: NEHGS, 1997).

Salem: *Town Records of Salem, Massachusetts, 1634–1691,* 3 vols. (Salem: Essex Institute, 1868, 1913, 1934).

Watertown: "Records of Town Proceedings — First and Second Books," Section One in *Watertown Records Comprising the First and Second Books of Town Proceedings* (Watertown: Historical Society, 1894).

Vital Records: New England towns generally began recording births, marriages, and deaths soon after settlement, and most of the original books survive. As one of the fundamental building blocks of New England genealogy, vital records are covered in depth for each state later in this book.

An important secondary source for early marriages is Clarence Almon Torrey's *New England Marriages Prior to 1700.* "Torrey" is both a marriage index and a guide to sources, and it covers an estimated 99 percent of New England marriages in or before 1700. The original twelve-volume work, created over thirty years at NEHGS, contains references to some 37,000 known or presumed marriages of New England couples before the year 1700. Torrey (1869–1962) abstracted every known work available to him—more than 2,500 printed works, including genealogies, journals, town histories, volumes of vital records, land records, probate records, and more. NEHGS has produced "Torrey" in several formats, including a CD-ROM (2002) and an indexed three-volume published set of the entire work, with sources (2011).

STAFF PICKS

For New England Research

Gordon DenBoer and George E. Goodridge Jr., comps., John H. Long, ed., *Atlas of Historical County Boundaries: New Hampshire, Vermont* (New York: Simon & Schuster, 1993).

Gordon DenBoer and John H. Long, comps., John H. Long, ed., *Atlas of Historical County Boundaries: Connecticut, Maine, Massachusetts, Rhode Island* (New York: Simon & Schuster, 1994).

Harriette Merrifield Forbes, *New England Diaries, 1602–1800: A Descriptive Catalogue of Diaries, Orderly Books and Sea Journals* (Topsfield, Mass.: privately printed, 1923).

Eric G. Grundset, ed., *Forgotten Patriots: African American and American Indian Patriots in the Revolutionary War: A Guide to Service, Sources and Studies* (Washington, D.C.: National Society Daughters of the American Revolution, 2008).

Patricia Law Hatcher, *Researching Your Colonial New England Ancestors* (Provo, Utah: Ancestry, 2006).

The New England Historical and Genealogical Register (Boston: NEHGS, 1847–present), vols. 1–165 available on *American Ancestors.org.*

Diane Rapaport, *New England Court Records: A Research Guide for Genealogists and Historians* (Burlington, Mass.: Quill Pen Press, 2006).

Timothy G. X. Salls and Judith Lucey, eds., *Manuscripts at the New England Historic Genealogical Society: R. Stanton Avery Special Collections*, First Comprehensive Edition (Boston, 2011).

Land Records: In his "Colonial English Research" article in *The Source*, Robert Charles Anderson points out that when the colonists had to devise a method for transferring real property, they faced an entirely new situation: "Almost no one in England in the seventeenth century had experience in the original transfer of land from the government to individuals since, with the exception of land recovered from the drained fens, virtually all the land in England had been granted at the time of William the Conqueror (and earlier)." [3]

In New England, land was first granted to groups of settlers, eventually known as proprietors, who intended to establish new towns. The proprietors parceled land out to individual landholders. Transfers of land were generally recorded by the town rather than the county. Although the methods could differ from town to town, the general principles of land granting were similar. On April 1, 1634, the Massachusetts Bay General Court ordered that each town compile an inventory of landholding. As compliance varied among towns, the Court periodically repeated this order, and towns submitted their inventories at different times. These inventories, often known collectively as a town's "Book of Possessions," survive for Boston, Cambridge, Charlestown, Hingham, Roxbury, and Watertown.

Church Records: Given that religion provided the impetus for immigration, establishing churches was a priority in early New England settlements. The church records that survive from the period vary in detail, and may include admissions of church members, disciplinary records, letters of dismissal, baptisms, deaths, burials, and, in Cambridge, a few detailed "confessions" made by church members upon admission. The most extensive church records survive for Boston and Roxbury.

Journals and Letters: Contemporary journals and letters can offer personal details and insights into life in New England that cannot be found in official records. The following selection of published works has been used frequently in the Great Migration Study Project:

Governor William Bradford's Letter Book (Boston: Massachusetts Society of Mayflower Descendants, 1906).

Sargent Bush Jr., ed., *The Correspondence of John Cotton* (Chapel Hill: University of North Carolina Press, 2001).

John Hull's Diary: Transactions and Collections of the American Antiquarian Society, Vol. III, pp. 141–250.

Everett Emerson, ed., *Letters from New England: The Massachusetts Bay Colony, 1629–1638* (Amherst: University of Massachusetts Press, 1976).

M. Halsey Thomas, ed., *The Diary of Samuel Sewall, 1674–1729,* 2 vols.(New York, Farrar, Straus and Giroux, 1973).

Glenn W. LaFantasie, ed., *The Correspondence of Roger Williams, 1629–1682,* 2 vols., (Providence: Rhode Island Historical Society, 1988).

John Winthrop, *The History of New England from 1630 to 1649,* James Savage, ed., 2 vols. (Boston: Phelps and Farnham, 1853). [This edition is preferred for its useful annotations.]

Winthrop Papers, 1498–1654, 6 vols., various editors (Boston, 1925–92).

---

[3] Robert Charles Anderson. "Colonial New England Research," in Loretto Dennis Szucs and Sandra Hargreaves Luebking, eds., *The Source: A Guidebook to American Genealogy,* 3rd ed. (Provo, Utah: Ancestry, 2006), 679.

New England Records

New England's governmental organization is different from other areas of the United States, which can confuse genealogical researchers from outside the region. One major difference is in geopolitical subdivisions. Unlike in other areas of the country, New England's primary unit of government is the town. With a few exceptions, all land in each state is part of a town or city. Unincorporated territory exists only in the three northern New England states (Maine, New Hampshire, and Vermont). There is no unincorporated territory in Connecticut, Massachusetts, or Rhode Island. Land is primarily divided into towns and cities. Large towns will often have villages within them, but the villages have no political significance, and no records are kept on the village level.

In other areas of the country, you will often find that the primary source of records is at the county level. This is not true for New England. Here you will discover many more records on the local level than the county level. Indeed, in Rhode Island, land, probate, and vital records are all recorded at the town level. And county governments in Massachusetts have mostly been abolished, with the state taking over the counties' former functions.

Vital records in the six New England states are recorded at the town level. In some locations and time periods you will also find marriage records at the county level, but in most instances the town clerk was the primary recorder. Land records will occasionally exist at both the town and county level. Probate matters were recorded at the town, district, or county level, depending on the state. Even if a probate district has the same name as a county or town, it is not necessarily concurrent.

In New England, each town acted as a small welfare state. Towns usually appointed overseers of the poor, who were paid from town funds to ensure that paupers and those who could not care for themselves were properly looked after. Records of these activities can often be found in the minutes of the town council, board of selectmen, and town

Above: "Colonists Going to Church." R. H. Howard and Henry Crocker, eds., *A History of New England* (1881), p. 23.

meeting. Records from the town treasurer might include information on payments to individuals charged with caring for the poor and indigent. This system continued through the nineteenth century and, in some areas, the early twentieth century.

The New England practice of warning people out of town is one with its roots in English Common Law. Colonies defined requirements for becoming a legal settler. Newcomers to a town who did not qualify as settlers, and appeared as if they would not be able to qualify at any time in the near future, were warned to leave town. Warnings were mainly given to prevent indigent individuals from becoming a public charge. Warning out records are available in many New England towns and can provide information on ages, children's names, and places of origin for a newly arrived family. For a longer discussion of warning out records, see Josiah Henry Benton, *Warning Out in New England* (Boston: W. B. Clarke, 1911; rpt. Bowie, Md.: Heritage Books, 1992).

Ear marks and cattle marks are another helpful New England town record. People marked their animals so that similar-looking animals could be differentiated from one another and ownership determined. Individual marks could be passed from father to son. Since only one son could inherit the father's mark, other sons created a version of their father's mark to use as their own.

Town meeting minutes may include information on appointments of town officers, election results, tax reports, poll lists, road surveys, and more. The exact information recorded will differ from town to town and state to state.

STAFF PICKS

Compilations

Martin E. Hollick, *New Englanders in the 1600s: A Guide to Genealogical Research Published Between 1980 and 2005* (Boston: NEHGS, 2006). An expanded edition, covering research published between 2005 and 2010 (but including the seventh volume of *The Great Migration,* published in 2011), is forthcoming in 2012.

Patty Barthell Myers, comp., *Female Index to Genealogical Dictionary of the First Settlers of New England by James Savage* (Baltimore: Genealogical Publishing Co., 2008).

Melinde Lutz Sanborn, *Third Supplement to Torrey's New England Marriages Prior to 1700* (Baltimore: Genealogical Publishing Co., 2003). [Includes all information from first and second supplements.]

James Savage, *A Genealogical Dictionary of the First Settlers of New England, Showing Three Generations of Those Who Came Before May, 1692, on the Basis of Farmer's Register,* 4 vols. (Boston, 1860–62, rpt. Baltimore, Md.: Genealogical Publishing Co., 1990).

Clarence Almon Torrey, *New England Marriages Prior to 1700,* 3 vols. (Boston: NEHGS, 2011).

Genealogical Journals

Several scholarly genealogical journals have published compiled genealogies as well as abstracts and transcriptions of original records.

The American Genealogist

Donald Lines Jacobus began publishing the *New Haven Genealogical Magazine* in 1922. After eight volumes, the name (and focus) changed to *The American Genealogist*. This journal is especially valuable for colonial-era New England and includes many articles on English origins. All but the most recent five years of *The American Genealogist* are also available on *AmericanAncestors.org*.

The Genealogist

The American Society of Genealogists is the honorary society for scholarly work in the field of genealogy. Founded in 1940, membership is limited to fifty living Fellows. Their journal, *The Genealogist*, has been published semi-annually since 1980.

The New England Historical and Genealogical Register

Published quarterly since 1847 by the New England Historic Genealogical Society, the *Register* is the flagship journal in the field of genealogy, publishing a wide variety of genealogies and source material, with an emphasis on New England. Authoritative compiled genealogies have always been a primary focus.

The National Genealogical Society Quarterly

Published quarterly since 1912, *NGSQ* focuses on all regions of the country and all ethnic groups. It offers compiled genealogies, abstracts and transcriptions of original records, case studies, and essays on methodology and resources.

"Trask's Rock," Castine, Maine. George A. Wheeler, *Castine Past and Present* (1896), facing p. 32.

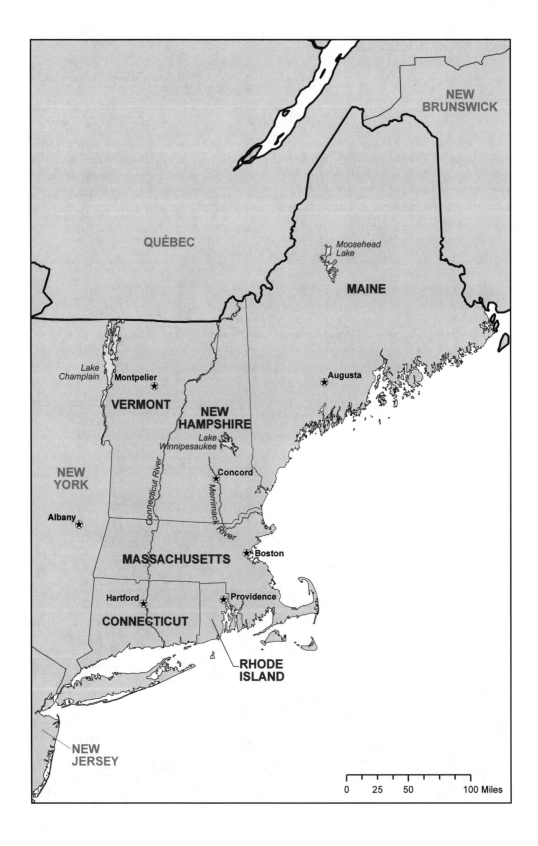

NEW
BRUNSWICK

QUÉBEC

Moosehead
Lake

MAINE

Lake
Champlain Montpelier ★ Augusta ★

VERMONT NEW
HAMPSHIRE

Lake
Winnipesaukee

NEW
YORK Concord ★

Albany ★

MASSACHUSETTS ★ Boston

Hartford ★ ★ Providence

CONNECTICUT

RHODE
ISLAND

NEW
JERSEY

0   25   50   100 Miles

New England Repositories

American Jewish Historical Society, New England Archives

99–101 Newbury Street
Boston, MA 02116
www.ajhsboston.org
(617) 226-1245; fax (617) 226-1248
reference@ajhsboston.org
Hours: M by appt. only; Tu–Th 9–5; F 9–2

The AJHS New England Archives, housed at NEHGS, serves as the archival repository for the documentary record of Jewish life in the Greater Boston area and New England communities, and is the home of the reference library of the Jewish Genealogical Society of Greater Boston. Extensive holdings include personal papers, organizational records, photographs, reports, and other materials for researching the history of the Jewish community of Boston.

General Society of Mayflower Descendants

4 Winslow Street
Plymouth, MA 02361

Mailing Address
PO Box 3297
Plymouth, MA 02361-3297

www.themayflowersociety.com
(617) 746-3188
gsmd.libr@verizon.net
Hours: M–F 10–3:30

The General Society of Mayflower Descendants oversees the state chapters, which are joined by individuals with proven descent from one of the passengers on the *Mayflower*. The research library is open year-round. Holdings include compiled genealogies, local histories, manuscripts, and microfilm of original records, as well as access to digital databases.

National Archives and Records Administration/Northeast Region

Frederick C. Murphy Federal Center
380 Trapelo Road
Waltham, MA 02451-6399
www.archives.gov/northeast/boston
(781) 663-0130; fax (781) 663-0154
boston.archives@nara.gov
Original records access: M–F 7–4:30;
Reference Room, M–W, F 7–4:30,
Th 7 a.m.–9 p.m.; one Saturday per month,
8–4:30 (see website for current schedule of Saturday openings)

The NARA research center at Waltham provides access to many online websites as well as microfilm and textual records of the federal government. Among the holdings are military records, bankruptcy proceedings, federal court records, draft records, tax lists, veterans' records, and more. NARA also sponsors many genealogy workshops and other free education programs. The genealogy research room of the Pittsfield branch of NARA closed permanently in October 2011.

New England Historic Genealogical Society

99–101 Newbury Street
Boston, MA 02116
www.AmericanAncestors.org
(617) 536-5740; fax (617) 536-7307
membership@nehgs.org
Hours: Tu, Th–Sat 9–5; W 9–9

Founded in Boston in 1845, NEHGS is the oldest and largest genealogical society in the country. *The New England Historical and Genealogical Register* is the flagship journal of American genealogy, published quarterly since 1847. Members also receive the quarterly *American Ancestors* magazine. The Society maintains a research library in Boston's Back Bay, including 200,000 published volumes and 28 million manuscript items. It makes many materials available as searchable databases on its website.

Genealogical Societies in New England

The following organizations are of interest to individuals tracing ancestors in the New England states. Researchers are also encouraged to explore the rich resources of New England's local historical societies.

Afro-American Historical and Genealogical Society, New England Chapter
42 Laurelwood Drive
Stoughton, MA 02072
www.aahgs-ne.org
See website for email

American-Canadian Genealogical Society
4 Elm Street
Manchester, NH 03103

Mailing Address
PO Box 6478
Manchester, NH 03108-6478

www.acgs.org
(603) 622-1554
acgs@acgs.org
Hours: W, F 9–9; Sat 9–4; 1st and
    3rd Sun 1–5

American-French Genealogical Society
78 Earle Street
Woonsocket, RI 02895
Mailing Address
PO Box 830
Woonsocket, RI 02895-0870

www.afgs.org
(401) 765-6141; fax (401) 765-6141
info@afgs.org
Hours: M 11–4; Tu 1–9; Sat 10–4.
Check website for summer hours.

Association for Gravestone Studies
Greenfield Corporate Center
101 Munson Street, Suite 108
Greenfield, MA 01301
www.gravestonestudies.org
(413) 772-0836
info@gravestonestudies.org
Hours: Tu–Th 9–3

Above: NEHGS reading room at 9 Ashburton Place, Boston, ca. 1925–1930. NEHGS Institutional Archives.

Association of Professional Genealogists, New England Chapter
PO Box 170204
Boston, MA 02117
www.neapg.org
See website for email

Berkshire Family History Association
PO Box 1437
Pittsfield, MA 01202-1437
www.berkshire.net/~bfha/index.html
bfhainc@gmail.com

Cape Cod Genealogical Society
PO Box 1394
Harwich, MA 02645
www.capecodgensoc.org
See website for email

Central Massachusetts Genealogical Society
PO Box 811
Westminster, MA 01473-0811
www.cmgs-inc.org
See website for email

Connecticut Ancestry Society
PO Box 249
Stamford, CT 06904-0249
www.connecticutancestry.org
See website for email

Connecticut Professional Genealogists Council
PO Box 4273
Hartford, CT 06147-4273
www.ctprofgen.org
membership@ctprofgen.org

Connecticut Society of Genealogists
172 Maple Street
East Hartford, CT 06118-2634

Mailing Address
PO Box 435
Glastonbury, CT 06033-0435

www.csginc.org
(860) 569-0002; fax (860) 569-0339
See website for email
Hours: M–F 9:30–4

Descendants of the Founders of Ancient Windsor
PO Box 39
Windsor, CT 06095
http://dfaw.blogspot.com
dfaw1633@yahoo.com

Essex Society of Genealogists
PO Box 313
Lynnfield, MA 01940-0313
www.esog.org
See website for email

Falmouth Genealogical Society
PO Box 2107
Falmouth, MA 02536
www.falgen.org
See website for email

Franco-American Genealogical Society of York County
PO Box 180
Biddeford, ME 05004
*www.mcarthur.lib.me.us/franco-american_
    genealogical_society.htm*

French-Canadian Genealogical Society of Connecticut
53 Tolland Green
Tolland, CT 06084

Mailing Address
PO Box 928
Tolland, CT 06084-0928

cont. on next page

French-Canadian Genealogical Society of Connecticut *(cont.)*

www.fcgsc.org
(860) 872-2597
See website for email
Hours: M,W 1–5; Sat 9–4; Sun 1–4

Genealogical Roundtable
PO Box 654
Concord, MA 01742-0654
www.genealogicalroundtable.com
information@genealogicalroundtable.com

Genealogical Society of Vermont
PO Box 14
Randolph, VT 05060-0014
www.genealogyvermont.org
See website for email

General Society of Mayflower Descendants
4 Winslow Street
Plymouth, MA 02360

Mailing Address
PO Box 3297
Plymouth, MA 02361-3297

www.themayflowersociety.com
(508) 746-3188; see website for email
Hours: M–F 10–3:30

Italian Genealogical Society of America
PO Box 3572
Peabody, MA 01961-3572
www.italianroots.org
See website for email

Jewish Genealogical Society of Greater Boston
PO Box 610366
Newton, MA 02461-0366
http://jgsgb.org
(866) 611-5698; *info@jgsgb.org*

Maine Genealogical Society
PO Box 221
Farmington, ME 04938
www.rootsweb.ancestry.com/~megs/contact.html
mainegenealogical@yahoo.com

Massachusetts Genealogical Council
PO Box 5393
Cochituate, MA 01778-5393
www.massgencouncil.org
info@massgencouncil.org

Massachusetts Society of Genealogists
PO Box 215
Ashland, MA 01721-0215
www.massachusettssocietyofgenealogists.org
See website for email

New England Historic Genealogical Society
99–101 Newbury Street
Boston, MA 02116
www.AmericanAncestors.org
(617) 536-5740; fax (617) 536-7307
membership@nehgs.org
Hours: Tu, Th–Sat 9–5; W 9–9

New England Regional Genealogical Conference
No physical address
www.nergc.org
See website for email

New Hampshire Society of Genealogists
PO Box 2316
Concord, NH 03302-2316
www.nhsog.org
(603) 431-6688; see website for email

Old Broad Bay Family History Association
No physical or postal address
www.rootsweb.ancestry.com/~meobbfha
See website for email

Polish Genealogical Society of Connecticut and the Northeast
8 Lyle Road
New Britain, CT 06053-2104
www.pgsctne.org
(860) 229-8873
pgsctne@yahoo.com

Rhode Island Black Heritage Society
101 Dyer Street
Providence, RI 02903
www.ribhs.org
(401) 421-0606; fax (401) 421-1111
ribhs1@gmail.com

Rhode Island Genealogical Society
PO Box 211
Hope, RI 02831
www.rigensoc.org
See website for email

Sons and Daughters of the First Settlers of Newbury, Massachusetts
PO Box 444
Newburyport, MA 01950
www.sonsanddaughtersofnewbury.org
See website for email

South Shore Genealogical Society
PO Box 396
Norwell, MA 02061

Strafford County Genealogical Society
PO Box 322
Dover, NH 03821-0322
www.straffgen.org
See website for email

Swedish Ancestry Research Association (SARA)
PO Box 70603
Worcester, MA 01607-0603
http://sarassociation.tripod.com
info@sarassociation.org

The Irish Ancestral Research Association (TIARA)
2120 Commonwealth Avenue
Auburndale, MA 02466
www.tiara.ie
(617) 244-3050
info@tiara.ie

Vermont French-Canadian Genealogical Society
Dupont Building
Fort Ethan Allen Complex
Colchester, VT 05439
Mailing Address
PO Box 65128
Burlington, VT 05460-5128
www.vt-fcgs.org
mail@vt-fcgs.org
Hours: Tu 3–9:30; Sat 10–4

Welsh-American Genealogical Society, Inc.
60 Norton Avenue
Poultney, VT 05764-1029
www.rootsweb.ancestry.com/~vtwags
wagsoff1990@yahoo.com
Hours by appt.

Western Massachusetts Genealogical Society
PO Box 418
West Springfield, MA 01090
www.rootsweb.ancestry.com/~mawmgs
westmassgen@gmail.com

Western Massachusetts Jewish Genealogical Society
26 Nutting Avenue
Florence, MA 01062
www.wmjgs.org
wmjgs@aol.com

York County Genealogical Society
PO Box 431
Eliot, ME 03903-0431
www.rootsweb.ancestry.com/~meyorkgs

Connecticut

Introduction by Christopher C. Child

Connecticut has a wealth of information available to researchers, ranging from the seventeenth-century settlements to the present state. Thanks primarily to Lucius Barnes Barbour, most of the vital records prior to 1850 have been published and most nineteenth-century records are available on microfilm. While some twentieth-century records are available, access to them is limited. Military and colonial records have been published and are easily available. Probate and land records are available on microfilm and other unique collections, such as the Hale Collection, are sources for cemetery and newspaper records.

Originally divided into New Haven Colony and Connecticut Colony, today Connecticut comprises eight counties. The county is fairly meaningless to Nutmeg State genealogists, however. While four counties were created in 1666, their role was limited to operating courts and jails, as Connecticut generally kept most power at the town level. County governments were completely abolished in 1960. Nearly all of the records discussed in this chapter were never kept at the county level.

Vital Records

Vital records survive from the earliest English settlement in Connecticut. Marriages were recorded as early as 1640, and recording births, marriages, and deaths became the town's responsibility by 1650. Since a fine was levied for not recording an event, many of the early towns have fairly extensive records. From the Revolutionary era until the mid-nineteenth century, town clerks were not as thorough in registering vital records. The State Board of Health was established in 1870, after which record-keeping in all towns improved.

Most vital records prior to 1850 are recorded in a series known by genealogists as the "Barbour Collection," named for its director, Lucius Barnes Barbour (1878–1934). In 1909, Barbour directed the publication of the vital records of Bolton and Vernon by the Connecticut Historical Society. Barbour became State Examiner of Public Records in 1911 (a position he held until his death), and directed the transcribing of most vital records prior to 1850. Of the several individuals he

The Connecticut state seal.

hired for this project, James Newell Arnold, who had previously published *Vital Record of Rhode Island, 1636–1850*, is the best known.

Several towns are omitted from the Barbour Collection, as records for these towns had already been published. These include Bolton and Vernon as mentioned above; Coventry (1897) and Mansfield (1898), transcribed by Susan Whitney Dimock; and New Haven (1917). Barbour himself was on the publications committee for the records of Norwich (1913) and Woodstock (1914), and thus the Barbour Collection version for these towns is a much smaller volume. Bicentennial publications were also published for Lyme and Saybrook Colony (including Chester, Deep River, Essex, Old Saybrook, and Westbrook). Articles in *The Connecticut Nutmegger* and *Connecticut Ancestry* have provided additional or corrected vital records.

After the towns' records were transcribed, the "Arnold" transcript was typed and then cut in small slips. The slips cited the town, volume, page, and original source from which the information was transcribed. The slips for each town were put into alphabetical order, typed onto sheets, and bound into one or two volumes. After all towns were completed, all of the slips were sorted alphabetically to create a statewide index. The statewide slip index exists as a card catalog at the Connecticut State Library (CSL) and was microfilmed by the Family History Library. It is available at FHL, NEHGS, and many other repositories. The statewide index also has yellow slips from private sources, such as diaries, interspersed with the vital records. Copies of the typescript volumes are available at CSL, NEHGS, and other repositories. Between 1994 and 2002, Lorraine Cook White compiled these records and published them with the Genealogical Publishing Company (GPC). In 2006, GPC published *The Ricker Compilation of Vital Records of Early Connecticut*, compiled by Jacquelyn Ladd Ricker from the Barbour Collection and other records.

STAFF PICKS

For Connecticut Research

The American Genealogical-Biographical Index, 206 vols. (Middletown, Conn.: Godfrey Library, 1952–2000).

Arthur H. Hughes and Morse S. Allen, *Connecticut Place Names* (Hartford, Conn.: Connecticut Historical Society, 1976).

Thomas Jay Kemp, *Connecticut Researcher's Handbook* (Detroit: Gale Research, 1981).

Roger N. Parks, ed., *Connecticut: A Bibliography of Its History* (Hanover, N.H.: University Press of New England, 1986).

Joyce S. Pendery, "Connecticut," pp. 85–104 of *A Guide to the Library of the New England Historic Genealogical Society,* Maureen A. Taylor and Henry B. Hoff, eds. (Boston: NEHGS, 2004).

From about 1850 to 1897, vital records survive mostly at the town level. The FHL has microfilmed these, and they are available at FHL and the Connecticut State Library. Town halls have the originals of their vital records for this time period as well.

Vital records from 1897 to the present are kept at the town level; the state holds a copy in Hartford as well. Many town clerks also transcribed their vital records in a nearly complete "index." Often these indexes are available in a more accessible format at the town hall; however, it is important to note that these are not the original records. The early indexes (i.e., 1900 to 1930s) often omit a town of marriage, and towns often have marriage records for residents of the town even if the marriage occurred elsewhere. The town clerk may also have transcribed some information incorrectly, and these indexes may have been compiled decades after the events. Therefore the original record should still be consulted.

Access to birth records less than one hundred years old for genealogical purposes is limited by Connecticut General Statutes Section 7-51 to members of genealogical societies incorporated or authorized by the Secretary of the State of Connecticut. A list of these societies is available at *www.cslib. org/genesoc.htm*. Appointments can be made at the Department of Health in Hartford to access vital records for the entire state. When going to a town hall, it can be useful to bring a copy of this statute, along with your genealogical society membership card, to explain why you are allowed to look at these records. More recent birth and marriage records can contain Social Security numbers, so if a town clerk prohibits you from looking at those records, you can ask them to photocopy the record and black out those numbers.

Probate Records

Probate records in Connecticut have been maintained under a variety of jurisdictions from the colonial period to the present. Probate courts were not created until 1698, so copies of most wills and administrations for New Haven Colony, which existed from 1638 to 1655, were included in the town records, and the originals were filed with the secretary of the colony. For Connecticut Colony, after 1639, estates were in the jurisdiction of the Particular Court (sometimes called the "Quarterly Court"). The Particular Courts were abolished with the new charter in 1662 and were replaced by the Court of Assistants. In 1666, the General Assembly established the original four counties of Connecticut—Hartford, New London, New Haven, and Fairfield. The Court of Sessions for these four county courts handled probate records until 1698. In that year specific probate districts were created for each of these four counties. Additional probate districts were created from 1719 on, often for a larger town and nearby towns, not always in the same county. Beginning in 2011 the number of probate districts was reduced to 54 from a high of 131.

Many of the probate records created prior to the formation of probate courts have been transcribed and published. The very useful Probate Estate Papers Index covers probate packets from the mid-1600s to 1948. The FHL microfilmed all estate papers (such as wills, administrations, and inventories) up to 1880, and most to 1915. Important probate documents were also transcribed by town clerks into probate volumes available at the town hall.

Adoptions

As in most states, adoptions in Connecticut were private matters until the turn of the twentieth century, with no formal action taken. Occasionally, a genealogy may record a child taken in by someone else within the family. Adoptions are handled by probate courts, but genealogists must have a court order to see original information. The birth certificate of someone who was adopted is marked as a "Confidential File," numbered, and removed from the normal volume of births for that year.

Land Records

Land records in Connecticut have always been kept at the town level. The only exceptions are border towns such as Woodstock and Suffield that were once part of Massachusetts. To locate records for these towns prior to their joining Connecticut, consult the Massachusetts county. In 1639, the Fundamental Orders of Connecticut required the recording of deeds in town records. The Connecticut General Court (later the Connecticut General Assembly) established town proprietors to distribute land that would be divided and sold in lots. Town clerks were responsible for recording land records. Most land records are available at the given town hall, and those to 1900 have been microfilmed by the FHL. Nothing is indexed on the county level and there is no statewide index.

Court Records

Court records are one of the few types of records in Connecticut that were kept at the county level. The earliest court records were under the jurisdiction of the Particular Court (which was the first recorder of probate records) from 1639 to 1663, when the 1662 charter abolished these courts. The records have been published in *Records of the Particular Court of Connecticut, 1639-1663*, volume 22 (Hartford: Collections of the Connecticut Historical Society, 1928). County courts began in 1665 with the original four counties; the Court of Assistants maintained trial court records from 1665 to 1711. Some of these court records have been transcribed; see Helen S. Ullmann, FASG, *Hartford County, Connecticut, County Court Minutes Volumes 3 and 4, 1663-1687, 1697* (Boston: NEHGS, 2005), and Ullmann, *Colony of Connecticut Minutes of the Court of Assistants, 1669–1711* (Boston: NEHGS, 2009).

The Court of Assistants was replaced by the Superior Court in 1711, and Superior Court districts were also at the county level. Matters not heard at the Superior level were tried at the county level. These courts existed until 1855 and their records are primarily available at the Connecticut State Library. After 1855, what had been handled by County Courts was divided between Superior Courts and Justice Courts. Courts of Common Pleas handled what the Justice and Superior Courts did not, until in 1961 the justice courts were abolished. The current system has district courts, county superior courts, and the State Supreme Court. Courts today generally keep criminal and civil records, including divorces and cases of paternity.

Above: Gravestone of Mary Hale, South Glastonbury, Connecticut. Harriette Merrifield Forbes, "New England Gravestones, 1653-1800" (R. Stanton Avery Special Collections, NEHGS, Mss 936, folder 10, p. 181).

Military Records

Military records in Connecticut have been published for nearly every conflict from the Pequot War (1634–38) up to World War I. The following compilations are available at NEHGS, CSL, FHL, and many other repositories:

- James Shepard, *Connecticut Soldiers in the Pequot War of 1637* (Meriden, Conn.: Journal Pub. Co., 1913)
- *Index to Compiled Service Records of Revolutionary War Soldiers Who Served with the American Army in Connecticut Military Organizations* (National Archives microfilm), available at the CSL, National Archives, and FHL.
- Connecticut Adjutant-General. *Record of Service of Connecticut Men in the War of the Revolution, War of 1812, Mexican War* (Hartford, 1889)
- Connecticut Adjutant-General. *Record of Service of Connecticut Men in the Army and Navy of the United States During the War of Rebellion* (Hartford, 1889)
- *Record of Service of Connecticut Men in the Army, Navy and Marine Corps of the United States in the Spanish-American War* (Hartford, 1919)

STAFF PICKS

Compilations

The American Genealogist, 1922–present, all but the most recent five years on *American Ancestors.org.* (The first eight volumes treat New Haven families; subsequent volumes often treat Connecticut families and records.)

Connecticut Ancestry (formerly *Bulletin of the Stamford Genealogical Society*) (Connecticut Ancestry Society, 1971–present).

The Connecticut Nutmegger (Connecticut Society of Genealogists, 1968–present), vols. 1–41 on *AmericanAncestors.org* as of fall 2011.

Charles William Manwaring, comp., *A Digest of the Early Connecticut Probate Records [Hartford District, 1635–1750],* 3 vols. (Hartford: R. S. Peck, 1904–6; rpt. Baltimore: Genealogical Publishing Co., 1995).

- *Service Records: Connecticut Men and Women in the Armed Forces of the United States During World War I, 1917-1920* (Hartford: Office of the Adjutant General, 1941)

Various volumes of the Collections of the Connecticut Historical Society are dedicated to colonial and Revolutionary Service. Each of the following is available at NEHGS, FHL, and the Connecticut State Library and has been digitized by Google Books:

- Volume 7: *Orderly Book and Journals Kept by Connecticut Men While Taking Part in the American Revolution, 1775-1778* (Hartford, 1899)
- Volume 8: *Rolls and Lists of Connecticut Men in the Revolution* (Hartford, 1901)

Above: "Anson Merriman and Wife." Francis Atwater, *History of Southington, Connecticut* (1924), p. 447.

- Volumes 9 and 10: *Rolls of Connecticut Men in the French and Indian War,* 2 vols. (Hartford, 1903, 1905)

- Volume 12: *Lists and Returns of Connecticut Men in the Revolution, 1775-1783* (Hartford, 1909)

Other Records

Collections of the Connecticut Archives

The Connecticut Archives holds records of the General Assembly up to about 1820. This includes papers and correspondence of the General Assembly, the Governor and Council, and other colony or state officials. The collection encompasses acts, resolves, drafts of bills, petitions, and other early government documents. The originals have been filed into 303 volumes, 66 boxes, and 55 index volumes. The originals are available at the CSL but can be accessed only if the microfilm is not legible. The microfilm is available in the History and Genealogy Reading Room at the CSL. The series is fully indexed, and the indexes are available in PDF format on the CSL website.

The official record books of the General Court/General Assembly are in *The Public Records of the Colony of Connecticut (1636-1776),* and *The Public Records of the State of Connecticut.* The colonial records are available online through the University of Connecticut at *www.colonialct.uconn.edu.* The state series has twelve published volumes encompassing records from 1776 to 1805.

The Jonathan Trumbull Papers are colonial and early state official papers from about 1631 to 1784, collected by Governor Jonathan Trumbull at the direction of the General Assembly. They were compiled into thirty volumes; volume 19 burned in 1825.

Cemetery Lists/Newspaper Records—The Hale Collection

Charles R. Hale's initial project, begun in 1916, was to find the graves of veterans in Connecticut cemeteries. It eventually expanded to a very large "slip index" and bound volumes encompassing cemetery transcriptions of more than two thousand Connecticut cemeteries, covering gravestones from the colonial period to the early twentieth century, which were transcribed from 1932 to 1935. Also filed in this index are marriage and death notices published in newspapers from about 1750 until 1865. The original index and bound volumes are available at the CSL; they have also been microfilmed by FHL. Copies of the microfilm are at NEHGS.

Passenger Lists

While many immigrants arrived through the ports of Boston and New York, Connecticut passenger lists that survive are part of the series *Copies of Lists of Passengers Arriving at Miscellaneous Ports on the Atlantic and Gulf Coasts and at Ports on the Great Lakes, 1820–1873.* These volumes include scattered lists for Bridgeport (1870), Fairfield (1820-21), Hartford (1837), New Haven (1820-73), New London (1820-47), and Saybrook (1820). They are available on microfilm from NARA and are on *Ancestry.com.*

State Census—Military Census of 1917

Unlike the other New England states, Connecticut never undertook a state census. One unique census ordered by the state was the Military Census of 1917. This listed all males between twenty to thirty years of age. Most towns reported the following information for men between sixteen and sixty: name, age, place of birth, number of dependents, occupation, and ability to perform certain tasks.

Church Records

The Congregational Church was the established church in Connecticut from the colonial period until 1818, and there is a Congregational church in the center of almost every Connecticut town. The CSL has originals or copies of records for more than 600 churches in Connecticut, many dating to the colonial period. The library also has a slip index, similar in design to the Barbour collection, which covers about one-quarter of these (mostly Congregational) church records. Arranged alphabetically by surname, then first name, the index provides a complete abstract of all baptisms, marriages, burials, membership admissions, or dismissals. The slip also has a citation to the original record, including the town, church, volume, and page. To check the accuracy of the transcription, one can consult the original church records on microfilm, which are available at the CSL and the FHL. Microfilm of the slip index is also available at NEHGS.

Above: "S. E. View of Humphreysville." John Warner Barber, *Connecticut Historical Collections* (1836), p. 200.

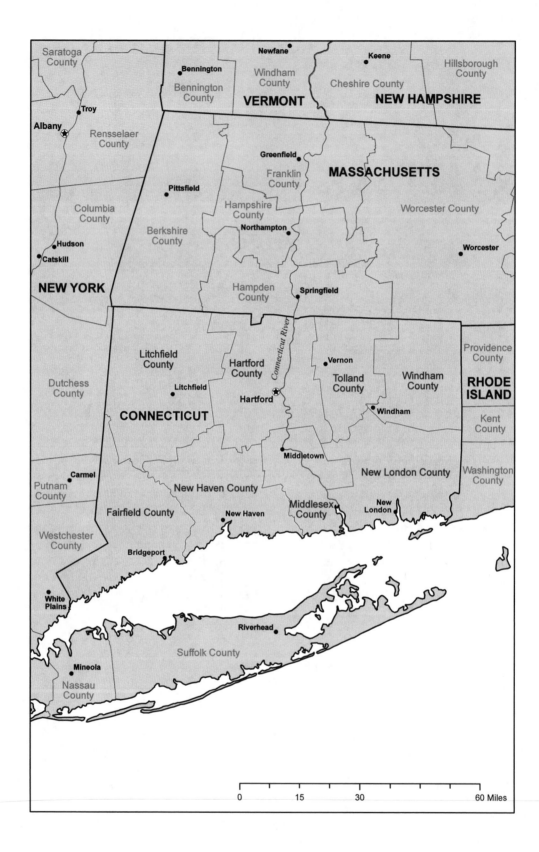

Connecticut Repositories

The following are major repositories with large collections of materials of interest to gene-alogists. Check with each repository prior to visiting to obtain the most recent information about hours and access to materials in the collection.

Connecticut State Archives

State Archives, Connecticut State Library
231 Capitol Avenue
Hartford, CT 06106
www.cslib.org/archives
(860) 757–6511; fax (860) 757–6542
See website for email
Hours: M–F 9–4:30

In 1909 the Connecticut State Library (CSL) became the official state archives. Today the archives holds more than 32,000 linear feet of records. It is a part of the Office of the Public Records Administration. Most of the genealogically significant materials can be accessed through the CSL's History and Genealogy Unit (see next entry).

Connecticut State Library

History and Genealogy Unit
231 Capitol Avenue
Hartford, CT 06106
www.cslib.org/archives
(860) 757–6580; fax (860) 757–6677
See website for email
Hours: Tu–F 10–4:15; Sat 9:15–1:45

The History and Genealogy Unit of the CSL holds original records from various levels of the three branches of state government. Major collections include original probate estate papers, military records, and transcriptions of vital, church, and cemetery records. Microfilm copies of land records are also available.

Above: "Interior View of the Southern New England Telephone Exchange, Bridgeport."
George Curtis Waldo, *The Standard's History of Bridgeport* (1897), p. 196.

Connecticut Department of Public Health State Office of Vital Records

410 Capitol Avenue
Hartford, CT 06134

Mailing Address
MS #11VRS
PO Box 340308
Hartford, CT 06134-0308

www.ct.gov/dph
(860) 509–7700; fax (860) 509–7964
Hours: M–F 8:15–3:45

The state office holds copies of birth, death, and marriage records from 1897 to the present; marriage indexes from 1959 to the present; and death indexes from 1949 to the present.

Connecticut Historical Society

One Elizabeth Street
Hartford, CT 06105
www.chs.org
(860) 236–5621; fax (860) 236–2664
research_center@chs.org
Hours: Tu–F 12–5; Sat 9–5

The CHS Research Center holds millions of objects, manuscripts, photographs, prints, books, maps, and original documents. Entrance is free to members. Non-members pay a day fee (discounted multi-day passes are available). Finding aids to some of the manuscript collections are available online.

Godfrey Memorial Library

134 Newfield Street
Middletown, CT 06457
www.godfrey.org
(860) 346–4375; fax (860) 347–9874
library@godfrey.org
Hours: M 9–8; Tu–F 9–4; Sat 9–1

The Godfrey is the publisher of the *American Genealogical Biographical Index* (AGBI), a 226-volume index to more than 800 genealogical books. The library contains more than 200,00 books and periodicals. There is no entrance fee. Members have access to numerous online resources.

New Haven Colony Historical Society

Whitney Library
114 Whitney Avenue
New Haven, CT 06510
www.newhavenmuseum.org
(203) 562–4183; fax (203) 2562–2002
info@newhavenmuseum.org
Hours: Tu–F 10–5; Sat 12–5

Founded in 1862, the Whitney Library provides information on New Haven and its families from the seventeenth century to the present. Collections include 30,000 printed volume, 300 manuscript collections, newspapers, photographs, and microfilms. Research guides are available online.

Right: Gravestone of John Hart, Farmington, Connecticut. Harriette Merrifield Forbes, "New England Gravestones, 1653–1800" (R. Stanton Avery Special Collections, NEHGS, Mss 936, folder 10, p 176).

Counties

Probate in Connecticut is administered through probate districts; see page 45. Deeds are administered through towns.

Name	Est.	Parent(s)	Deed District(s)
Fairfield	1666	Original County	Towns
Hartford	1666	Original County	Towns
Litchfield	1751	Fairfield and Hartford	Towns
Middlesex	1785	Hartford and New Haven	Towns
New Haven	1666	Original County	Towns
New London	1666	Original County	Towns
Tolland	1785	Windham	Towns
Windham	1726	New London	Towns

Above: Tower at Roseland Park, Woodstock, Connecticut. Clarence Winthrop Bowen Papers (R. Stanton Avery Special Collections, NEHGS, Mss 1007, Folder 1638).

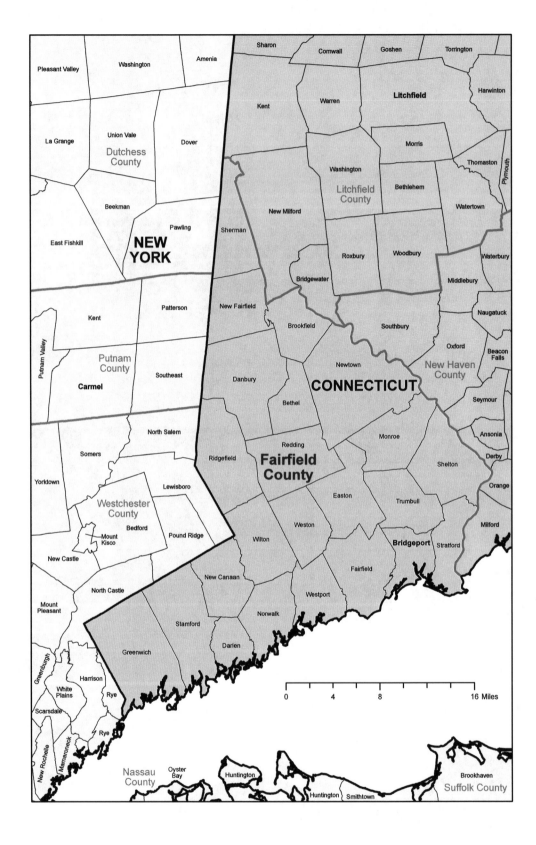

Fairfield County

Founded	1666
Original County	
County Seat	Fairfield (1666–1853); Bridgeport (1853–1960)

Towns

Bethel, Bridgeport, Brookfield, Danbury, Darien, Easton, Fairfield, Greenwich, Monroe, New Canaan, New Fairfield, Newtown, Norwalk, Redding, Ridgefield, Shelton, Sherman, Stamford, Stratford, Trumbull, Weston, Westport, Wilton

Extinct

Huntington

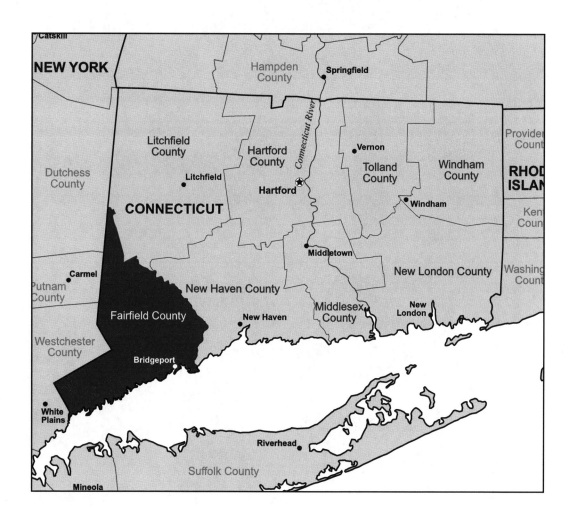

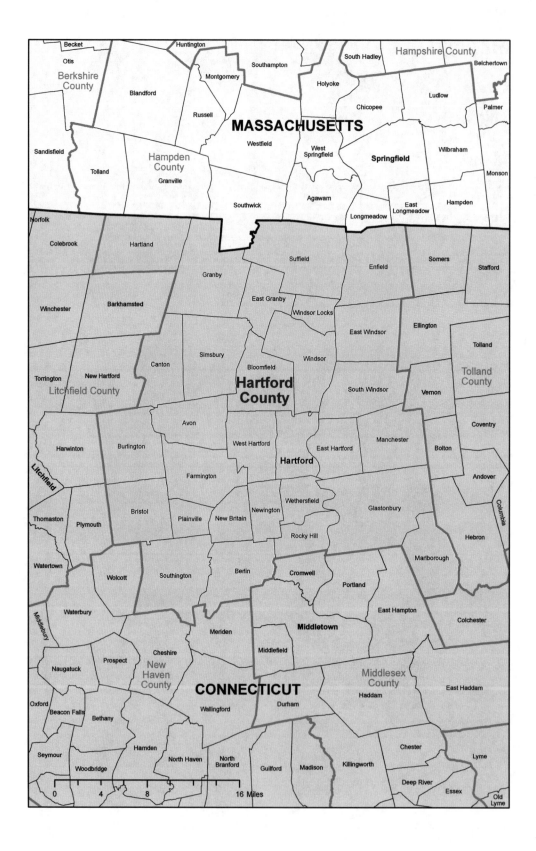

Hartford County

Founded	1666
Original County	
County Seat	Hartford (until 1960)

Towns

Avon, Berlin, Bloomfield, Bristol, Burlington, Canton, East Granby, East Hartford, East Windsor, Enfield, Farmington, Glastonbury, Granby, Hartford, Hartland, Manchester, Marlborough, New Britain, Newington, Plainville, Rocky Hill, Simsbury, South Windsor, Southington, Suffield, West Hartford, Wethersfield, Windsor, Windsor Locks

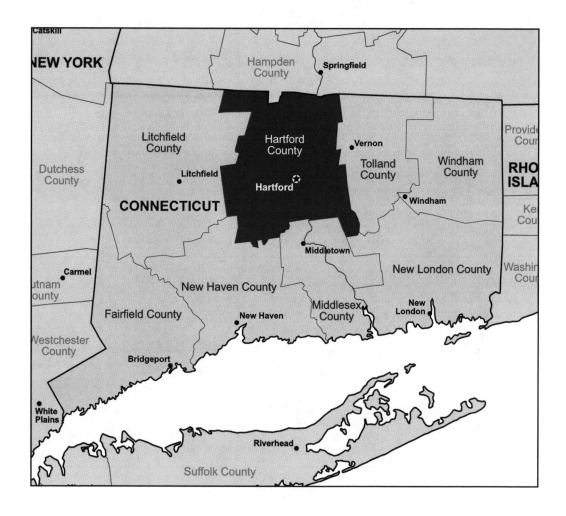

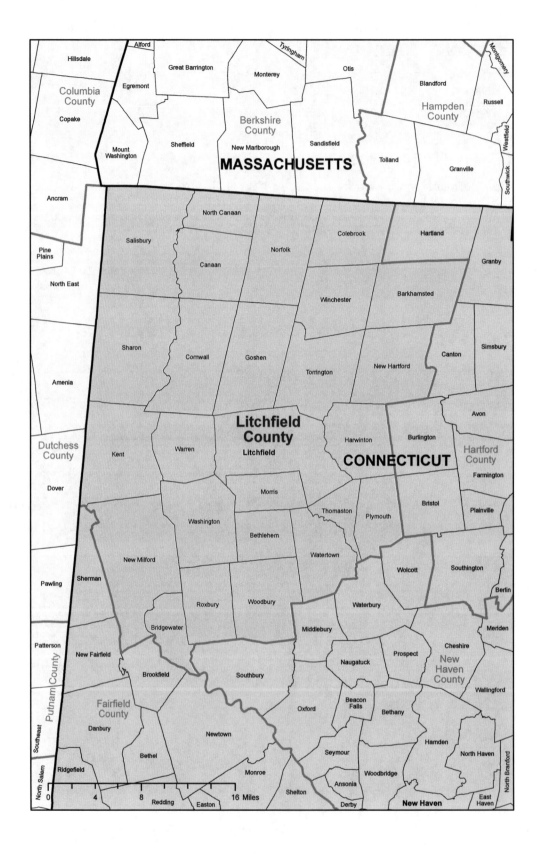

Litchfield County

Founded	1751
Parent Counties	Fairfield, Hartford
County Seat	Litchfield (until 1960)

Towns

Barkhamsted, Bethlehem, Bridgewater, Canaan, Colebrook, Cornwall, Goshen, Harwinton, Kent, Litchfield, Morris, New Hartford, New Milford, Norfolk, North Canaan, Plymouth, Roxbury, Salisbury, Sharon, Thomaston, Torrington, Warren, Washington, Watertown, Winchester, Woodbury

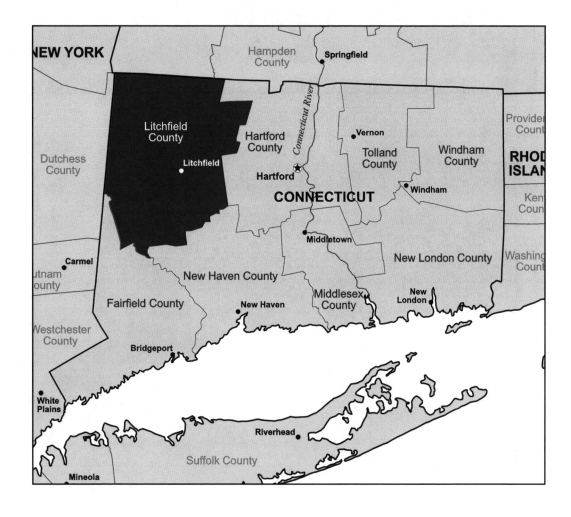

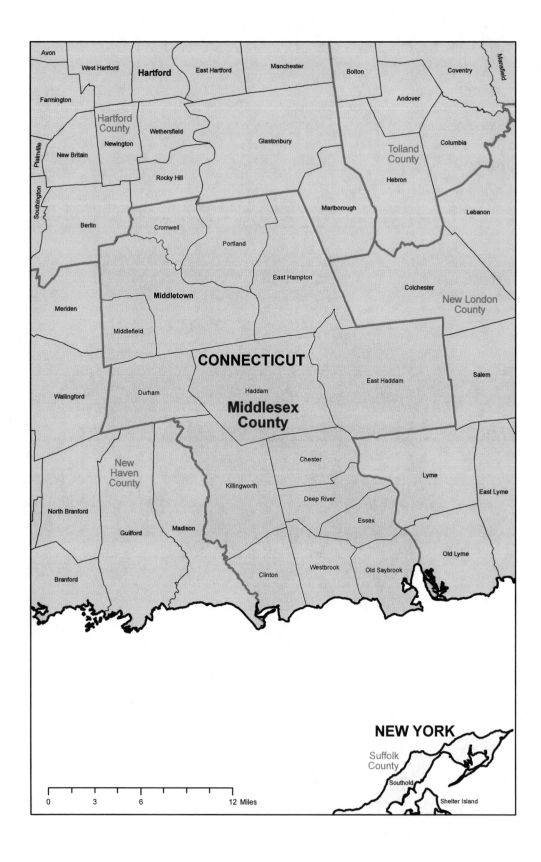

Middlesex County

Founded	1785
Parent Counties	Hartford, New Haven, New London
County Seat	Middletown (until 1960)

Towns

Chester, Clinton, Cromwell, Deep River, Durham, East Haddam, East Hampton, Essex, Haddam, Killingworth, Middlefield, Middletown, Old Saybrook, Portland, Westbrook

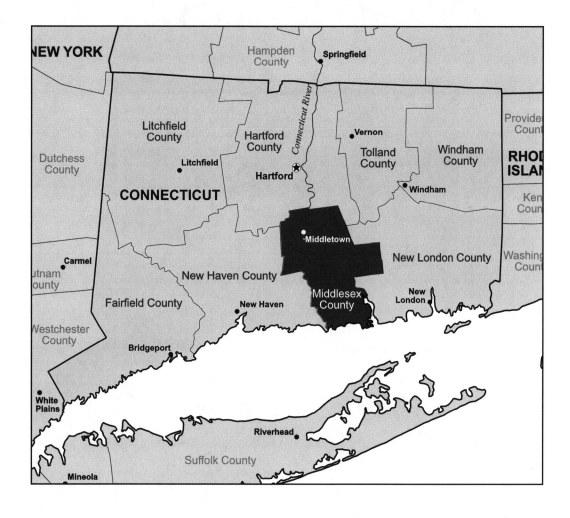

New Haven County

Founded	1666
Original County	
County Seat	New Haven (until 1960)

Towns

Ansonia, Beacon Falls, Bethany, Branford, Cheshire, Derby, East Haven, Guilford, Hamden, Madison, Meriden, Middlebury, Milford, Naugatuck, New Haven, North Branford, North Haven, Orange, Oxford, Prospect, Seymour, Southbury, Wallingford, Waterbury, West Haven, Wolcott, Woodbridge

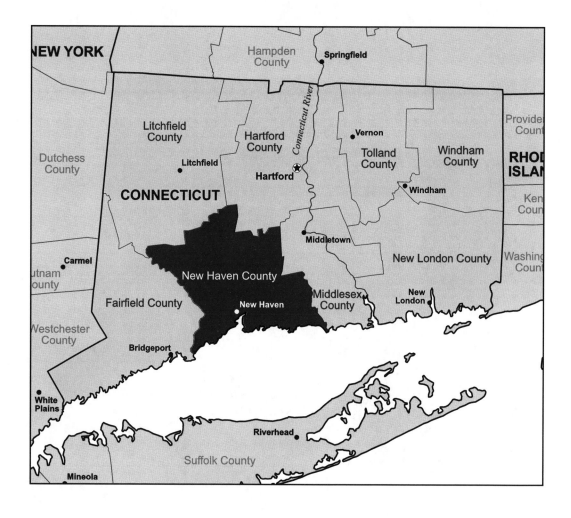

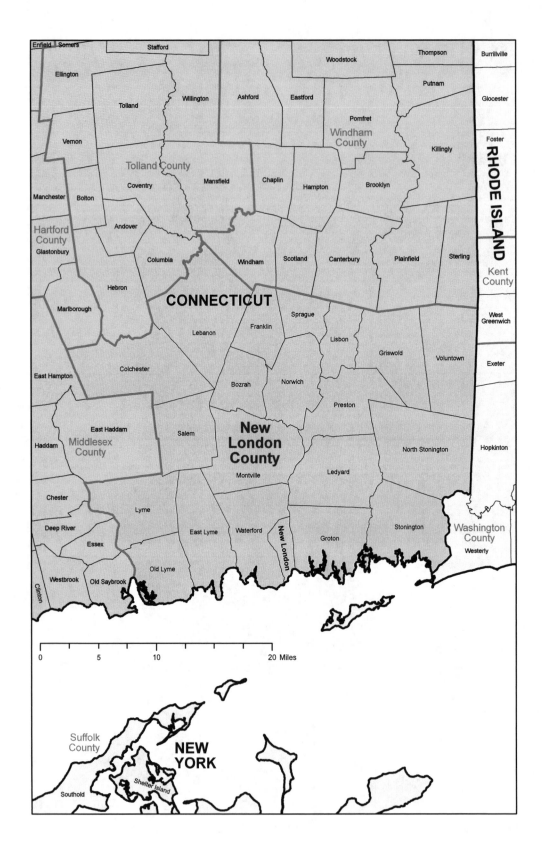

New London County

Founded	1666
Original County	
County Seat	New London (until 1960)

Towns

Bozrah, Colchester, East Lyme, Franklin, Griswold, Groton, Lebanon, Ledyard, Lisbon, Lyme, Montville, New London, North Stonington, Norwich, Old Lyme, Preston, Salem, Sprague, Stonington, Voluntown, Waterford

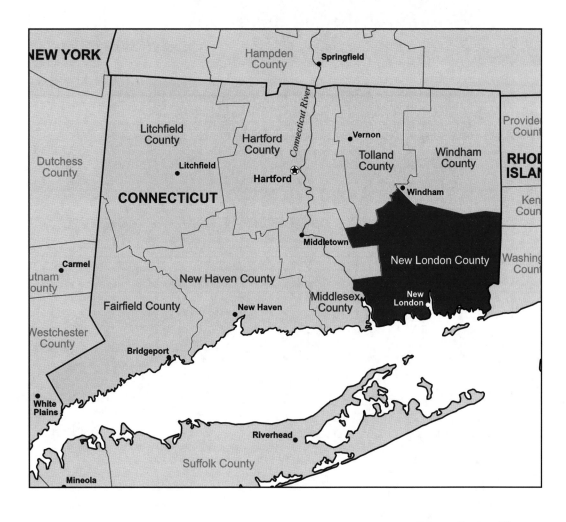

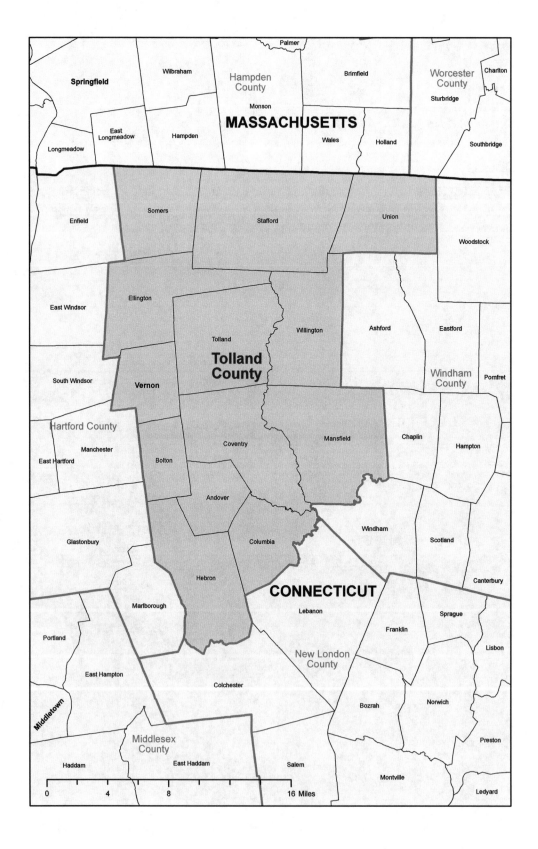

Tolland County

Founded	1785
Parent County	Windham
County Seat	Tolland (1785–1889), Rockville [now part of Vernon] (1819–1960)

Towns

Andover, Bolton, Columbia, Coventry, Ellington, Hebron, Mansfield, Somers, Stafford, Tolland, Union, Vernon, Willington

Extinct

Rockville

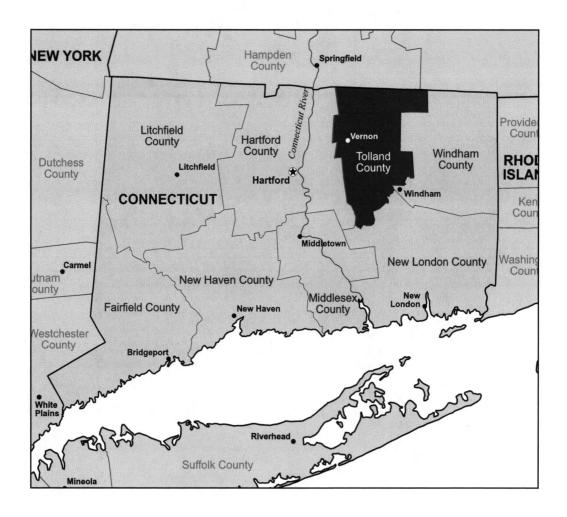

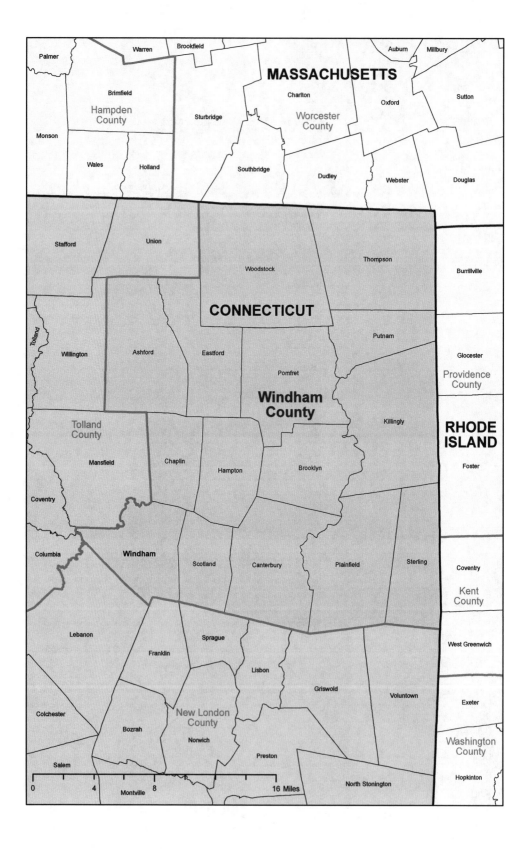

Windham County

Founded	1726
Parent Counties	Hartford, New London
County Seat	Windham (1726–1819), Brooklyn (1819–95), Willimantic (1895–1960)

Towns

Ashford, Brooklyn, Canterbury, Chaplin, Eastford, Hampton, Killingly, Plainfield, Pomfret, Putnam, Scotland, Sterling, Thompson, Windham, Woodstock

Extinct

Willimantic

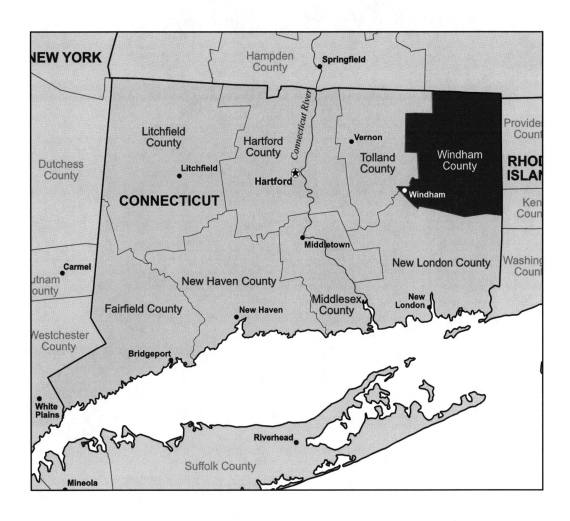

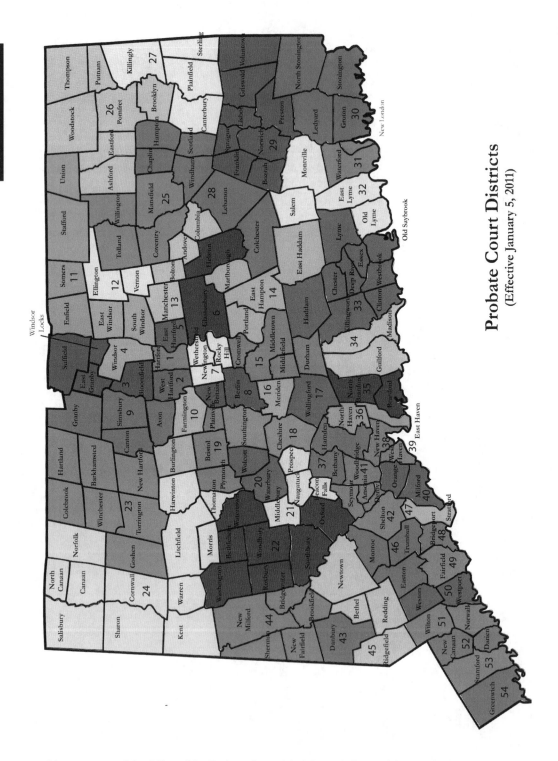

Probate Court Districts
(Effective January 5, 2011)

Map courtesy of the Office of the Probate Court Administrator, State of Connecticut

Probate Records

Probate in Connecticut is administered through probate districts, which have changed over time. In 2011 the state reduced the number of districts to 54. Districts are listed in numerical order. Check the note field in the town table beginning on page 71 to determine the probate district of the town you are researching.

The Probate Estate Papers Index (for probates from the mid-1600s through 1880, at least), available on microfilm at NEHGS, CSL, and FHL, lists individuals by surname, with year of probate, town of residence, probate district, and case number. This index provides the quickest way to determine the district of a particular person's probate. For a list of towns and probate districts over time—up until the 2011 change—consult the Connecticut State Library's guide at *www.cslib.org/probate/index.htm.*

1 Hartford Probate District
250 Constitution Plaza, 3rd floor
Hartford, CT 06103
www.jud.ct.gov/probate
(860) 757-9150; fax (860) 724-1503
Hours: M–F 8–4

Town served: Hartford

2 West Hartford Probate District
50 South Main Street, Rm. 318
West Hartford, CT 06107
www.jud.ct.gov/probate
(860) 561-7940; fax (860) 561-7591
Hours: M–F 8:30–4:30

Town served: West Hartford

3 Tobacco Valley Probate District
Town Office Building
50 Church Street
Windsor Locks, CT 06096
www.jud.ct.gov/probate
(860) 627-1450; fax (860) 654-8919
Hours: M–W 8–4; Th 8–6; F 8–1

Towns served: Bloomfield, East Granby, Suffield, Windsor Locks

4 Greater Windsor Probate District
Town Hall
1540 Sullivan Avenue
South Windsor, CT 06074
www.jud.ct.gov/probate
(860) 644-2511 ext. 371; fax (860) 648-5047
Hours: M–F 8–4

Towns served: East Windsor, South Windsor, Windsor

5 East Hartford Probate District
Town Hall
740 Main Street
East Hartford, CT 06108
www.jud.ct.gov/probate
(860) 291-7278; fax (860) 291-7211
Hours: M–F 8:30–4:30

Town served: East Hartford

6 Glastonbury-Hebron Probate District
2155 Main Street
Glastonbury, CT 06033-6523

Mailing Address
PO Box 6523
Glastonbury, CT 06033-6523

www.jud.ct.gov/probate
(860) 652-7629; fax (860) 368-2520
Hours: M, W–F 8:30–4:30; Tu 8:30–7

Towns served: Glastonbury, Hebron

7 Newington Probate District
66 Cedar Street, Rear
Newington, CT 06111
www.jud.ct.gov/probate
(860) 665-1285; fax (860) 665-1331
Hours: M, W, Th 8:30–4:30; Tu 8:30–5:30;
    F 8:30–4

Towns served: Newington, Rocky Hill, Wethersfield

8 Berlin Probate District
One Liberty Square
New Britain, CT 06050-0400

Mailing Address
PO Box 400
New Britain, CT 06050-0400

www.jud.ct.gov/probate
(860) 826-2696; fax (860) 826-2695
Hours: M–F 8:30–4:30

Towns served: Berlin, New Britain

9 Simsbury Regional Probate District
933 Hopmeadow Street
Simsbury, CT 06070-0495

Mailing Address
PO Box 495
Simsbury, CT 06070-0495

www.jud.ct.gov/probate
(860) 658-3277; fax (860) 658-3204
Hours: M–F 8:30–4:30

Towns served: Avon, Canton, Granby,
Simsbury

10 Farmington-Burlington Probate District
One Monteith Drive
Farmington, CT 06032
www.jud.ct.gov/probate
(860) 675-2360; fax (860) 673-8262
Hours: M, W–F 8:30–4:30; Tu 8:30–6

Towns served: Burlington, Farmington

11 North Central Connecticut Probate District
820 Enfield Street
Enfield, CT 06082
www.jud.ct.gov/probate
(860) 253-6305; fax (860) 253-6388
Hours: M–F 9–5

Towns served: Enfield, Somers, Stafford,
Union

12 Ellington Probate District
14 Park Place
Vernon, CT 06066

Mailing Address
PO Box 268
Vernon, CT 06066

www.jud.ct.gov/probate
(860) 872-0519; fax (860) 870-5140
Hours: M–W 8:15–4:30; Th 8:15–7;
    F 8:30–1

Towns served: Ellington, Vernon

13 Greater Manchester Probate District
66 Center Street
Manchester, CT 06040
www.jud.ct.gov/probate
(860) 647-3227; fax (860) 647-3236
Hours: M–F 8:30–4:30

Towns served: Andover, Bolton, Columbia,
Manchester

14 Region #14 Probate District
9 Austin Drive
Marlborough, CT 06447

Mailing Address
PO Box 29
Marlborough, CT 06447

www.jud.ct.gov/probate
(860) 295-6239; fax (860) 295-6122
Hours: M–F 8–4

Towns served: East Haddam, East
Hampton, Marlborough, Portland

15 Middletown Probate District
94 Court Street
Middletown, CT 06457
www.jud.ct.gov/probate
(860) 347-7424 ext.1; fax (860) 346-1520
Hours: M–F 8:30–4:30

Towns served: Cromwell, Durham, Middlefield, Middletown

16 Meriden Probate District

City Hall, Rm. 113
142 E. Main Street
Meriden, CT 06450
www.jud.ct.gov/probate
(203) 630-4150; fax (203) 630-4043
Hours: M–F 8–4

Town served: Meriden

17 Wallingford Probate District

Town Hall
45 S. Main Street, Rm. 114
Wallingford, CT 06492
www.jud.ct.gov/probate
(203) 294-2100; fax (203) 294-2109
Hours: M–F 9–5

Town served: Wallingford

18 Cheshire-Southington Probate District

84 South Main Street
Cheshire, CT 06410
www.jud.ct.gov/probate
(203) 271-6608; fax (203) 271-3735
Hours: M–F 8:15–4:15

Towns served: Cheshire, Southington

19 Region #19 Probate District

City Hall, 3rd floor
111 N. Main Street
Bristol, CT 06010
www.jud.ct.gov/probate
(860) 584-6230; fax (860) 584-3818
Hours: M–F 8:30–5

Towns served: Bristol, Plainville, Plymouth

20 Waterbury Probate District

49 Leavenworth Street
Waterbury, CT 06702
www.jud.ct.gov/probate
(203) 755-1127; fax (203) 597-0824
Hours: M–F 8–4

Towns served: Waterbury, Wolcott

21 Naugatuck Probate District

Town Hall
229 Church Street
Naugatuck, CT 06770
www.jud.ct.gov/probate
(203) 720-7046; fax (203) 720-5476
Hours: M–F 8–5

Towns served: Beacon Falls, Middlebury,
Naugatuck, Prospect

22 Region #22 Probate District

501 Main Street, South
Southbury, CT 06488

Mailing Address
PO Box 674
Southbury, CT 06488

Website *www.jud.ct.gov/probate*
(203) 262-0641; fax (203) 264-9310
Hours: M–F 8:30–4:30

Towns served: Bethlehem, Oxford,
Roxbury, Southbury, Washington,
Watertown, Woodbury

23 Torrington Area Probate District

Municipal Building
140 Main Street
Torrington, CT 06790
www.jud.ct.gov/probate
(860) 489-2215; fax (860) 496-5910
Hours: M–W 8–4:30; Th 8–6:30; F 8–12:30

Towns served: Barkhamsted, Colebrook,
Goshen, Hartland, New Hartford,
Torrington, Winchester

24 Litchfield Hills Probate District

74 West Street
Litchfield, CT 06759

Mailing Address
PO Box 505
Litchfield, CT 06759

www.jud.ct.gov/probate
(860) 567-8065; fax (860) 567-2538
Hours: M–F 8:30–4:30

cont. on next page

24 Litchfield Hills Probate District *(cont.)*

Towns served: Harwinton, Kent, Litchfield, Morris, Thomaston, Warren

Satellite Office
100 Pease Street
Canaan, CT 06018

Mailing Address
PO Box 849
Canaan, CT 06018

www.jud.ct.gov/probate
(860) 824-7012; fax (860) 824-7428
Hours: M–F 9–4

Towns served: Canaan, Cornwall, Norfolk, North Canaan, Salisbury, Sharon

25 Tolland-Mansfield Probate District

21 Tolland Green
Tolland, CT 06084
www.jud.ct.gov/probate
(860) 871-3640; fax (860) 871-3641
Hours: M–F 8–4:30; Th 8–7:30; F 8–11 a.m.

Towns served: Coventry, Mansfield, Tolland, Willington

26 Northeast Probate District

815 Riverside Drive
North Grosvenordale, CT 06255

Mailing Address
PO Box 40
North Grosvenordale, CT 06255

www.jud.ct.gov/probate
(860) 923-2203; fax (860) 923-9105
Hours: M–W 8:30–4:30; Th 8:30–6; F 8:30–3

Towns served: Ashford, Brooklyn, Eastford, Pomfret, Putnam, Thompson, Woodstock

27 Plainfield-Killingly Probate District

Town Hall
8 Community Avenue
Plainfield, CT 06374
www.jud.ct.gov/probate
(860) 230-3031; fax (860) 230-3033
Hours: M–F 8:30–4:30

Towns served: Canterbury, Killingly, Plainfield, Sterling

28 Windham-Colchester Probate District

979 Main Street,
Willimantic, CT 06226

Mailing Address
PO Box 34
Willimantic, CT 06226

www.jud.ct.gov/probate
(860) 465-3049; fax (860) 465-2162
Hours: M–F 8–5; Th 8–7:30; F 8–12

Towns served: Chaplin, Hampton, Scotland, Windham

Satellite Office
Town Hall
127 Norwich Avenue
Colchester, CT 06415

www.jud.ct.gov/probate
(860) 537-7290; fax (860) 537-7298
Hours: W–Th 11–4

Towns served: Colchester, Lebanon

29 Norwich Probate District

100 Broadway, Rm. 122
Norwich, CT 06360-0038

Mailing Address
PO Box 38
Norwich, CT 06360-0038

www.jud.ct.gov/probate
(860) 887-2160; fax (860) 887-2401
Hours: M–F 8:30–4:30

Towns served: Bozrah, Franklin, Griswold, Lisbon, Norwich, Preston, Sprague, Voluntown

30 Southeastern Connecticut Regional Probate District

Town Hall
45 Fort Hill Road
Groton, CT 06340
www.jud.ct.gov/probate
(860) 441-6655; fax (860) 441-6657
Hours: M–F 8:30–4:30

Towns served: Groton, Ledyard, North Stonington, Stonington

---

31 New London Probate District
181 State Street, Rm. 2
New London, CT 06320

Mailing Address
PO Box 148
New London, CT 06320

www.jud.ct.gov/probate
(860) 443-7121; fax (860) 437-8155
Hours: M–F 8:30–4

Towns served: New London, Waterford

---

32 Niantic Regional Probate District
118 Pennsylvania Avenue
Niantic, CT 06357

Mailing Address
PO Box 519
Niantic, CT 06357

www.jud.ct.gov/probate
(860) 739-6052; fax (860) 739-6738
Hours: M–F 8:30–4:30

Towns served: East Lyme, Montville, Old Lyme, Salem

---

33 Saybrook Probate District
302 Main Street, 2nd floor
Old Saybrook, CT 06475
www.jud.ct.gov/probate
(860) 510-5028; fax (860) 388-3734
Hours: M–F 8:30–4:30

Towns served: Chester, Clinton, Deep River, Essex, Haddam, Killingworth, Lyme, Old Saybrook, Westbrook

---

34 Madison-Guilford Probate District
8 Campus Drive
Madison, CT 06443
www.jud.ct.gov/probate
(203) 245-5661; fax (203) 245-5653
Hours: M–F 8:30–4:30

Towns served: Guilford, Madison

---

35 Branford-North Branford Probate District
1019 Main Street
Branford, CT 06405-0638

Mailing Address
PO Box 638
Branford, CT 06405-0638

www.jud.ct.gov/probate
(203) 488-0318; fax (203) 315-4715
Hours: M–F 8:30–4:30

Towns served: Branford, North Branford

---

36 East Haven-North Haven Probate District
Town Hall
250 Main Street
East Haven, CT 06512
www.jud.ct.gov/probate
(203) 468-3895, (203) 468-5155
Hours: M–F 8:30–4:30

Towns served: East Haven, North Haven

---

37 Hamden-Bethany Probate District
Government Center
2750 Dixwell Avenue
Hamden, CT 06518
www.jud.ct.gov/probate
(203) 287-7082; fax (203) 287-7087
Hours: M–F 8:30–4:30

Towns served: Bethany, Hamden

---

38 New Haven Probate District
200 Orange Street, 1st floor
New Haven, CT 06504

Mailing Address
PO Box 905
New Haven, CT 06504

www.jud.ct.gov/probate
(203) 946-4880; fax (203) 946-5962
Hours: M–F 9–5

Town served: New Haven

39 West Haven Probate District
355 Main Street
West Haven, CT 06516

Mailing Address
PO Box 127
West Haven, CT 06516

www.jud.ct.gov/probate
(203) 937-3552; fax (203) 937-3556
Hours: M–F 8:30–5

Town served: West Haven

40 Milford-Orange Probate District
Parsons Government Center
70 West River Street
Milford, CT 06460-0414

Mailing Address
PO Box 414
Milford, CT 06460-0414

www.jud.ct.gov/probate
(203) 783-3205; fax (203) 783-3364
Hours: M–F 8:30–4:30

Towns served: Milford, Orange

41 Derby Probate District
City Hall
253 Main Street, 2nd floor
Ansonia, CT 06401
www.jud.ct.gov/probate
(203) 734-1277; fax (203) 736-1434
Hours: M–Th 8:30–5:30; F 8:30–2:30

Towns served: Ansonia, Derby, Seymour,
Woodbridge

42 Shelton Probate District
40 White Street
Shelton, CT 06484

Mailing Address
PO Box 127
Shelton, CT 06484

www.jud.ct.gov/probate
(203) 924-8462; fax (203) 924-8943
Hours: M–F 9–5

Town served: Shelton

43 Danbury Probate District
City Hall Building
155 Deer Hill Avenue
Danbury, CT 06810
www.jud.ct.gov/probate
(203) 797-4521; fax (203) 796-1563
Hours: M–Th 7:30–5:30

Town served: Danbury

44 Housatonic Probate District
Town Hall
10 Main Street
New Milford, CT 06776
www.jud.ct.gov/probate
(860) 355-6029; fax (860) 355-6024
Hours: M–F 8:30–5

Towns served: Bridgewater, Brookfield,
New Fairfield, New Milford, Sherman

**45 Northern Fairfield County
Probate District**
1 School Street
Bethel, CT 06801
www.jud.ct.gov/probate
(203) 794-8508; fax (203) 778-7517
Hours: M–F 8:30–4:30

Towns served: Bethel, Newtown, Redding,
Ridgefield

46 Trumbull Probate District
Town Hall
5866 Main Street
Trumbull, CT 06611-5416
www.jud.ct.gov/probate
(203) 452-5068; fax (203) 452-5092
Hours: M–F 8:30–4:03

Towns served: Easton, Monroe, Trumbull

47 Stratford Probate District
468 Birdseye Street, 2nd floor
Stratford, CT 06615
www.jud.ct.gov/probate
(203) 385-4023; fax (203) 375-6253
Hours: M–F 8:30–4:30

Town served: Stratford

48 Bridgeport Probate District

202 State Street, McLevy Hall, 3rd floor
Bridgeport, CT 06604
www.jud.ct.gov/probate
(203) 576-3945; fax (203) 576-7898
Hours: M–Th 8:30–4:30; F 8:30–4

Town served: Bridgeport

49 Fairfield Probate District

Sullivan Independence Hall
725 Old Post Road
Fairfield, CT 06824
www.jud.ct.gov/probate
(203) 256-3041; fax (203) 256-3044
Hours: M–F 8:30–4:30

Town served: Fairfield

50 Westport Probate District

Town Hall
110 Myrtle Avenue, Rm. 100
Westport, CT 06880
www.jud.ct.gov/probate
(203) 341-1100; fax (203) 341-1102
Hours: M–F 8:30–4:30

Towns served: Weston, Westport

51 Norwalk-Wilton Probate District

125 East Avenue
Norwalk, CT 06852-2009

Mailing Address
PO Box 2009
Norwalk, CT 06852-2009
www.jud.ct.gov/probate
(203) 854-7737; fax (203) 854-7825
Hours: M–F 8:30–4:30

Towns served: Norwalk, Wilton

52 Darien-New Canaan Probate District

Town Hall
2 Renshaw Road
Darien, CT 06820
www.jud.ct.gov/probate
(203) 656-7342; fax (203) 656-0774
Hours: M–F 8:30–4:30

Towns served: Darien, New Canaan

53 Stamford Probate District

Stamford Gov't Center, 8th floor
888 Washington Blvd.
Stamford, CT 06904-2152

Mailing Address
PO Box 10152
Stamford, CT 06904-2152

www.jud.ct.gov/probate
(203) 323-2149; fax (203) 964-1830
Hours: M–F 8:30–4:30

Town served: Stamford

54 Greenwich Probate District

Town Hall
101 Field Point Road
Greenwich, CT 06836-2540

Mailing Address
PO Box 2540
Greenwich, CT 06836-2540

www.jud.ct.gov/probate
(203) 622-7879; fax (203) 622-6451
Hours: M–F 8–4

Town served: Greenwich

CT

Land Records

Land transactions in Connecticut are recorded on the town level. Town and city clerks are responsible for maintaining land transactions. Some towns have made records available online. A number of town clerks have grouped together to create the Connecticut Town Clerks Portal, which provides access to records online for a fee at *https://connecticut-townclerks-records.com*; check that site in addition to checking the individual town and town clerk sites listed here.

Andover
Town Office Building
17 School Road
Andover, CT 06232
*http://andoverconnecticut.org/
    services-government/town-clerk*
(860) 742-7305; fax (860) 742-7535
Hours: M 8:15–7; Tu–Th 8:15–4

Ansonia
53 Main Street
Ansonia, CT 06401
www.cityofansonia.com
(203) 736-5980; fax (203) 736-5982
See website for email
Hours: M–W 8:30–4:30; Th 8:30–5;
    F 8:30–1

Ashford
Ashford Town Offices
5 Town Hall Road
Ashford, CT 06278

*www.ashfordtownhall.org/government/
    admin-and-finance/town-clerk*
(860) 487-4401; fax (860) 487-4431
See website for email
Hours: M–Tu 8:30–3; W 8:30–3, 7-9;
    Th closed; F 8:30–3

Avon
60 West Main Street (Route 44)
Avon, CT 06001
*www.town.avon.ct.us/Public_Documents/
    AvonCT_Clerk/clerk*
(860) 409-4311; fax (860) 677-8428
See website for email
Hours: M–F 8:30–4:30

Barkhamsted
67 Ripley Hill Road
Pleasant Valley, CT 06063-0558

Above: "Shaker houses, Enfield." John Warner Barber, *Connecticut Historical Collections* (1836), p. 85.

Mailing Address
PO Box 558
Pleasant Valley, CT 06063-0558

http://barkhamsted.us
(860) 379-8665; fax (860) 379-9284
See website for email
Hours: M, Tu, Th 9–4; W 10–6; F 9–12

Beacon Falls

10 Maple Avenue
Beacon Falls, CT 06403
www.beaconfalls-ct.org
(203) 729-4340; fax (203) 720-8254
See website for email
Hours: M–W 9–12:30, 1–4:30; Th 9–12:30,
    1–8; F 9–12:30, 1–2:30

Berlin

240 Kensington Road
Berlin, CT 06037
www.town.berlin.ct.us
(860) 828-7035; fax (860) 828-8628
See website for email
Hours: M–W 8:30–4:30; Th 8:30–7;
    F 8:30–1

Bethany

40 Peck Road
Bethany, CT 06524-3338
www.bethany-ct.com/townoffices/t_TownClerk.asp
(203) 393-2100, x 105; fax (203) 393-0821
See website for email
Hours: M, 9–4:30 6:30– 7:30; Tu–F 9–4:30

Bethel

Clifford J. Hurgin Municipal Center
1 School Street
Bethel, CT 06801
www.bethelct.org/clerk/town_clerk.html
www.bethel-landrecords.org
(203) 794-8505; (203) 794-8506;
    fax (203) 778-7516
See website for email
Hours: M–F 8:30–4:30

Bethlehem

36 Main Street South
Bethlehem, CT 06751
www.ci.bethlehem.ct.us/government.htm
(203) 266-7510; fax (203) 266-7670
townclerkbethlehem@snet.net
Hours: Tu–Sat 7–12

Bloomfield

800 Bloomfield Avenue
Bloomfield, CT 06002
www.bloomfieldct.org/dept_town_clerk.php
(860) 769-3507; fax (860) 769-3597
See website for email
Hours: M–F 9–5

Bolton

222 Bolton Center Road
Bolton, CT 06043
http://bolton.govoffice.com/
(860) 649-8066, x 106; fax (860) 643-0021
See website for email
Hours: M, W, Th 8:30–4; Tu 8:30–6:30;
    F 8:30–1

Bozrah

1 River Road
Bozrah, CT 06334
www.munic.state.ct.us/BOZRAH/bozrah.htm
(860) 889-2689; fax (860) 877-5449
See website for email
Hours: M–Th 9–4; F 9–12; or by appointment

Branford

1019 Main Street
Branford, CT 06405
www.branford-ct.gov
(203) 315-0678; fax (203) 889-4807
townclerk@branford-ct.gov
Hours: M–F 8:30–4

Bridgeport

45 Lyon Terrace
Bridgeport, CT 06604
*www.bridgeportct.gov/TownClerk/Pages/
    TownClerk.aspx*
(203) 576-7208
See website for email
Hours: M–F 9–12, 1–4:30

Bridgewater

44 Main Street South
Bridgewater, CT 06752

Mailing Address
PO Box 216
Bridgewater, CT 06752

www.bridgewatertownhall.org/townclerk.html
(860) 354-5102; fax (860) 350-5944
See website for email
Hours: M 8–12:30; Tu 8–3:30; W 8–12:30;
    Th closed; F 8–12:30

Bristol

111 North Main Street
Bristol, CT 06010
www.ci.bristol.ct.us
(860) 584-6200; fax (860) 584-6199
Hours: M–F 8:30–5

Brookfield

Town Hall, 1st floor, Rm. 115
100 Pocono Road
Brookfield, CT 06804

Mailing Address
PO Box 5106
Brookfield, CT 06804
www.brookfieldct.gov/offices/townclerk.html
(203) 775-7313; fax (203) 775-5231
townclerk@brookfieldct.gov
Hours: M–W, F 8:30–4:15; Th 8:30–6:15
    (call first)

Brooklyn

4 Wolf Den Road
Brooklyn, CT 06234

Mailing Address
PO Box 356
Brooklyn, CT 06234

www.brooklynct.org/townclerk.htm
(860) 779-5032; fax (860) 774-5732
See website for email
Hours: M, Tu, W 8–5; Th 8–6

Burlington

200 Spielman Highway
Burlington, CT 06013
*http://burlingtonct.us/departments/burlington-
    town-clerk.php*
(860) 673-6789, ext. 2; fax (860) 675-9312
See website for email
Hours: M–Th 8:30–4; F 8:30–1:30

Canaan

108 Main Street
Falls Village, CT 06031

Mailing Address
PO Box 47
Falls Village, CT 06031-0047

www.canaanfallsvillage.org
(860) 824-0707, ext. 10; fax (860) 824-4506
See website for email
Hours: M–Th 9–3

Canterbury

1 Municipal Drive
Canterbury, CT 06331

Mailing Address
PO Box 27
Canterbury, CT 06331

www.canterburyct.org
(860) 546-9377; fax (860) 546-9295
See website for email
Hours: M–W 9–4; Th 9–6:30; F 9–1:30

Canton

4 Market Street
Collinsville, CT 06022

Mailing Address
PO Box 168
Collinsville, CT 06022

www.townofcantonct.org
(860) 693-7870; fax (860) 693-7840
See website for email
Hours: M–Tu, Th 8:15–4:30; W 8:15–6:45;
F 8:15–12

Chaplin

495 Phoenixville Road
Chaplin, CT 06235
www.chaplinct.org
(860) 455-0073 ext. 312; fax (860) 455-0027
townclerk@chaplinct.org
Hours: M, W, Th 9–3; Tu 1-7

Cheshire

84 South Main Street
Cheshire, CT 06410
www.cheshirect.org/town-clerk
(203) 271-6601; fax (203) 271-6639
See website for email
Hours: M–F 8:30–4

Chester

203 Middlesex Avenue
Chester, CT 06412
www.chesterct.com
(860) 526-0013; fax (860) 526-0004
TownClerk@chesterct.org
Hours: M, W–Th 9–4; Tu 9–7; F 9–12

Clinton

54 E. Main Street
Clinton, CT 06413
www.clintonct.org/townclerk.htm
(860) 669-9333 ext. 30; fax (860) 669-0890
See website for email
Hours: M–W 9–4; Th 9–7; F 9–12

Colchester

127 Norwich Avenue, Suite 101
Colchester, CT 06415
www.colchesterct.gov
(860) 537-7215; (860) 537-7216; fax
(860) 537-0547
townclerk@colchesterct.gov
Hours: M–W, F 8:30–4:30; Th 8:30–7

Colebrook

562 Colebrook Road
Route 183
Colebrook, CT 06021
www.townofcolebrook.org
(860) 379-1551; fax (860) 379-2342
See website for email
Hours: Nov.–May, M–F 1–5
May–Nov., M, F 10–4:30; Tu–Th 1–5

Columbia

323 Route 87
Columbia, CT 06237
www.columbiact.org
(860) 228-3284; fax (860) 228-2335
townclerk@columbiact.org
Hours: M–W 8–4; Th 8–6; F 8–12

Cornwall

26 Pine Street
Cornwall, CT 06753

Mailing Address
PO Box 97
Cornwall, CT 06753

www.cornwallct.org
(860) 672-2709; fax (860) 672-4069
cwltownclerk@optonline.net
Hours: M–Th 9–12, 1–4

Coventry

1712 Main Street
Coventry, CT
www.coventryct.org
(860) 742-7966; fax (860) 742-8911
See website for email
Hours: M–W 8:30–4:30; Th 8:30–6:30;
F 8:30–1:30

Cromwell

Town Hall, 2nd floor
41 West Street
Cromwell, CT 06416
www.cromwellct.com
(860) 632-3440; fax (860) 632-3425
townclerk@cromwellct.com
Hours: M–F 8:30 a.m–4

Danbury

155 Deer Hill Avenue
Danbury, CT 06810
www.ci.danbury.ct.us
(203) 797-4531; fax (203) 796-8087
See website for email
Hours: M–W 7:30–6; Th 7:30–6:30

Darien

Town Hall, Rm. 101
2 Renshaw Road
Darien, CT 06820
www.darienct.gov
(203) 656-7307; fax (203) 656-7380
See website for email
Hours: M–F 8:30–4:30

Deep River

174 Main Street
Deep River, CT 06417
www.deepriverct.com/town_clerk
(860) 526-6024; fax (860) 526-6023
townclerk@deepriverct.us
Hours: M–W, F 9–4; Th 9–7

Derby

1 Elizabeth Street
Derby, CT 06418
http://electronicvalley.org/derby/govern
(203) 736-1462; fax (203) 736-1548
See website for email
Hours: M–F 9–5

Durham

30 Townhouse Road
Durham, CT 06422

Mailing Address
PO Box 428
Durham, CT 06422

www.townofdurhamct.org
(860) 349-3453; fax (860) 343-6733
See website for email
Hours: M, W, Th–F 8:30–4:30; Tu 8:30–7;
and by appointment.

East Granby

9 Center Street
East Granby, CT 06026

Mailing Address
PO Box 1858
East Granby, CT 06026

www.eastgranby.net
(860) 653-2576; fax (860) 653-4017
info@egtownhall.com
Hours: M–Th 8–4; F 8–1

East Haddam

7 Main Street
East Haddam, CT 06423

Mailing Address
PO Box K
East Haddam, CT 06423

www.easthaddam.org
(860) 873-5027; fax (860) 873-5042
townclerk@easthaddam.org
Hours: M, W–Th 9–4; Tu 9–7; F 9–12

East Hampton

20 East High Street
East Hampton, CT 06424
www.easthamptonct.org
(860) 267-2519, ext 311; fax (860) 267-1027
See website for email
Hours: M, W, Th 8–4; Tu, 8–7:30; F 8–12:30

East Hartford

Town Hall, 1st floor
740 Main Street
East Hartford, CT 06108
www.ci.east-hartford.ct.us
(860) 291-7230, (860) 291-7232; fax (860)
291-7238
See website for email
Hours: M–W, F 8:30–4:30; Th 8:30–6

East Haven

Town Hall, Upper Level
250 Mail Street
East Haven, CT 06512
www.townofeasthavenct.org/tclerk.shtml
(203) 468–3201, (203) 468–3202,
(203) 468–3203; fax (203) 468-2422
Hours: M–F 8:30–4:30

East Lyme

108 Pennsylvania Avenue
Niantic, CT 06357

Mailing Address
PO Box 519
Niantic, CT 06357

www.eltownhall.com/town-clerk
(860) 739-6931 ext 120; fax (860) 739-6930
See website for email
Hours: M–F 8–4

East Windsor

11 Rye Street
Broad Brook, CT 06016
www.eastwindsor-ct.gov
(860) 292-8255; fax (860) 623-4798
See website for email
Hours: M–W 8:30–4:30; F 8:30–1

Eastford

16 Westford Road
Eastford, CT 06242

Mailing Address
PO Box 207
Eastford, CT 06242
www.townofeastford.org
(860) 974-0133; fax (860) 974-0624
Town.of.Eastford@SNET.net
Hours: Tu, W 10–12, 1–4; 2nd & 4th Tu
5:30-7:30

Easton

225 Center Road
Easton, CT 06612

Mailing Address
PO Box 61
Easton, CT 06612

www.eastonct.gov
(203) 268-6291; fax (203) 261-6080
townclerk@eastonct.gov
Hours: M–F 8:30–3:30

Ellington

55 Main Street
Ellington, CT 06029
www.ellington-ct.gov
(860) 870-3105; fax (860) 870-3158
townclerk@ellington-ct.gov
Hours: M 8:30–6; Tu–Th 8:30–4;
F 8:30–1:30

Enfield

820 Enfield Street
Enfield, CT 06082
www.enfield-ct.gov
(860) 253-6440; fax (860) 253-6331
townclerk@enfield.org
Hours: M–F 9–5

Essex

29 West Avenue
Essex, CT 06426
www.essexct.gov/departments/townclerk.html
(860) 767-4340, ext 129; fax (860) 767-4560
See website for email
Hours: M–F 9–4

Fairfield

Old Town Hall
611 Old Post Road
Fairfield, CT 06824
www.fairfieldct.org
(203) 256-3090
See website for email
Hours: M–F 8:30–4:30

Farmington

1 Monteith Drive
Farmington, CT 06032
www.farmington-ct.org
(860) 675-2380; fax (860) 675-2389
See website for email
Hours: M–F 8:30–4:30

Franklin

7 Meeting House Hill Road
Franklin, CT 06254
www.franklinct.com
(860) 642-7352, ext 18; see website for fax
franklintownclerk@99main.com
Hours: M, W–Th 8:30–3; Tu 8:30–3, 6–8

Glastonbury

2155 Main Street
Glastonbury, CT 06033

Mailing Address
PO Box 6523
Glastonbury, CT 06033-6523

www.glastonbury-ct.gov
(860) 652-7616; fax (860) 652-7639
townclerk@glastonbury-ct.gov
Hours: M–F 8–4:30

Goshen

42C North Street
Goshen, CT 06756
www.goshenct.gov
(860) 491-3647
Hours: M–Th 9–12, 1-4; F 9–1; and
   by appt.

Granby

15 North Granby Road
Granby, CT 06035
www.granby-ct.gov
(860) 844-5308; fax (860) 653-4769
See website for email
Hours: M, Tu, W 8–4; Th 8–6:30;
   F 8–12:30

Greenwich

101 Field Point Road
Greenwich, CT 06830
www.greenwichct.org/TownClerk/TownClerk.asp
(203) 622-7897; fax (203) 622-3767
See website for email
Hours: M–F 8–4

Griswold

28 Main Street
Jewett City, CT 06351

Mailing Address
PO Box 369
Jewett City, CT 06351

www.griswold-ct.org/townclerk.html
(860) 376-7060, ext 101; fax (860) 376-7070
See website for email
Hours: M–W 8:30–4; Th 8:30–6:30;
   F 8:30–1

Groton

45 Fort Hill Road
Groton, CT 06340
www.groton-ct.gov/depts/twnclk/
(860) 441-6642; fax (860) 441-6703
townclerk@groton.ct.us
Hours: M–F 8:30–4:30

Guilford

31 Park Street
Guilford, CT 06437
www.ci.guilford.ct.us/town-clerk.htm
http://ctguilford.cotthosting.com/
(203) 453-8001
See website for email
Hours: M–F 8:30–4:30

Haddam

Town Office Building
30 Field Park Drive
Haddam, CT 06438
www.haddam.org/town_clerk.shtml
(860) 345-8531, ext 212; fax (860) 345-3730
townclerk@haddam.org
Hours: M–W 9–12, 1–4; Th 9–12, 12:30–5,
    5:30–7; F 9–12

Hamden

Hamden Government Center
2750 Dixwell Avenue
Hamden, CT 06518
www.hamden.com
(203) 287-7112
Hours: M–F 8:45–4

Hampton

164 Main Street (Route 97)
Hampton, CT 06247

Mailing Address
PO Box 143
Hampton, CT 06247

www.hamptonct.org
(860) 455-9132, ext 1; fax (860) 455-0517
townclerk@hamptonct.org
Hours: Tu 9–4; Th 10–7

Hartford

550 Main Street, Rm. 105
Hartford, CT 06103
http://townclerk.hartford.gov
(860) 757-9751; fax (860) 722-8041
See website for email
Hours: M–F 8:15–4:45

Hartland

22 South Road
East Hartland, CT 06027
(860) 653-0285; fax (860) 653-0452
Hours: M–W 10–12, 1–4

Harwinton

100 Bentley Drive
Harwinton, CT 06791
www.harwinton.us
(860) 485-9051; fax (860) 485-0051
Hours: M–Tu, Th 8:30–4; W 8:30–6;
    F 8:30–12:30

Hebron

Town Office Building and Horton House
15 Gilead Street
Hebron, CT 06248
www.hebronct.com/townclerkofc.htm
www.uslandrecords.com/ctlr
(860) 228-5971; fax (860) 228-4859
See website for email
Hours: M–W 8–4; Th 8–6; F 8–1

Kent

41 Kent Green Boulevard
Kent, CT 06757

Mailing Address
PO Box 843
Kent, CT 06757

www.townofkentct.org/town-clerk
(860) 927-3433; fax (860) 927-4541
townclerk@townofkentct.org
Hours: M–F 9–4; July–Labor Day: M–Th
    9–4, F 9–12

Killingly

172 Main Street
Danielson, CT 06239

Mailing Address
PO Box 6000
Danielson, CT 06239-1832

www.killingly.org
(860) 779-5308; fax (860) 779-5316
See website for email
Hours: M–F 8:30–4:30

Killingworth

323 Route 81
Killingworth, CT 06419
www.killingworthct.com/town.shtml
(860) 663-1765 ext 502; fax (860) 663-4050
See website for email
Hours: M–F 8–12, 1–4
Website *www.killingworthct.com/town.shtml*

Lebanon

579 Exeter Road
Lebanon, CT 06249
www.lebanontownhall.org
(860) 642-7319; fax (860) 642-7716
townclerk@lebanontownhall.org
Hours: M, W–Th F 8–4; Tu 8–6

Ledyard

741 Colonel Ledyard Highway
Ledyard, CT 06339-1511
www.town.ledyard.ct.us
(860) 464-3257, (860) 464-3230;
    fax (860) 464-1126
town.clerk@ledyardct.org
Hours: M–F 8:30–4:30

Lisbon

Route 138 and Route 169
Lisbon, CT 06351
www.lisbonct.com
(860) 376-3400
See website for email
Hours: M–Tu, Th 9–3; W 6–9; F 9–12

Litchfield

Town Offices
74 West Street
Litchfield, CT 06759

Mailing Address
PO Box 488
Litchfield, CT 06759

www.townoflitchfield.org
(860) 567-7561
townclerk@townoflitchfield.org
Hours: M–F 9–4:30

Lyme

480 Hamburg Road (Route 156)
Lyme, CT 06371
www.townlyme.org
(860) 434-7733
townclerk@townlyme.org
Hours: M–F 9–4

Madison

8 Campus Drive
Madison, CT 06443
www.madisonct.org/clerk/clerkhome.htm
(203) 245-5672; fax (203) 245-5672
Hours: M–F 8:30–4

Manchester

41 Center Street
Manchester, CT 06045

Mailing Address
PO Box 191
Manchester, CT 06045-0191

www.townofmanchester.org/Town_Clerk
(860) 647-3037; fax (860) 647-3029
Hours: M–F 8:30–5

Mansfield

Audrey P. Beck Municipal Building
4 South Eagleville Road
Storrs, CT 06268
www.mansfieldct.gov
(860) 429-3302
townclerk@mansfieldct.org
Hours: M–W 8:15–4:30; Th 8:15–6:30;
    F 8–12

Marlborough
26 North Main Street
Marlborough, CT 06447
(860) 295-6206; fax (860) 295-0317
Hours: M, W, Th 8–4:30; Tu 8–7

Meriden
142 East Main Street, Rm. 124
Meriden, CT 06450
www.cityofmeriden.org
(203) 630-4030; fax (203) 630-4059
Hours: M–F 8–5

Middlebury
1212 Whittemore Road
Middlebury, CT 06762
www.middlebury-ct.org
(203) 758-2557; fax (203) 758-2915
townclerk@middlebury-ct. org
Hours: M–F 9–5

Middlefield
393 Jackson Hill Road
Middlefield, CT 06455

Mailing Address
PO Box 179
Middlefield, CT 06455-1208

www.middlefieldct.org
(860) 349-7116; fax (860) 349-7115
See website for email
Hours: M 9–5; Tu–Th 9–4; F 9–3

Middletown
Municipal Building, 1st floor
245 deKoven Drive
Middletown, CT 06457
www.cityofmiddletown.com
(860) 344-3459
townclerk@cityofmiddletown.com
Hours: M–F 8:30–4:30

Milford
70 W. River Street
Milford, CT 06460
www.ci.milford.ct.us
(203) 783-3210; fax (203) 783-4856
See website for email
Hours: M–F 8:30–5

Monroe
Town Hall, Rm. 201
7 Fan Hill Road
Monroe, CT 06468
www.monroect.org/townclerk.aspx
(860) 452-2811; fax (860) 452-6581
See website for email
Hours: M–Th 8–4; F 8–1

Montville
Town Hall, Rm. 5
310 Norwich-New London Turnpike
Uncasville, CT 0638
www.montville-ct.org
(860) 848-3030 ext 384; fax (860) 848-9784
See website for email
Hours: M–F 8–4:30

Morris
3 East Street
Morris, CT 06763

Mailing Address
PO Box 66
Morris, CT 06763

www.townofmorrisct.org
(860) 567-7433; fax (860) 567-7432
townclerk@townofmorris.org
Hours: M, Tu, W 8:30–12, 1–4;
     Th 8:30–12, 1–5; F 8:30–12

Naugatuck
229 Church Street, 2nd floor
Naugatuck, CT 06770-4199
www.naugatuck-ct.gov
(203) 720-7055; fax (203) 720-7099
townclerknaug@sbcglobal.net
Hours: M–F 8:30–4

New Britain

27 West Main Street, Rm. 109
New Britain, CT 06051
www.newbritainct.gov
http://landrecords.newbritainct.gov
(860) 826-3344; fax (860) 826-3348
See website for email
Hours: M–F 8:15–3:45; last Th 8:15–6:45

New Canaan

Town Hall, 1st floor
77 Main Street
New Canaan, CT 06840
www.newcanaan.info
http://townclerk.ci.new-canaan.ct.us/resolution
(203) 594-3070; fax (203) 594-3073
See website for email
Hours: M–F 8:30–4

New Fairfield

4 Brush Hill Road
New Fairfield, CT 06812
www.newfairfield.org
(203) 312-5616; fax (203) 312-5612
See website for email
Hours: M–Th 8:30–5; F 8:30–12

New Hartford

530 Main Street
New Hartford, CT 06057

Mailing Address
PO Box 316
New Hartford, CT 06057
www.town.new-hartford.ct.us
http://cotthosting.com/ctnewhartford
(860) 379-5037; fax (860) 379-1367
nhtownclerk@town.new-hartford.ct.us
Hours: M–Tu, Th 8–4; W 8–6; F 8–12

New Haven

200 Orange Street
New Haven, CT 06510
www.cityofnewhaven.com
www.uslandrecords.com/ctlr

(203) 46-8346; fax (203) 946-6974
See website for email
Hours: M–F 8–5

New London

181 State Street
New London, CT 06320
http://ci.new-london.ct.us
(860) 447-5205; fax (860) 447-1644
See website for email
Hours: M–F 8:30 –4

New Milford

10 Main Street
New Milford, CT
www.newmilford.org
(860) 355-6020; fax (860) 210-2096
town_clerk@newmilford.org
Hours: M–F 8:30 – 4:30

Newington

131 Cedar Street
Newington, CT 06111
www.newingtonct.gov
(860) 665-8500; fax (860) 665-8551
See website for email
Hours: M-F 8:30–4:30

Newtown

Newtown Municipal Center
3 Primrose Street
Newtown, CT 06470
www.newtown-ct.gov
(203) 270-4210; fax (203) 270-4213
town.clerk@newtown-ct.gov
Hours: M–F 8–4:30

Norfolk

19 Maple Avenue
Norfolk, CT 06058

Mailing Address
PO Box 552
Norfolk, CT 06058

www.norfolkct.org
(860) 542-5679; fax (860) 542-5274
nfkclerk@snet.net
Hours: M–Th 8:30–12, 1–4; F 8:30–12

North Branford
909 Foxon Road
North Branford, CT 06471
www.townofnorthbranfordct.com
(203) 484-6015; fax (203) 484-6025
townclerk@townofnorthbranfordct.com
Hours: M–F 8:30–4:30

North Canaan
100 Pease Street
North Canaan, CT 06018
www.northcanaan.org
(860) 824-3138; fax (860) 824-3139
no.canaan.clerk@snet.net
Hours: M-Th 9–12, 1–4

North Haven
18 Church Street
North Haven, CT 06473
www.town.north-haven.ct.us
(203) 239-5321; fax (203) 985-8370
townclerk@town.north-haven.ct.us
Hours: M–F 8:30–4:30

North Stonington
40 Main Street
North Stonington, CT 06359
www.northstoningtonct.gov
(860) 535-2877, ext 21; fax (860) 535-4554
See website for email
Hours: M–F 8–4

Norwalk
125 East Avenue
Norwalk, CT 06851
www.norwalkct.org
(203) 854-7747; fax (203) 854-7802
See website for email
Hours: M–W F 8:30–4:30;Th 8:30–7

Norwich
City Hall, Rm. 215
100 Broadway
Norwich, CT 06360-4431
www.cityofnorwich.com
(860) 823-3732; fax (860) 823-3790
cityclerk@cityofnorwich.com
Hours: M–F 8:30–4:30

Old Lyme
52 Lyme Street
Old Lyme, CT 06371
www.oldlyme-ct.gov
(860) 434-1605, ext 221; fax (860) 434-1400
townclerk@oldlyme-ct.gov
Hours: M–F 9–12, 1–4

Old Saybrook
302 Main Street
Old Saybrook, CT 06475
www.oldsaybrookct.org
(860) 395-3135l fax (860) 395-5014
See website for email
Hours: M–F 8:30–4:30

Orange
617 Orange Center Road
Orange, CT 06477
www.orange-ct.gov
(203) 891-4730; fax (203) 891-2185
See website for email
Hours: M–F 8:30–4:30

Oxford
486 Oxford Road
Oxford, CT 06478-1298
www.oxford-ct.gov
(203) 888-2543, x 3024;
    fax (203) 888-2136
townclerk@oxford-ct.gov
Hours: M–Th 9–5; M,Th 7–9

Plainfield
8 Community Avenue
Plainfield, CT 06374
(860) 230-3001; fax (860) 230-3033
See website for email
Hours: M–F 8:30–4:30

Plainville
Plainville Municipal Center
One Central Square
Plainville, CT 06062
www.plainville-ct.gov
(860) 793-0221; fax (860) 793-2285
Hours: M–W 8–4; Th 8–7; F 8–12

Plymouth
80 Main Street
Terryville, CT 06786
www.plymouthct.us
(860) 585-4039; fax (860) 585-4015
See website for email
Hours: M–F 8:30–4:30

Pomfret
5 Haven Road
Pomfret Center, CT 06259

Mailing Address
PO Box 286
Pomfret Center, CT 06259-0286

www.pomfretct.org
(860) 974-0343; fax (860) 974-3950
See website for email
Hours: M, Tu, Th 8:30–5; W 8:30–6

Portland
33 East Main Street
Portland, CT 06480

Mailing Address
PO Box 71
Portland, CT 06480-0071

www.portlandct.org
(860) 342-6743; fax (860) 342-0001

See website for email
Hours: M, W, Th 8:30–4:30; Tu 8:30–7;
    F 8:30–12

Preston
389 Route 2
Preston, CT 06365
www.preston-ct.org
(860) 887-5581, ext 111; fax (860) 885-1905
townclerk@preston-ct.org
Hours: Tu–W, F 9–4:30; Th 9–6:30

Prospect
36 Center Street
Prospect, CT 06712
www.townofprospect.org
(203) 758-4461; fax (203) 758-7230
town.clk.prospect@snet.net
Hours: M–F 8:30–4

Putnam
126 Church Street
Putnam, CT 06260
www.putnamct.us
(860) 963-6807; fax (860) 963-5360
See website for email
Hours: M–F 8:30–4

Redding
100 Hill Road
Redding Center, CT 06875
www.townofreddingct.org
(203) 936-2377; fax (203) 938-5000
townclerk@townofreddingct.org
Hours: M–W 8:30–5:30; Th 8:30–6

Ridgefield
400 Main Street
Ridgefield, CT 06877-4610
www.ridgefieldct.org
(203) 431-2783; fax (203) 431-2722
townclerk@ridgefieldct.org
Hours: M–F 8:30–4

Rocky Hill

761 Old Main Street
Rocky Hill, CT 06067
www.ci.rocky-hill.ct.us
(860) 258-2705; fax (860) 258-2787
See website for email
Hours: M–F 8:30–4:30

Roxbury

29 North Street
Roxbury, CT 06783

Mailing Address
PO Box 203
Roxbury, CT 06783

www.roxburyct.com
(860) 354-9938; fax (860) 354-0560
townclerk@roxburyct.com
Hours: Tu, Th 9–12, 1–4; W, F 9–12

Salem

270 Hartford Road
Salem, CT 06420
www.salemct.gov
(860) 859-3873, ext 7; fax (860) 859-1184
See website for email
Hours: M–W 8–5; Th 8–6

Salisbury

27 Main Street
Salisbury, CT 06068

Mailing Address
PO Box 548
Salisbury, CT 06068-0548

www.salisburyct.us/offices/townclerk
(860) 435-5182; fax (860) 435-5172
townclerk@salisburyct.us
Hours: M–F 9–4

Scotland

9 Devotion Road
Scotland, CT 06264

Mailing Address
PO Box 122
Scotland, CT 06264

www.scotlandct.org
(860) 423-9634; fax (860) 423-3666
scotlandtownclerk@yahoo.com
Hours: M, Tu–Th 9–3; W 12–8

Seymour

1 First Street
Seymour, CT 06483
www.seymourct.org/Departments/town_clerk.htm
(203) 888-0519; fax (203) 881-5005
See website for email
Hours: M–Th 8–5:30

Sharon

63 Main Street
Sharon, CT 06069

Mailing Address
PO Box 224
Sharon, CT 06069-0224

www.sharonct.org
(860) 364-5224; fax (860) 492-7025
sharontownclerk@yahoo.com
Hours: M–Th 8:30–12, 1–4; F 8:30–12

Shelton

54 Hill Street
Shelton, CT 06484

Mailing Address
PO Box 364
Shelton, CT 06484-0364

www.cityofshelton.org
(203) 924-1555, ext 377; fax (203) 924-1721
See website for email
Hours: M–F 8–5:30

Sherman
Mallory Town Hall
9 Route 39 North
Sherman, CT 06784

Mailing Address
PO Box 39
Sherman, CT 06784

www.townofshermanct.org
(860) 354-5281; fax (860) 350-5041
See website for email
Hours: Tu–F 9–12, 1–4; Sat 9–12

Simsbury
933 Hopmeadow Street
Simsbury, CT 06070

Mailing Address
PO Box 495
Simsbury, CT 06070-1822

www.simsbury-ct.gov
(860) 658-3243; fax (860) 658-3206
See website for email
Hours: M 8:30–7; Tu–F 8:30–4:30

Somers
600 Main Street
Somers, CT 06071-2119
www.somersct.gov/townclerk.cfm
(860) 763-8206; fax (860) 763-8228
See website for email
Hours: M–W 8:30–4:30; Th 8:30–7; F 8:30–1

South Windsor
1540 Sullivan Avenue
South Windsor, CT 06074
www.southwindsor.org
(860) 644-2511, ext 325; fax (860) 644-3781
See website for email
Hours: M–F 8–4:30

Southbury
501 Main Street South
Southbury, CT 06488
www.southbury-ct.org
(203) 262-0657; fax (203) 264-9762
townclerk@southbury-ct.gov
Hours: M–F 8:30–4:30

Southington
75 Main Street
Southington, CT 06489

Mailing Address
PO Box 152
Southington, CT 06489

www.southington.org
(860) 276-6211; fax (860) 276-6229
See website for email
Hours: M–W, F 8:30–4:30; Th 8:30–7

Sprague
1 Main Street
Baltic, CT 06330

Mailing Address
PO Box 677
Baltic, CT 06330

www.ctsprague.org
(860) 822-3000, ext 220; fax (860) 822-3013
townclerk@ctsprague.org
Hours: M–Th 8–4:30; W 8:30–5:30

Stafford
Warren Memorial Town Hall
1 Main Street
Stafford Springs, CT 06076

Mailing Address
PO Box 11
Stafford Springs, CT 06076-0011

www.staffordct.org/clerk.php
(860) 684-1765; fax (860) 684-1795
clerk@staffordct.org
Hours: M–W 8–4:30; Th 8–6:30

Stamford
Town Clerk
Stamford Government Center
888 Washington Boulevard
Government Center Lobby
Stamford, CT 06901
www.ci.stamford.ct.us
(203) 977-4054; fax (203) 977-4943
Hours: M–F 8–3:45

Sterling

1183 Plainfield Pike
Sterling, CT 06377

Mailing Address
PO Box 157
Oneco, CT 06373
www.sterlingct.us/townclerk.htm
(860) 564-2904; fax (860) 564-1660
townclerk@sterlingct.us
Hours: M, Tu 8–4:30; W 8–6; Th 8–4

Stonington

152 Elm Street
Stonington, CT 06378
www.stonington-ct.gov
(860) 535-5060; fax (860) 535-5062
See website for email
Hours: M–F 8:30–4

Stratford

2725 Main Street, Rm. 106
Stratford, CT 06615
www.townofstratford.com
(203) 385-4020; fax (203) 385-4005
See website for email
Hours: M–F 8–4

Suffield

83 Mountain Road
Suffield, CT 06078
www.suffieldtownhall.com
(860) 668-3880; fax (860) 668-3312
See website for email
Hours: M–W 8–4:30; Th 8–6; F 8–1

Thomaston

158 Main Street, Level 3
Thomaston, CT 06787
www.thomastonct.org
(860) 283-4141; fax (860) 283-1013
See website for email
Hours: M–W 8–4; Th 9–6:30; F 8:30–12

Thompson

815 Riverside Drive
North Grosvenordale, CT 06255

Mailing Address
PO Box 899
North Grosvenordale, CT 06255
www.thompsonct.org
(860) 923-9900; fax (860) 923-3836
See website for email
Hours: M–W 8:30–4:30; Th 8:30–6;
  F 8:30–3

Tolland

21 Tolland Green, 5th Level
Tolland, CT 06084
www.tolland.org
(860) 871-3630; fax (860) 871-3663
See website for email
Hours: M–W 8–4:30; Th 8–7:30

Torrington

140 Main Street, 2nd floor, Rm. 209
Torrington, CT 06790
www.torringtonct.org
(860) 489-2236; fax (860) 489-2548
See website for email
Hours: M–W 8:30–4; Th 8:30–6:30;
  F 8:30–12:30

Trumbull

5866 Main Street, 1st floor
Trumbull, CT 06611
www.trumbull-ct.gov
(203) 452-5035; fax (203) 452-5094
See website for email
Hours: M–F 9–5

Union

1043 Buckley Hwy.
Union, CT 06076
www.unionconnecticut.org
(860) 684-3770; fax (860) 684-3370
townclerk@union.necoxmail.com
Hours: Tu, Th 9–12; W 9–12, 1–3

Vernon

14 Park Place
Vernon, CT 06066
www.vernon-ct.gov
(860) 870-3662; fax (860) 870-3683
townclerk@vernon-ct.gov
Hours: M–W 8:30–4:30; Th 8:30–7;
    F 8:30–1:30

Voluntown

115 Main Street
Voluntown, CT 06384
www.voluntown.gov
(860) 376-4089; fax (860) 376-3295
See website for email
Hours: M–F 9–4; Tu, 6–8

Wallingford

45 South Main Street, Rm. 108
Wallingford, CT 06492
www.town.wallingford.ct.us
(203) 294-2145; fax (203) 294-2150
Hours: M–F 9–5

Warren

50 Cemetery Road
Warren, CT 06754
www.warrenct.org
(860) 868-7881, ext 101; fax (860) 868-7746
townclerk@warrenct.org
Hours: M, F 9–1; W–Th 9–4

Washington

Bryan Memorial Town Hall
2 Bryan Plaza
Washington Depot, CT 06794
www.washingtonct.org/townclerk.html
(860) 868-2786; fax (860) 868-3103
townclerk@washingtonct.org
Hours: M–F 9–12, 1–4:45

Waterbury

Chase Municipal building
236 Grand Street
Waterbury, CT 06702

www.waterburyct.org
(203) 574-6806; fax (203) 574-6887
See website for email
Hours: M–F 8:50–4:50

Waterford

20 Rope Ferry Road
Waterford, CT 06385-2886
www.waterfordct.org
(860) 444-5831; fax (860) 437-0352
clerk@waterfordct.org
Hours: M–F 8–4

Watertown

37 DeForest Street
Watertown, CT 06795
www.watertownct.org
(860) 945-5230; fax 945-2706
See website for email
Hours: M–F 9–5

West Hartford

50 South Main Street, Rm. 313
West Hartford, CT 06107
www.westhartford.org
(860) 561-7500; fax (860) 561-7400
See website for email
Hours: M, W 8:30–4:30; Tu 7:30–4:30;
    Th 8:30–7

West Haven

355 Main Street
West Haven, CT 06516
www.cityofwesthaven.com
(203) 937-3534; fax (203) 937-3504
See website for email
Hours: M–F 9–5

Westbrook

866 Boston Post Road
Westbrook, CT 06498
www.westbrookct.us/townclerk.php
https://connecticut-townclerks-records.com
(860) 399-3044, ext 118; fax (860) 399-3092
See website for email
Hours: M–W 9–4; Th 9–7; F 9–12

Weston

56 Northfield Road
Weston, CT 06883

Mailing Address
PO Box 1007
Weston, CT 06883

www.westonct.gov
(203) 222-2616; fax (203) 222-2516
See website for email
Hours: M–F 9–4:30

Westport

110 Myrtle Avenue, Rm. 105
Westport CT 06880
www.westportct.gov
(203) 341-1110; fax (203) 341-1112
See website for email
Hours: M–F 9–4:30

Wethersfield

505 Silas Deane Highway
Wethersfield, CT 06109
www.wethersfieldct.com
(860) 721-2800; fax (860) 721-2994
See website for email
Hours: M-W 8–4:30; Th 8–6; F 8–1

Willington

40 Old Farms Road
Willington, CT 06279
www.willingtonct.org
(860) 487-3121; fax (860) 487-3103
See website for email
Hours: M, 12:30–7:30; Tu-F 9–2

Wilton

238 Danbury Road
Wilston, CT 06897
www.wiltonct.org
(203) 563-0106; fax 834-6246
See website for email
Hours: M–F 8:30–4:30

Winchester

338 Main Street
Winsted, CT 06098
www.townofwinchester.org
(860) 738-6963, ext 342; fax (860) 738-6595
townclerk@townofwinchester.org
Hours: M-W 8–4; Th 8–7; F 8–12

Windham

979 Main Street
Windham, CT 06226

Mailing Address
PO Box 96
Windham, CT 06226

www.windhamct.com
(860) 465-3013; fax (860) 465-3012
townclerksoffice@windhamct.com
Hours: M-W 8–5; Th 8–7:30; F 8–12

Windsor

275 Broad Street
Windsor, CT 06095
www. townofwindsorct.com
(860) 285-1902; fax (860) 285-1909
townclerk@townofwindsorct.com
Hours: M–F 8–5

Windsor Locks

50 Church Street
Windsor Locks, CT 06096
www.windsorlocksct.org
(860) 627-1441, ext 312; fax (860) 292-1121
See website for email
Hours: M-W 8–4; Th 8–6; F 8–1

Wolcott

10 Kenea Avenue
Wolcott, CT 06716
www.wolcottct.org
(203) 879-8100; fax (203) 879-8105
townclerk@wolcottct.org
Hours: M-W 8–4:30; Th 8–5:30; F 8–12

Woodbridge
11 Meetinghouse Lane
Woodbridge, CT 06525
www.woodbridgect.org
(203) 389-3400; fax (203) 389-3480
See website for email
Hours: M-F 8:30–4

Woodbury
271 Main Street South
Woodbury, CT 06798

Mailing Address
PO Box 369
Woodbury, CT 06798

www.woodburyct.org
(203) 263-2144; fax (203) 263-5477
See website for email
Hours: M-F 8–4

Woodstock
415 Route 169
Woodstock, CT 06281-3039
www.woodstockct.gov
(860) 928-6595, ext 320; fax (860) 963-7557
townclerk@woodstockct.gov
Hours: M-Tu, Th 8:30–4:30; W 8:30–6;
     F 8:30–3

Towns

Today there are 169 towns in the state of Connecticut. Each of these towns has villages and post offices and may also contain incorporated cities and boroughs. For example, the well-known village of Mystic is part of both Groton and Stonington.

The following chart lists the name of the town, the date of its incorporation as a town, the county, towns from which it was formed (or from which land was later added to the town), towns that were formed from it (or to which land was added from it), and notes about the town. In the Parent Towns column, towns from which other towns were formed are indicated in **bold** type. Parts of other towns later annexed are in regular type.

The chart also shows which vital records and church records are available as manuscripts, typescripts, published books, or online. Extinct towns (those that are no longer extant or that were annexed by other towns) are listed in the second table. "PD" in the note field indicates the current probate district for that town.

For more information, see the Connecticut State Library's helpful online lists of towns and cities, *www.cslib.org/cttowns.htm*.

VR and CR codes

B   Barbour Collection
F   Church records and other records published by French–Canadian societies
M   NEHGS microfilm
N   Manuscript or typescript at NEHGS
P   Published volume
W   Database on *AmericanAncestors.org*

Town	Inc.	County	Parent Town(s)	Daughter Town(s)	Notes	VRs	CRs
Andover	1848	Tolland	Coventry, Hebron		PD-13	B, W	
Ansonia	1889	New Haven	Derby		PD-41		
Ashford	1714	Windham		Eastford	PD-26	B, W	
Avon	1830	Hartford	Farmington		PD-9	B, W	
Barkhamsted	1779	Litchfield			PD-23	B, W	
Beacon Falls	1871	New Haven	Bethany, Naugatuck, Oxford, Seymour		PD-21		
Berlin	1785	Hartford	Farmington, Middletown, Wethersfield	New Britain	PD-8	B, W	
Bethany	1832	New Haven	Woodbridge	Beacon Falls, Naugatuck	PD-37	B, W	N
Bethel	1855	Fairfield	Danbury		PD-45		
Bethlehem	1787	Litchfield	Woodbury		PD-22	B, W	
Bloomfield	1835	Hartford	Farmington, Simsbury, Windsor		PD-3	B, W	
Bolton	1720	Tolland			PD-13	P, W	
Bozrah	1786	New London	Norwich		PD-29. Created from part of Norwich called Norwich Farms.	B, W	N, W
Branford	1685	New Haven	New Haven	North Branford	PD-35. Settled 1639–44 under New Haven jurisdiction. Named 1653.	B, W	
Bridgeport	1821	Fairfield	Fairfield, Stratford		PD-48. Called Newfield to 1821.	B, W	
Bridgewater	1856	Litchfield	New Milford		PD-44		
Bristol	1785	Hartford	Farmington, Southington	Burlington	PD-19	B, W	W
Brookfield	1788	Fairfield	Danbury, New Milford, Newtown		PD-44	B, W	
Brooklyn	1786	Windham	Canterbury, Pomfret	Hampden	PD-26	B, W	N
Burlington	1806	Hartford	Bristol		PD-10	B, W	
Canaan	1739	Litchfield		North Canaan	PD-24	B, W	
Canterbury	1703	Windham	Plainfield	Brooklyn, Hampden	PD-27		
Canton	1806	Hartford	Simsbury		PD-9	B, W	

Town	Inc.	County	Parent Town(s)	Daughter Town(s)	Notes	VRs	CRs
Chaplin	1822	Windham	Hampton, Mansfield, Windham		PD-28	B, W	
Cheshire	1780	New Haven	Wallingford	Prospect	PD-18	B, W	
Chester	1836	Middlesex	Deep River (Saybrook)		PD-33	B, W	
Clinton	1838	Middlesex	Killingworth		PD-33	B, N, W	
Colchester	1698	New London		Marlborough, Salem	PD-28. Named 1699.	B, W	
Colebrook	1779	Litchfield			PD-23	B, W	
Columbia	1804	Tolland	Lebanon		PD-13	B, W	
Cornwall	1740	Litchfield			PD-24	B, W	
Coventry	1712	Tolland		Andover	PD-25	P, W	
Cromwell	1851	Middlesex	Middletown		PD-15		
Danbury	1687	Fairfield		Bethel, Brookfield	PD-43. Settled 1685.	B, W	N
Darien	1820	Fairfield	Stamford		PD-52	B, W	N
Deep River	1635	Middlesex		Chester, Lyme, Old Saybrook, Westbrook	PD-33. Called Saybrook to 1947.	B, P, W	
Derby	1675	New Haven		Andover, Oxford, Seymour	PD-41	B, W	
Durham	1708	Middlesex			PD-15. Settled 1699. Named 1704.	B, W	
East Granby	1858	Hartford	Granby, Windsor Locks		PD-3	P, W	
East Haddam	1734	Middlesex	Haddam		PD-14	B, W	N, W
East Hampton	1767	Middlesex	Middletown		PD-14. Called Chatham to 1915.	B, W	
East Hartford	1783	Hartford	Hartford	Manchester	PD-5	B, W	N, W
East Haven	1785	New Haven	New Haven		PD-36	B, W	
East Lyme	1839	New London	Lyme, Waterford		PD-32	B, W	
East Windsor	1768	Hartford	Windsor	Ellington, South Windsor	PD-4	B, W	
Eastford	1847	Windham	Ashford		PD-26	B, W	N
Easton	1845	Fairfield	Weston		PD-46		
Ellington	1786	Tolland	East Windsor		PD-12	B, W	

Town	Inc.	County	Parent Town(s)	Daughter Town(s)	Notes	VRs	CRs
Enfield	1683	Hartford		Somers	PD-11. Called Freshwater to 1683. Annexed from Mass. 1749.		
Essex	1852	Middlesex	**Old Saybrook**		PD-33. Split from Old Saybrook and named Essex 1854.		
Fairfield	1639	Fairfield		Bridgeport, Redding, Westport	PD-49. Named 1645.	B, W	
Farmington	1645	Hartford		Avon, Berlin, Bloomfield, Bristol, Plainville, Southington	PD-10	B, W	
Franklin	1786	New London	**Norwich**	Sprague	PD-29	B, W	
Glastonbury	1693	Hartford	**Wethersfield**	Marlborough	PD-6. Established 1690.	B, W	
Goshen	1739	Litchfield			PD-23. Called New Bantam to 1737.	B, W	
Granby	1786	Hartford	**Simsbury**	East Granby	PD-9	B, W	
Greenwich	1665	Fairfield	**Stamford**		PD-54. Settled 1640.	B, W	N, W
Griswold	1815	New London	**Preston**		PD-29	B, W	
Groton	1705	New London	**New London**	Ledyard	PD-30	B, W	
Guilford	1643	New Haven		Madison	PD-34. Settled 1639.	B, W	
Haddam	1668	Middlesex		East Haddam	PD-33	B, W	
Hamden	1786	New Haven	**New Haven**		PD-37	B, W	
Hampton	1786	Windham	**Brooklyn, Canterbury, Mansfield, Pomfret, Windham**	Chaplin	PD-28	B, W	
Hartford	1784	Hartford		East Hartford, West Hartford	PD-1. Settled 1635.	B, N, W	N, P, W
Hartland	1761	Hartford			PD-23	B, W	
Harwinton	1737	Litchfield			PD-24	B, W	
Hebron	1708	Tolland		Andover, Marlborough	PD-6	B, W	
Kent	1739	Litchfield		Warren, Washington	PD-24	B, W	
Killingly	1708	Windham		Putnam, Thompson	PD-27	B, W	N, W
Killingworth	1667	Middlesex		Clinton	PD-33	B, W	
Lebanon	1700	New London		Columbia	PD-28	B, W	
Ledyard	1836	New London	**Groton**		PD-30	B, W	
Lisbon	1786	New London	**Norwich**	Sprague	PD-29	B, W	

Town	Inc.	County	Parent Town(s)	Daughter Town(s)	Notes	VRs	CRs
Litchfield	1719	Litchfield		Morris, Washington	PD-24	B, W	N
Lyme	1667	New London	Deep River (Saybrook)	East Lyme, Old Lyme (South Lyme), Salem	PD-33. Set off from Saybrook (now Deep River) 1665.	B, N, P, W	N
Madison	1826	New Haven	Guilford		PD-34	B, N,W	N
Manchester	1823	Hartford	East Hartford		PD-13	B	
Mansfield	1702	Tolland	Windham	Chaplin	PD-25	P, W	
Marlborough	1803	Hartford	Colchester, Glastonbury, Hebron		PD-14	B, W	N
Meriden	1806	New Haven	Wallingford		PD-16	B, W	
Middlebury	1807	New Haven	Southbury, Waterbury, Woodbury		PD-21	B, W	
Middlefield	1866	Middlesex	Middletown		PD-15		
Middletown	1651	Middlesex		Berlin, Cromwell, East Hampton (Chatham)	PD-15. Named 1653.	B, W	
Milford	1639	New Haven		Orange, Woodbridge	PD-40. Named 1640.	B, W	W
Monroe	1823	Fairfield	Huntington		PD-46	B, W	
Montville	1786	New London	New London	Salem	PD-32	B, W	
Morris	1859	Litchfield	Litchfield		PD-24		
Naugatuck	1844	New Haven	Bethany, Oxford, Waterbury	Beacon Falls	PD-21	B, W	
New Britain	1850	Hartford	Berlin		PD-8. Taken from Berlin 1871.		
New Canaan	1801	Fairfield	Norwalk, Stamford		PD-52	B, W	
New Fairfield	1740	Fairfield			PD-44		N
New Hartford	1738	Litchfield			PD-23	B, W	
New Haven	1784	New Haven		Branford, East Haven, North Haven, Orange, Woodbridge	PD-38. Settled 1638. Named 1640.	P, S, W	P
New London	1784	New London		Groton, Montville, Waterford	PD-31. Settled 1646. Named 1658.	B, W	

Town	Inc.	County	Parent Town(s)	Daughter Town(s)	Notes	VRs	CRs
New Milford	1712	Litchfield		Bridgewater, Brookfield, Washington	PD-44	B, W	W
Newington	1871	Hartford	**Wethersfield**		PD-7		
Newtown	1711	Fairfield		Brookfield	PD-45	B, N, W	
Norfolk	1758	Litchfield			PD-24	B, W	W
North Branford	1831	New Haven	**Branford**		PD-35	B, W	
North Canaan	1858	Litchfield	**Canaan**		PD-24		
North Haven	1786	New Haven	**New Haven**		PD-36	B, W	
North Stonington	1807	New London	**Stonington**		PD-30	B, W	
Norwalk	1651	Fairfield		New Canaan, Westport, Wilton	PD-51	B, W	
Norwich	1662	New London		Bozrah, Franklin, Lisbon	PD-29. Settled 1659.	B, P, W	N, W
Old Lyme	1855	New London	**Lyme**		PD-32. Called South Lyme to 1857.		
Old Saybrook	1854	Middlesex	**Deep River (Saybrook)**	Essex	PD-33. Established 1852. Name changed 1854.		
Orange	1822	New Haven	**Milford, New Haven**	West Haven	PD-40	B, W	
Oxford	1798	New Haven	**Derby, Southbury**	Beacon Falls, Naugatuck	PD-22	B, W	
Plainfield	1699	Windham		Canterbury	PD-27. Called Quinabaug to 1700.	B, W	
Plainville	1869	Hartford	**Farmington**		PD-19		
Plymouth	1795	Litchfield	**Watertown**	Thomaston	PD-19	B, W	
Pomfret	1713	Windham		Brooklyn, Hampden, Putnam	PD-26	B, W	
Portland	1841	Middlesex	**Chatham**		PD-14	B, W	
Preston	1687	New London		Griswold	PD-29	B, W	W
Prospect	1827	New Haven	**Cheshire, Waterbury**		PD-21	B, W	
Putnam	1855	Windham	**Killingly, Pomfret, Thompson**		PD-26		
Redding	1767	Fairfield	**Fairfield**		PD-45	B, W	N
Ridgefield	1709	Fairfield			PD-45. Settled 1708.	B, W	
Rocky Hill	1843	Hartford	**Wethersfield**		PD-7	B, W	

Town	Inc.	County	Parent Town(s)	Daughter Town(s)	Notes	VRs	CRs
Roxbury	1796	Litchfield	**Woodbury**		PD-22	B, W	N
Salem	1819	New London	**Colchester, Lyme, Montville**		PD-32	B, W	
Salisbury	1741	Litchfield			PD-24	B, W	
Scotland	1857	Windham	**Windham**		PD-28		
Seymour	1850	New Haven	**Derby**	Beacon Falls	PD-41	P, W	
Sharon	1739	Litchfield			PD-24	B, P	N
Shelton	1789	Fairfield	**Stratford**	Monroe	PD-42		
Sherman	1802	Fairfield	**New Fairfield**		PD-44	B, W	
Simsbury	1670	Hartford		Bloomfield, Granby, Simsbury	PD-9	B, W	P
Somers	1734	Tolland	**Enfield**		PD-11. Annexed from Massachusetts 1749.	B, W	
South Windsor	1845	Hartford	**East Windsor**		PD-4	B, W	
Southbury	1787	New Haven	**Woodbury**	Middlebury, Oxford	PD-22	B, W	
Southington	1779	Hartford	**Farmington**	Wolcott	PD-18	B, W	
Sprague	1861	New London	**Franklin, Lisbon**		PD-29		
Stafford	1719	Tolland			PD-11	B, W	
Stamford	1641	Fairfield		Darien, Greenwich, New Canaan	PD-53. Named 1642.	B, W	
Sterling	1794	Windham	Voluntown		PD-27	B, W	
Stonington	1662	New London		North Stonington	PD-30. Settled 1649. Named 1666.	B, W	N, W
Stratford	1639	Fairfield		Bridgeport, Huntington, Shelton, Trumbull	PD-47	B, W	
Suffield	1674	Hartford			PD-11. Annexed from Massachusetts 1749.	B, P	W
Thomaston	1875	Litchfield	**Plymouth**		PD-24		
Thompson	1785	Windham	**Killingly**	Putnam	PD-26	B, W	
Tolland	1722	Tolland			PD-25. Named 1715.	B, W	F
Torrington	1740	Litchfield			PD-23	BV	
Trumbull	1797	Fairfield	Stratford		PD-42		
Union	1734	Tolland			PD-11	B, W	

CT

Town	Inc.	County	Parent Town(s)	Daughter Town(s)	Notes	VRs	CRs
Vernon	1808	Tolland	**Bolton, Rockville**		PD-12	W	
Voluntown	1721	New London		Sterling	PD-29. Called Volunteers' Town to 1721.	B, W	
Wallingford	1670	New Haven		Cheshire, Meriden	PD-17	B, W	
Warren	1786	Litchfield	**Kent**		PD-24	B, W	
Washington	1779	Litchfield	**Kent, Litchfield, New Milford, Woodbury**		PD-22	B, W	
Waterbury	1686	New Haven		Middlebury, Naugatuck, Prospect, Watertown, Wolcott	PD-20	B, W	F
Waterford	1801	New London	**New London**	East Lyme	PD-31	B, W	
Watertown	1780	Litchfield	**Waterbury**	Plymouth	PD-22	B, W	
West Hartford	1854	Hartford	**Hartford**		PD-2		
West Haven	1921	New Haven	**Orange**		PD-39		
Westbrook	1840	Middlesex	**Deep River (Saybrook)**		PD-33	B, W	
Weston	1787	Fairfield	**Fairfield**	Easton, Westport	PD-50	B, W	
Westport	1835	Fairfield	**Fairfield, Norwalk, Weston**		PD-50	B, W	
Wethersfield	1822	Hartford		Berlin, Glastonbury, Newington, Rocky Hill	PD-7. Settled 1634. Named 1637.	B, W	
Willington	1727	Tolland			PD-25. Called Wellington to 1727.	B, W	
Wilton	1802	Fairfield	**Norwalk**		PD-51	B, W	
Winchester	1771	Litchfield			PD-23		
Windham	1692	Windham	Willimantic	Chaplin, Hampden, Mansfield, Scotland, Willimantic	PD-28. Consolidated with Willimantic 1983.	B, P, W	W
Windsor	1633	Hartford		Bloomfield, East Windsor, Windsor Locks	PD-4. Named 1637.	B, W	
Windsor Locks	1854	Hartford	**Windsor**	East Granby	PD-3		
Wolcott	1796	New Haven	**Southington, Waterbury**		PD-20		
Woodbridge	1784	New Haven	**Milford, New Haven**	Bethany	PD-41		

Town	Inc.	County	Parent Town(s)	Daughter Town(s)	Notes	VRs	CRs
Woodbury	1673	Litchfield		Bethlehem, Middlebury, Roxbury, Southbury, Washington	PD-22	B, W	
Woodstock	1690	Windham			PD-26. Settled 1686. Called New Roxbury to 1690. Annexed from Massachusetts 1749.	B, P, W	

Extinct Towns

Town	Est.	County	Parent Town (s)	Daughter Town(s)	Notes	VRs	CRs
Huntington	1789	Fairfield	Stratford	Monroe, Shelton	Annexed to Shelton 1919.	B, W	
Rockville	1889	Tolland	Vernon	Vernon	Created from Vernon 1889 and annexed back 1965.		
Willimantic	1893	Windham	Windham	Windham	Created from Windham 1893 and annexed back 1983.		

"View of Litchfield Taken about 1860." Emily Noyes Vanderpoel, comp., *Chronicles of A Pioneer School* (1903), facing p. 14.

Maine

Introduction by Michael J. Leclerc

In 1607 the first English settlement was established in what is now Maine. The Plymouth Company founded Popham Colony near the mouth of the Kennebec River, but the ill-fated settlement lasted only a year. The area encompassing present-day Maine became part of the Massachusetts Bay Colony in 1652, but continued to be contested by the French, who considered the land to be part of Acadia. Maine's border with New Brunswick would remain in dispute until the Webster-Ashburton Treaty of 1842.

In 1679 Maine became physically separated from the rest of Massachusetts when the colony of New Hampshire was formed. By the beginning of the nineteenth century, many Maine residents wanted to secede from Massachusetts and form a new state. Maine was admitted as the twenty-third state on March 15, 1820, as part of the Missouri Compromise, which kept a balance between free and slave states.

Unlike other parts of the country, New England generally has very little unincorporated territory. Maine is a major exception to that rule. Vast amounts of territory in this state are still wilderness. This is especially true in Aroostook, Piscataquis, and Somerset Counties. Wilderness townships are often indicated on maps with a code of letters and numbers. A number of towns in Maine have disappeared through the years as the population dwindled away. Even today, many towns have very small populations.

Vital Records

Few Maine vital records survive from the seventeenth century. Recordkeeping during this period was spotty, and the availability of records varies widely from town to town. Legislation in the 1860s attempted to establish a centralized system of vital records, but it took the passage of additional legislation in 1892 to firmly establish statewide reporting.

With the later legislation, the state requested all towns to report their earlier records as well. Unfortunately, only eighty towns complied with that request. These "delayed returns" were microfilmed and are available at many repositories. This pre-1892 series is

The Maine state seal

arranged alphabetically by surname, then by year. Within each year the births appear first, then marriages, then deaths.

Records from 1892 through 1955 are available on microfilm. The films are subdivided into four groups: 1892–1907, 1908–22, 1923–35, and 1936–55. The records are organized in the same manner as the pre-1892 records. Marriages always appear under the groom's name. A cross-index for marriage records is also available on microfilm. Counties started recording marriages at various times throughout the nineteenth century.

County marriage records through 1892 are microfilmed separately from the delayed returns. Records for the counties of Cumberland, Hancock, Lincoln, Penobscot, Waldo, and York have been published.

Divorce records from 1892 through 1963 are available on microfilm, as is an index for divorces from 1964 through 1983. Searchable indexes for marriage records (1892–1966, 1976–2009) and death records (1960–2009) are available online at *AmericanAncestors.org* and the Maine State Archives (MSA). Among the databases that the MSA offers for down-loading to your personal computer is an index to divorces between 1800 and 1891.

A few towns published their early vital records at the beginning of the twentieth century. Other towns periodically published records, and in the last few years Picton Press has published a large number of town vital records, focusing specifically on the towns that did not file delayed returns.

Vital records through 1922 have been transferred to the custody of the MSA. Records of birth, marriage, death, divorce, and domestic partnership are available through the Maine Department of Public Health. Records less than 100 years old are considered private records, and access is limited to the following:

- The person named on the record
- The person's spouse or registered domestic partner
- The parent(s) named on the record
- Descendants of the person named on the record (including children, grandchildren, and great-grandchildren to the most remote degree)

Above: "First Settlers of Maine." John Warner Barber, *The History and Antiquities of New England, New York, New Jersey, and Pennsylvania* (1856), p. 174.

ME

- The legal custodian, guardian, or authorized representative of the person named on the record
- Genealogists who have a researcher card issued by the Maine Center for Disease Control and Prevention, Office of Data, Research and Vital Statistics

Genealogists can obtain a researcher card by filling out an application (available on the vital records website) and paying the annual registration fee. The researcher card is good for one year and will allow the bearer to view or purchase non-certified copies of birth, death, and marriage records registered in Maine that are less than 100 years old. Certified copies of records can only be purchased by someone who meets one of the first five criteria above.

Church Records

Church records are excellent supplements or substitutes for vital records. In denominations that practice infant baptism, christening records can help establish an approximate date of birth. Funeral and burial records can assist in establishing dates of death. Marriage records should, in theory, carry the same date as the civil record. In many denominations the ecclesiastical records were considered the property of the minister. Thus they would leave the church when the minister left, and they may be located in localities far distant from the Maine town in which the events occurred. Check online catalogs for ministers' records that might be available in manuscript collections.

Few churches in Maine have had records published. Some have put records on deposit with historical societies and archives to ensure their preservation. Town histories often list local or area churches, and can help establish which churches were in existence during a given time period. Check online catalogs for manuscript collections of church and other records. The church records listed in the town table reflect only known published church ecclesiastical records and copies in the NEHGS manuscript collection. It does not include published church histories, which may provide lists of members but rarely information on baptism, burial, and marriage.

Probate Records

Records of the administration of estates are under the jurisdiction of the state judiciary's probate court system. These courts oversee estates and trusts, adoptions, name changes, guardianships, and protective proceedings. The probate courts are county courts, not state courts, and sit without a jury. Each county has probate judges who serve part-time and are elected to the position. Each county also has an elected register of probate. There is no uniform method of recording probate matters throughout the state. Each court keeps its own records. In addition to the original probate dockets, many records have been transferred into copy books.

Some jurisdictions kept separate books for each part of the administration (wills, inventories, guardianships, etc.), while others simply kept records chronologically, mixing different types of records throughout a volume. Most microfilm of probate records in Maine was made from the copy books.

Additional probate information may be found in the records of the Supreme Judicial Court (SJC), the highest court in the state. The SJC has appellate jurisdiction for all probate matters. The probate records for some counties have been lost to fire or other disasters. Most notable among these losses are the pre-1908 records for Cumberland County.

York County covered all of Maine until Cumberland and Lincoln counties were created in 1760. William M. Sargent published *Maine Wills, 1640–1760* (Portland: Brown, Thurston, and Co., 1887), which includes full transcriptions of all wills probated in the state during this period. *Maine Wills* was published on CD-ROM by NEHGS in 2006 and is now searchable as part of the Maine Early Wills & Deeds database on *AmericanAncestors.org*. John E. Frost published the early records of all counties in his two-volume *Maine Probate Abstracts, 1687–1800* (Camden, Me.: Picton Press, 1991). Joseph Crook Anderson II extended this in 1997 with his work *York County, Maine Will Abstracts, 1801–1858* (Camden, Me.: Picton Press, 1997). The Family History Library has microfilmed probate records of each county. The exact dates of coverage vary from county to county.

Land Records

Early land grant records for Maine are located at the Massachusetts State Archives. Some of these early records were abstracted in volumes 4 through 8 of the *Maine Historical and Genealogical Recorder* (Portland: S. M. Watson, 1884–98).

In 1783, the Massachusetts General Court created the Massachusetts Committee for the Sale of Eastern Lands. The goal was to generate revenues through new settlements in the Maine wilderness. Revenue generation was critical in the post-Revolutionary War era to pay off wartime debt. Later the General Court authorized the granting of land in lieu of pensions to veterans of the American Revolution and the War of 1812.

The committee later became the Maine Land Office, and many of that organization's records are available at the MSA.

Among the databases that the MSA offers for download is an index to Revolutionary War Land Grant and Pension Applications that provides the names of veterans and/or their widows.

Like Massachusetts, land registration in Maine is handled on the county level. Each county has an elected registrar of deeds. The Registry of Deeds holds land transactions from the time of the formation of the county. The Family History Library has microfilmed land records from each county. The exact dates vary from county to county.

Above: "Lobster Pot." Samuel Adams Drake, *Nooks and Corners of the New England Coast* (1875), p. 85.

The first eighteen volumes of York County deeds (covering all of Maine through about 1736) were published by the state between 1887 and 1910. These records are also available online in the Maine Early Wills & Deeds database on *AmericanAncestors.org*.

Court Records

The court system exercises judicial power, interpreting and applying the state constitution and statutes and resolving disputes between parties. Parties are either plaintiffs (the party bringing suit) or defendants (the party accused of wrongdoing). Prior to 1820 the court system was part of the Massachusetts judiciary. See the Massachusetts chapter for a discussion of the courts in that time period.

After statehood, justices of the peace held trials for civil matters involving $20 or less and criminal cases carrying a fine of $5 or less. The Court of Common Pleas was established to hear civil and other criminal cases and appeals from justices of the peace. The Court of Sessions dealt with highways, licenses, jails, taxes, and the like. The Supreme Judicial Court had original jurisdiction over specific civil matters and serious criminal cases (including capital crimes), and served as the court of appeal for the lower courts. It is the final court of appeal for matters of state law.

During the nineteenth century, town, municipal, and police courts were formed throughout the state. In 1839, the Courts of Common Pleas were replaced with District Courts. In 1852, the District Courts were abolished, and the SJC was divided into three districts (Eastern, Middle, and Western) to hear cases formerly heard by the District Courts. In 1961, the state reintroduced District Courts, dividing the state into thirty-three judicial districts.

The Maine Historical Society published a six-volume series of judicial records entitled *Province and Court Records of Maine* (Portland: Maine Historical Society, 1928–75). These

For Maine Research

Joseph C. Anderson II, "Maine," in *A Guide to the Library of the New England Historic Genealogical Society*, Maureen A. Taylor and Henry B. Hoff, eds. (Boston: NEHGS, 2004), pp. 105–26.

Charles E. Clark, *The Eastern Frontier: The Settlement of Northern New England, 1610–1763* (Hanover, N.H.: University Press of New England, 1987).

John E. Frost, *Maine Genealogy: A Bibliographical Guide* (Portland: Maine Historical Society, 1985).

John D. Haskell, *Maine: A Bibliography of Its History* (Boston: G. K. Hall, 1977).

George J. Varney, *A Gazetteer of the State of Maine* (1881; rpt. Bowie, Md.: Heritage Books, 1991).

include records from many different courts held between 1646 and 1727.

The MSA holds judicial records dating back to 1636. Many of these have been microfilmed by the Family History Library, but others exist only in the original. Court clerks used different systems of recordkeeping, and researchers may find dockets, records books, or original case files, depending on the court and the time period.

Among the databases that the MSA offers for download are two containing court records. The Courts 1696–1854 database indexes early cases from the York County Court of Common Pleas (1696–1760), the Kennebec County Supreme Court (1799–1854), and the Washington County District Court (1839–46), including depositions and decisions. A second database indexes records of the Hancock County Court of Sessions from 1788 to 1881.

ME

Military Records

Military records in Maine date back to the colonial wars of the seventeenth century. Muster rolls and account books often document the service of the volunteer militia. Once again, see the Massachusetts chapter for a discussion of sources for pre-statehood records.

One helpful resource for Revolutionary War service is Charles J. House, comp., *Names of Soldiers of the American Revolution Who Applied for State Bounty Under Resolves of March 17, 1835, March 24, 1836, and March 20, 1836, as Appears of Record in Land Office* (Augusta: State of Maine, 1893; rpt. Baltimore: Genealogical Publishing Company, 1967). This work includes the soldier's residence at time of enlistment, which was often in a place other than Maine.

Soldiers, Sailors, and Patriots of the Revolutionary War: Maine (Louisville, Ky.: National Society of the Sons of the American Revolution, 1982) and *Supplement to Soldiers, Sailors, and Patriots of the Revolutionary War: Maine* (Rockport, Me.: Picton Press, 1998), both by Carleton E. Fisher and Sue G. Fisher, provide information on people involved in the Revolutionary War who are buried in the state of Maine.

For information on those who served in World War I, see James W. Hanson, *Roster of Maine in the Military Service of the United States and Allies in the World War, 1917–1919* (Augusta, Me.: State Legislature, 1929). It covers the Army, Navy, Marine Corps, Coast Guard, and Nurse Corps. This two-volume work gives name, place of birth, age or date of birth, date and place of enlistment, rank, service, and discharge status. It is also available as a searchable database, Maine Soldiers in World War I (1917–19), on *AmericanAncestors.org*.

Other Records

Early Families of Maine

Two compendia are very helpful for researching seventeenth- and early-eighteenth-century residents. The first is Charles Henry Pope, *The Pioneers of Maine and New Hampshire 1623 to 1660: A Descriptive List, Drawn from Records of the Colonies, Towns, Churches, Courts, and Other Contemporary Sources* (Boston: C. H. Pope, 1908; rpt. Baltimore: Genealogical Publishing Company, 1973). Pope lists surnames in alphabetical order. Under each surname is a list of individuals in alphabetical order by first name, with a brief account of records in which they appear during the given time period.

The second compendium was authored by three noted genealogists of the early twentieth century: Sybil Noyes, Charles Thornton Libby, and Walter Goodwin Davis. Their *Genealogical Dictionary of Maine and New Hampshire* was originally privately published between 1928 and 1939. The Genealogical Publishing Company began reprinting it in 1972, with numerous reprintings since; NEHGS reprinted it as a paperback, with an introduction by David Curtis Dearborn, in 2012. The book begins with some early lists of records, followed by an alphabetical (by surname, then first name) dictionary of record abstractions for each individual. The number of records examined and amount of information abstracted varies from individual to individual. The timespan is more extensive than Pope's, going into the first third of the eighteenth century.

Maine Families in 1790

In 1988 the Maine Genealogical Society embarked on a major project to document the families of heads of household in the 1790 U.S. census for the District of Maine. This is an ongoing series that has documented thousands of families in ten volumes to date.

State Census and Substitutes

Two useful sets of data are available at the Maine State Archives: the 1837 Revenue Sharing Census and certificates of land ownership. The 1837 Revenue Sharing Census—which includes only Bangor, Portland, and the unincorporated towns—records the head of household and the number of inhabitants per dwelling. Certificates of land ownership given by the Maine Land Office to settlers are available for many northern Maine townships and unincorporated territories. They are indexed by name and town. Also at the MSA are a number of reports prepared by town assessors for the state government for various reasons.

Maine Old Cemetery Association

The Maine Old Cemetery Association (MOCA) was formed in 1969 to locate old cemeteries in the state of Maine, encourage their care and protection, and preserve the historical information within and about those cemeteries.

MOCA has so far published three series of cemetery transcriptions. They have been microfilmed and are available at NEHGS, through the Family History Library, and at other major repositories. A number of their records are also available for purchase on CD-ROM. The two-volume *Maine Cemetery Inscriptions York County* (Camden, Me.: Picton Press, 1995) contains thousands of transcriptions from current-day York County cemeteries collected by MOCA over the previous twenty-five years. You can find out more about MOCA at *www.rootsweb.ancestry.com/~memoca/moca.htm*.

STAFF PICKS

Compilations

Carleton E. and Sue G. Fisher, *Soldiers, Sailors and Patriots of the Revolutionary War, Maine* (Louisville, Ky.: National Society of the Sons of the American Revolution, 1982).

_____, *Supplement to Soldiers, Sailors and Patriots of the Revolutionary War: Maine* (Rockport, Me.: Picton Press, 1998).

The Maine Genealogist (formerly *Maine Seine*) (Maine Genealogical Society, 1977–present).

Massachusetts and Maine Direct Tax Census of 1798, microfilm (Boston: NEHGS, 1978), available as a database at *AmericanAncestors.org*.

Sybil Noyes, Charles Thornton Libby, and Walter Goodwin Davis, *Genealogical Dictionary of Maine and New Hampshire* (1928–39; rpt. Baltimore: Genealogical Publishing Co., 1976; rpt. Boston: NEHGS, 2012).

Charles Henry Pope, *The Pioneers of Maine and New Hampshire, 1623–1660* (1908; rpt. Baltimore: Genealogical Publishing Co., 1973).

Bettye Hobbs Pruitt, ed., *The Massachusetts Tax Valuation List of 1771* (Camden, Me.: Picton Press, 1998).

QUÉBEC

NEW
BRUNSWICK

Aroostook County

Houlton

Piscataquis
County

*Moosehead
Lake*

Somerset
County

MAINE

Penobscot
County

Dover-
Foxcroft

Washington
County

Franklin
County

Skowhegan

Bangor

Machias

Coos
County

Farmington

Hancock
County

Guildhall

Ellsworth

Lancaster

Oxford
County

Kennebec
County

Waldo
County

South Paris

Augusta

Belfast

Carroll
County

Auburn

Rockland

*Lake
Winnipesaukee*

Ossipee

Cumberland
County

Bath

Wiscasset

Knox County

Laconia

Portland

Lincoln
County

Alfred

Concord

York
County

Sagadahoc
County

Dover

Androscoggin
County

Exeter

Rockingham
County

NEW HAMPSHIRE

Nashua

Essex
County

Merrimack
County

Salem

Cambridge

MASSACHUSETTS

Boston

Dedham

Norfolk County

Plymouth County

| 0 | 25 | 50 | 100 Miles |

With love
G.M.S.

Fort Popham, Me., Boston Boat Passing Fort Popham.

Maine Repositories

The following are major repositories with large collections of materials of interest to gene-alogists. Check with each repository prior to visiting to obtain the most recent information about hours and access to materials in the collection.

Maine State Archives
230 State Street
Augusta, ME 04333

Mailing Address
84 State House Station
Augusta, ME 04333–0084

www.maine.gov/sos/arc
(207) 287–5790; fax (207) 287–6035
Hours: M–F 8–4

While Maine towns continue to gener-ate and have custody of their vital records (and are the appropriate jurisdiction from which to obtain *certified* records of births, etc. prior to 1923), copies have been sent to the Maine State Archives since 1892. The MSA has custody of all statewide vital rec-ords from the start of registration in 1892 through 1922. Microfilm copies of births, marriages, and deaths are available for 1923–55. Certified copies of all records from 1923 to the present must come from Maine Vital Statistics. Other records include court rec-

Above: Postcard, private collection.

ords, Land Office records, militia rolls, rec-ords of the office of the Adjutant General, and records of the state legislature. Several databases are available for online searching or for download.

Maine State Library
230 State Street
Augusta, ME 04333

Mailing Address
64 State House Station
Augusta, ME 04333–0064

www.maine.gov/msl/index.shtml
(207) 287–5790; fax (207) 287–6035
Hours: M, W, Th 9–6; Tu 9–6; F 9–5;
    Sat 9–2

The Maine State Library has more than 350,000 published volumes and more than 250,000 government documents, as well as microfilms of vital records through 1955. Dozens of newspaper titles from throughout the state are available, including several titles serving the French-Canadian population. Users can submit an online request for an obituary search.

Maine Division of Public Health Systems Office of Data, Research, and Vital Statistics

244 Water Street
Augusta, ME 04333–0011

Mailing Address
Vital Records
11 State House Station
Augusta, ME 04333–0011

*www.maine.gov/dhhs/boh/phs/odrvs/
vital-records/order*
(207) 287–3181, (888) 664–9491
Hours: M–F 8–5

Holds records of birth, marriage, domestic partnership, divorce, and death from 1923 to the present. Records prior to 1923 are held at the Maine State Archives. Contact the Vital Records office for current access restrictions.

Maine Historical Society

489 Congress Street
Portland, ME 04101
www.mainehistory.org; www.mainememory.net
(207) 774–1822; fax (207) 775–4301
info@mainehistory.org
Hours: Tu–Sat 10–4

The Maine Historical Society is the third oldest statewide historical society, founded in 1822. Its Brown Research Library (recently renovated and expanded to include state of the art archival storage) is a major repository for the study of Maine local and family history. In addition to more than 100,000 published titles, it includes several million manuscript pages of letters, diaries, business, town and church records, maps (printed and manuscript), 150,000 photographs, and other materials of use to the historian or genealogist, including copies of the 1892–1955 state VRs microfilm discussed above, which has been restricted elsewhere.

Everett S. Stackpole, *History of Winthrop, Maine* (1925), p. 185.

Counties

Name	Est.	Parent(s)	Probate District(s)	Deed District(s)	Note
Androscoggin	1854	Cumberland, Kennebec, Lincoln, and Oxford	Androscoggin	Androscoggin	
Aroostook	1839	Penobscot, Piscataquis, Somerset, Washington	Aroostook	Southern and Northern	
Cumberland	1760	York	Cumberland	Cumberland	
Franklin	1838	Kennebec, Oxford, and Somerset	Franklin	Franklin	
Hancock	1789	Lincoln	Hancock	Hancock	
Kennebec	1799	Cumberland and Lincoln	Kennebec	Kennebec	
Knox	1860	Lincoln and Waldo	Knox	Knox	
Lincoln	1760	York	Lincoln	Lincoln	
Oxford	1805	Cumberland and York	Oxford	Eastern and Western	
Penobscot	1816	Hancock	Penobscot	Penobscot	
Piscataquis	1838	Penobscot and Somerset	Piscataquis	Piscataquis	
Sagadahoc	1854	Lincoln	Sagadahoc	Sagadahoc	
Somerset	1809	Kennebec	Somerset	Somerset	
Waldo	1827	Hancock	Waldo	Waldo	
Washington	1789	Lincoln	Washington	Washington	
York	1652	Original County	York	York	Called Yorkshire 1658–91.

Extinct Counties

Name	Est.	Dissolved	Note
Cornwall	1635	1683	Called Devon or Devonshire 1673–83. Encompassed the territory from the Kennebec River to the Penobscot River. (See Old Lincoln, below)
New Somerset	1635	1639	Included the land from the Piscataqua River to the Kennebec River.
New Ireland			Proposed in 1780 as a British colony that would include the territory between the Penobscot River and the St. Croix River. It was never organized, as this area became part of the U.S. after the Treaty of Paris in 1783.
Old Lincoln	1652	1691	Part of the Massachusetts Bay Colony 1652–83. It included the territory from the Penobscot River to Nova Scotia. In 1683 the territory of Cornwall was annexed and became part of the Colony of New York until Old Lincoln was dissolved in 1691. Also called the Province of Sagadahoc and the Sagadahoc Territory.

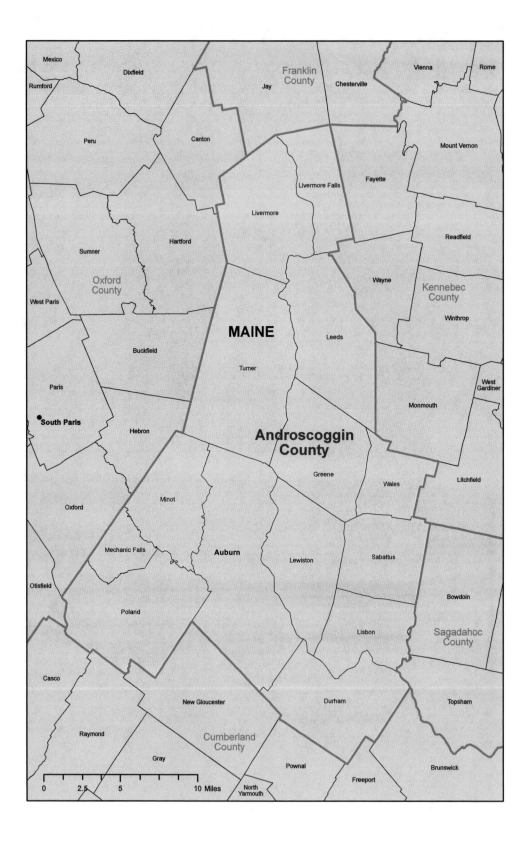

Mexico
Rumford
Dixfield
Jay
Franklin
County
Chesterville
Vienna
Rome
Peru
Canton
Mount Vernon
Livermore Falls
Fayette
Livermore
Readfield
Hartford
Sumner
Oxford
County
Wayne
Kennebec
County
West Paris
Winthrop
MAINE
Leeds
Buckfield
Turner
Paris
West
Gardiner
● South Paris
Hebron
Monmouth
Androscoggin
County
Greene
Wales
Litchfield
Minot
Oxford
Mechanic Falls
Auburn
Lewiston
Sabattus
Otisfield
Bowdoin
Poland
Lisbon
Sagadahoc
County
Casco
New Gloucester
Durham
Topsham
Raymond
Cumberland
County
Pownal
Brunswick
Gray
Freeport
0   2.5   5   10 Miles
North
Yarmouth

ME

Androscoggin County

Founded	1854
Parent Counties	Cumberland, Kennebec, Lincoln, Oxford
County Seat	Auburn

Towns

Auburn, Durham, Greene, Leeds, Lewiston, Lisbon, Livermore, Livermore Falls, Mechanic Falls, Minot, Poland, Sabattus, Turner, Wales

Extinct

Danville

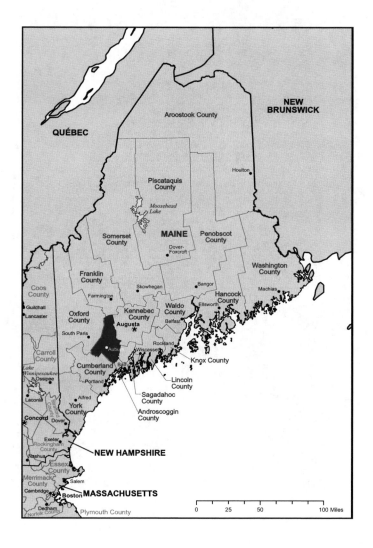

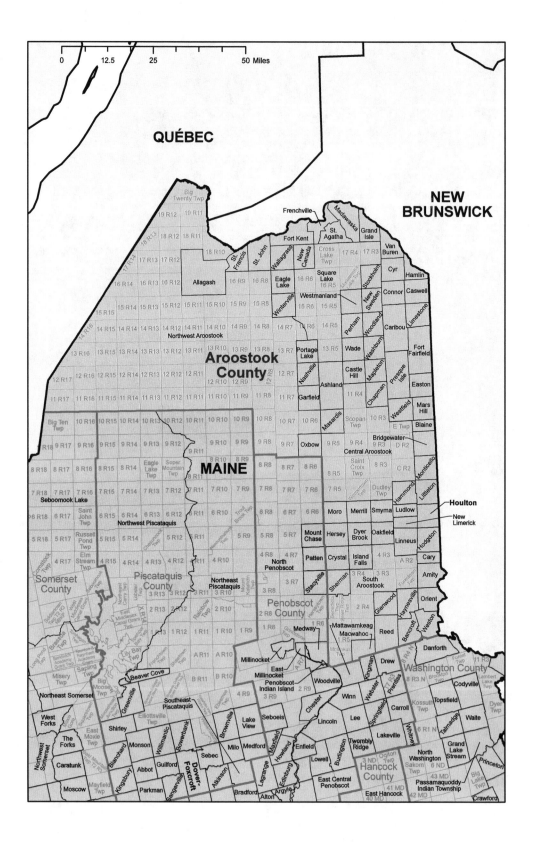

QUÉBEC

NEW BRUNSWICK

0   12.5   25   50 Miles

Big Twenty Twp

19 R12   19 R11

18 R13   18 R12   18 R11

18 R10

Frenchville

Madawaska

St. Agatha

Grand Isle

Fort Kent

Van Buren

17 R14   17 R13   17 R12

St. Francis   St. John   Wallagrass   New Canada   Cross Lake Twp   17 R4   17 R3

Cyr   Hamlin

16 R14   16 R13   16 R12   Allagash   16 R9   16 R8   Eagle Lake   16 R6   Square Lake 16 R5   Stockholm   Connor   Caswell

15 R14   15 R13   15 R12   15 R11   15 R10   15 R9   15 R8   Winterville   Westmanland   15 R6   15 R5   New Sweden   Woodland   Limestone

14 R16   14 R15   14 R14   14 R13   14 R12   14 R11   14 R10   14 R8   14 R7   14 R6   14 R5   Perham   Washburn   Caribou   Fort Fairfield

Northwest Aroostook

13 R15   13 R14   13 R13   13 R12   13 R11   13 R10   13 R9   13 R8   13 R7   Portage Lake   13 R5   Wade   Mapleton   Presque Isle

Aroostook County

12 R17   12 R16   12 R15   12 R14   12 R13   12 R12   12 R11   12 R10   12 R9   12 R8   12 R7   Nashville   Castle Hill   Chapman   Easton

Ashland   11 R4   Westfield   Mars Hill

11 R17   11 R16   11 R15   11 R14   11 R13   11 R12   11 R11   11 R10   11 R9   11 R8   11 R7   Garfield

Big Ten Twp

10 R16   10 R15   10 R14   10 R13   10 R12   10 R11   10 R10   10 R9   10 R8   10 R7   10 R6   Masardis   Scopan Twp   10 R3   Blaine

R18   9 R17   9 R16   9 R15   9 R14   9 R13   9 R12   9 R11   9 R10   9 R9   9 R8   9 R7   Oxbow   9 R5   9 R4   Bridgewater 9 R3   E Twp   D R2

MAINE

8 R18   8 R17   8 R16   8 R15   8 R14   Eagle Lake Twp   Soper Mountain Twp   8 R10   8 R9   8 R8   8 R7   8 R6   Saint Croix Twp   8 R5   8 R3   C R2   Monticello

7 R18   7 R17   7 R16   7 R15   7 R14   7 R13   7 R12   7 R11   7 R10   7 R9   7 R8   7 R7   7 R6   7 R5   Dudley Twp   Hammond   Littleton

Seboomook Lake

6 R18   6 R17   Saint John Twp   6 R14   6 R13   6 R12   6 R11   6 R10   6 R9   6 R8   6 R7   6 R6   Moro   Merrill   Smyrna   Ludlow   **Houlton**

Northwest Piscataquis

New Limerick

5 R18   5 R17   Russell Pond Twp   5 R15   5 R14   5 R13   5 R12   5 R11   5 R10   5 R9   5 R8   5 R7   Mount Chase   Hersey   Dyer Brook   Oakfield   Linneus   Hodgdon

4 R17   Elm Stream Twp   4 R15   4 R14   4 R13   4 R12   4 R11   4 R10   4 R9   4 R8   4 R7   North Penobscot   Patten   Crystal   Island Falls   4 R3   Cary

Comstock Twp

Somerset County

3 R13   3 R12   3 R11   3 R10   3 R9   3 R8   3 R7   Stacyville   Sherman   South Aroostook   3 R4   3 R3   Amity

Northeast Piscataquis

Piscataquis County

Orient

2 R13   2 R12   2 R11   2 R10   2 R9   2 R8   2 R4   Glenwood   Haynesville

Penobscot County

1 R13   1 R12   1 R11   1 R10   1 R9   1 R8   1 R6   Medway   Mattawamkeag   Reed   Bancroft   Weston

Macwahoc   1 R5

A R11   A R10   Millinocket   East Millinocket   Penobscot Indian Island   2 R9   Woodville   Kingman   Webster   Drew   Prentiss   Danforth

B R11   B R10   **Washington County**   Codyville

Beaver Cove

Misery Twp   Big Moose Twp   Greenville   4 R9   Chester   Winn   Carroll   Springfield   Kossuth Twp   Topsfield   Dyer Twp

Northeast Somerset   Southeast Piscataquis   Lake View   Seboeis   Lincoln   Lee   Lakeville   Whitney   Talmadge   Waite

West Forks   Shirley   Elliottsville Twp   Brownville   Lowell   Burlington   Twombly Ridge   6 R1 N   Grand Lake Stream

Willimantic   Milo   Medford   Enfield   Princeton

The Forks   East Moxie Twp   Blanchard   Monson   Sebec   Howland   Lowell   Hancock   North Washington   Sakom   6 ND   Big Lake Twp

Caratunk   Abbot   Guilford   **Dover-Foxcroft**   Edinburg   East Central Penobscot   3 ND   Ogton Twp   43 MD   Passamaquoddy Indian Township   42 MD

Moscow   Mayfield Twp   Kingsbury   Parkman   Atkinson   Sangerville   Bradford   Alton   Argyle   East Hancock   41 MD   40 MD   Crawford

Aroostook County

Founded	1839
Parent Counties	Penobscot, Piscataquis, Somerset, Washington
County Seat	Houlton

Towns

Allagash, Amity, Ashland, Bancroft, Blaine, Bridgewater, Caribou, Cary Plantation, Castle Hill, Caswell, Chapman, Crystal, Cyr Plantation, Dyer Brook, Eagle Lake, Easton, Fort Fairfield, Fort Kent, Frenchville, Garfield Plantation, Glenwood Plantation, Grand Isle, Hamlin, Hammond, Haynesville, Hersey, Hodgdon, Houlton, Island Falls, Limestone, Linneus, Littleton, Ludlow, Macwahoc Plantation, Madawaska, Mapleton, Mars Hill, Masardis, Merrill, Monticello, Moro Plantation, Nashville Plantation, New Canada, New Limerick, New Sweden, Oakfield, Orient, Oxbow Plantation, Perham, Portage Lake, Presque Isle, Reed Plantation, Saint Agatha, Saint Francis, Saint John Plantation, Sherman, Smyrna, Stockholm, Van Buren, Wade, Wallagrass, Washburn, Westfield, Westmanland, Weston, Winterville Plantation, Woodland

Extinct or Unincorporated

Benedicta, Connor, Maysville, Silver Ridge Plantation

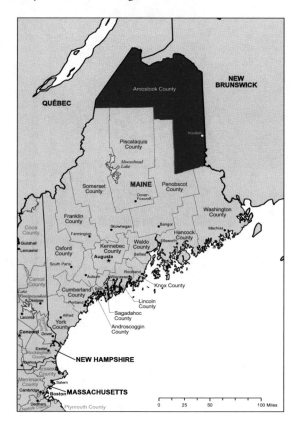

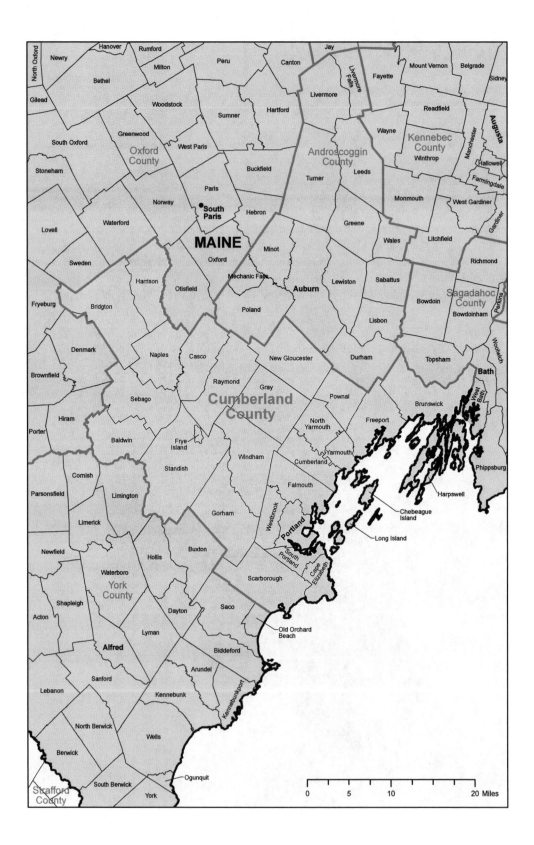

MAINE

Hanover
Rumford
Newry
Milton
Peru
Canton
Jay
North Oxford
Bethel
Livermore Falls
Fayette
Mount Vernon
Belgrade
Gilead
Woodstock
Livermore
Readfield
Sidney
Sumner
Hartford
Wayne
Kennebec County
Manchester
Augusta
South Oxford
Greenwood
Oxford County
West Paris
Androscoggin County
Winthrop
Hallowell
Stoneham
Buckfield
Turner
Leeds
Farmingdale
Paris
Monmouth
West Gardiner
Lovell
Norway
South Paris
Hebron
Greene
Waterford
MAINE
Minot
Wales
Litchfield
Gardiner
Sweden
Oxford
Wales
Richmond
Harrison
Mechanic Falls
Lewiston
Sabattus
Fryeburg
Otisfield
Auburn
Bowdoin
Sagadahoc County
Bridgton
Poland
Lisbon
Bowdoinham
Denmark
Naples
Casco
New Gloucester
Durham
Topsham
Perkins
Brownfield
Raymond
Gray
Woolwich
Hiram
Sebago
Cumberland County
Pownal
Brunswick
Bath
Porter
Baldwin
Frye Island
North Yarmouth
Freeport
West Bath
Cornish
Standish
Windham
Yarmouth
Parsonsfield
Limington
Cumberland
Chebeague Island
Harpswell
Newfield
Gorham
Falmouth
Phippsburg
Limerick
Westbrook
Portland
Long Island
Waterboro
Hollis
Buxton
South Portland
Shapleigh
York County
Scarborough
Cape Elizabeth
Acton
Dayton
Saco
Alfred
Lyman
Old Orchard Beach
Sanford
Biddeford
Lebanon
Arundel
Kennebunk
Kennebunkport
North Berwick
Wells
Berwick
Strafford County
South Berwick
Ogunquit
York

0   5   10   20 Miles

Cumberland County

Founded	1760
Parent County	York
County Seat	Portland

Towns

Baldwin, Bridgton, Brunswick, Cape Elizabeth, Casco, Chebeague Island, Cumberland, Falmouth, Freeport, Frye Island, Gorham, Gray, Harpswell, Harrison, Long Island, Naples, New Gloucester, North Yarmouth, Portland, Pownal, Raymond, Scarborough, Sebago, South Portland, Standish, Westbrook, Windham, Yarmouth

Extinct

Deering

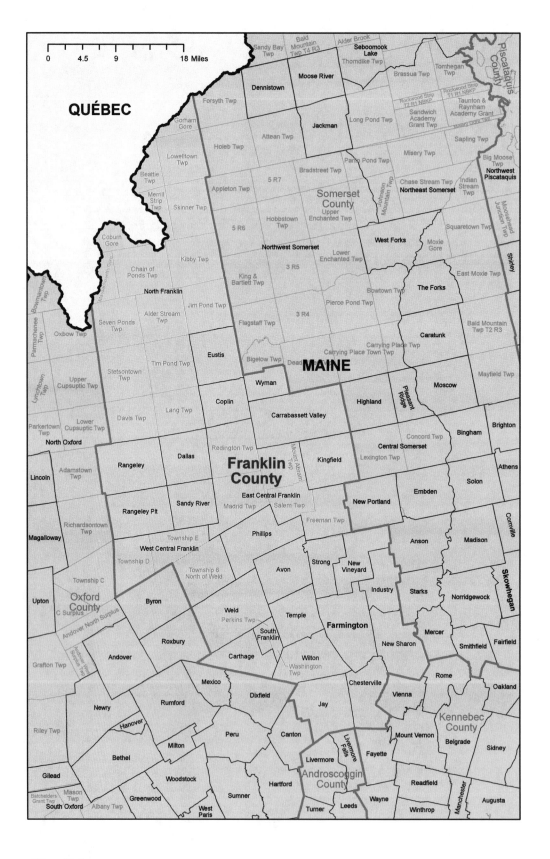

Franklin County

Founded	1838
Parent Counties	Kennebec, Oxford, Somerset
County Seat	Farmington

Towns

Avon, Carrabassett Valley, Carthage, Chesterville, Coplin Plantation, Dallas Plantation, Eustis, Farmington, Industry, Jay, Kingfield, New Sharon, New Vineyard, Phillips, Rangeley, Rangeley Plantation, Sandy River Plantation, Strong, Temple, Weld, Wilton

Extinct or Unincorporated

Berlin, Freeman, Madrid, Perkins, Salem

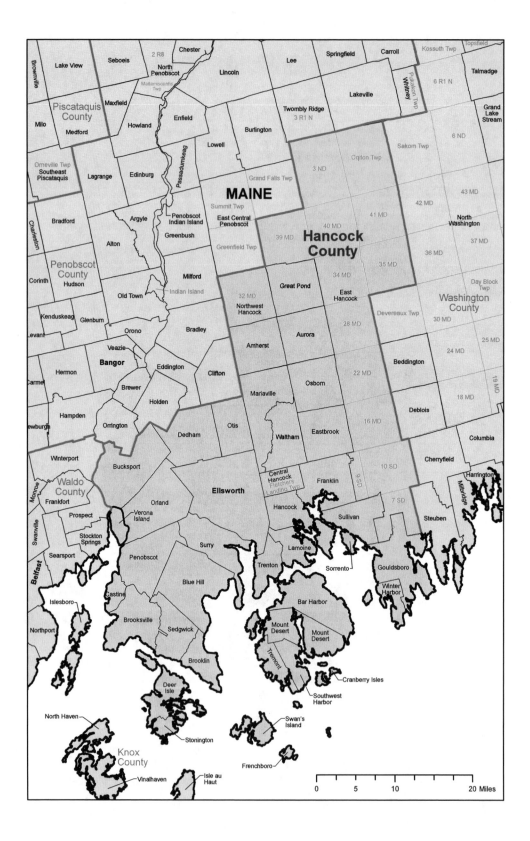

Hancock County

Founded	1789
Parent County	Lincoln
County Seat	Ellsworth

Towns

Amherst, Aurora, Bar Harbor, Blue Hill, Brooklin, Brooksville, Bucksport, Castine, Cranberry Isles, Dedham, Deer Isle, Eastbrook, Ellsworth, Franklin, Frenchboro, Gouldsboro, Great Pond, Hancock, Lamoine, Mariaville, Mount Desert, Orland, Osborn, Otis, Penobscot, Sedgwick, Sorrento, Southwest Harbor, Stonington, Sullivan, Surry, Swan's Island, Tremont, Trenton, Verona Island, Waltham, Winter Harbor

Extinct

Seaville

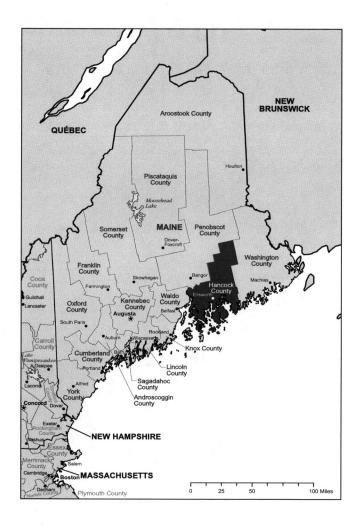

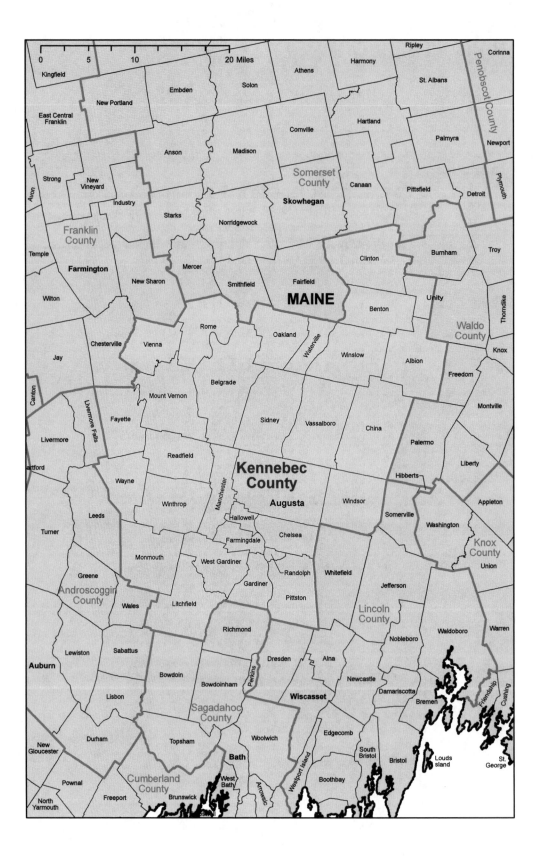

Kennebec County

Founded	1799
Parent Counties	Cumberland, Lincoln
County Seat	Augusta

Towns

Albion, Augusta, Belgrade, Benton, Chelsea, China, Clinton, Farmingdale, Fayette, Gardiner, Hallowell, Litchfield, Manchester, Monmouth, Mount Vernon, Oakland, Pittston, Randolph, Readfield, Rome, Sidney, Vassalboro, Vienna, Waterville, Wayne, West Gardiner, Windsor, Winslow, Winthrop

Extinct or Unincorporated

Dearborn, Harlem, Unity

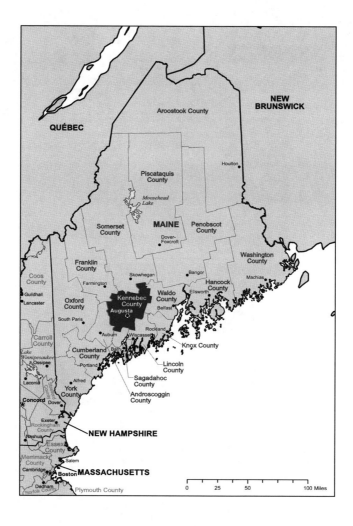

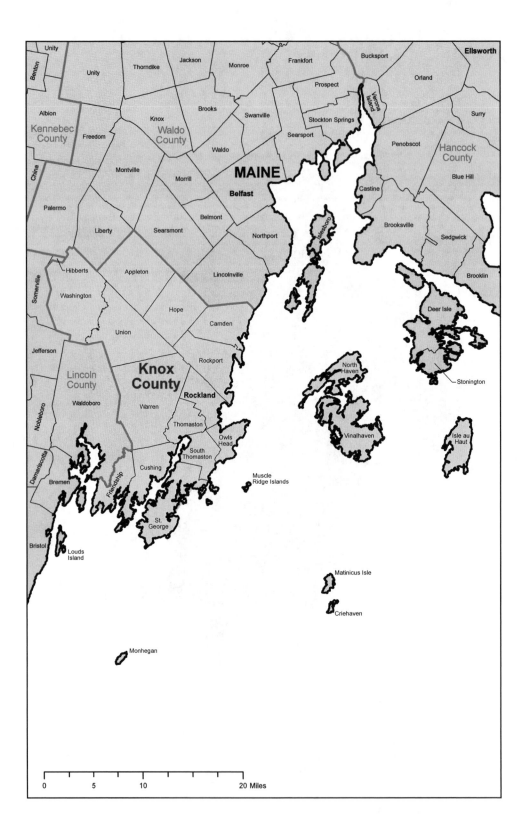

Knox County

Founded	1860
Parent Counties	Lincoln, Waldo
County Seat	Rockland

Towns

Appleton, Camden, Cushing, Friendship, Hope, Isle Au Haut, Matinicus Isle Plantation, North Haven, Owls Head, Rockland, Rockport, Saint George, South Thomaston, Thomaston, Union, Vinalhaven, Warren, Washington

Extinct

Hurricane Isle

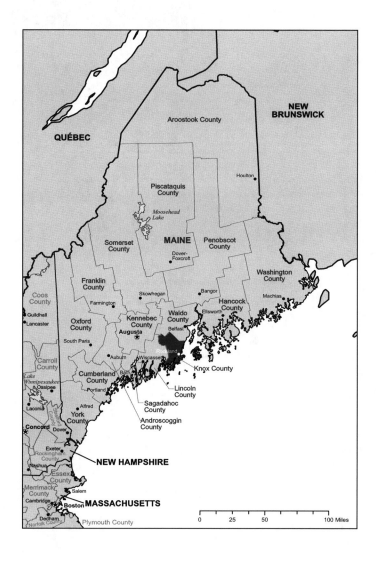

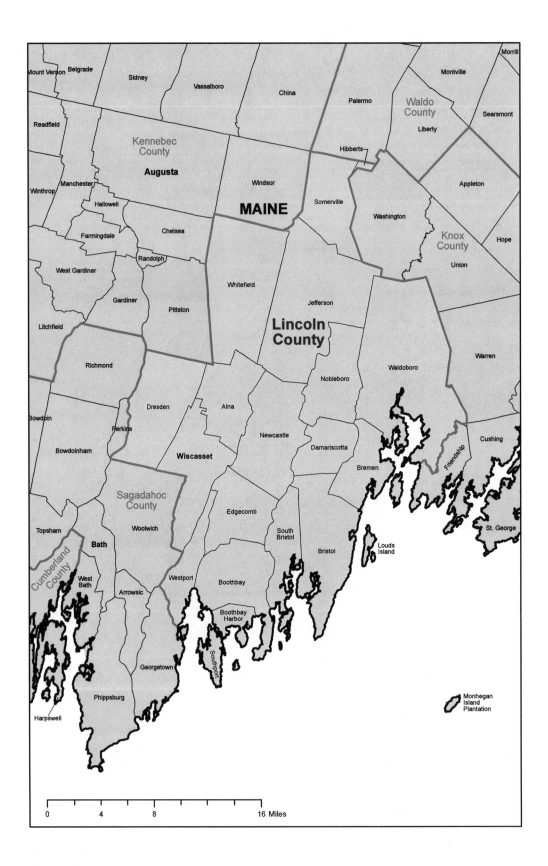

Mount Vernon Belgrade Sidney Vassalboro China Palermo Morrill Montville

Waldo County

Searsmont

Readfield

Kennebec County

Liberty

Hibberts

Augusta

Windsor

MAINE

Somerville

Appleton

Washington

Winthrop Manchester

Hallowell

Knox County

Chelsea

Hope

Farmingdale

Randolph

Union

West Gardiner

Whitefield

Jefferson

Gardiner

Pittston

Lincoln County

Litchfield

Warren

Richmond

Waldoboro

Nobleboro

Dresden

Alna

Cushing

Bowdoin

Perkins

Newcastle

Damariscotta

Friendship

Bowdoinham

Wiscasset

Bremen

St. George

Sagadahoc County

Edgecomb

Topsham

Woolwich

South Bristol

Bath

Bristol

Louds Island

Cumberland County

West Bath

Westport

Arrowsic

Boothbay

Boothbay Harbor

Monhegan Island Plantation

Georgetown

Southport

Phippsburg

Harpswell

0   4   8   16 Miles

Lincoln County

Founded	1760
Parent County	York
County Seat	Wiscasset

Towns

Alna, Boothbay, Boothbay Harbor, Bremen, Bristol, Damariscotta, Dresden, Edgecomb, Jefferson, Monhegan Island Plantation, Newcastle, Nobleboro, Somerville, South Bristol, Southport, Waldoboro, Westport, Whitefield, Wiscasset

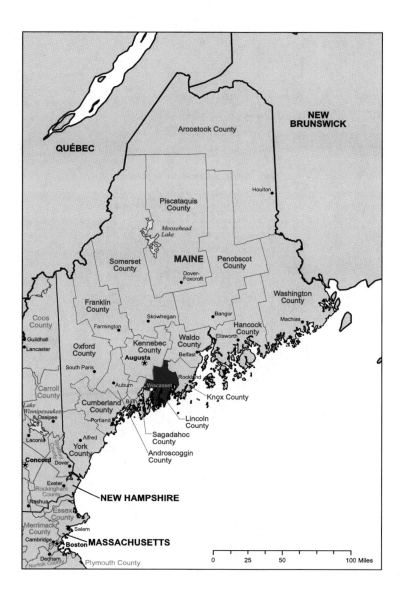

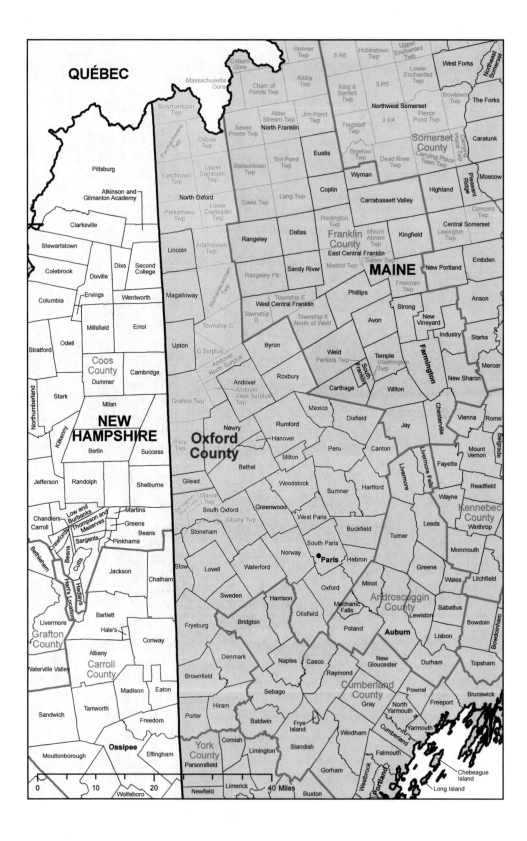

QUÉBEC

Massachusetts Gore

Bowmantown Twp

Pittsburg

Atkinson and Gilmanton Academy

Coburn Gore

Skinner Twp

5 R6

Hobbstown Twp

Upper Enchanted Twp

West Forks

Northeast Somerset

Chain of Ponds Twp

Kibby Twp

King & Bartlett Twp

3 R5

Lower Enchanted Twp

Alder Stream Twp

Jim Pond Twp

Northwest Somerset

Pierce Pond Twp

Bowtown Twp

The Forks

Seven Ponds Twp

North Franklin

Flagstaff Twp

3 R4

Caratunk

Somerset County

Oxbow Twp

Eustis

Bigelow Twp

Dead River Twp

Carrying Place Town Twp

Moscow

Clarksville

Lynchtown Twp

Upper Cupsuptic Twp

Stetsontown Twp

Tim Pond Twp

Wyman

Pleasant Ridge

Stewartstown

North Oxford

Coplin

Carrabassett Valley

Highland

Concord Twp

Central Somerset

Colebrook

Parkertown Twp

Lower Cupsuptic Twp

Davis Twp

Lang Twp

Redington Twp

Mount Abram Twp

Kingfield

Lexington Twp

Embden

Dixville

Dixs

Second College

Lincoln

Adamstown Twp

Rangeley

Dallas

Franklin County

East Central Franklin

MAINE

Madrid Twp

Salem Twp

New Portland

Ervings

Wentworth

Magalloway

Rangeley Plt

Sandy River

Freeman Twp

Columbia

Millsfield

Errol

Upton

West Central Franklin

Phillips

Strong

Anson

Township E

Avon

New Vineyard

Industry

Starks

Odell

Coos County

Cambridge

Township C

Township D

Township 6 North of Weld

Mercer

Stratford

Dummer

Byron

Weld

Temple

New Sharon

Stark

Milan

C Surplus

Andover North Surplus

Perkins Twp

South Franklin

Washington Twp

Wilton

Farmington

NEW HAMPSHIRE

Grafton Twp

Andover
Andover West Surplus Twp

Roxbury

Carthage

Wilton

Chesterville

Vienna

Rome

Kilkenny

Newry

Mexico

Dixfield

Jay

Mount Vernon

Belgrade

Berlin

Success

Riley Twp

Oxford County

Hanover

Rumford

Peru

Canton

Livermore

Livermore Falls

Fayette

Readfield

Jefferson

Randolph

Shelburne

Gilead

Milton

Bethel

Hartford

Wayne

Kennebec County

Chandlers
Carroll

Low and Burbanks

Martins

Mason Twp

Woodstock

Sumner

Greens

Thompson and Meserves

South Oxford

Greenwood

Leeds

Winthrop

Sargents

Pinkhams

Albany Twp

West Paris

Buckfield

Turner

Monmouth

Bethlehem

Beans

Cutts

Jackson

Stoneham

Norway

South Paris

Hebron

Greene

Wales

Litchfield

Hadleys

Chatham

Stow

Lovell

Waterford

Paris

Oxford

Minot

Androscoggin County

Sabattus

Bowdoin

Livermore

Bartlett

Hale's

Sweden

Harrison

Otisfield

Mechanic Falls

Lewiston

Lisbon

Bowdoinham

Grafton County

Conway

Fryeburg

Bridgton

Poland

Auburn

Waterville Valley

Albany

Carroll County

Denmark

Naples

Casco

New Gloucester

Durham

Topsham

Madison

Eaton

Brownfield

Raymond

Pownal

Cumberland County

Freeport

Brunswick

Sandwich

Tamworth

Freedom

Hiram

Sebago

Gray

North Yarmouth

Porter

Baldwin

Frye Island

Windham

Yarmouth

Chebeague Island

Ossipee

Effingham

Comish

Limington

Standish

Falmouth

Moultonborough

York County

Parsonsfield

Gorham

Westbrook

Portland

Long Island

0   10   20   Wolfeboro

Newfield

Limerick

40 Miles

Buxton

Oxford County

Founded	1805
Parent Counties	Cumberland, York
County Seat	Paris

Towns

Andover, Bethel, Brownfield, Buckfield, Byron, Canton, Denmark, Dixfield, Fryeburg, Gilead, Greenwood, Hanover, Hartford, Hebron, Hiram, Lincoln Plantation, Lovell, Magalloway Plantation, Mexico, Newry, Norway, Otisfield, Oxford, Paris, Peru, Porter, Roxbury, Rumford, Stoneham, Stow, Sumner, Sweden, Upton, Waterford, West Paris, Woodstock

Extinct or Unincorporated

Albany, Franklin Plantation, Mason, Milton

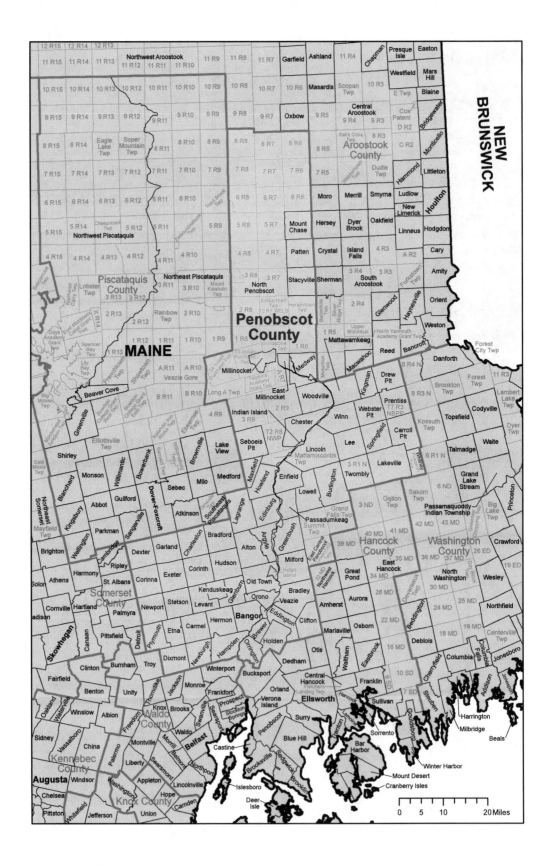

Penobscot County

Founded	1816
Parent County	Hancock
County Seat	Bangor

Towns

Alton, Bangor, Bradford, Bradley, Brewer, Burlington, Carmel, Carroll Plantation, Charleston, Chester, Clifton, Corinna, Corinth, Dexter, Dixmont, Drew Plantation, East Millinocket, Eddington, Edinburg, Enfield, Etna, Exeter, Garland, Glenburn, Greenbush, Hampden, Hermon, Holden, Howland, Hudson, Indian Island, Kenduskeag, Lagrange, Lakeville, Lee, Levant, Lincoln, Lowell, Mattawamkeag, Maxfield, Medway, Milford, Millinocket, Mount Chase, Newburgh, Newport, Old Town, Orono, Orrington, Passadumkeag, Patten, Plymouth, Seboeis Plantation, Springfield, Stacyville, Stetson, Veazie, Webster Plantation, Winn, Woodville

Extinct or Unincorporated

Argyle, East Central Penobscot, Grand Falls Plantation, Greenfield, Kingman, Mattamiscontis, North Penobscot, Prentiss Plantation, Twombly, Whitney

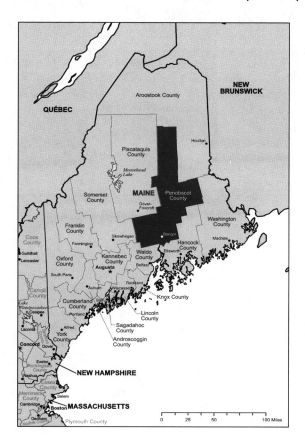

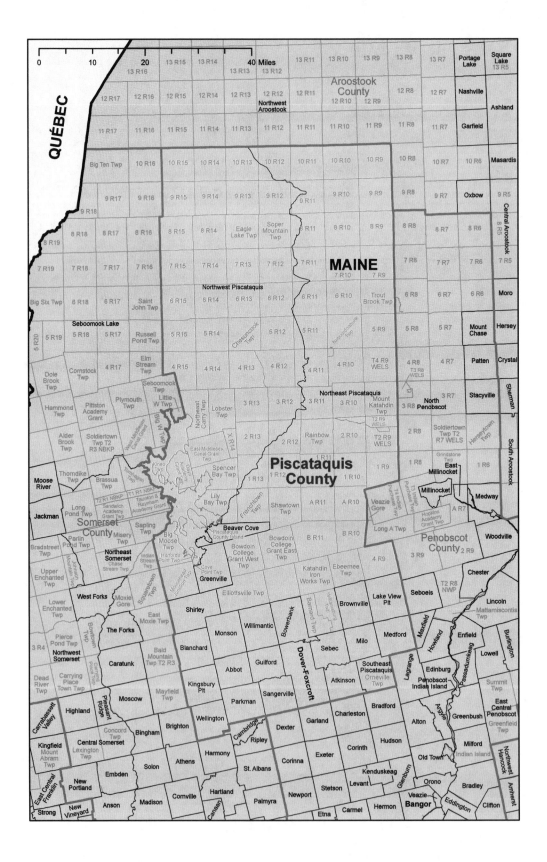

Piscataquis County

Founded	1838
Parent Counties	Penobscot, Somerset
County Seat	Dover-Foxcroft

Towns

Abbot, Atkinson, Beaver Cove, Bowerbank, Brownville, Dover-Foxcroft, Greenville, Guilford, Kingsbury Plantation, Lake View Plantation, Medford, Milo, Monson, Parkman, Sangerville, Sebec, Shirley, Wellington, Willimantic

Extinct or Unincorporated

Barnard, Blanchard, Elliotsville, Northeast Piscataquis, Northwest Piscataquis, Orneville, Southeast Piscataquis, Williamsburg, Wilson

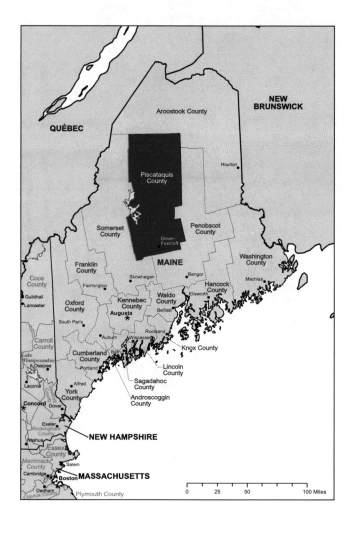

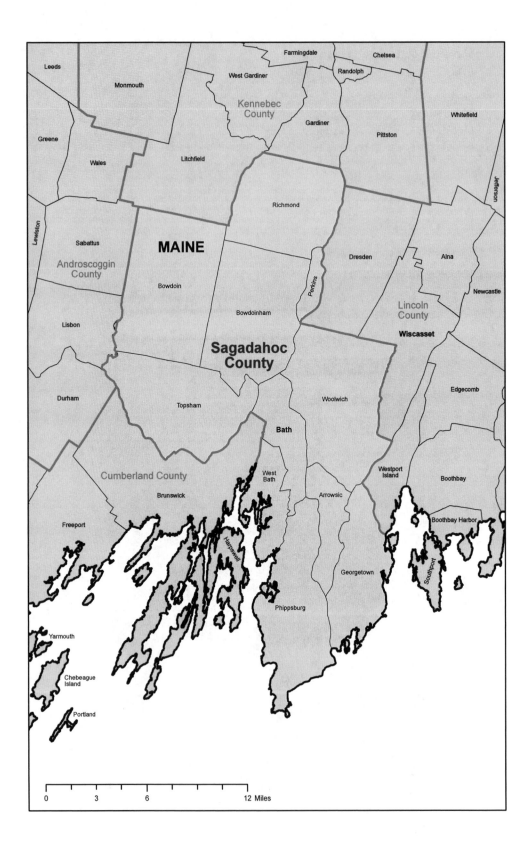

Sagadahoc County

Founded	1854
Parent County	Lincoln
County Seat	Bath

Towns

Arrowsic, Bath, Bowdoin, Bowdoinham, Georgetown, Phippsburg, Richmond, Topsham, West Bath, Woolwich

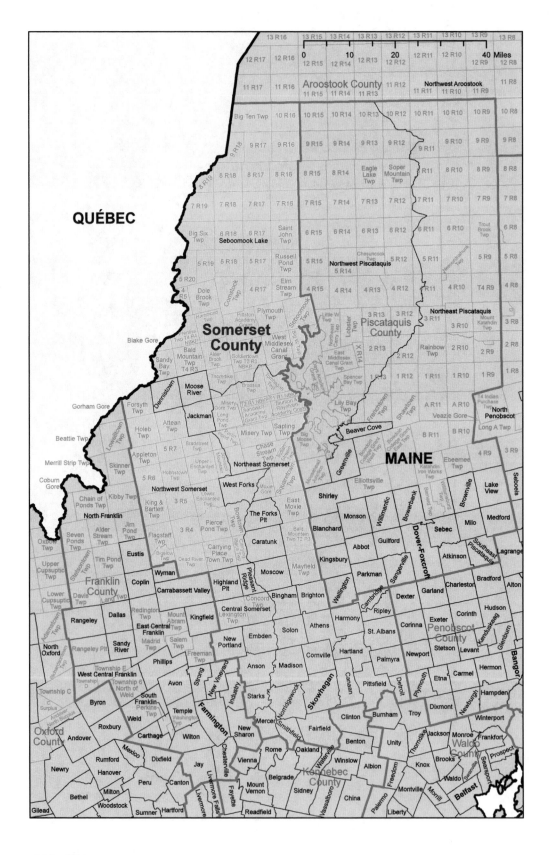

Somerset County

Founded	1809
Parent County	Kennebec
County Seat	Skowhegan

Towns

Anson, Athens, Bingham, Brighton Plantation, Cambridge, Canaan, Caratunk Plantation, Cornville, Dennistown Plantation, Detroit, Embden, Fairfield, The Forks Plantation, Harmony, Hartland, Highland Plantation, Jackman, Madison, Mercer, Moose River, Moscow, New Portland, Norridgewock, Palmyra, Pittsfield, Pleasant Ridge Plantation, Ripley, Saint Albans, Skowhegan, Smithfield, Solon, Starks, West Forks Plantation

Extinct or Unincorporated

Central Somerset, Concord, Northeast Somerset, Northwest Somerset, Seboomook Lake

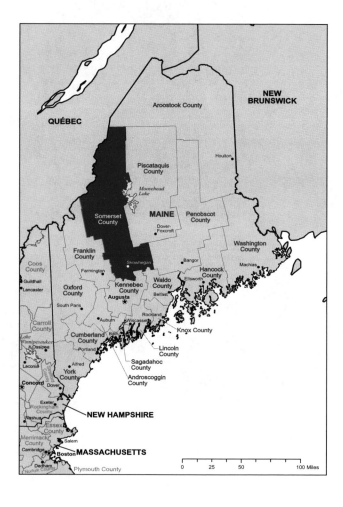

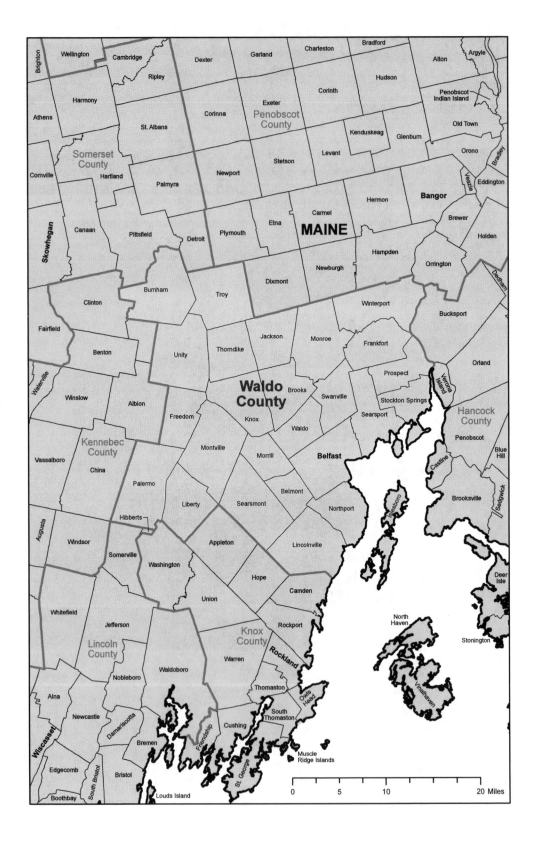

Waldo County

Founded	1827
Parent County	Hancock
County Seat	Belfast

Towns

Belfast, Belmont, Brooks, Burnham, Frankfort, Freedom, Islesboro, Jackson, Knox, Liberty, Lincolnville, Monroe, Montville, Morrill, Northport, Palermo, Prospect, Searsmont, Searsport, Stockton Springs, Swanville, Thorndike, Troy, Unity, Waldo, Winterport

Extinct

North Anson

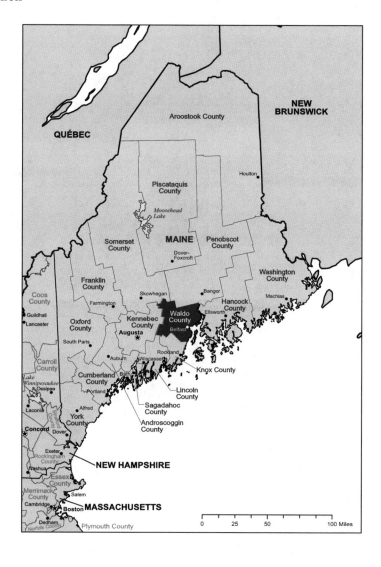

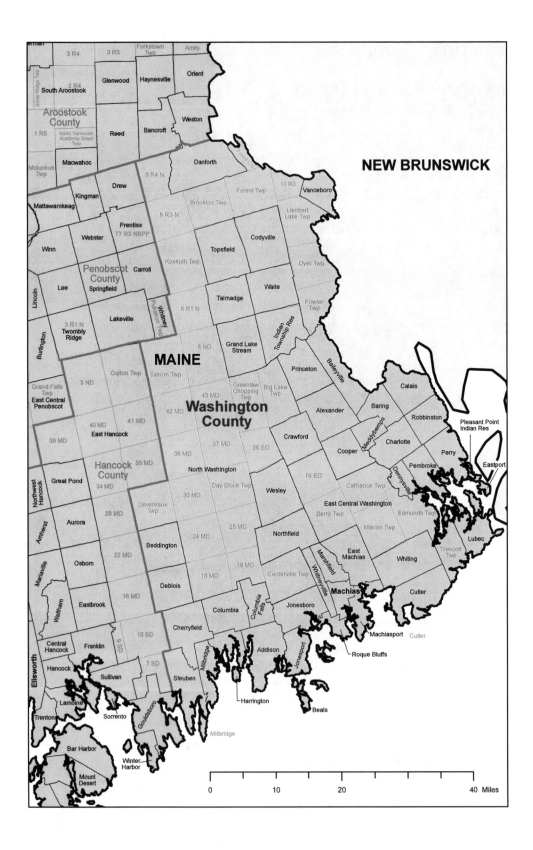

NEW BRUNSWICK

MAINE

Washington County

Penobscot County

Aroostook County

Hancock County

Washington County

Founded	1789
Parent County	Lincoln
County Seat	Machias

Towns

Addison, Alexander, Baileyville, Beals, Beddington, Calais, Centerville, Charlotte, Cherryfield, Codyville Plantation, Columbia, Columbia Falls, Cooper, Crawford, Cutler, Danforth, Deblois, Dennysville, East Machias, Eastport, Grand Lake Stream Plantation, Harrington, Indian Township Reservation [of Passamaquoddy], Jonesboro, Jonesport, Lubec, Machias, Machiasport, Marshfield, Meddybemps, Milbridge, Northfield, Pembroke, Perry, Pleasant Point Indian Reservation, Princeton, Robbinston, Roque Bluffs, Steuben, Talmadge, Topsfield, Vanceboro, Waite, Wesley, Whiting, Whitneyville

Extinct or Unincorporated

Baring, Brookton, East Central Washington, Eaton, Edmunds, Forest City, North Washington, Trescott

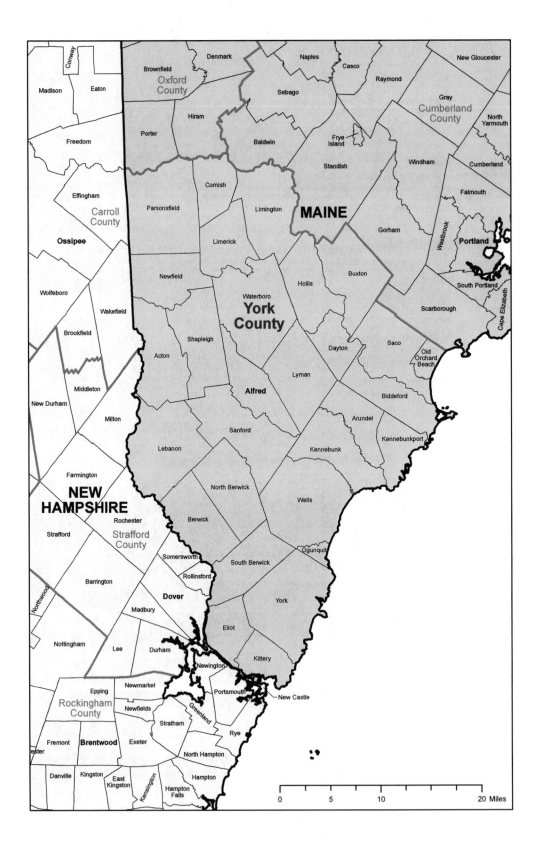

York County

Founded	1636 (called Yorkshire 1658–91)
Original County	
County Seat	Alfred

Towns

Acton, Alfred, Arundel, Berwick, Biddeford, Buxton, Cornish, Dayton, Eliot, Hollis, Kennebunk, Kennebunkport, Kittery, Lebanon, Limerick, Limington, Lyman, Newfield, North Berwick, Ogunquit, Old Orchard Beach, Parsonsfield, Saco, Sanford, Shapleigh, South Berwick, Waterboro, Wells, York

Probate Records

Probate in Maine is recorded on the county level. Older records will usually be found at the county probate court. Access to originals may be restricted if copies are available on microfilm.

Androscoggin County
Androscoggin County Probate Court
2 Turner Street
Auburn, ME 04210
www.maineprobate.net/Androscoggin.html
(207) 782–0281; fax (207) 782–1135
Hours: M–F 8:30 –5

Aroostook County
Aroostook County Probate Court
26 Court Street, Suite 103
Houlton, ME 04730
http://aroostook.me.us/probate.html
(207) 532–1502
See website for email
Hours: M–F 8–4:30

Cumberland County
Cumberland County Probate Court
142 Federal Street
Portland, ME 04101
www.maineprobate.net/Cumberland.html
(207) 871–8382; fax (207) 791–2658
Hours: M–F 8:30–4:15

Franklin County
Franklin County Probate Court
140 Main Street
Farmington, ME 04938
www.maineprobate.net/Franklin.html
(207) 778–5888; fax (207) 778–5899
Hours: M–F 8:30–4:15

Hancock County
Hancock County Probate Court
50 State Street
Ellsworth, ME 04605
www.*maineprobate.net/Hancock.html*
(207) 667–8434; fax (207) 667–5316
Hours: M–F 8:30–4

Kennebec County
Kennebec County Probate Court
95 State Street
Augusta, ME 04330
www.maineprobate.net/Kennebec.html
(207) 622–7558; fax (207) 621–1639
kenprob@gwi.net
Hours: M–F 8–4

Above: "Members of the extended Gammon family of Peru, Maine." Hollis Turner, *The History of Peru in the County of Oxford and State of Maine* (1912), facing p. 126.

Knox County

Knox County Probate Court
62 Union Street
Rockland, ME 04841
http://knoxcounty.midcoast.com/departments/
probate.html
(207) 594–0427; fax (207) 594–0863
probate@knoxcountymaine.gov
Hours: M–F 8–4

Lincoln County

Lincoln County Probate Court
32 High Street
Wiscasset, ME 04578
Mailing Address
PO Box 249
Wiscasset, ME 04578
www.maineprobate.net/Lincoln.html
(207) 882–7392; fax (207) 882–4324
Hours: M–F 8–4

Oxford County

Oxford County Probate Court
26 Western Avenue
South Paris, ME 04281
Mailing Address
PO Box 179
South Paris, ME 04281
www.maineprobate.net/Oxford.html
(207) 743–6671 ; fax (207) 743–4255
register@oxfordcounty.org
Hours: M–F 8–4

Penobscot County

Penobscot County Probate Court
97 Hammond Street
Bangor, ME 04401
www.maineprobate.net/Penobscot.html
(207) 942–8769; fax (207) 941–8499
Hours: M–F 8–4

Piscataquis County

Piscataquis County Probate Court
159 East Main Street
Dover–Foxcroft, ME 04426
www.maineprobate.net/Somerset.html

(207) 564–2431; fax (207) 564–3022
probate@piscataquis.us
Hours: M–F 8–4:30

Sagadahoc County

Sagadahoc County Probate Court
752 High Street
Bath, ME 04530
http://sagcounty.com/sag_probate.html
(207) 443–8218; fax (207) 443–8217
sagprob@sagcounty.com
Hours: M–F 8:30–4:30

Somerset County

Somerset County Probate Court
41 Court Street
Skowhegan, ME 04976
www.maineprobate.net/Somerset.html
(207) 474–3322; fax (207) 858–4235
Hours: M–F 8–4:30

Waldo County

Waldo County Probate Court
39A Spring Street, PO Box 323
Belfast, ME 04915
www.maineprobate.net/Waldo.html
(207) 338–2780; fax (207) 338–2360
Hours: M–F 8–4

Washington County

Washington County Probate Court
85 Court Street, PO Box 297
Machias, ME 04654
www.washingtoncountymaine.com/probate
(207) 255–6591
probate@washingtoncountymaine.com
Hours: M–F 8–4

York County

York County Probate Court
45 Kennebunk Road
Alfred, ME 04002
www.maineprobate.net/York.html
(207) 324–1577; fax (207) 324–0163
probate@co.york.me.us
Hours: M–F 8–12:30, 1–4

ME

Land Records

Deeds and other land records are filed at the county level in Maine. Aroostook and Oxford Counties have two registration districts. Counties have begun to digitize their records and make them available online, though online access varies from county to county. The counties of Cumberland, Kennebec, Knox, Oxford (East District), Piscataquis, Somerset, Waldo, and Washington make records available at *www.mainelandrecords.com*. The Maine Registers of Deeds Association runs a website, *www.maineregistryofdeeds.us*, through which you can access information from any of the eighteen registries of deeds.

Androscoggin County

Androscoggin County Registry of Deeds
2 Turner Street
Auburn, ME 04210–5943
http://androscoggindeeds.com
(207) 782–0191
Hours: M–F 8–5

Aroostook County

Aroostook County Northern
Registry of Deeds
22 Hall Street, Suite 201
Fort Kent, ME 04743–0047

Mailing Address
PO Box 47
Fort Kent, ME 04743-0047

www.AroostookDeedsNorth.com
(207) 834–3925; fax (207) 834–3138
Hours: M–F 8–4:30

Aroostook County Southern
Registry of Deeds
26 Court Street, Suite 102
Houlton, ME 04730
www.AroostookDeedsSouth.com
(207) 532–1500; fax (207) 532–1506
Hours: M–F 8–4:30

Cumberland County

Cumberland County Registry of Deeds
142 Federal Street
Portland, ME 04101

Mailing Address
PO Box 7230
Portland, ME 04101
www.cumberlandcounty.org/Deeds
(207) 871–8389; fax (207) 772–4162
Hours: M–F 8–4:30

Franklin County

Franklin County Registry of Deeds
140 Main Street
Farmington, ME 04938
www.franklincountydeedsme.com
(207) 778–5889; fax (207) 778–5899
Hours: M–F 8:30–4

Hancock County

Hancock County Registry of Deeds
50 State Street
Ellsworth, ME 04605
www.co.hancock.me.us/reg_deeds/index.html
(207) 667– 8353
Hours: M–F 8:30–4

Kennebec County

Kennebec County Registry of Deeds
1 Weston Court
Augusta, ME 04330
https://gov.propertyinfo.com/me-kennebec/
(207) 622-0431
Hours: M–F 8–4

Knox County

Knox County Registry of Deeds
62 Union Street
Rockland, ME 04841

Mailing Address
PO Box 943
Rockland, ME 04841

www.knoxcounty.midcoast.com/departments/deeds.html
(207) 594–0422; fax (207) 594–0446
Hours: M–F 8–4

Lincoln County

Lincoln County Registry of Deeds
Lincoln County Courthouse
32 High Street
Wiscasset, ME 04578

Mailing Address
PO Box 249
Wiscasset, ME 04578

http://co.lincoln.me.us/dep.html
(207) 882–7431, (207) 882–7515;
    fax (207) 882–4061
Hours: M–F 8–4

Oxford County

Oxford County Registry of Deeds
Eastern District
26 Western Avenue
South Paris, ME 04281

Mailing Address
PO Box 179
South Paris, ME 04281

https://oxfordcounty.org/deeds-east.php
(207) 743– 6211; fax (207) 743–2656
Hours: M–F 8–4

Towns served: Andover, Bethel, Buckfield,
Byron, Canton, Dixfield, Gilead, Green-
wood, Hanover, Hartford, Hebron, Lincoln
Plantation, Magalloway Plantation, Mexico,
Newry, Norway, Otisfield, Oxford, Paris,
Peru, Roxbury, Rumford, Sumner, Sweden,
Upton, Waterford, West Paris, Woodstock

Oxford County Registry of Deeds
Western District
38 Portland Street
Fryeburg, ME 04037
www.oxfordcounty.org/deeds-west.php
(207) 935–2565; fax (207) 935–4183
Hours: M–F 9–4

Towns served: Brownfield, Denmark,
Fryeburg, Hiram, Lovell, Porter, Stoneham,
Stow

Penobscot County

Penobscot County Registry of Deeds
97 Hammond Street
Bangor, ME 04401
https://penobscotdeeds.com
(207) 942–8797
Hours: M–F 8–4:30

Piscataquis County

Piscataquis County Registry of Deeds
159 East Main Street
Dover-Foxcroft, ME 04426
https://i2a.uslandrecords.com/ME/Piscataquis
(207) 564–2411; fax (207) 564–7708
deeds@piscataquis.us
Hours: M–F 8:30–4:30

Sagadahoc County

Sagadahoc County Registry of Deeds
752 High Street
Bath, ME 04530–0246

Mailing Address
PO Box 246
Bath, ME 04530-0246

www.sagcounty.com
(207) 443-8214; fax (207) 443-8216
Hours: M–F 8–3

Somerset County

Somerset County Registry of Deeds
41 Court Street
Skowhegan, ME 04976
www.mainelandrecords.com
(207) 474–9861; (207) 474–7405
Hours: M–F 8:30–4:30

Waldo County

Waldo County Registry of Deeds
137 Church Street
Belfast, ME 04915

Mailing Address
PO Box D
Belfast, ME 04915

www.waldocountyme.gov/rod/
(207) 338–1710; fax (207) 338–6360
Hours: M–F 8–4

Washington County

Washington County Registry of Deeds
85 Court Street
Machias, ME 04654

Mailing Address
PO Box 297
Machias, ME 04654

www.washingtoncountymaine.com/deeds/
(207) 255–6512; fax (207) 255–3838
deeds@washingtoncountymaine.com
Hours: M–F 8–4

York County

York County Registry of Deeds
45 Kennebunk Road
Alfred, ME 04002
www.govpropertyinfo.com/ME-York
(207) 324–1576; fax (207) 324–2886
Hours: M–F 8:30–4:30

Towns

Today there are 434 towns, 34 plantations, and 22 cities in the state of Maine. Plantations were common government structures in the Massachusetts Bay Colony, but today Maine is the only state to continue using this form of government. Originally created to guide a community through the process of incorporation as a town by the state legislature, plantations have survived as a smaller form of government for communities that need far fewer services than more populated areas. Plantations are mostly rural, heavily forested areas with very small populations. By the end of the twentieth century, two-thirds of plantations had populations of less than 100.

The following chart lists the name of each town, the date of its incorporation as a town, the county, towns from which it was formed (or from which land was later added to the town), towns that were formed from it (or to which land was added from it), and notes about the town. In the Parent Towns column, towns from which other towns were formed are indicated in **bold** type. Parts of other towns later annexed are in regular type.

It also shows which vital records and church records are available as manuscripts, typescripts, published books, or online. Extinct towns (those that are no longer extant or that were annexed by other towns) are listed in the second table. For more information, see *www.maine. gov/local* or the Maine Secretary of State's interactive archive, *www.maine.gov/cgi-bin/archives*.

VR and CR codes

D   Delayed returns
F   Catholic Church records and other records published by French-Canadian societies
M   NEHGS microfilm
N   Manuscript or typescript at NEHGS
P   Published volume
S   Published substitute records (e.g., newspapers, vital records, etc.)
W   Records available on *AmericanAncestors.org*

Town	Inc.	County	Parent	Daughter	Note	VR	CR
Abbot	1827	Piscataquis			Settled 1805. Organized as plantation 1854.		
Acton	1830	York	**Shapleigh**	Shapleigh			
Addison	1797	Washington			Settled 1780.	M, P	
Albion	1804	Kennebec	Clinton, Unity, Winslow	Benton (Sebasticook), China	Called Fairfax to 1821. Called Lygonia to 1824.	D, P	
Alexander	1825	Washington	Cooper	Crawford	Settled 1810.	M, P	
Alfred	1808	York	**Sanford**, Waterboro	Sanford	Created as district 1794.	D, P	
Allagash Plantation	1886	Aroostook			Organization repealed 1933. Reorganized as town 1978.		
Alna	1794	Lincoln	Jefferson, Newcastle, White-field, **Wiscasset (Pownalborough)**	Dresden, White-field, Wiscasset (Pownalborough)	Called New Milford to 1811.	M	
Alton	1844	Penobscot	**Argyle**	Old Town			
Amherst	1831	Hancock	Mariaville				
Amity	1836	Aroostook			Settled 1825.	M	
Andover	1804	Oxford			Settled 1780. Called East Andover to 1820.		
Anson	1798	Somerset	Embden, New Vineyard, North Anson	Industry, New Portland, North Anson	Settled 1775.	P	
Appleton	1829	Knox	Hope		Settled 1775.	M, P	
Arrowsic	1841	Sagadahoc	**Georgetown**				
Arundel	1915	York	**Kennebunkport**		Kennebunkport called Arundel between 1719 and 1821. Called North Kennebunkport to 1957.		
Ashland	1862	Aroostook	Sheridan Planta-tion (Buchanan)		Settled 1835. Called Ashland to 1869. Called Dalton to 1876. Re-named Ashland 1876.		
Athens	1804	Somerset	Brighton (North Hill), Hartland		Settled 1782.		
Atkinson	1819	Piscataquis	Orneville (Milton)		Settled 1804.	D	
Auburn	1842	Androscoggin	Danville, **Minot**			M	F

ME

Town	Inc.	County	Parent	Daughter	Note	VR	CR
Augusta	1797	Kennebec	**Hallowell**, Manchester	Hallowell, Manchester (Kennebec), Winthrop	Called Harrington to 1797.	P, W	F
Aurora	1831	Hancock			Settled 1805. Called Hampton to 1833.		
Avon	1802	Franklin		Strong	Settled 1779.	M	
Baileyville	1828	Washington	Princeton		Sometimes called Woodland (distinct from Woodland, Aroostook Co.).		
Baldwin	1802	Cumberland		Hiram, Sebago	Settled 1735.		
Bancroft	1889	Aroostook		Weston	Settled 1830. Organized as plantation 1878.		
Bangor	1791	Penobscot	Veazie	Veazie	Settled 1768.	M, P	
Bar Harbor	1796	Hancock		Trenton	Settled 1786. Called Eden to 1913.	D	
Bath	1781	Sagadahoc		West Bath		D, W	
Beals	1925	Washington	Jonesport				
Beaver Cove	1975	Piscataquis			Organized as plantation 1975 and as town 1978.		
Beddington	1833	Washington					
Belfast	1773	Waldo		Searsport	Settled 1769.	M, W	
Belgrade	1796	Kennebec	Dearborn, Rome, Sidney	Mount Vernon	Settled 1774.	M	
Belmont	1814	Waldo	**Greene Plantation**	Morrill (North Belmont)	Petition for incorporation asked that town be called Gilead, but named Belmont by legislature.		
Benton	1842	Kennebec	Albion, **Clinton**, Unity Gore	Fairfield	Called Sebasticook to 1850.	M	
Berwick	1713	York	**Kittery**	North Berwick, South Berwick		D, N, P	F, P
Bethel	1796	Oxford	Hanover	Hanover	Settled 1774.	M	
Biddeford	1653	York		Saco (Pepperellborough)	Settled 1630.	D, P	F
Bingham	1812	Somerset			Settled 1784.	M	F
Blaine	1874	Aroostook			Settled 1842.		
Blue Hill	1789	Hancock	Sedgwick	Penobscot	Settled 1762.	W	

Town	Inc.	County	Parent	Daughter	Note	VR	CR
Boothbay	1764	Lincoln		Boothbay Harbor, Southport (Townsend)	Settled 1630.	D	
Boothbay Harbor	1889	Lincoln	**Boothbay**				
Bowdoin	1788	Sagadahoc		Lisbon (Thompson)	Settled 1725.	M, P, W	
Bowdoinham	1762	Sagadahoc	Pittston (Gardinerston), Richmond Plantation, Topsham	Richmond, Topsham			
Bowerbank	1839	Piscataquis		Sebec	Settled 1825. Incorporation repealed 1869. Organized as plantation 1895. Reincorporated as town 1907.		
Bradford	1831	Penobscot			Settled 1803.		
Bradley	1835	Penobscot			Settled 1817.	D, M	
Bremen	1828	Lincoln	**Bristol,** Waldoboro	Waldoboro			
Brewer	1812	Penobscot	Bucksport (Buckstown), Dedham, **Orrington**	Eddington, Holden			
Bridgewater	1858	Aroostook			Settled 1827.		
Bridgton	1794	Cumberland	Denmark, Fryeburg	Harrison, Naples	Settled 1769.	M, P	
Brighton Plantation	1816	Somerset		Athens	Settled 1801. Called North Hill until 1827. Name changed to Brighton 1827. Incorporation repealed and organized as plantation 1895.	D	
Bristol	1765	Lincoln		Bremen, Damariscotta, Nobleboro, South Bristol	Settled 1625.	M, P	
Brooklin	1849	Hancock	**Sedgwick**		Called Port Watson June–July 1849.	M, W	
Brooks	1816	Waldo	Monroe (Lee)	Monroe (Lee), Swanville	Settled 1798.	D	P
Brooksville	1817	Hancock	**Castine, Penobscot, Sedgwick**			P, W	

ME

Town	Inc.	County	Parent	Daughter	Note	VR	CR
Brownfield	1802	Oxford		Denmark, Fryeburg, Hiram, Porter	Settled 1765.		
Brownville	1824	Piscataquis			Settled 1795.	M, P	F
Brunswick	1737	Cumberland		Freeport, North Yarmouth		M, P	
Buckfield	1793	Oxford	Hartford, Sumner	Paris	Settled 1776.	M	
Bucksport	1792	Hancock		Brewer, Dedham, Orrington	Settled 1764. Called Buckstown to 1817.	M, P	
Burlington	1832	Penobscot	Lowell (Hunt-ressville), Two Mile Strip			M	
Burnham	1824	Waldo	Clinton Gore, Pittsfield (Warsaw)	Troy (Joy), Unity	Originally called Twenty-fivemile Pond Planta-tion. Settled 1795.	M	
Buxton	1772	York		Standish (Pearsontown)	Settled 1748.	M, W	P
Byron	1833	Oxford				M	
Calais	1809	Washington			Settled 1779.	D, M, P, S	
Cambridge	1834	Somerset	**Ripley**	Wellington	Settled 1804.		
Camden	1791	Knox	Warren	Rockport	Settled 1769.	D, P	
Canaan	1788	Somerset	Clinton, Hart-land, Pittsfield (Warsaw)	Bloomfield, Clin-ton, Skowhegan (Milburn)	Settled 1770.	M	
Canton	1821	Oxford	Hartford, **Jay**	Peru	Settled 1792.		
Cape Elizabeth	1775	Cumberland	**Falmouth**	South Portland	Created as district 1765.	M	
Caratunk Plantation	1840	Somerset					
Caribou	1859	Aroostook	Eaton Grant, Forestville, Sheridan	Connor	Settled 1839. Called Lyndon to Feb. 1869. Called Caribou to March 1869. Renamed Lyndon 1877. Renamed Caribou 1877.	P	
Carmel	1811	Penobscot	Etna		Settled 1798.	P, S	
Carrabassett Valley	1972	Franklin				M	

Town	Inc.	County	Parent	Daughter	Note	VR	CR
Carroll Plantation	1845	Penobscot			Settled 1831. Incorporation repealed and organized as plantation 1937.		
Carthage	1826	Franklin		Dixfield	Previously called 4 AP. Settled 1803.		
Cary Plantation	1858	Aroostook			Settled 1824. Organized as Plantation No. 11 1859. Organized as Cary Plantation 1883.	M	
Casco	1841	Cumberland	Dingley Islands, Poland, **Raymond**, Songo, Gore				
Castine	1796	Hancock	**Penobscot**	Brooksville		P, W	
Castle Hill	1903	Aroostook			Settled 1843.	M	
Caswell	1879	Aroostook			Organized as Pleasant Ridge Plantation 1878.		
Centerville	1842	Washington	Columbia	Northfield		D	
Chapman	1915	Aroostook			Plantation from 1874.	M	
Charleston	1811	Penobscot			Settled 1795. Called New Charleston to 1827.		
Charlotte	1825	Washington		Meddybemps	Settled 1807.		N
Chebeague Island	2007	Cumberland	**Cumberland**				
Chelsea	1850	Kennebec	**Hallowell**	Pittston		M	
Cherryfield	1816	Washington	Steuben	Columbia	Settled 1757.	M	
Chester	1834	Penobscot			Settled 1823.		
Chesterville	1802	Franklin	Wilton	Vienna	Settled 1782.	M	
China	1818	Kennebec	**Albion (Fairfax), Harlem, Winslow**	Vassalboro		D, P	
Clifton	1848	Penobscot			Settled as Jarvis Gore 1812. Called Maine 1848–49.	M	
Clinton	1795	Kennebec	Benton (Sebasticook), Canaan, Clinton Gore, Pittsfield (Warsaw)	Albion (Fairfax), Canaan		M, P	
Codyville Plantation	1845	Washington					
Columbia	1796	Washington	Jonesboro	Centreville, Cherryfield, Columbia Falls, Harrington	Settled 1770.	M	

Town	Inc.	County	Parent	Daughter	Note	VR	CR
Columbia Falls	1863	Washington	Columbia		Settled 1780.	M	
Cooper	1822	Washington		Alexander, Meddybemps	Settled 1812.	M	
Coplin Plantation	1895	Franklin					
Corinna	1816	Penobscot			Settled 1815.	M, P	
Corinth	1811	Penobscot			Settled 1792.	M	
Cornish	1794	York			Settled 1776.	N	P
Cornville	1798	Somerset	Mile-and-a-half Strip	Skowhegan (Milburn)	Settled 1794.	M	
Cranberry Isles	1830	Hancock	Mount Desert				
Crawford	1828	Washington	Alexander		Founded as Adams 11 February 1828. Renamed Crawford 23 February 1828.		
Crystal	1878	Aroostook		Sherman	Settled 1839. Incorporated as town 1901.		
Cumberland	1821	Cumberland	**North Yarmouth**	Portland, Chebeague Island		M, P	
Cushing	1789	Knox	Friendship, Warren	Friendship, Saint George, Warren	Settled 1733.		
Cutler	1826	Washington			Settled 1765.	M	
Cyr Plantation	1870	Aroostook					
Dallas Plantation	1845	Franklin			Called Plantation No. 2 and 3 to 1845. Called Dallas Plantation to 1852. Called Rangeley Plantation to 1895. Renamed Dallas Plantation 1895.		
Damariscotta	1848	Lincoln	**Bristol, Nobleboro**				
Danforth	1860	Washington	Eaton, Weston		Settled 1829.		
Dayton	1854	York	**Hollis**			D	
Deblois	1852	Washington					
Dedham	1837	Hancock	Bucksport (Buckstown)	Brewer, Ellsworth	Settled 1810.		
Deer Isle	1789	Hancock		Isle Au Haut, Stonington	Settled 1762.	P	

Town	Inc.	County	Parent	Daughter	Note	VR	CR
Denmark	1807	Oxford	**Brownfield,** Fosters Gore, Fryeburg, Fryeburg Academy Grant (Pleasant Mountain Gore)	Bridgton, Sebago			
Dennistown Plantation	1895	Somerset					
Dennysville	1818	Washington		Pembroke	Settled 1786.		
Detroit	1828	Somerset		Pittsfield	Called Chandlerville until 1841.	D	
Dexter	1816	Penobscot			Settled 1801.	D	
Dixfield	1803	Oxford	Carthage (4 AP)	Carthage	Settled 1795.		
Dixmont	1807	Penobscot			Settled 1799.	P	
Dover-Foxcroft	1922	Piscataquis	**Dover, Foxcroft**		Towns merged in 1915, effective 1922. (See extinct towns.)		
Dresden	1794	Lincoln	Alna (New Milford), **Wiscasset (Pownalborough)**	Perkins		M	
Drew Plantation	1921	Penobscot	Reed	Prentiss, Reed	Settled 1825. Incorporation repealed 1933. Organized as plantation 1934.		
Durham	1789	Androscoggin	Danville (Pejobscot)		Settled 1763.	D	
Dyer Brook	1891	Aroostook			Organized as plantation 1858. Reorganized 1880.		
Eagle Lake	1911	Aroostook			Settled 1840. Organized as plantation 1859.	M	
East Machias	1826	Washington			Renamed Machisses 1840. Name reverted to East Machias 1841.		
East Millinocket	1907	Penobscot					
Eastbrook	1837	Hancock	Waltham		Settled 1800.		
Easton	1865	Aroostook					
Eastport	1798	Washington	Dudleys or Allens Island	Lubec	Settled 1772.	M, S	
Eddington	1811	Penobscot	Brewer, Clifton (Jarvis Gore)		Settled 1787.		
Edgecomb	1774	Lincoln		Westport	Settled 1744.	M	

Town	Inc.	County	Parent	Daughter	Note	VR	CR
Edinburg	1835	Penobscot			Settled 1827.		
Eliot	1810	York	**Kittery**	Kittery		D	
Ellsworth	1800	Hancock	Dedham, Surry, Trenton	Surry	Settled 1763.	S	
Embden	1804	Somerset		Anson	Settled 1779.	M	
Enfield	1835	Penobscot			Settled 1820.		
Etna	1820	Penobscot		Carmel, Plymouth	Settled 1807. Originally called Aetna; name changed almost immediately.		
Eustis	1871	Franklin			Organized as Jackson 1850. Organized as Eustis 1857.		
Exeter	1811	Penobscot			Settled 1801.	M	
Fairfield	1788	Somerset	Benton (Sebasticook)	Bloomfield, Norridgewock	Settled 1774.	D, P	
Falmouth	1718	Cumberland	Westbrook (Stroudwater)	Cape Elizabeth, Deering, Portland, Westbrook (Stroudwater)			P
Farmingdale	1852	Kennebec	**Gardiner, Hallowell, West Gardiner**	Manchester (Kennebec)		M, P, W	
Farmington	1794	Franklin	Industry, Strong		Settled 1776.	D, W	
Fayette	1795	Kennebec		Mount Vernon		M	
The Forks Plantation	1895	Somerset					
Fort Fairfield	1858	Aroostook	DR1 WELS, Plymouth (Sarsfield)		Settled 1816.		
Fort Kent	1869	Aroostook			Settled 1841.		
Frankfort	1789	Waldo		Hampden, Monroe (Lee), Prospect, Searsport, Swanville, Winterport	Settled 1760.	P	
Franklin	1825	Hancock	9 SD BPP (wild land township), 10 SD BPP (wild land township), Hancock		Settled 1784.		
Freedom	1813	Waldo			Settled 1794.	D, P	

Town	Inc.	County	Parent	Daughter	Note	VR	CR
Freeport	1789	Cumberland	**North Yarmouth**	Brunswick, Pownal		M	
Frenchboro	1979	Hancock			Incorporated as Island-port 1857. Incorporation repealed 1858. Organized as Long Island Plantation. Incorporated as Frenchboro 1979.		
Frenchville	1869	Aroostook		Saint Agatha	Called Dickeyville to 1871.		
Friendship	1807	Knox	Cushing	Cushing	Settled 1770.	M	
Frye Island	1998	Cumberland	**Standish**				
Fryeburg	1777	Oxford		Bridgton; Conway, N.H.; Denmark	Settled 1762.	M	
Gardiner	1803	Kennebec	Hallowell, **Pittston**	Farmingdale, West Gardiner		D, M, P, W	
Garfield Plantation	1895	Aroostook					
Garland	1811	Penobscot			Settled 1802.		
Georgetown	1716	Sagadahoc				M, P	
Gilead	1804	Oxford			Settled 1780.	D	
Glenburn	1822	Penobscot		Kenduskeag, Old Town	Settled 1805. Called Dutton to 1837.	M	
Glenwood Plantation	1867	Aroostook			Incorporated as town 1867. Incorporation repealed 1868. Organized as plantation 1877.		
Gorham	1764	Cumberland	Scarboro, Standish (Pearsontown)		Settled 1736.	D, M, P	
Gouldsboro	1789	Hancock	7 SD BPP (wild land township), Hancock	Winter Harbor	Settled 1700.	D	
Grand Isle	1869	Aroostook			Settled 1805. Called Grant Isle to 1872.		
Grand Lake Stream Plantation	1897	Washington					
Gray	1778	Cumberland			Settled 1750.	M, W	
Great Pond	1981	Hancock			Organized as Plantation Number 33 MD 5 1895. Named 1969.		

Town	Inc.	County	Parent	Daughter	Note	VR	CR
Greenbush	1834	Penobscot			Settled 1812.		
Greene	1788	Androscoggin	**Lewiston**	Lewiston, Sabattus (Webster)	Settled 1773.	M	
Greenville	1836	Piscataquis	Wilson		Settled 1824. Organized as Haskell 1836.		
Greenwood	1816	Oxford		Woodstock	Settled 1802.	M	
Guilford	1816	Piscataquis	Parkman, Sangerville.		Settled 1806.	M	
Hallowell	1771	Kennebec	Augusta (Harrington), Manchester (Kennebec), Winthrop	Chelsea, Gardiner, Manchester (Kennebec), Pittston	Settled 1754.	D, M, P, W	
Hamlin	1975	Aroostook		Van Buren	Organized as plantation 1859.		
Hammond	1978	Aroostook			Organized as plantation 1885.	M	
Hampden	1794	Penobscot	**Frankfort**, Hermon, Newburgh		Settled 1768.	P	
Hancock	1828	Hancock	**8 SD BPP (wild land township)**, Lamoine, **Sullivan, Trenton**	Franklin, Gouldsboro, Lamoine		M	
Hanover	1843	Oxford	**Bethel**, Howard's Gore	Bethel		D	
Harmony	1803	Somerset			Settled 1796.	M	
Harpswell	1758	Cumberland	**North Yarmouth**, Phippsburg		Settled 1720.	M	
Harrington	1797	Washington	Columbia	Milbridge, Steuben	Settled 1765.	W	
Harrison	1805	Cumberland	**Bridgton, Otisfield**	Naples			
Hartford	1798	Oxford	Chandler's Gore, Plantation Number 1	Buckfield, Canton	Settled 1783.	M, P	
Hartland	1820	Somerset		Athens, Canaan, Pittsfield (Warsaw), Saint Albans	Settled 1800.		
Haynesville	1876	Aroostook	**Haynesville, Leavitt Plantation, Forkstown, Glenwood Plantation**		Settled 1828.		
Hebron	1792	Oxford	Paris	Oxford	Settled 1774.	D	
Hermon	1816	Penobscot		Hampden	Settled 1790.	M	

Town	Inc.	County	Parent	Daughter	Note	VR	CR
Hersey	1873	Aroostook			Settled 1839.		
Highland Plantation	1871	Somerset				M	
Hiram	1814	Oxford	Baldwin, Brownfield		Settled 1774. Created as district 1807.	M	
Hodgdon	1832	Aroostook			Settled 1824.	M	
Holden	1852	Penobscot	**Brewer**			M	
Hollis	1798	York	Limington, Waterboro	Dayton	Settled 1753. Called Phillipsburgh until 1812.	D	N, S
Hope	1804	Knox		Appleton	Settled 1782.	M, P	
Houlton	1831	Aroostook	Williams College Grant		Settled 1805.		
Howland	1826	Penobscot		Mattamiscontis	Settled 1820.		
Hudson	1825	Penobscot		Old Town	Settled 1800. Called Kirkland to 1855.	P	
Indian Island		Penobscot					
Indian Township Reservation		Washington					
Industry	1803	Franklin	Anson, New Sharon, New Vineyard, Starkes	New Farmington, New Sharon	Settled 1793.	D	
Island Falls	1872	Aroostook			Settled 1843.		
Isle Au Haut	1874	Knox	Deer Isle		Settled 1772.		
Islesboro	1789	Waldo			Settled 1769.	P	
Jackman	1895	Somerset					
Jackson	1818	Waldo			Settled 1798.	D, P	F, P
Jay	1795	Franklin	Canton, Letter A	Canton	Settled 1776.	M	
Jefferson	1807	Lincoln	Somerville (Patricktown)	Alna (New Milford), Newcastle, Whitefield	Called Ballstown to 1807.	D, W	
Jonesboro	1809	Washington		Columbia, Jonesport, Roque Bluffs	Settled 1763.	D	
Jonesport	1832	Washington		Beals	Settled 1764.		
Kenduskeag	1852	Penobscot	**Glenburn, Levant**			D	
Kennebunk	1820	York	**Wells**			M	

Town	Inc.	County	Parent	Daughter	Note	VR	CR
Kennebunk-port	1653	York		Arundel (North Kennebunkport)	Originally created 1653 as Cape Porpoise/Porpus. Under jurisdiction of Saco (Pepperellborough) between 1688 and 1719. Settlement abandoned during Indian Wars. Reorganized as Arundel. Name changed 1821.	M	
Kingfield	1816	Franklin			Settled 1806.	M	
Kingsbury Plantation	1836	Piscataquis			Incorporation repealed 1885. Organized as plantation 1895.	M	
Kittery	1652	York	Berwick, Isle of Shoals	Berwick, Eliot	Settled 1623.	M, P	N
Knox	1819	Waldo	Montville, Thorndike		Settled 1800.	D, P	
Lagrange	1832	Penobscot					
Lake View Plantation	1892	Piscataquis					
Lakeville	1981	Penobscot			Settled 1855. Organized as plantation 1868.		
Lamoine	1870	Hancock	Hancock, **Trenton**	Hancock		M	
Lebanon	1767	York	Sanford, Shapleigh	Shapleigh	Settled 1743.	D, P	
Lee	1832	Penobscot			Settled 1824.	P	
Leeds	1801	Androscoggin	Livermore, Monmouth	Sabattus (Webster), Wales, Wayne	Settled 1779.	D	
Levant	1813	Penobscot		Kenduskeag	Settled 1789.	M	
Lewiston	1795	Androscoggin	Greene, Sabattus (Webster), Webster	Greene, Sabattus (Webster)	Settled 1770.	M, P	F
Liberty	1827	Waldo	Montville		Settled 1800.	P	
Limerick	1787	York	Limington (Little Ossipee Plantation)		Settled 1775.	P	
Limestone	1869	Aroostook			Settled 1847.		
Limington	1792	York		Hollis (Phillipsburgh), Limerick	Settled 1773 as Little Ossipee Plantation. Renamed Limington 1792.	D	
Lincoln	1829	Penobscot			Settled 1825. Called Mattanawcook to 1829.		

ME

Town	Inc.	County	Parent	Daughter	Note	VR	CR
Lincoln Plantation	1875	Oxford					
Lincolnville	1802	Waldo			Settled 1780.	M, P	
Linneus	1836	Aroostook					
Lisbon	1799	Androscoggin	**Bowdoin**, Little River Plantation, Sabattus (Webster)	Sabattus (Webster)	Called Thompsonborough 1802.	M, P	F
Litchfield	1795	Kennebec		Bowdoinham, Manchester (Kennebec), Sabattus (Webster), Wales, West Gardiner	Settled 1776. Called Smithfield and Smithtown to 1795.	M	
Littleton	1856	Aroostook			Settled 1835.		
Livermore	1795	Androscoggin	Chandler's Gore	Leeds, Livermore Falls (East Livermore), Wayne	Settled 1770.	M	
Livermore Falls	1843	Androscoggin	**Livermore**		Called East Livermore to 1929.		
Long Island	1993	Cumberland	**Portland**				
Lovell	1800	Oxford		Sweden	Settled 1777.	M	
Lowell	1837	Penobscot	Cold Stream Settlement, Passadumkeag, Two Mile Strip	Burlington	Settled 1819. Called Huntressville to 1838.		
Lubec	1811	Washington	**Eastport**, Trescott	Eastport	Settled 1780.	M, P	
Ludlow	1864	Aroostook		New Limerick	Settled 1825.		
Lyman	1778	York			Settled 1767. Called Coxhall until 1803. Incorporation suspended between Oct. 1778 and April 1790.		
Machias	1784	Washington	Jonesboro	East Machias, Machiasport, Marshfield, Whitneyville	Settled 1763. Subdivided to form East Machias, West Machias, and Machiasport 1826. West Machias reverted to Machias 1830.		
Machiasport	1826	Washington	Machias				
Macwahoc Plantation	1851	Aroostook			Settled 1830.		
Madawaska	1869	Aroostook				D	
Madison	1804	Somerset		Norridgewock	Settled 1780.		

ME

Town	Inc.	County	Parent	Daughter	Note	VR	CR
Magalloway Plantation	1883	Oxford					
Manchester	1850	Kennebec	**Augusta**, Farmingdale, **Hallowell**, **Litchfield**, **Readfield**, **Winthrop**	Hallowell, Readfield, Winthrop	Called Kennebec to 1854.		
Mapleton	1878	Aroostook			Settled 1842. Organized as plantation 1878.		
Mariaville	1836	Hancock	Tilden, Waltham (14 MD BPP, Mariaville South)	Tilden, Waltham (14 MD BPP, Mariaville South)	Settled 1802.		
Mars Hill	1867	Aroostook			Settled 1844.		
Marshfield	1846	Washington	**Machias**			M	
Masardis	1839	Aroostook			Settled 1833.		
Matinicus Isle Plantation	1840	Knox		Criehaven		M	
Mattawamkeag	1860	Penobscot					
Maxfield	1824	Penobscot			Settled 1814.	M	
Mechanic Falls	1893	Androscoggin	**Minot, Poland**				
Meddybemps	1841	Washington	**Baring, Charlotte, Cooper**				
Medford	1824	Piscataquis			Settled 1808. Called Kilmarnock to 1856. Incorporation repealed 1940. Organized as plantation 1942. Organization repealed 1945. Reincorporated as town 1967.		
Medway	1875	Penobscot			Settled 1838.		
Mercer	1804	Somerset	Starks	New Sharon, Norridgewock, Smithfield	Settled 1784.	M	
Merrill	1911	Aroostook			Settled 1840. Organized as plantation 1895.		
Mexico	1818	Oxford		Roxbury	Settled 1780.	D	
Milbridge	1848	Washington	**Harrington**, Steuben			D	
Milford	1833	Penobscot					
Millinocket	1901	Penobscot					

Town	Inc.	County	Parent	Daughter	Note	VR	CR
Milo	1823	Piscataquis			Settled 1803.		
Minot	1823	Androscoggin	**Poland**	Auburn, Mechanic Falls		M, P	N
Monhegan Island Plantation	1839	Lincoln				M	
Monmouth	1792	Kennebec		Leeds, Wales, Winthrop		M	
Monroe	1818	Waldo	Brooks, Frankfort	Brooks	Settled 1800. Organized as Lee 1812. Incorporated as town and renamed Monroe 1822.	D	
Monson	1822	Piscataquis			Settled 1818.	M, P	
Monticello	1846	Aroostook			Settled 1830.	D	
Montville	1807	Waldo		Knox, Liberty	Settled 1780.	D, M	
Moose River	1957	Somerset			Settled 1820. Organized as plantation 1857.		
Moro Plantation	1850	Aroostook			Settled 1837. Organized as Rockabema 1850. Reorganized as Moro 1860.		
Morrill	1855	Waldo	Belmont, The Gore		Originally called North Belmont.	M	
Moscow	1816	Somerset			Settled 1773.	D	
Mount Chase	1864	Penobscot			Incorporation repealed and organized as plantation 1936. Reincorporated as town 1979.	P	
Mount Desert	1789	Hancock		Cranberry Isles, Seaville, Tremont (Mansel)	Settled 1613.	M	
Mount Vernon	1792	Kennebec	Belgrade, Fayette, Readfield, Rome, Vienna (Goshen)	Readfield	Settled 1774.	M	
Naples	1834	Cumberland	**Bridgton, Harrison, Otisfield, Raymond, Sebago**				
Nashville Plantation	1889	Aroostook					
New Canada	1881	Aroostook			Incorporated as town 1976.		

Town	Inc.	County	Parent	Daughter	Note	VR	CR
New Gloucester	1774	Cumberland	Thompson Pond Plantation		Settled 1738.	D	
New Limerick	1837	Aroostook	**Ludlow**		Settled 1775.		
New Portland	1808	Somerset	Anson, Freeman, New Vineyard		Settled 1783.		
New Sharon	1794	Franklin	Industry, Mercer	Industry		D	
New Sweden	1895	Aroostook			Settled 1870.	D	
New Vineyard	1802	Franklin	New Portland, Strong	Anson, Industry, New Portland	Settled 1791.		
Newburgh	1819	Penobscot		Hampden	Settled 1794.	M	
Newcastle	1753	Lincoln	**Jefferson (Ballstown)**	Alna (New Milford)	Created as district 1753.		
Newfield	1794	York	**Shapleigh**		Settled 1778.		
Newport	1814	Penobscot			Settled 1807.		
Newry	1805	Oxford	**Andover West Surplus, Grafton**		Settled 1781.	M	
Nobleboro	1788	Lincoln	**Bristol**	Damariscotta	Settled 1730	P	
Norridgewock	1788	Somerset	**East Pond Plantation, Fairfield, Madison, Mercer, Smithfield, Starks**	Skowhegan (Milburn)	Settled 1773.	M	
North Berwick	1831	York	**Berwick**			D, P	
North Haven	1846	Knox	Hurricane Isle, **Vinalhaven**		Called Fox Isle to 1847.	M, P	
North Yarmouth	1683	Cumberland		Brunswick, Cumberland, Freeport, Georgetown, Harpswell, Pownal, Yarmouth		P	
Northfield	1838	Washington	Centreville				
Northport	1796	Waldo			Settled 1780.	P	
Norway	1797	Oxford	Paris	Paris		M	
Oakfield	1897	Aroostook			Settled 1831. Incorporated as town 1897.	M	
Oakland	1873	Kennebec	**Waterville**		Called West Waterville to 1883.		
Ogunquit	1980	York	**Wells**				
Old Orchard Beach	1883	York	**Saco**		Called Old Orchard until 1929.		F

Town	Inc.	County	Parent	Daughter	Note	VR	CR
Old Town	1840	Penobscot	Alton, Argyle Plantation, Glenburn, Hudson (Kirkland), **Orono**			M, P	F
Orient	1856	Aroostook			Settled 1830.		
Orland	1800	Hancock			Settled 1764.	M	
Orono	1806	Penobscot		Old Town	Settled 1774.	M	
Orrington	1788	Penobscot	Bucksport (Buckstown)	Brewer		M	
Osborn	1895	Hancock			Called Plantation No. 21 MD BPP to 1923. Incorporated as town 1976.		
Otis	1835	Hancock			Settled 1808.		
Otisfield	1798	Oxford	Phillips Gore, Poland, Thompson Pond Plantation	Harrison, Naples, Oxford	Settled 1776.	D, P	
Owls Head	1921	Knox		**South Thomaston**			
Oxbow Plantation	1895	Aroostook			Settled 1840.		
Oxford	1829	Oxford	**Hebron**, Otisfield, Paris		Settled 1774.	M	
Palermo	1804	Waldo		Washington	Settled 1778.		
Palmyra	1807	Somerset		Pittsfield (Warsaw)		M	
Paris	1793	Oxford	Buckfield, Norway, Woodstock	Hebron, Norway, Oxford, Woodstock	Settled 1779.	M	
Parkman	1822	Piscataquis	Wellington	Guilford, Wellington	Settled 1810.	D	
Parsonsfield	1785	York			Settled 1772.	P	
Passadumkeag	1835	Penobscot		Lowell (Huntressville)	Settled 1819.		
Patten	1841	Penobscot			Settled 1828.	M	
Pembroke	1832	Washington	**Dennysville**		Settled 1786.	M	
Penobscot	1787	Hancock	Blue Hill, Sedgwick, Surry	Brooksville, Castine, Surry	Settled 1760.	P	
Perham	1878	Aroostook			Settled and organized 1860. Reorganized 1867. Incorporated as town 1897.		

ME

Town	Inc.	County	Parent	Daughter	Note	VR	CR
Perry	1818	Washington			Settled 1780.	M	
Peru	1821	Oxford	Canton, Fox's Grant, Franklin Plantation (Plantation No. 2), Lunt's Upper and Lower Grant, Rumford, Thompson's Grant	Rumford	Organized as No. 1, Partridgetown to 1812.	M	
Phillips	1812	Franklin	Berlin (6 AP)	Salem (North Salem)	Settled 1791.	M	
Phippsburg	1814	Sagadahoc	**Georgetown**	Harpswell		M, P	
Pittsfield	1819	Somerset	Detroit (Chandlersville), Hartland	Burnham (Twentyfivemile Pond Plantation), Canaan, Clinton	Settled 1794. Organized as Plymouth Gore 1815. Called Warsaw from incorporation 1819 to 1824.	D	
Pittston	1779	Kennebec	Chelsea, Hallowell	Bowdoinham, Gardiner, Randolph (West Pittston)		D, M, P, W	
Pleasant Point Indian Reservation		Washington					
Pleasant Ridge Plantation	1895	Somerset	Concord	Concord	Settled 1786.	M	
Plymouth	1826	Penobscot	**Etna**		Settled 1815.		
Poland	1795	Androscoggin	Eighty Rod Strip, Thompson Pond	Danville (Pejobscot), Mechanic Falls, Otisfield		D	
Portage Lake	1895	Aroostook			Organized as plantation 1872. Incorporated as town 1909.	M	
Porter	1807	Oxford		Brownfield	Settled 1784.		
Portland	1786	Cumberland	Cumberland, Deering, **Falmouth**, Westbrook	Long Island		D, P	
Pownal	1808	Cumberland	**Freeport**, North Yarmouth	North Yarmouth		M	
Presque Isle	1859	Aroostook	Maysville		Settled 1828.	D	
Princeton	1832	Washington		Baileyville	Settled 1815.	M	
Prospect	1794	Waldo	**Frankfort**	Searsport, Stockton (Stockton Springs)		M, P	

Town	Inc.	County	Parent	Daughter	Note	VR	CR
Randolph	1887	Kennebec	**Pittston**		Called West Pittston to 17 March 1887.	P. W	
Rangeley	1855	Franklin			Settled 1815.	D	
Rangeley Plantation	1895	Franklin			Organized 1859.		
Raymond	1803	Cumberland	Eighty Rod Strip, Gray Surplus, Standish	Casco, Naples	Settled 1771.	D	
Readfield	1791	Kennebec	Manchester (Kennebec), Mount Vernon, Wayne, Winthrop	Manchester (Kennebec), Mount Vernon, Winthrop		M	
Reed Plantation	1878	Aroostook	Drew	Drew	Settled 1830.		
Richmond	1823	Sagadahoc	**Bowdoinham**			D	W
Ripley	1816	Somerset		Cambridge, Saint Albans	Settled 1804.		
Robbinston	1811	Washington			Settled 1787.		
Rockland	1848	Knox	**Thomaston**	Thomaston	Called East Thomaston to 1850.	D, S	P
Rockport	1891	Knox	**Camden**				N
Rome	1804	Kennebec		Belgrade, Mount Vernon, Vienna	Settled 1780.	M	
Roque Bluffs	1891	Washington	**Jonesboro**				
Roxbury	1835	Oxford		Mexico			
Rumford	1800	Oxford	Franklin Plantation, Peru (No. 1, Partridgetown)		Settled 1777. Called New Penacook to 1800.	D	
Sabattus	1840	Androscoggin	Greene, Lewiston, **Lisbon**, Litchfield, Wales	Lewiston, Lisbon	Called Webster to 1971.	M	
Saco	1762	York	Scarboro	Old Orchard Beach (Old Orchard)	Settled 1631. Called Pepperellborough to 1805.		F, P, W
Saint Agatha	1899	Aroostook	**Frenchville**	Frenchville			
Saint Albans	1813	Somerset	Hartland, Ripley	Hartland		M	
Saint Francis	1870	Aroostook			Organized as plantation 1870. Incorporated as town 1966.		
Saint George	1803	Knox	**Cushing**			M, P	
Saint John Plantation	1870	Aroostook					

Town	Inc.	County	Parent	Daughter	Note	VR	CR
Sandy River Plantation	1905	Franklin	Greenvale Plantation				
Sanford	1768	York	Alfred, Shapleigh	Alfred, Lebanon, Shapleigh	Settled 1740.	D	F
Sangerville	1814	Piscataquis		Guilford		M	
Scarborough	1658	Cumberland		Gorham, Saco (Pepperellborough)	Settled 1630.		N
Searsmont	1814	Waldo	**Greene Plantation**		Settled 1804.	P	
Searsport	1845	Waldo	**Belfast, Frankfort, Prospect**			P	
Sebago	1826	Cumberland	**Baldwin**, Denmark	Naples		M	
Sebec	1812	Piscataquis		Bowerbank	Settled 1803.	M	
Seboeis Plantation	1895	Penobscot					
Sedgwick	1789	Hancock		Blue Hill, Brooksville, Brooklin, Penobscot	Settled 1763.	M	
Shapleigh	1785	York		Acton, Sanford, Lebanon, Newfield, Waterboro	Settled 1772.	D	
Sherman	1862	Aroostook	Crystal, Silver Ridge			M	
Shirley	1834	Piscataquis	Wilson		Settled 1825.	M	
Sidney	1792	Kennebec	**Vassalboro**	Belgrade		M	
Skowhegan	1823	Somerset	**Canaan**, Cornville, Fairfield Norridgewock	Bloomfield	Called Milburn to 1836.	M	F, W
Smithfield	1840	Somerset	**Dearborn, East Pond Plantation, Mercer**	Norridgewock		M	
Smyrna	1839	Aroostook			Settled 1830		
Solon	1809	Somerset			Settled 1782. Called Spauldingtown to 1809.	M	
Somerville	1858	Lincoln		Jefferson	Called Patricktown Plantation to 1858. Incorporation repealed 1937. Organized as plantation 1938. Reincorporated as town 1974.		
Sorrento	1895	Hancock	**Sullivan**				
South Berwick	1814	York	**Berwick**, York			P	F, M

Town	Inc.	County	Parent	Daughter	Note	VR	CR
South Bristol	1915	Lincoln	**Bristol**				
South Portland	1895	Cumberland	**Cape Elizabeth**				
South Thomaston	1848	Knox	Saint George, Thomaston	Owl's Head		M	N
Southport	1842	Lincoln	**Boothbay**		Called Townsend to 1850.	M	
Southwest Harbor	1905	Hancock	**Tremont**				
Springfield	1834	Penobscot			Settled 1830.		
Stacyville	1883	Penobscot			Settled 1850. Organized as plantation 1860, ratified 1883. Incorporated as town 1953.		
Standish	1785	Cumberland	Buxton	Gorham, Raymond	Called Pearsontown to 1785.	P, W	
Starks	1795	Somerset		Industry, Mercer, Norridgewock	Settled 1774.		
Stetson	1831	Penobscot			Settled 1800.		
Steuben	1795	Washington	Harrington	Cherryfield, Milbridge	Settled 1760.	M	
Stockholm	1911	Aroostook			Organized 1895.		
Stockton Springs	1857	Waldo	Prospect		Called Stockton to 1889.	D	
Stoneham	1834	Oxford	Batchelder's Grant, Fryeburg Academy Grant		Called Stoneham to 1841. Called Usher 1841–43. Renamed Stoneham 1843.	M	
Stonington	1897	Hancock	**Deer Isle**				
Stow	1833	Oxford	Bradley's Grant, Eastman's Grant, Fryeburg Addition		Settled 1770.		
Strong	1801	Franklin	Avon	Farmington, New Vineyard	Settled 1748.		
Sullivan	1789	Hancock	7 SD BPP	Hancock, Sorrento	Settled 1762.	M	
Sumner	1798	Oxford	Franklin Plantation (Plantation No. 2)	Buckfield	Settled 1783.	M	
Surry	1803	Hancock	Ellsworth, Penobscot	Ellsworth	Settled 1785.	M, W	
Swan's Island	1897	Hancock	Calf Island, West Black Island		Organized 1834.		

ME

Town	Inc.	County	Parent	Daughter	Note	VR	CR
Swanville	1818	Waldo	Brooks, Frankfort	Waldo		P	
Sweden	1813	Oxford	**Lovell**		Settled 1784.	D	
Talmadge	1875	Washington					
Temple	1803	Franklin	Wilton		Settled 1796.	M	
Thomaston	1777	Knox	Cushing, Rockland (East Thomaston), Saint George Plantation, Warren	Rockland (East Thomaston), South Thomaston		M, S	
Thorndike	1819	Waldo		Knox		M, P	
Topsfield	1838/ 1960	Washington			Incorporation revoked and organized as plantation 1939. Organization repealed 1941. Reincorporated as town 1960.	M	
Topsham	1764	Sagadahoc	Bowdoinham	Bowdoinham	Settled 1730.	P	
Tremont	1848	Hancock	Mount Desert, Seaville	Southwest Harbor	Called Mansel from June 1848 to Aug. 1848.	M	
Trenton	1789	Hancock	Bar Harbor (Eden)	Ellsworth, Hancock, Lamoine	Settled 1763.	M	
Troy	1812	Waldo	Burnham (Twentyfivemile Pond Plantation)		Called Kingville from 1812–14. Called Joy 1814–26.	P	
Turner	1786	Androscoggin			Settled 1690.	D, P	
Union	1786	Knox		Washington (Putnam)	Called Sterlington to 1786. Also called Taylortown.	M, P, W	W
Unity	1804	Waldo	Burnham (Twentyfivemile Pond Plantation)		Settled 1782.		
Upton	1860	Oxford					
Van Buren	1881	Aroostook	Hamlin		Settled 1791.		
Vanceboro	1874	Washington					
Vassalboro	1771	Kennebec	China	Sidney	Settled 1760.	P	
Veazie	1853	Penobscot	**Bangor**	Bangor		M	
Verona Island	1861	Hancock					

Town	Inc.	County	Parent	Daughter	Note	VR	CR
Vienna	1802	Kennebec	Rome	Chesterville, Mount Vernon	Settled 1786. Called Goshen and Wyman prior to 1802.		
Vinalhaven	1789	Knox		Hurricane Isle, North Haven (Fox Isle)	Settled 1765.	P	
Wade	1913	Aroostook			Settled 1846. Organized 1859. Reorganized 1874. Organized as plantation 1895.		
Waite	1876	Washington			Settled 1832.		
Waldo	1845	Waldo	Swanville, Gore Between Waldo and Knox		Organized 1821.	D	
Waldoboro	1773	Lincoln	Bremen	Bremen	Settled 1740.	D, P	
Wales	1816	Androscoggin	Leeds, Litchfield (Smithfield/ Smithtown), Monmouth	Sabattus (Webster)	Settled 1773.	M	
Wallagrass	1870	Aroostook			Incorporated as town 1986.		
Waltham	1833	Hancock	**Mariaville**	Eastbrook			
Warren	1776	Knox		Camden, Cushing, Thomaston	Settled 1736.	P	P
Washburn	1861	Aroostook			Settled 1826.		
Washington	1811	Knox	Palermo, **Union**		Called Putnam to 1823.	M, P	
Waterboro	1787	York		Alfred, Hollis (Phillipsburgh), Shapleigh	Settled 1768.	D	
Waterford	1797	Oxford	Albany		Settled 1775.	D	
Waterville	1802	Kennebec	Dearborn, **Winslow**	Oakland (West Waterville)		M, W	F
Wayne	1798	Kennebec	Leeds, Livermore	Readfield, Winthrop	Settled 1773.		
Webster Plantation	1856	Penobscot			Settled 1843.		
Weld	1816	Franklin			Settled 1800.		
Wellington	1828	Piscataquis	Parkman	Cambridge, Parkman	Settled 1814.	D	
Wells	1653	York	Kennebunk	Kennebunk	Settled 1640.	M, P, W	
Wesley	1833	Washington					

Town	Inc.	County	Parent	Daughter	Note	VR	CR
West Bath	1844	Sagadahoc	**Bath**	Bath		M	
West Forks Plantation	1893	Somerset					
West Gardiner	1850	Kennebec	Farmingdale, **Gardiner**, Litchfield	Farmingdale		M, P	
West Paris	1957	Oxford	**Paris**				
Westbrook	1814	Cumberland	Cape Elizabeth, **Falmouth**	Deering, Falmouth, Portland	Incorporated as Stroudwater Feb. 1814. Renamed Westbrook June 1814.	P	
Westfield	1905	Aroostook			Incorporated as town 1905. Settled 1839.		
Westmanland	1895	Aroostook					
Weston	1835	Aroostook	Bancroft	Danforth	Settled 1825.		
Westport	1828	Lincoln	**Edgecomb**			M	
Whitefield	1809	Lincoln	**Jefferson (Ballstown)**	Alna (New Milford), Windsor (Gerry)		M	
Whiting	1825	Washington	Orangetown, Plantation No. 12		Settled 1780.		
Whitneyville	1845	Washington					
Willimantic	1881	Piscataquis			Settled 1849. Called Howard to 1883.	M	
Wilton	1803	Franklin		Chesterville, Temple	Settled 1789.	M	
Windham	1762	Cumberland			Settled 1735.		
Windsor	1809	Kennebec	Whitefield	Whitefield	Settled 1790. Called Windsor to 1821. Called Gerry to 1822. Renamed Windsor 1822.		
Winn	1857	Penobscot			Settled 1820.		
Winslow	1771	Kennebec		China, Fairfax, Harlem, Waterville	Settled 1764.	P, W	
Winter Harbor	1895	Hancock	**Gouldsboro**				
Winterport	1860	Waldo	**Frankfort**				
Winterville Plantation	1895	Aroostook			Briefly renamed Hill in 1903 before reverting back. Settled 1846.		

Town	Inc.	County	Parent	Daughter	Note	VR	CR
Winthrop	1771	Kennebec	Augusta (Harrington), Manchester (Kennebec), Monmouth, Wayne	Hallowell, Manchester (Kennebec), Readfield	Settled 1760.	F	
Wiscasset	1760	Lincoln	Alna (New Milford)	Alna (New Milford), Dresden	Called Pownalborough to 1802. Settled 1663.	D	
Woodland	1880	Aroostook			Organized as plantation 1861. (Different from Baileyville, Washington Co., which was sometimes called Woodland.)	M	
Woodstock	1815	Oxford	Greenwood, Hamilton's Grant, Milton, Paris	Paris	Settled 1793.	M	
Woodville	1895	Penobscot			Settled 1832.		
Woolwich	1775	Sagadahoc	**Georgetown**		Created as district in 1759.	M	
Yarmouth	1849	Cumberland	**North Yarmouth**			M	
York	1652	York		South Berwick	Settled 1624.	D, P	

ME

Extinct or Unincorporated Places

The following areas have never had large populations. In many instances they exist only on paper. Few, if any, records exist for these locations.

Town	Est.	County	Parent Town(s)	Child Town(s)	Notes	VR	CR
Albany	1803	Oxford		Waterford	Settled 1784.	D	
Argyle	1839	Penobscot	**Argyle Plantation**	Alton, Old Town	Settled 1810. Incorporation repealed 1937.		
Baring Plantation	1825	Washington		Meddybemps	Settled 1786. Incorporation repealed 1841. Reorganized as plantation 1961.		
Barnard	1834	Piscataquis	**Williamsburg**		Incorporation repealed 1877. Reorganized as plantation 1895. Organization surrendered 1982.		
Benedicta	1873	Aroostook			Settled 1834. Now part of South Aroostook.		
Berlin	1824	Franklin			Previously called 6 AP. Incorporation repealed 1942.		

Town	Est.	County	Parent Town(s)	Daughter Town(s)	Note	VR	CR
Blanchard	1831	Piscataquis			Incorporation repealed and organized as plantation 1951. Organization repealed 1984.		
Brookton	1883	Washington			Incorporation repealed 1941.		
Central Somerset		Somerset					
Concord	1821	Somerset	Pleasant Ridge Plantation	Pleasant Ridge Plantation	Incorporation repealed and organized as plantation 1921. Organization repealed 1935.		
Connor	1877	Aroostook	Caribou		Incorporated as town 1913. Incorporation repealed 1945.		
Danville	1802	Androscoggin	Poland	Auburn, Durham	Settled 1764. Called Pejobscot to 1867. Called Danville from 1818. (Sometimes referred to as Danville or Old Danville from the 17th century.) Part annexed to Auburn and Durham in 1821 and 1823. Remainder annexed to Auburn 1859 and 1867.	D, N	
Dearborn	1812	Kennebec		Belgrade, Smithfield, Waterville	Organization repealed 1841. Annexed to Waterville 1843.		
Deering	1871	Cumberland	**Falmouth, Westbrook**		Annexed to Portland 1889.		
Dover	1822	Piscatiquis			Merged with Foxcroft to form Dover-Foxcroft 1915, effective 1922.		
East Central Penobscot		Penobscot					
East Central Washington		Washington					
East Plantation		Aroostook					
Eaton	1860	Washington		Danforth, Forest City	Settled 1829. Part was set off to form Forest City 1889. Remainder annexed to Danforth.		
Edmunds	1828	Washington	Trescott		Settled 1775. Incorporation repealed 1837.		

ME

Town	Est.	County	Parent Town(s)	Daughter Town(s)	Note	VR	CR
Elliotsville	1835	Piscataquis	Wilson		Incorporation repealed 1858. Organized as plantation 1886.		
Forest City	1889	Washington	**Eaton**		Settled 1829. Incorporation repealed 1937.		
Foxcroft	1812	Piscataquis			Merged with Foxcroft to form Dover-Foxcroft 1915, effective 1922.		
Franklin Plantation	1841	Oxford		Peru, Sumner	Originally called Plantation No. 2. Abolished 1899 and annexed to Peru and Rumford.		
Freeman	1808	Franklin		New Portland, Salem (North Salem)	Settled 1797. Incorporation repealed 1937.		
Grand Falls Plantation	1878	Penobscot			Settled 1830. Organized 1840. Organization surrendered 1981.		
Greenfield	1834	Penobscot			Settled 1812. Incorporation repealed 1993.		
Harlem	1796	Kennebec	Winslow		Part annexed to China 1818. Remainder annexed 1882.		
Hurricane Isle	1878	Knox	**Vinalhaven**	North Haven, Vinalhaven	Incorporation repealed 1921.		
Kingman	1873	Penobscot			Incorporation repealed and Kingman Plantation organized 1935. Organization repealed 1945.		
Madrid		Franklin					
Mason	1843	Oxford	**Batchelders Grant**, Fryeburg Academy Grant		Incorporation repealed 1935.		
Mattamiscontis	1839	Penobscot	Howland		Incorporation repealed 1907.		
Maysville	1859	Aroostook			Annexed to Presque Isle 1883.		
Milton	1842	Oxford		Woodstock	Organization repealed 1939.		
North Anson	1845	Waldo	**Anson**		Annexed back to Anson in 1855.		
North Penobscot		Penobscot					
North Washington		Washington					

Town	Est.	County	Parent Town(s)	Daughter Town(s)	Note	VR	CR
Northeast Piscataquis		Piscataquis					
Northeast Somerset		Somerset					
Northwest Piscataquis		Piscataquis					
Northwest Somerset		Somerset					
Orneville	1832	Piscataquis	Atkinson		Called Milton to 1841. Called Almond 1841–43. Incorporation repealed 1939.		
Perkins	1847	Franklin	**Dresden**		Settled 1663. Formerly called Swan Island. Incorporation repealed 1917.		
Prentiss Plantation	1858	Penobscot	Drew		Settled 1838. Incorporation repealed 1939. Organized as plantation 1950. Organization repealed1990.		
Salem	1823	Franklin	Freeman, Mount Abraham, Phillips		Called North Salem to 1834.		
Seaville		Hancock					
Seboomook Lake		Somerset					
Silver Ridge Plantation	1863	Aroostook	Sherman		Organization repealed 1941.		
Southeast Piscataquis		Piscataquis					
Southwest Harbor		Hancock					
Trescott	1827	Washington		Edmunds, Lubec	Settled 1780. Incorporation repealed 1945.		
Twombly		Penobscot					
Unity	1853	Kennebec		Albion	Organization repealed 1941.		
Whitney		Penobscot					
Williamsburg	1820	Piscataquis	Barnard		Incorporation repealed 1939.	D	
Wilson	1836	Piscataquis		Elliotsville, Greenville, and Shirley	Town divided and annexed to Elliotsville, Greenville, and Shirley 1848.		

Massachusetts

Introduction by Michael J. Leclerc

Massachusetts researchers are lucky to have many valuable resources at their disposal. Records survive from the earliest settlements of the Plymouth and Massachusetts Bay Colonies, the first surviving European settlements in New England (1620 and 1630). Many records have been published, and many others are widely available on microfilm and/or in digital form.

Most Massachusetts county governments were abolished in the 1990s. Of the fourteen counties, only six (Barnstable, Bristol, Dukes, Nantucket, Norfolk, and Plymouth) still have a county government. The other eight counties are run by the Commonwealth of Massachusetts, and they are considered part of the state government. Accordingly, the records of these counties may be found at state repositories instead of at the local level.

The borders between Massachusetts and surrounding states were not completely settled until the nineteenth century. Entire towns were transferred from one state to another. This is especially important to keep in mind for Essex County, where some towns combined with towns now in New Hampshire to form the original Norfolk County in the Massachusetts Bay Colony (see Old Norfolk County discussion on p. 194). The towns of Barrington, Bristol, Little Compton, Tiverton, and Warren, Rhode Island, were originally part of Bristol County in Massachu-setts. In 1747 they were ceded to Rhode Island as part of a settlement of the border. Part of the town of Attleboro was ceded to Rhode Island and incorporated into the towns of Cumberland and Pawtucket. East Providence, Rhode Island, was created in 1861 when part of the town of Seekonk was ceded to Rhode Island. Researching families in these towns requires examining records in both states.

One helpful resource for Massachusetts researchers is *Report on the Custody and Condition of the Public Records of Parishes, Towns, and Counties* (Boston: Wright and Potter, 1889) by Carroll D. Wright, Commissioner of Public Records. This inventory of town, church, and county records shows not only what records existed, but the condition of those records in the late nineteenth century. Proprietors' records, church records, town and vital records, civil and criminal court records, probate records, land records, and the records of county commissioners are included in this massive work. This book is available for free online through Google Books.

MA

The Massachusetts state seal.

Vital Records

Vital records were kept even in the earliest years of English settlement. In September 1639, the legislature ordered that in addition to wills, administrations, and inventories, records should be kept of "the days of every marriage, birth, & death of every person within this jurisdiction." Unfortunately, many towns ignored this, and in June 1642 a system was implemented to pay each town three pence for each birth and death recorded. The records were to be delivered to the recorder of the court in each jurisdiction, and towns were to be penalized 20 shillings each time they neglected to do so. Towns were also ordered to compile births and deaths dating to the town's founding. In 1657 the penalty was again increased in response to improper and incomplete reporting.

Recording births, marriages, and deaths in Massachusetts was the responsibility of the town clerk. Even for those towns whose records survive, there may be gaps or obvious missing records. Sometimes it is easy to note where a volume may have been lost, as there may be a gap of years with no events recorded. Other times, it is difficult or impossible to say with any accuracy how many records are missing, or the reason for their absence.

When NEHGS received a bequest from Robert Henry and Annie (Goddard) Eddy in 1900, $20,000 was set aside for publishing vital records of Massachusetts towns. In 1902 the General Court authorized funds to purchase 500 copies of each volume to be distributed to local libraries and historical societies. This created a market that allowed NEHGS, the Essex Institute, Topsfield Historical Society, Systematic History Fund, and other institutions to publish these records. Often called the tan books (because of the color of the cloth on the cover) or the "official series," the records of 206 towns, mostly in central and eastern Massachusetts, were published by 1945. Some towns produced their own books. (The town chart at the

For Massachusetts Research

Richard LeBaron Bowen, *Massachusetts Records: A Handbook for Genealogists, Historians, Lawyers, and Other Researchers* (Rehoboth, Mass., 1957).

Ellen M. Coty, "Research Aids: Genealogy in Western Massachusetts" *Historical Journal of Western Massachusetts* 6 [1978]: 42–47.

Ann S. Lainhart, *A Researcher's Guide to Boston* (Boston: NEHGS, 2003).

David Allen Lambert, *A Guide to Massachusetts Cemeteries,* 2nd ed. (Boston: NEHGS, 2009).

Helen Schatvet Ullmann, "Massachusetts," in *A Guide to the Library of the New England Historic Genealogical Society,* Maureen A. Taylor and Henry B. Hoff, eds. (Boston: NEHGS, 2004), pp. 127–46.

end of this chapter lists all towns, whether or not their early records were published or were part of the "official series.") For more information about the publication of Massachusetts vital records, see Lynn Betlock, "Massachusetts Vital Records Debut Online at *www.NewEnglandAncestors.org,*" *New England Ancestors* 3, no. 4 (2002): 44–45, 48.

Many records of towns in the Connecticut Valley and western Massachusetts were abstracted and are available at NEHGS in manuscript, on microfilm, and on *AmericanAncestors.org.*

In the interest of public health, the General Court mandated in 1841 that towns report specific information concerning births, marriages, and deaths in the Commonwealth. As with the earlier vital records, not all cities and towns complied. Boston was one of the biggest violators, almost completely ignoring the requirements for nearly a decade. More stringent regulations were implemented in 1850, and from that year records are mostly complete.

Because an event was recorded at the town level and a copy sent to the state, two copies should exist for all vital records: one in the town clerk's office and one at the state Department of Public Health. The information contained in these two records, especially from the nineteenth through the early twentieth centuries, may not be identical. For example, statewide death records may report the town of burial, but local copies may name the exact cemetery.

Massachusetts state law provides complete access to records more than ninety years old. As the original indexes were compiled in five-year increments, records are usually transferred to the state archives every five years. More recent records may have restrictions on access. Chief among these are records of illegitimate children and of adopted indi-

viduals, whose birth records are sealed when an adoption is complete and for whom a new birth certificate is issued with the adoptive parents' names on it. Contact the Massachusetts Department of Public Health, Division of Vital Records, for the most up-to-date information on access to modern records. Records more than ninety years old are housed at the Massachusetts Archives.

Probate Records

Records of the administration of estates are under the jurisdiction of the state judiciary's probate court system. Each county is assigned a probate court, which serves as the original court of record. Each court has a judge of probate as well as a register of probate.

The executor of a testate estate (an estate with a legally valid will) was required to begin administration of the estate within a specific time period, or face penalties. Executors were often family members, but they could also be neighbors or friends. Intestate estates also had to be reported to the court, and an administrator was appointed to oversee the distribution of the estate. The costs of administering the estate were refunded to the executor/administrator out of the estate prior to its distribution to creditors and/or heirs.

There is no uniform method of recording probate matters throughout the state. Each court kept its own records. Many records from the original probate dockets were transferred into books. Some jurisdictions kept separate books for each part of the administration (wills, inventories, guardianships, etc.), while others simply kept records chronologically, mixing types of records throughout a volume. Most probate records in Massachusetts were microfilmed from the copy books. Notable exceptions are the counties of Bristol, Middlesex, and Hampshire, where the original docket files were filmed.

Additional probate information may be found in the records of the Supreme Judicial Court (SJC), the highest court in the state. The SJC has appellate jurisdiction for all probate matters.

Above: Five children in Jamaica Plain. George Norman Albree Collection (R. Stanton Avery Special Collections, NEHGS, Mss 674).

Adoptions

Until the early twentieth century, most adoptions were a private matter. No formal action was required. People took orphaned or abandoned children into their homes, and eventually they became part of the family. Formal adoptions prior to 1852 were handled by action of the General Court, and these records are available through the Massachusetts Archives. Beginning in 1852, jurisdiction over adoptions was transferred to the probate courts. Access to these records is restricted. Contact the probate court for the town where your ancestor was adopted to find out more about requesting access to the records.

Church Records

The material contained in church records varies widely between deominations—and, within denominations, from church to church. In many denominations the ecclesiastical records were considered the minister's property. Thus they would leave the church when the minister left. Many of these ministerial records are now in private hands, as well as historical societies, archives, and libraries, sometimes far from the town in which the events occurred.

Potter's *Records of Parishes, Towns, and Counties,* listing existing and extinct churches in 1889, is a good reference for identifying churches past and present for a particular location.

Records of extinct churches may be held at historical societies, libraries, and archives. Some denominations, such as the Roman Catholics, maintain their own archives. See p. 164 for a list of key religious repositories in Massachusetts.

Land Records

The transfer of land from the government to individuals was different in New England than in other areas of the country. In Massachusetts, the crown originally granted land to Plymouth Colony and the Massachusetts Bay Colony. Proprietors were given land for specified towns by colony leaders. The proprietors then examined the land, determining the best location for house lots, pasture land, land for crops, marshland, etc., and subdivided the land into enough lots for each family in the town. A portion of the land was reserved for the common use of all families. These common lands included roads, burying grounds, churches, schools, common grazing land, and more. As more families moved to the town, a second division would be made for the new population. Families drew lots to determine which lands they received.

Some towns maintained separate books of proprietors' records in the early years. Others combined them with other town records (town meetings, vital records, etc.). Maps were often drawn showing lot numbers, which can identify your ancestor's property.

After the first transfer to individuals, land was traded between individuals. In Massachusetts, these transactions were recorded at the county level. Each county elected a registrar of deeds who would record the transactions and copy the records into ledger books.

In addition to outright sales, quitclaims, mortgages, leases, assignments, divisions, partitions, and more will be found in the books of proprietors' records. Some counties elected to maintain separate sets of books for each type of record, while others combined them all into one set of books.

Land transactions can also be found in other types of records. Land transferred from a deceased person to his or her heirs may be recorded in probate records. Division of

lands or orders of partition are also common in both testate and intestate probate matters.

In some cases, land was transferred silently through inheritance. The heirs may have seen no need to record the transfer. The only way to find such transactions is to examine the records of bordering landowners and note when the owner of your ancestor's property changed.

Court Records

The court system exercises judicial power. The courts interpret and apply the constitution and statutes and resolve disputes between parties. Parties are either plaintiffs (the party bringing suit) or defendants (the party accused of wrongdoing).

In the seventeenth century, civil matters involving small sums and criminal misdemeanors were heard by inferior courts. Quarter Courts were established in the Massachusetts Bay Colony for these matters. They were replaced by county courts in 1643. The Court of Assistants tried jury cases and heard appeals from lower courts.

The judicial system was overhauled in 1685, and the county courts were divided into two jurisdictions. Courts of Common Pleas (later Inferior Courts of Common Pleas) heard civil cases while General Sessions of the Peace were responsible for criminal actions. Justices of the Peace were appointed by the governor and council to hear small cases at the local level. The Superior Court of Judicature was created in 1687 and was the highest trial and appellate court, responsible for capital criminal trials, larger civil cases, and matters of equity.

After the Revolution, the Superior Court of Judicature became the Supreme Judicial Court (SJC). In addition to its previous responsibilities, the SJC also heard divorce cases. With the partition of Maine into a separate state, the judiciary was again reorganized in 1821. Courts of Common Pleas became mid-level courts for civil and criminal cases. In addition to justices of the peace, a new system of police, municipal, and district Courts was created to handle small cases. In 1859 the Superior Court replaced the courts of common pleas and took over the trial function of the SJC as well. By the 1870s, the district courts replaced justices of the peace and police courts. (The General Court is not a part of the judiciary. In the Commonwealth of Massachusetts, the General Court is the name of the state legislature.)

In addition to their trial and appellate responsibilities, courts were in charge of

Above: "Quincy Centre." Daniel Munro Wilson, *Where American Independence Began: Quincy, its Famous Group of Patriots, Their Deeds, Homes, and Descendants* (1904), facing p. 250.

naturalization. Prior to 1906, an alien could become a naturalized citizen in any court of record. The complex court system makes locating early naturalization records difficult in some jurisdictions. Fortunately, the Works Progress Administration created an extremely comprehensive index to pre-1906 naturalizations in Massachusetts (see National Archives and Record Administration/ Northeast Region, p. 11).

The Judicial Archives has jurisdiction over court records. While many of these records are stored at the Massachusetts Archives on Columbia Point, their staff cannot access the materials. Requests to access materials must be addressed to the Judicial Archives (p. 163).

Military Records

Military records in Massachusetts date to the colonial wars of the seventeenth century. Muster rolls and account books often document the service of the volunteer militia. Records of the General Court also include valuable information, such as payment for service and pensions for those who served as well as for their widows and children.

In the 1970s and 1980s, NEHGS published a series of abstractions of muster rolls and other records for those who served in colonial wars through the American Revolution. The information is also available in the databases of *AmericanAncestors.org*.

Two widely available compendia can help researchers trace ancestors who served in the Revolutionary War, the War of 1812, or the Civil War: *Massachusetts Soldiers and*

Sailors of the Revolutionary War: A Compilation from the Archives (Boston: Wright & Potter, 1896–1908) and *Massachusetts Soldiers, Sailors, and Marines in the Civil War* (Norwood, Mass.: Norwood Press, 1931–37). For the War of 1812, see *Records of the Massachusetts Volunteer Militia . . . during the War of 1812–14* (Boston: Wright & Potter, 1913).

The Adjutant General's Office maintains a large collection of information on those who served in the Mexican War, Civil War, Spanish-American War, World War I, and World War II. Records through World War I are housed at the Massachusetts National Guard Museum in Worcester. Records from World War II and later can be accessed through the Military Records Branch of the Adjutant General's Office in Boston.

Other Records

Massachusetts Archives Collection

The Massachusetts Archives Collection is a reference work that should not be confused with the Massachusetts Archives itself. The Massachusetts Archives Collection (sometimes called the Felt Collection) documents the Massachusetts Bay Colony government, and land records, from 1630 to 1800. It includes original records of the governor, council, General Court, secretary of state, and treasurer. A wide variety of records are included in the collection, including land grants, divorces, contested estates, papers relating to the towns (including formation, petitions, remonstrances, etc.), military records, tax valuation lists, and more.

The records are bound into 328 volumes. Most, but not all, of the volumes have a table of contents. A number of them have indexes. A card catalog at the Archives indexes surnames and place names for about 25 percent of the collection. The Archives also has a database on its website that indexes seventeen volumes.

Passenger Lists

Starting in 1848, the Commonwealth recorded the names of immigrants who arrived by ship. This process was separate from federal record keeping. In 1891, federal record-keeping programs superseded those of the state. More than a million individuals entered through the port of Boston during this period. The Massachusetts Archives is in the process of creating an online index to the 1848–91 records. Unfortunately, the Archives has no records for the smaller Massachusetts ports.

State Census

Only two state censuses, from 1855 and 1865, survive for Massachusetts. The 1855 census has nine categories:

1. Dwelling houses, numbered in order of visitation
2. Families, numbered in order of visitation
3. The name of every person whose usual place of abode on the first day of June, 1855, was in this family
4. Age (subdivided into five-year increments up to age 20 then ten-year increments up to age 100, with a column for "over 100")
5. Sex
6. Color—white, black, or mulatto
7. Profession, occupation, or trade of each male person over 15 years of age
8. Place of birth (state, territory, or country)
9. Whether deaf and dumb, blind, insane, idiotic, pauper, or convict

The 1865 census expanded to 14 categories:

1. Dwelling houses, numbered in order of visitation
2. Families, numbered in order of visitation
3. The name of every person whose usual place of abode on the first day of May, 1865, was in this family
4. Age
5. Sex
6. Color—white, black, mulatto, or Indian
7. Place of birth (state, territory, or country)
8. "Condition"—single, married, or widowed
9. Profession, occupation, or trade, of every person over 15 years of age
10. Persons over 20 years of age who cannot read or write
11. Whether deaf, dumb, blind, insane, idiotic, pauper, or convict
12. Ratable polls [eligible voters]
13. Legal voters
14. Naturalized voters

Transcriptions for Essex, Middlesex, and Plymouth Counties are available on *AmericanAncestors.org*. The original records, for all counties, are available on *FamilySearch.org*.

STAFF PICKS

Compilations

General Society of Mayflower Descendants, *Mayflower Families Through Five Generations: Descendants of the Pilgrims Who Landed at Plymouth, Mass., December 1620*, 23 vols. to date (Plymouth, Mass.: General Society of Mayflower Descendants, 1975–).

Massachusetts Soldiers and Sailors of the Revolutionary War, 17 vols. (Boston: Wright & Potter, 1896–1908).

Mayflower Descendant (Massachusetts Society of Mayflower Descendants, 1899–1937, 1985–present), vols. 1–20 on *AmericanAncestors.org*; five-volume increments will be added quarterly.

Charles Henry Pope, *The Pioneers of Massachusetts, 1623 to 1660: A Descriptive List, drawn from Records of the Colonies, Towns, Churches, Courts, and Other Contemporary Sources* (Boston: C. H. Pope, 1900).

Report of the Boston Record Commissioners [titles vary], 39 vols. (Boston: City of Boston, 1875–1909).

MA

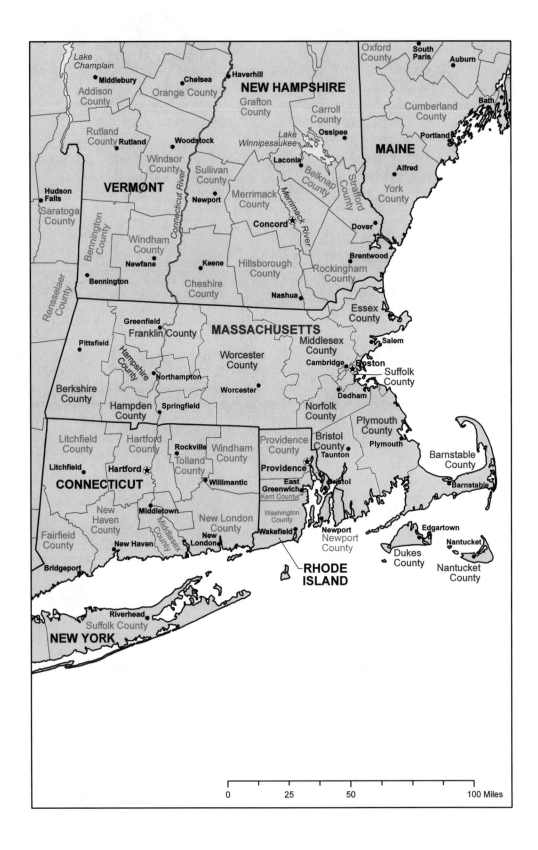

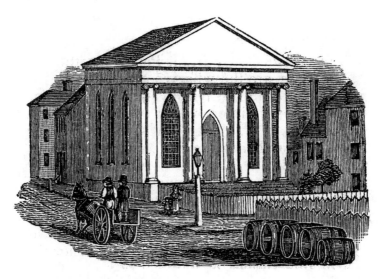

Massachusetts Repositories

The following are major repositories with large collections of materials of interest to genealogists. Check with each repository prior to visiting to obtain the most recent information about hours and access to materials in the collection.

Massachusetts State Archives
220 Morrissey Boulevard
Dorchester, MA 02125-3384
www.sec.state.ma.us/arc/arcidx.htm
(617) 727-2816; fax (617) 288-8429
archives@sec.state.ma.us
Hours: M–F 9–5

Massachusetts State Library
24 Beacon Street
State House, Rm. 341
Boston, MA 02133-1030
www.mass.gov
(617) 727-2590; fax (617) 727-9730
See website for email
Hours: M–F 9–5

Massachusetts Judicial Archives
Supreme Judicial Court Archives
16th floor, Highrise Court House
3 Pemberton Square
Boston, MA 02108
www.sec.state.ma.us/arc/arccol/colidx.htm
(617) 557-1082; hours by appointment

Massachusetts Adjutant General's Office, Military Records Branch
239 Causeway Street
Boston, MA 02114
(617) 727-2964

Massachusetts Historical Society
1154 Boylston Street
Boston, MA 02215
www.masshist.org
(617) 646–0532; fax (617) 859–0074
library@masshist.org
Hours: M–W, F 9–4:45; Th 9–7:45;
    Sat 9–4

Massachusetts Registry of Vital Records and Statistics
150 Mount Vernon Street, 1st floor
Dorchester, MA 02125-3105
www.mass.gov/dph/rvrs
(617) 740–2600
Hours: M, Th 2–4:30; Tu, F 9–12

Above: "Athenæum of Nantucket." John Warner Barber, *Historical Collections . . . Relating to the History and Antiquities of Every Town in Massachusetts* (1848), p. 446.

American Antiquarian Society
185 Salisbury Street
Worcester, MA 01609–1634
www.americanantiquarian.org
(508) 755–5221; fax (508) 753–3311
library@americanantiquarian.org
Hours: M, Tu, Th, F 9–5; W 10–8

Archdiocese of Boston Archives
66 Brooks Drive
Braintree, MA 02184-3839
www.bostoncatholic.org/Archives.aspx
(617) 746–5795; fax (617) 779–4561
See website for email
Hours by appt.

Boston Athenaeum
10½ Beacon Street
Boston, MA 02108
www.bostonathenaeum.org
(617) 227–0270
reference@bostonathenaeum.org
Hours: M, W 8:30–8; Tu, Th, F 8:30–5:30;
  Sat 9–4

City of Boston Archives
201 Rivermoor Street
West Roxbury, MA 02131
www.cityofboston.gov/archivesandrecords
(617) 635–1195; fax (617) 635–1194
Archives@cityofboston.gov
Hours: M–F 9:30–4

Connecticut Valley Historical Museum
220 State Street
Springfield, MA 01103
www.springfieldmuseums.org/museums/history
(413) 263-6800; fax (413) 263–6807
info@springfieldmuseums.org

Congregational Library / Congregational Christian Historical Society
14 Beacon Street
Boston, MA 02108
www.congregationallibrary.org
(617) 523–0470; fax (617) 523–0491
See website for email
Hours: M–F 9–5

National Guard Museum and Archives
44 Salisbury Street
Worcester, MA 01609
http://states.ng.mil/sites/MA/resources/museum
(508) 797-0334
museum@ng.army.mil
Hours: M–F 9–4

Old Colony Historical Society
66 Church Green
Taunton, MA 02780
www.oldcolonyhistoricalsociety.org
(508) 822-1622
oldcolony@oldcolonyhistoricalsociety.org
Hours: Tu–Sat 10–4

Above: "West view of Leicester." John Warner Barber, *Historical Collections . . . Relating to the History and Antiquities of Every Town in Massachusetts* (1848), p. 580.

Peabody-Essex Museum, Phillips Library
Plummer Hall
161 Essex Street
Salem, MA 01970
www.pem.org/library/information
(978) 745–9500, (866) 745–1876;
   fax (978) 741–9012
Hours: W 10–5; Th 1–5

[Closed for renovations until 2014; until then patrons can use an off-site research center.]

University of Massachusetts, W.E.B. Dubois Library
154 Hicks Way
University of Massachusetts / Amherst
Amherst, MA 01003–9275
www.umass.edu/learningcommons
(413) 545–0150
ref@library.umass.edu
Hours, academic year: 24 hours per day,
   11 a.m. Sun– 9 p.m. Fri; Sat. 9–9
Hours, summer: 24 hours per day, 8 a.m. M–
   7 p.m. Thu; F 8–5; Sat 10–5

Counties

Name	Est.	Parent(s)	Probate District(s)	Deed District(s)	Note
Barnstable	1685	New Plymouth Colony	Barnstable	Barnstable	
Berkshire	1761	Hampshire	Berkshire	Northern, Middle, Southern	
Bristol	1685	New Plymouth Colony	Bristol	Northern, Southern, Fall River	
Dukes	1683 (N.Y.) 1695 (Mass)	Original County	Dukes	Dukes	
Essex	1643	Original County	Essex	Northern, Southern	
Franklin	1811	Hampshire	Franklin	Franklin	
Hampden	1812	Hampshire	Hampden	Hampden	See next entry
Hampshire	1662	Middlesex	Hampshire	Hampshire	Pre-1812 land records held in Hampden Co.
Middlesex	1643	Original County	Middlesex	Northern, Southern	
Nantucket	1695	Dukes	Nantucket	Nantucket	
Norfolk	1793	Suffolk	Norfolk	Norfolk	
Plymouth	1685	New Plymouth Colony	Plymouth	Plymouth	
Suffolk	1643	Original County	Suffolk	Suffolk	
Worcester	1731	Middlesex and Suffolk	Worcester	Northern, Worcester	

Extinct County

Name	Est.	Parent(s)	Probate District(s)	Deed District(s)	Note
"Old" Norfolk	1643	Original County	Old Norfolk	Old Norfolk	Abolished 1679, but recorded deeds through 1714.

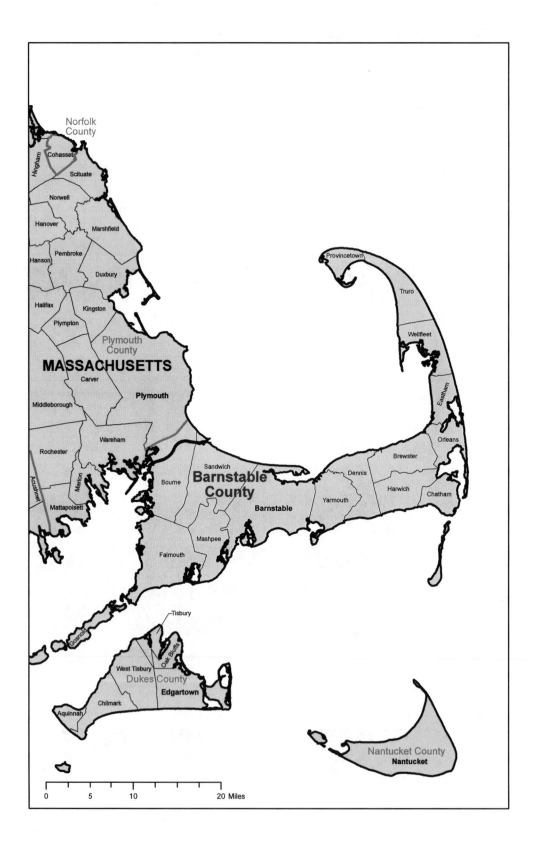

Barnstable County

Established	1685
Parent County	New Plymouth Colony
County Seat	Barnstable

Towns

Barnstable, Bourne, Brewster, Chatham, Dennis, Eastham, Falmouth, Harwich, Mashpee, Orleans, Provincetown, Sandwich, Truro, Wellfleet, Yarmouth

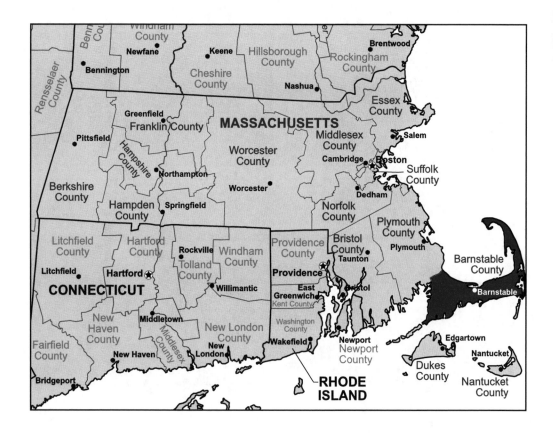

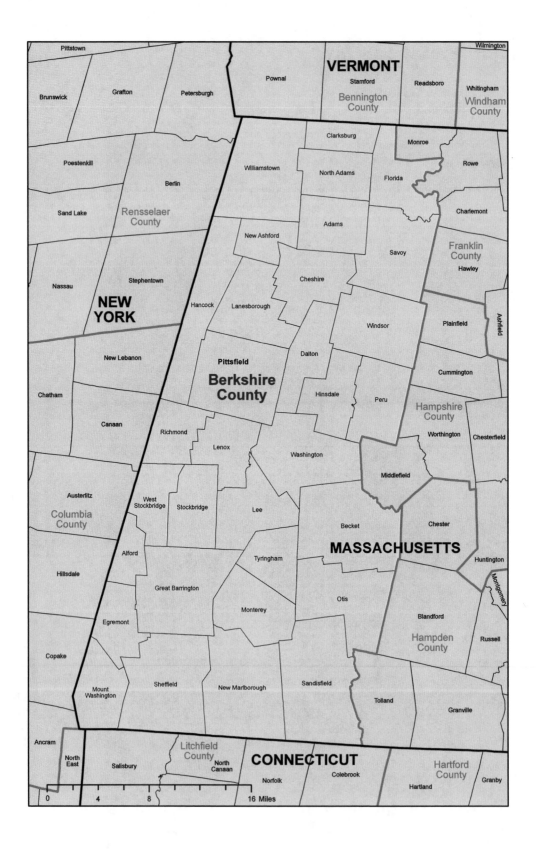

MA

Berkshire County

Established	1761
Parent County	Hampshire
County Seat	Pittsfield

Towns

Adams, Alford, Becket, Cheshire, Clarksburg, Dalton, Egremont, Florida, Great Barrington, Hancock, Hinsdale, Lanesborough, Lee, Lenox, Monterey, Mount Washington, New Ashford, New Marlborough, North Adams, Otis, Peru, Pittsfield, Richmond, Sandisfield, Savoy, Sheffield, Stockbridge, Tyringham, Washington, West Stockbridge, Williamstown, Windsor

Extinct

Boston Corner District, District of Bethlehem, District of Southfield, Zoar (never incorporated)

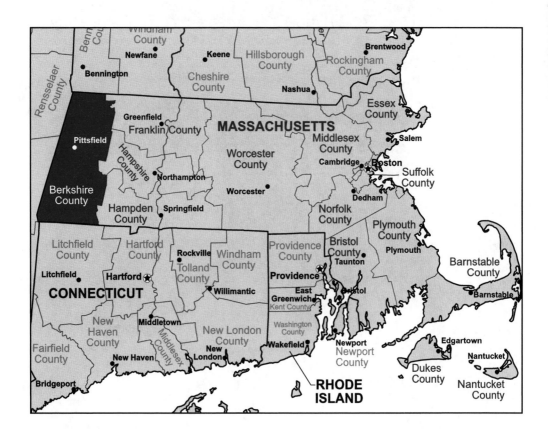

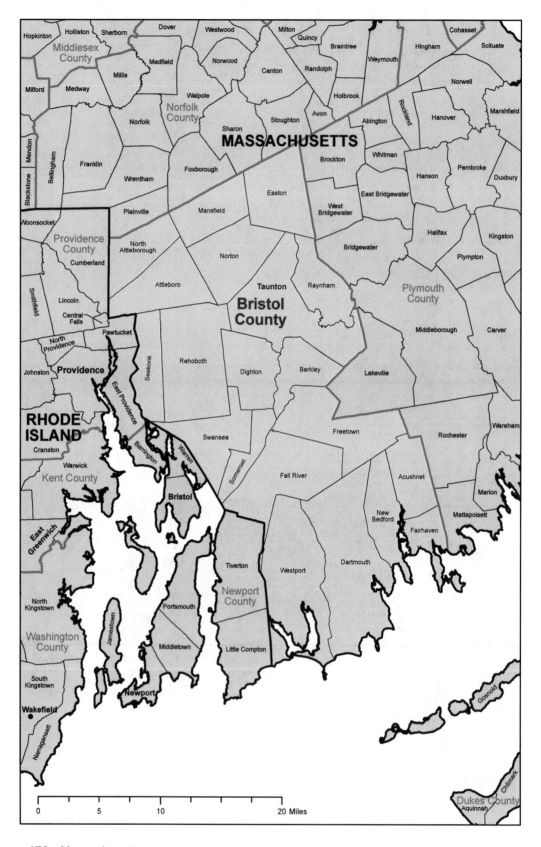

Bristol County

Established	1685
Parent County	New Plymouth Colony
County Seat	Taunton

Towns

Acushnet, Attleboro, Berkley, Dartmouth, Dighton, Easton, Fairhaven, Fall River, Freetown, Mansfield, New Bedford, North Attleborough, Norton, Raynham, Rehoboth, Seekonk, Somerset, Swansea, Taunton, Westport

Extinct

Barrington, Bristol, Little Compton, Tiverton, Warren, Wellington

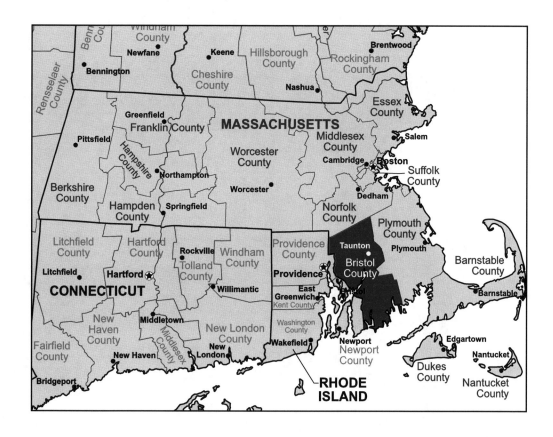

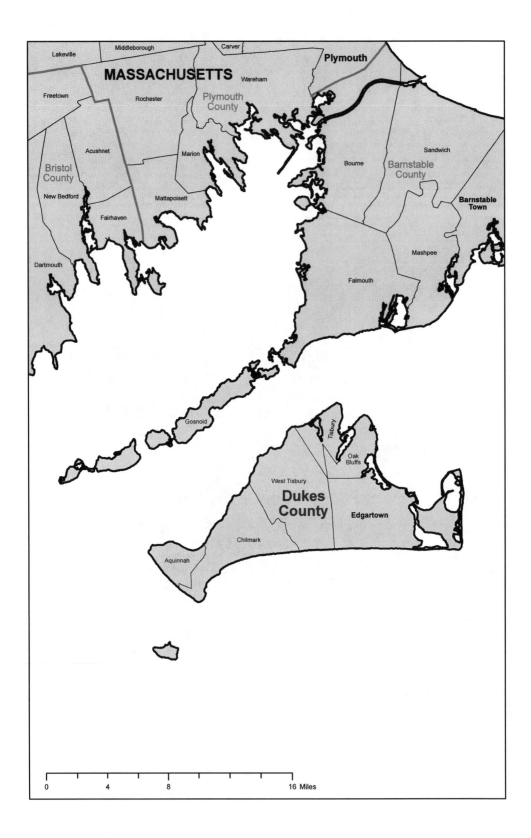

Dukes County

Established	1683 (New York), 1695 (Massachusetts)
Original County	
County Seat	Edgartown

Towns

Aquinnah, Chilmark, Edgartown, Gosnold, Oak Bluffs, Tisbury, West Tisbury

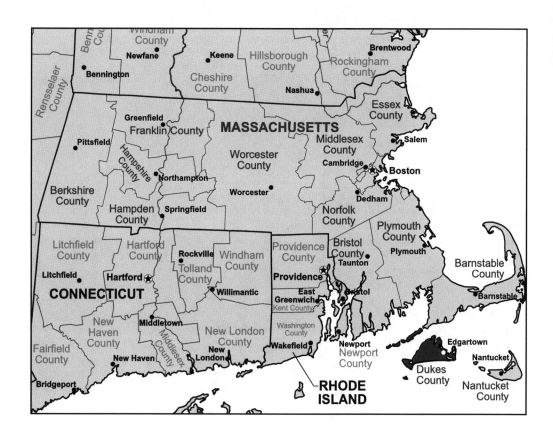

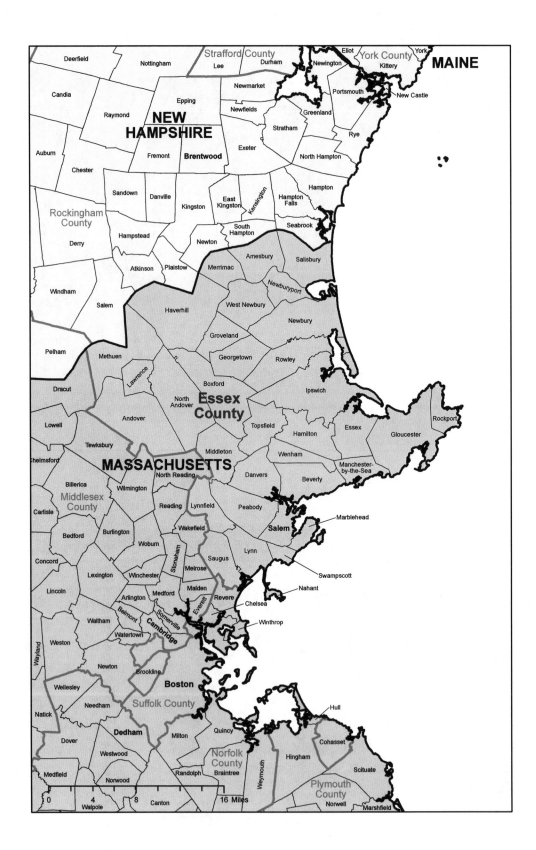

Essex County

Established	1643
Original County	
County Seat	Salem

Towns

Amesbury, Andover, Beverly, Boxford, Danvers, Essex, Georgetown, Gloucester, Groveland, Hamilton, Haverhill, Ipswich, Lawrence, Lynn, Lynnfield, Manchester-by-the-Sea, Marblehead, Merrimac, Methuen, Middleton, Nahant, Newbury, Newburyport, North Andover, Peabody, Rockport, Rowley, Salem, Salisbury, Saugus, Swampscott, Topsfield, Wenham, West Newbury

Extinct

Bradford

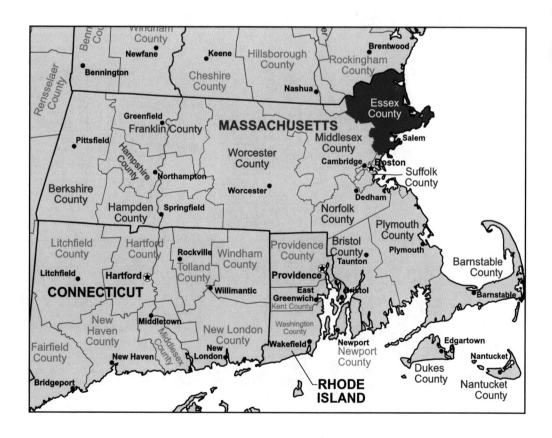

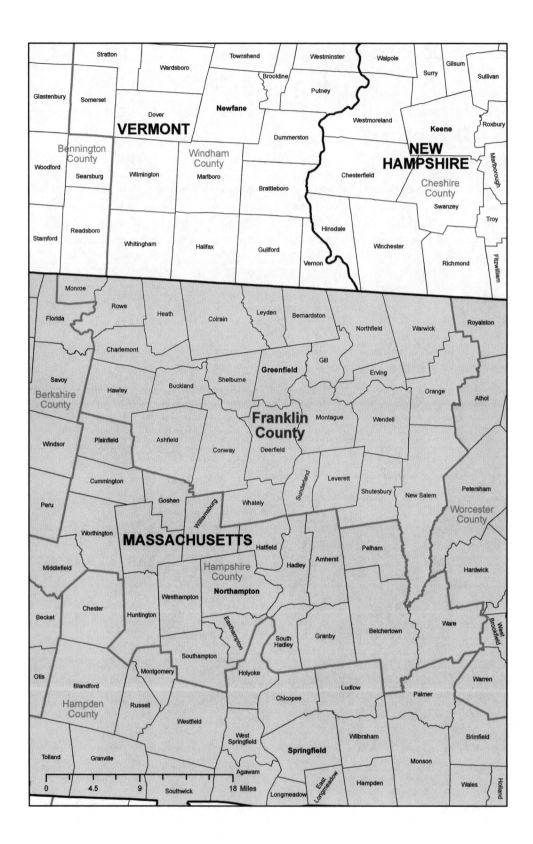

Franklin County

Established	1811
Parent County	Hampshire
County Seat	Greenfield

Towns

Ashfield, Bernardston, Buckland, Charlemont, Colrain, Conway, Deerfield, Erving, Gill, Greenfield, Hawley, Heath, Leverett, Leyden, Monroe, Montague, New Salem, Northfield, Orange, Rowe, Shelburne, Shutesbury, Sunderland, Warwick, Wendell, Whately

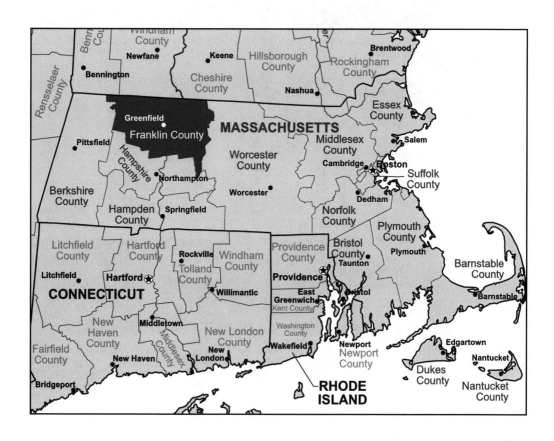

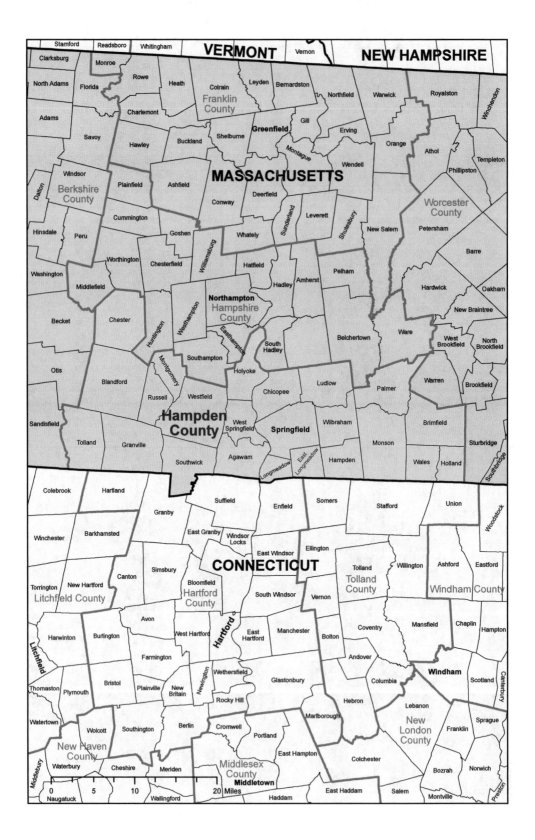

Hampden County

Established	1812
Parent County	Hampshire
County Seat	Springfield

Towns

Agawam, Blandford, Brimfield, Chester, Chicopee, East Longmeadow, Granville, Hampden, Holland, Holyoke, Longmeadow, Ludlow, Monson, Montgomery, Palmer, Russell, Southwick, Springfield, Tolland, Wales, West Springfield, Westfield, Wilbraham

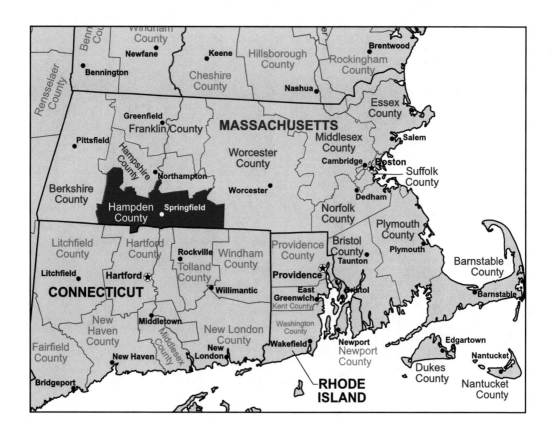

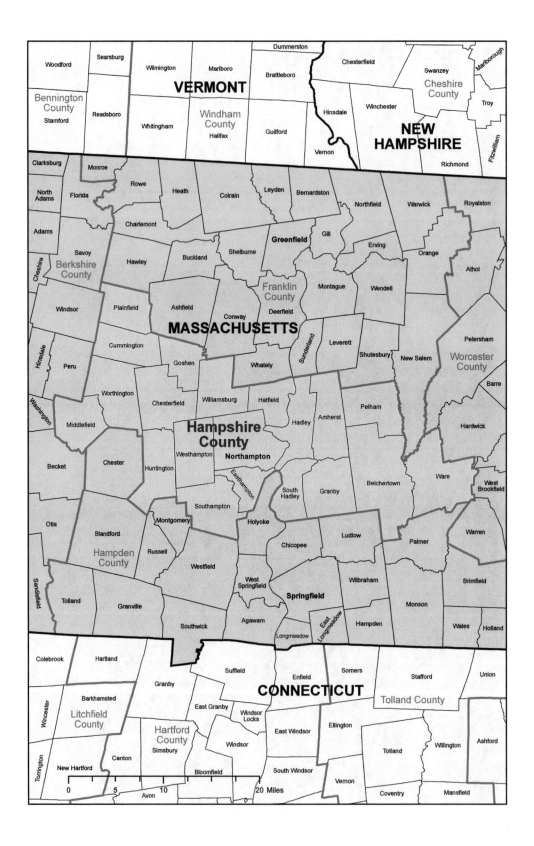

Hampshire County

Established	1662
Parent County	Middlesex
County Seat	Northampton

Towns

Amherst, Belchertown, Chesterfield, Cummington, Easthampton, Goshen, Granby, Hadley, Hatfield, Huntington, Middlefield, Northampton, Pelham, Plainfield, South Hadley, Southampton, Ware, Westhampton, Williamsburg, Worthington

Extinct

Enfield, Greenwich, Prescott

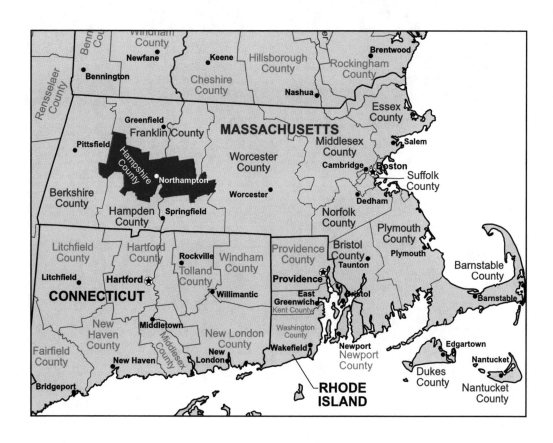

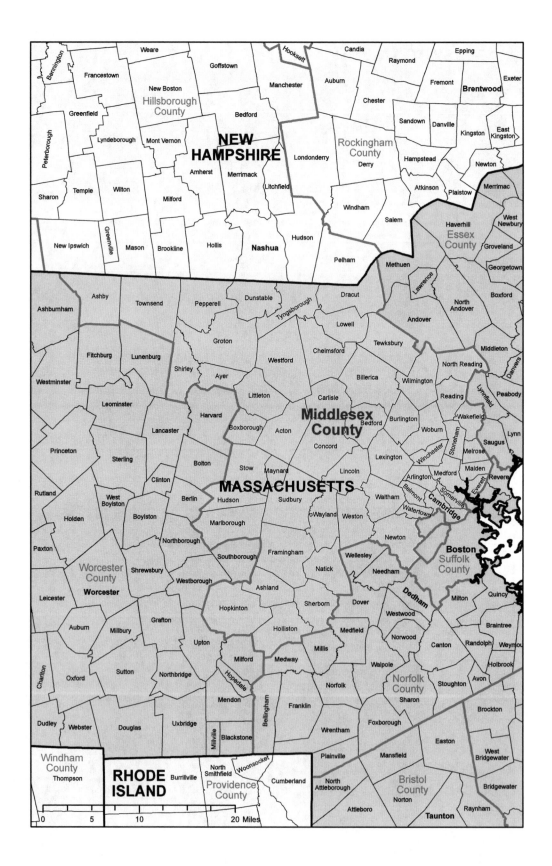

Middlesex County

Established	1643
Original County	
County Seat	Cambridge

Towns

Acton, Arlington, Ashby, Ashland, Ayer, Bedford, Belmont, Billerica, Boxborough, Burlington, Cambridge, Carlisle, Chelmsford, Concord, Dracut, Dunstable, Everett, Framingham, Groton, Holliston, Hopkinton, Hudson, Lexington, Lincoln, Littleton, Lowell, Malden, Marlborough, Maynard, Medford, Melrose, Natick, Newton, North Reading, Pepperell, Reading, Sherborn, Shirley, Somerville, Stoneham, Stow, Sudbury, Tewksbury, Townsend, Tyngsborough, Wakefield, Waltham, Watertown, Wayland, Westford, Weston, Wilmington, Winchester, Woburn

Extinct

Brighton, Charlestown, Litchfield, Nottingham

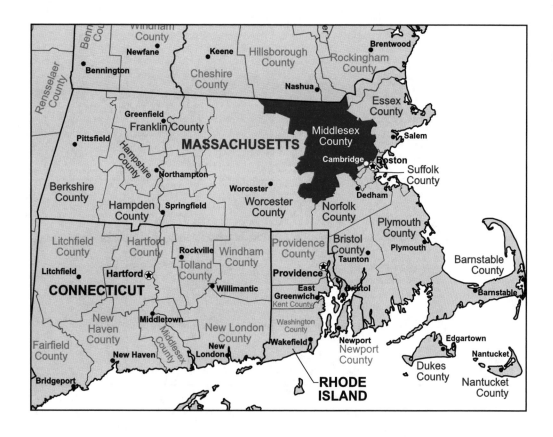

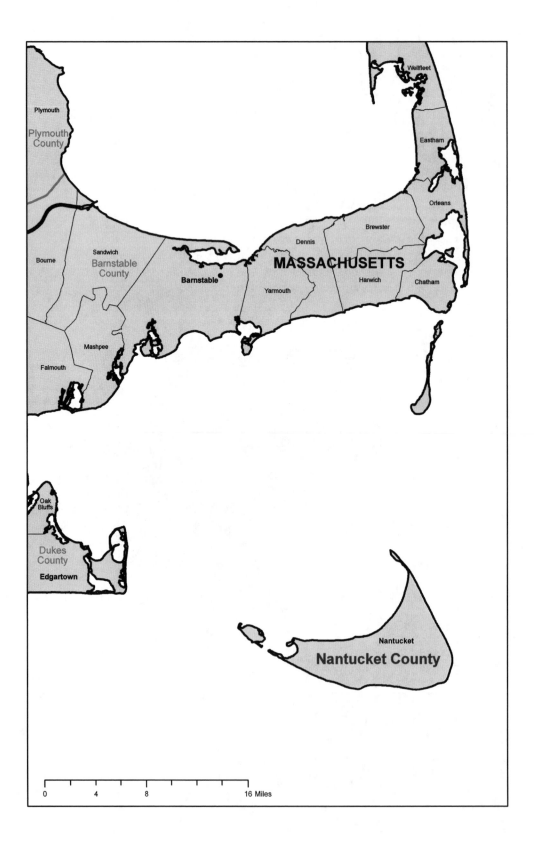

Nantucket County

Established	1695
Parent County	Dukes
County Seat	Nantucket

Town

Nantucket

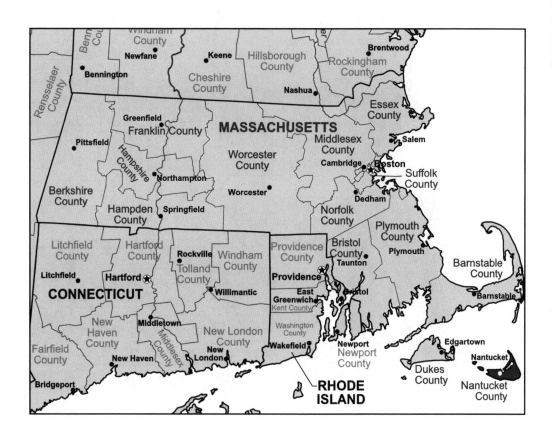

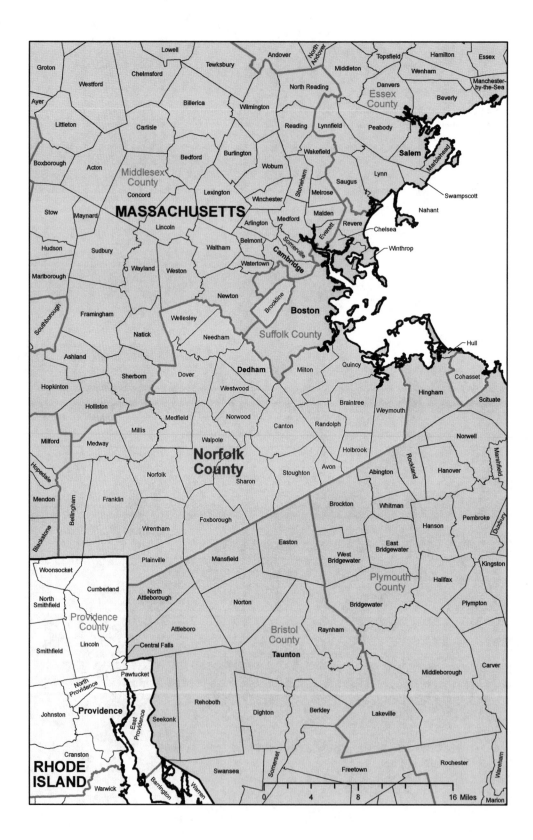

Norfolk County

Established	1793
Parent County	Suffolk
County Seat	Dedham

Towns

Avon, Bellingham, Braintree, Brookline, Canton, Cohasset, Dedham, Dover, Foxborough, Franklin, Holbrook, Medfield, Medway, Millis, Milton, Needham, Norfolk, Norwood, Plainville, Quincy, Randolph, Sharon, Stoughton, Walpole, Wellesley, Westwood, Weymouth, Wrentham

Extinct

Dorchester, Roxbury, West Roxbury

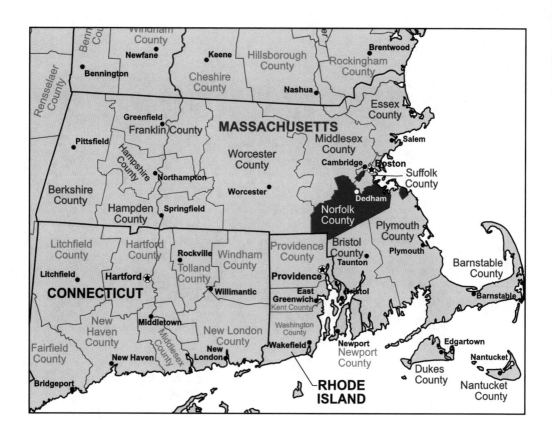

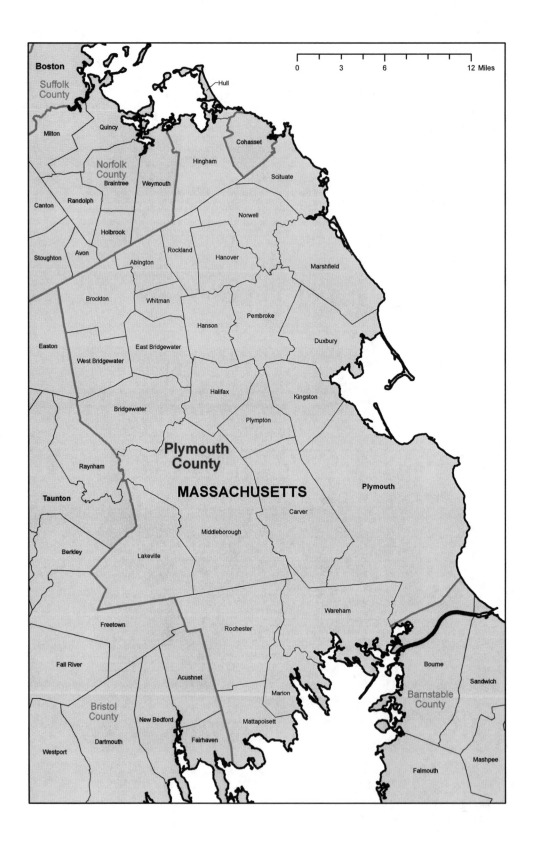

Boston

Suffolk
County

Hull

Milton

Quincy

Cohasset

Norfolk
County

Hingham

Braintree   Weymouth

Scituate

Canton

Randolph

Norwell

Holbrook

Stoughton   Avon

Rockland

Hanover

Marshfield

Abington

Brockton   Whitman

Pembroke

Easton

Hanson

Duxbury

West Bridgewater   East Bridgewater

Bridgewater

Halifax

Kingston

Plympton

**Plymouth
County**

Raynham

MASSACHUSETTS

Plymouth

Taunton

Carver

Middleborough

Berkley

Lakeville

Freetown

Wareham

Rochester

Boume

Fall River

Acushnet

Sandwich

Marion

Barnstable
County

Bristol
County

New Bedford

Mattapoisett

Westport   Dartmouth   Fairhaven

Mashpee

Falmouth

MA

Plymouth County

Established	1685
Parent County	New Plymouth Colony
County Seat	Plymouth

Towns

Abington, Bridgewater, Brockton, Carver, Duxbury, East Bridgewater, Halifax, Hanover, Hanson, Hingham, Hull, Kingston, Lakeville, Marion, Marshfield, Mattapoisett, Middleborough, Norwell, Pembroke, Plymouth, Plympton, Rochester, Rockland, Scituate, Wareham, West Bridgewater, Whitman

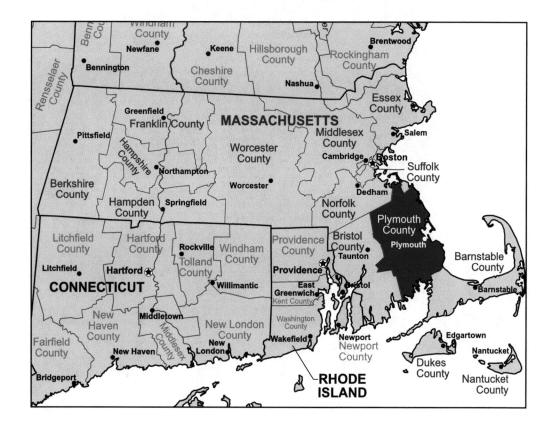

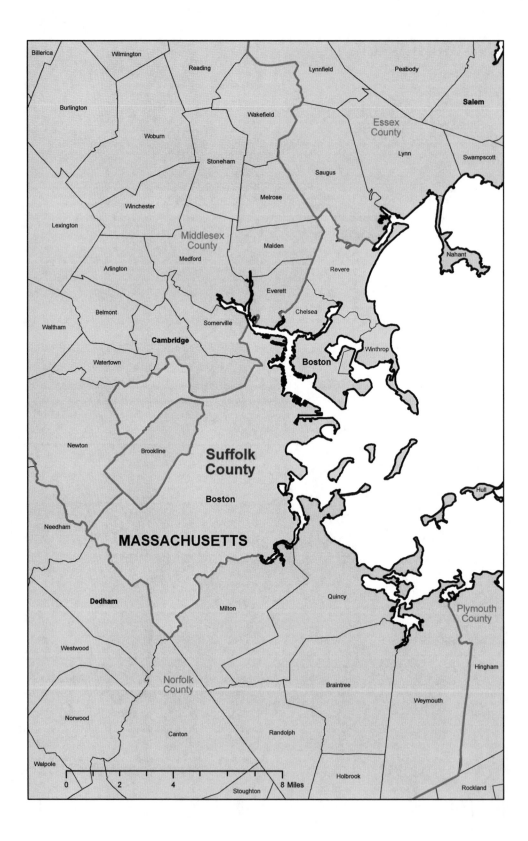

Billerica
Wilmington
Reading
Lynnfield
Peabody
Salem
Burlington
Wakefield
Essex County
Woburn
Lynn
Swampscott
Stoneham
Saugus
Melrose
Winchester
Lexington
Middlesex County
Malden
Medford
Nahant
Arlington
Revere
Belmont
Everett
Waltham
Somerville
Chelsea
Cambridge
Winthrop
Watertown
Boston
Newton
Brookline
Suffolk County
Hull
Boston
Needham
MASSACHUSETTS
Dedham
Quincy
Milton
Plymouth County
Westwood
Hingham
Norfolk County
Braintree
Weymouth
Norwood
Canton
Randolph
Walpole
Holbrook
0   2   4   8 Miles
Stoughton
Rockland

Suffolk County

Established	1643
Original County	
County Seat	Boston

Towns

Boston, Chelsea, Revere, Winthrop

Extinct

Hyde Park

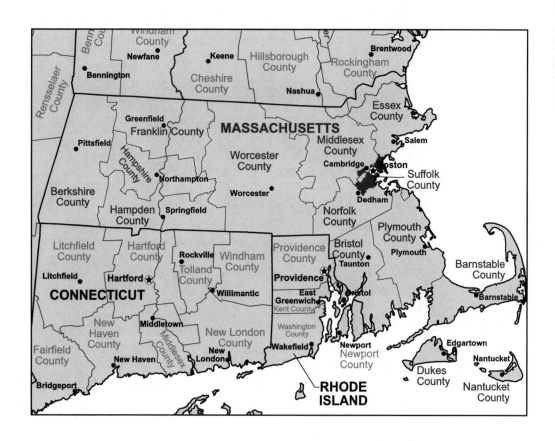

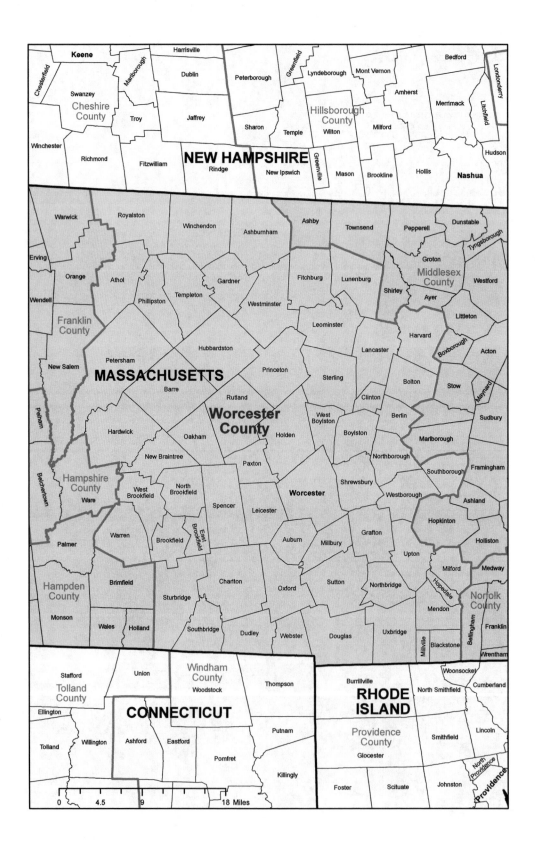

Worcester County

Established	1731
Parent Counties	Middlesex, Suffolk
County Seat	Worcester

Towns

Ashburnham, Athol, Auburn, Barre, Berlin, Blackstone, Bolton, Boylston, Brookfield, Charlton, Clinton, Douglas, Dudley, East Brookfield, Fitchburg, Gardner, Grafton, Hardwick, Harvard, Holden, Hopedale, Hubbardston, Lancaster, Leicester, Leominster, Lunenburg, Mendon, Milford, Mendon, Millbury, Millville, New Braintree, North Brookfield, Northborough, Northbridge, Oakham, Oxford, Paxton, Petersham, Phillipston, Princeton, Royalston, Rutland, Shrewsbury, Southborough, Southbridge, Spencer, Sterling, Sturbridge, Sutton, Templeton, Upton, Uxbridge, Warren, Webster, West Boylston, West Brookfield, Westborough, Westminster, Winchendon, Worcester

Extinct

Dana, Suffield, Woodstock

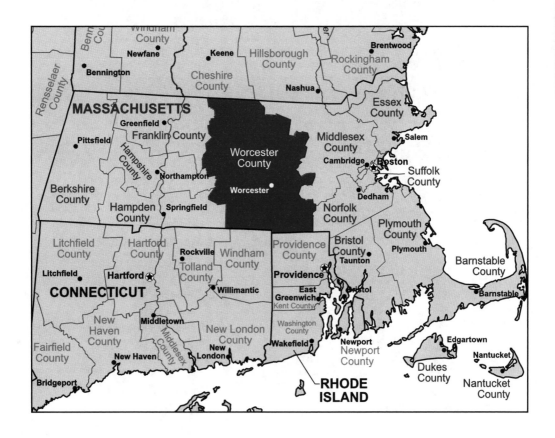

Norfolk County (extinct)

Norfolk County was originally established in 1643. It included the towns of Amesbury, Haverhill, Salisbury, Dover, Exeter, and Portsmouth—and, from 1668, Amesbury. In 1679 Dover, Exeter, and Portsmouth were joined with Hampton to form the royal province of New Hampshire. Amesbury, Haverhill, and Salisbury returned to Essex County. Although abolished, Norfolk County continued to record deeds through 1714. The originals of those records are now at the Essex County Registry of Deeds. The name of Norfolk was again used in 1793 when Suffolk County was subdivided. For more information, see David C. Dearborn, "The Old Norfolk County Records," *The Essex Genealogist* 3 (1983): 194–96.

Above: "Map of Old Norfolk County, 1643," *The Essex Antiquarian* 1 (1897), facing p. 19.

Probate Records

Probate in Massachusetts is recorded on the county level. In the twentieth century some counties opened satellite offices to better administer to the needs of the residents. Check with satellite offices before visiting to ensure that the records you are seeking are there. Older records will usually be found at the main county probate court or at the Massachusetts Judicial Archives. General information about the probate courts can be found at *www.mass.gov/courts*, where you can also obtain information about changes in court hours.

Barnstable County

Barnstable Probate and Family Court
Probate and Family Court Department,
Barnstable Division
3195 Main Street
Barnstable, MA 02630

Mailing Address
PO Box 346
Barnstable, MA 02630

www.barnstablecountypfc.com
Probate/estates: (508) 375–6725
Guardianships: (508) 375–6730
Equity: (508) 375–6728
Domestic relations/divorce: (508) 375–6722
Fax (Registry): (508) 362–3662
barnstableprobate@barnstablecountypfc.com
Hours: M–F 8:30–4:30

Berkshire County

Berkshire Probate and Family Court
44 Bank Row
Pittsfield, MA 01201
*www.mass.gov/courts/courtsandjudges/courts/
    berkprobmain.html*
(413) 442–6941; fax (413) 443–3430
Hours: M–F 8:30–4

Bristol County

Bristol Probate and Family Court
21 Father DeValles Boulevard
Fall River, MA 02723
www.bristolcountyprobate.com
(508) 672–4669; fax (508) 672–0043
info@bristolcountyprobate.com
Hours: M–F 8–1, 2–4:30

Fall River Satellite
289 Rock Street
Fall River, MA 02720
www.bristolcountyprobate.com
(508) 672–1751; fax (508) 673–4714
info@bristolcountyprobate.com
Hours: M–F 8–1, 2–4:30

New Bedford Satellite
505 Pleasant Street
New Bedford, MA 02740
www.bristolcountyprobate.com
(508) 999–5249; fax (508) 999–1269
info@bristolcountyprobate.com
Hours: M–F 8–1, 2–4:30

Dukes County

Dukes Probate and Family Court
Dukes County Courthouse
81 Main Street
Edgartown, MA 02539

Mailing Address
PO Box 237
Edgartown, MA 02539

*www.dukescounty.org/pages/DukesCountyMA_
    Courts*
(508) 627–4703, (508) 627–4704;
    fax (508) 627–7664
info@dukescounty.org
Hours: M–F 8:30–4:30

Essex County

Essex Probate and Family Court
36 Federal Street
Salem, MA 01970
*www.mass.gov/courts/courtsandjudges/courts/
    essexprobmain.html*

cont. on next page

Essex County (cont.)

Main telephone: (978) 744–1020; probate,
(978) 744–1020 ext 383;
TTY (978) 745–0350;
fax (978) 741–2957
Hours: M–F 8:30–3

Lawrence Satellite
Essex Probate and Family Court
2 Appleton Street
Lawrence, MA 01840
*www.mass.gov/courts/courtsandjudges/courts/
essexprobmain.html*
(978) 686–9692; TTY (978) 975–2429;
fax (978) 687–3694
Hours: M–F 8–4:30

Franklin County

Franklin Probate and Family Court
Franklin County Courthouse
425 Main Street
Greenfield, MA 01302

Mailing Address
PO Box 590
Greenfield, MA 01302

*www.mass.gov/courts/courtsandjudges/courts/
frankprobmain.html*
(413) 774–7011, (413) 774–7012, (413)
774–7013; TTY (413) 774–3364;
fax (413) 774–3829
Hours: M–F 8–4:30

Hampden County

Hampden Probate and Family Court
Probate and Family Court Department
50 State Street
Springfield, MA 01102–0559
*www.mass.gov/courts/courtsandjudges/courts/
hampdenprobmain.html*
Adoptions: (413) 748–7754
Divorce: (413) 748–7740
Office Manager: (413) 735–6058
Paternity: (413) 748–7728
Probate & Equity: (413) 748–7745
Vault/Records Management: (413) 748–7766
Fax (413) 781–5605
Hours: M–F 8–4:30

Hampshire County

Hampshire County Probate and Family Court
33 King Street, Suite 3
Northampton, MA 01060
www.hampshireprobate.com
(413) 586–8500; fax (413) 584–1132
hampshireprobate@dacbase.com
Hours: M–F 8–4:30

Middlesex County

Middlesex Probate and Family Court
Probate and Family Court Department,
Middlesex County Division
208 Cambridge Street
East Cambridge, MA 02141–0006

Mailing Address
PO Box 410480
East Cambridge, MA 02141–0006

*www.mass.gov/courts/courtsandjudges/courts/
middprobmain.html*
Adoptions: (617) 768–5898
Copy: (617) 768–5905
Divorce: (617) 768–5850
Equity: (617) 768–5909
Register's Office: (617) 768–5989
Fax (617) 225–0781
Hours: M–F 8–4:30

Cambridge Satellite Session
121 Third Street
Cambridge, MA 02141
Hours: M–F 8–4:30

Concord Satellite Session
305 Walden Street
Concord, MA 01742
Hours: M–F 8–4:30

Marlborough Satellite Session
45 Williams Street
Marlborough, MA 01752
Hours: M–F 8–4:30

Lowell Satellite Session
360 Gorham Street
Lowell, MA 01852
Hours: M–F 8–4:30

Nantucket County

Nantucket Probate and Family Court
Town and County Building
16 Broad Street
Nantucket, MA 02554

Mailing Address
PO Box 1116
Nantucket, MA 02554

*www.mass.gov/courts/courtsandjudges/courts/
nanprobmain.html*
(508) 228–2669, (508) 228–6852;
fax (508) 228–3662
Hours: M–F 8:15–4

Norfolk County

Norfolk Probate and Family Court
35 Shawmut Road
Canton, MA 02021
*www.mass.gov/courts/courtsandjudges/courts/
norfolkprobmain.html*
(781) 830–1200; fax (Registry)
(781) 830–4310
Hours: M–F 8:30–4:30

Plymouth County

Plymouth Probate and Family Court
52 Obery Street, Suite 1130
Plymouth, MA 02360
www.pcpfc.com
(508) 747–6204
plymouthprobate@dacbase.com
Hours: M–F 8:30–4:30

Brockton Satellite Session
215 Main Street, Suite 220
Brockton, MA 02301
www.pcpfc.com/
(508) 897–5400
plymouthprobate@dacbase.com
Hours: M–F 8:30–4:30

Suffolk County

Suffolk Probate and Family Court
Edward W. Brooke Courthouse
24 New Chardon Street, 3rd floor
Boston, MA 02114

Mailing Address
PO Box 9667
Boston, MA 02114

*www.mass.gov/courts/courtsandjudges/courts/
suffprobmain.html*
(617) 788–8300; fax (617) 788–8962
Hours: M–F 8–5

Worcester County

Worcester Probate and Family Court
225 Main Street
Worcester, MA 01608
*www.mass.gov/courts/courtsandjudges/courts/
worcesterprobmain.html*
(508) 831–2200; fax (508) 752–6138
Hours: M–F 8–4:30

"Little Canada." George F. Kenngott, *The Record of a City: A Social Survey of Lowell, Massachu-setts* (1912), between pp. 52–53.

Land Records

Deeds and other matters dealing with land are recorded at the county level in Massachusetts. Some counties have multiple registration districts. Many registries have now digitized records and make them available online, though fees may apply. Registries also make their records available online through *www.masslandrecords.com*.

Barnstable County

Barnstable County Registry of Deeds
3195 Main Street
Barnstable, MA 02630

Mailing Address
PO Box 368
Barnstable, MA 02630
www.barnstabledeeds.org
(508) 362–7733; fax (508) 362–5065
Hours: M–F 7:45–4:15

Berkshire County

Berkshire Middle Registry of Deeds
44 Bank Row
Pittsfield, MA 01201
www.berkshiremiddledeeds.com
(413) 443–7438; fax (413) 448–6025
Hours: M–F 8:30–3:59

Towns served: Becket, Dalton, Hinsdale, Lee, Lenox, Otis, Peru, Pittsfield, Richmond, Stockbridge, Tyringham, Washington

Berkshire North Registry of Deeds
65 Park Street
Adams, MA 01220
www.sec.state.ma.us/rod/rodbrknth/brknthidx.htm
(413) 743–0035; fax (413) 743–1003
nbrd@sec.state.ma.us
Hours: M–F 8:30–4

Towns served: Adams, Cheshire, Clarksburg, Florida, Hancock, Lanesborough, New Ashford, North Adams, Savoy, Williamstown, Windsor

Southern Berkshire Registry of Deeds
334 Main Street
Great Barrington, MA 01230
www.sec.state.ma.us/rod/rodbrksth/brksthidx.htm
(413) 528–0146; fax (413) 528–6878
SBRD@sec.state.ma.us
Hours: M–F 8:30–4

Towns served: Alford, Egremont, Great Barrington, Monterey, Mount Washington, New Marlborough, Sandisfield, Sheffield, West Stockbridge

Bristol County

Northern Bristol Registry of Deeds
11 Court Street
Taunton, MA 02780
www.tauntondeeds.com
(508) 822–0502; fax (508) 880–4975
registry@tauntondeeds.com
Hours: M–F 8–4:30

Attleboro Satellite
75 Park Street
Attleboro, MA 02703
(508) 455–6100; fax (508) 455–6104

Towns served: Attleboro, Berkley, Dighton, Easton, Mansfield, North Attleborough, Norton, Raynham, Rehoboth, Seekonk, Taunton

Fall River District Registry of Deeds
441 North Main Street
Fall River, MA 02720
www.fallriverdeeds.com
(508) 673–2910; fax (508) 673–7633
frdeeds@verizon.net
Hours: M–F 8 –4:30

Towns served: Assonet, Fall River, Freetown, Somerset, Swansea

Southern Bristol Registry of Deeds
26 North 6th Street
New Bedford, MA 02740
www.newbedforddeeds.org
(508) 993–2605; fax (508) 997–4250
nbregistry@gis.net

Towns served: Acushnet, Dartmouth, Fairhaven, New Bedford, Westport

Dukes County

Dukes County Registry of Deeds
81 Main Street
Edgartown, MA 02539
www.masslandrecords.com
(508) 627–4025; fax (508) 627–7821
registry@dukescounty.org
Hours: M–F 8:30–4

Essex County

Northern Essex District Registry of Deeds
354 Merrimack Street
Suite 304 (Entry C)
Lawrence, MA 01843
www.lawrencedeeds.com
(978) 683–2745; fax (978) 681–5409
Hours: M–F 8:30–4:30

Towns served: Andover, Lawrence, Methuen, North Andover

Southern Essex District Registry of Deeds
Shetland Park
45 Congress Street, Suite 4100
Salem, MA 01970
www.salemdeeds.com
(978) 741–0201; fax (978) 744–5865
southernessexcustomerservice@sec.state.ma.us
Hours: M–F 8–4:30

Towns served: Amesbury, Beverly, Boxford, Danvers, Essex, Georgetown, Gloucester, Groveland, Hamilton, Haverhill, Ipswich, Lynn, Lynnfield, Manchester-by-the-Sea, Marblehead, Merrimac, Middleton, Nahant, Newbury, Newburyport, Peabody, Rockport, Rowley, Salem, Salisbury, Saugus, Swampscott, Topsfield, Wenham, West Newbury

Franklin County

Franklin County Registry of Deeds
425 Main Street
Greenfield, MA 01302
www.franklindeeds.com
(413) 772–0239; fax (413) 774–7150
franklinreg@sec.state.ma.us
Hours: M–F 8:30–4:30

Hampden County

Hampden County Registry of Deeds
50 State Street
Springfield, MA 01103
www.hampdendeeds.com
(413) 755–1722; fax (413) 731–8190
Hours: M–F 8:30–4:30

cont. on next page

Above: "Pynchon House, Springfield, erected about 1660." John Warner Barber, *Historical Collections . . . Relating to the History and Antiquities of Every Town in Massachusetts* (1848), p. 292.

Hampden County *(cont.)*
Westfield Satellite Office
59 Court Street
Westfield, MA 01085
www.hampdendeeds.com
(413) 568–2290; fax (413) 568–4869
See website for email
Hours: M, W, F 8:30–4, closed 1–2

Hampshire County
Hampshire District Registry of Deeds
33 King Street
Northampton, MA 01060
www.hampshiredeeds.com
(413) 584–3637; fax (413) 584–4136
hampshirereg@sec.state.ma.us
Hours: M–F 8:30–4:30

Note: Pre-1812 land records are held in Hampden County.

Middlesex County
Middlesex Northern District Registry of Deeds
360 Gorham Street
Lowell, MA 01852
www.lowelldeeds.com
(978) 322–9000; fax (978) 322–9001
lowelldeeds@comcast.net
Hours: M–F 8:30–4:30

Towns served: Billerica, Carlisle, Chelmsford, Dracut, Dunstable, Lowell, Tewksbury, Tyngsborough, Westford, Wilmington

Middlesex Southern District Registry of Deeds
208 Cambridge Street
Cambridge, MA 02141
(617) 679–6310; fax (617) 494–9083
middlesexsouth@sec.state.ma.us
Hours: M–F 8–3:45

Towns served: Acton, Arlington, Ashby, Ashland, Ayer, Bedford, Belmont, Boxborough, Burlington, Cambridge, Concord, Everett, Framingham, Groton, Holliston, Hopkinton, Hudson, Lexington, Lincoln, Littleton, Malden, Marlborough, Maynard, Medford, Melrose, Natick, Newton, North Reading, Pepperell, Reading, Sherborn, Shirley, Somerville, Stoneham, Stow, Sudbury, Townsend, Wakefield, Waltham, Watertown, Wayland, Weston, Winchester, Woburn

Nantucket County
Nantucket County Registry of Deeds
Town Building, 16 Broad Street
Nantucket, MA 02554
www.masslandrecords.com/Nantucket
(508) 228–7250; fax (508) 325–5331
See website for email
Hours: M–F 8–4

Norfolk County
Norfolk County Registry of Deeds
649 High Street
Dedham, MA 02026–1831

Mailing Address
PO Box 69
Dedham, MA 02026–0069

www.norfolkdeeds.org
(781) 461–6122; fax (781) 326–4742
See website for email
Hours: M–F 8–4:30

Plymouth County
Plymouth County Registry of Deeds
50 Obery Street
Plymouth, MA 02361
www.plymouthdeeds.org
(508) 830–9200; fax (508) 830–9280
admin@plymouthdeeds.org
Hours: M–F 8:15–4:30

Suffolk County
Suffolk Registry of Deeds
24 New Chardon Street
Boston, MA 02114
www.suffolkdeeds.com
(617) 788–8575; fax (617) 720–4163
suffolk.deeds@sec.state.ma.us
Hours: M–F 8:30–4:45

Worcester County

Worcester Northern District Registry of Deeds
Putnam Place
166 Boulder Drive, Suite 202
Fitchburg, MA 01420
www.fitchburgdeeds.com
(978) 342–2132; fax (978) 345–2865
fitchreg@sec.state.ma.us
Hours: M–F 8:30–4:30

Towns served: Ashburnham, Fitchburg, Leominster, Lunenburg, Westminster

Worcester South District Registry of Deeds
90 Front Street
Worcester, MA 01608
www.worcesterdeeds.com
(508) 798–7717; fax (508) 798–0000

See website for email
Hours: M–F 8:15–4:30

Towns served: Athol, Auburn, Barre, Berlin, Blackstone, Bolton, Boylston, Brookfield, Charlton, Clinton, Douglas, Dudley, East Brookfield, Gardner, Grafton, Hardwick, Harvard, Holden, Hopedale, Hubbardston, Lancaster, Leicester, Mendon, Milford, Mendon, Millbury, Millville, New Braintree, North Brookfield, Northborough, Northbridge, Oakham, Oxford, Paxton, Petersham, Phillipston, Princeton, Royalston, Rutland, Shrewsbury, Southborough, Southbridge, Spencer, Sterling, Sturbridge, Sutton, Templeton, Upton, Uxbridge, Warren, Webster, West Boylston, West Brookfield, Westborough, Winchendon, Worcester

Towns

There are currently 55 cities and 296 towns in the Commonwealth of Massachusetts. The following chart lists the name of each town, the date of its incorporation as a town, the county, towns from which it was formed (or from which land was later added to the town), towns that were formed from it (or to which land was added from it), and notes about the town. In the Parent Towns column, towns from which other towns were formed are indicated in **bold** type. Parts of other towns later annexed are in regular type.

It also shows vital records and church records that are available as manuscript, typescript, published books, or online. Extinct towns (those that are no longer extant or that were annexed by other towns or ceded to other states) are listed in the second table.

For more information, see the Massachusetts Secretary of State's online listing of city and town incorporation and settlement dates at *www.sec.state.ma.us/cis/cisctlist/ctlistalph.htm*.

VR and CR codes

A   James N. Arnold, *Vital Record of Rhode Island, 1636–1850*
B   Rollin H. Cooke Collection
C   Corbin Collection
D   DAR Library (Daughters of the American Revolution), Washington, D.C.
F   Catholic Church records and other records published by French-Canadian societies
H   Holbrook Microfiche (Archives Publishing)
K   Published church records
M   *Mayflower Descendant*
N   Manuscript or typescript at NEHGS
P   Miscellaneous published volumes, not part of the "official series"
R   *New England Historical and Genealogical Register*
S   Published in the "official series"
T   Records on microfilm
W   Records available on *AmericanAncestors.org*

Town	Inc.	County	Parent Town(s)	Daughter Town(s)	Notes	VR	CR
Abington	1712	Plymouth	**Bridgewater**	Whitman (South Abington), Hanover, Rockland	Settled 1668.	H, S	N
Acton	1735	Middlesex	**Concord**	Carlisle	Settled 1680.	H, S	
Acushnet	1860	Bristol	**Fairhaven**	New Bedford	Settled 1659.	H	
Adams	1778	Berkshire		Cheshire, North Adams	Settled 1762. Originally East Hoosuck Plantation.	H, F	N
Agawam	1855	Hampden	**West Springfield**		Settled 1635.	H	
Alford	1775	Berkshire	**Great Barrington,** West Stockbridge		Settled 1740. Established as district from part of Great Barrington 1773.	H, S	
Amesbury	1666	Essex	**Salisbury**		Settled 1654. Called Salisbury-new-towne to 1668. Also called Amsbury/Emesbury.	H, S	
Amherst	1775	Hampshire	**Hadley**		Settled 1703. Created as district of Hadley 1759.	C, H	K, N
Andover	1646	Essex		Middleton, Lawrence, North Andover	Settled 1642.	H, S	
Aquinnah	1870	Dukes			Settled 1669. District of Gay Head created 1855. Called Gay Head to 1995.		

Above: "The Shepard School Float." *City of Lynn, Massachusetts, Semi-Centennial of Incorporation* (1900), facing p. 241.

Town	Inc.	County	Parent Town(s)	Daughter Town(s)	Notes	VR	CR
Arlington	1807	Middlesex	**Cambridge, Charlestown**	Belmont, Winchester	Settled 1630. Called West Cambridge to 1867.	H, S	
Ashburnham	1765	Worcester	**Dorchester-Canada,** Gardner, Westminster	Ashby, Gardner	Settled 1736.	H, S	
Ashby	1767	Middlesex	**Ashburnham, Fitchburg, Townsend**		Settled 1676.	H, P	
Ashfield	1765	Franklin			Settled as grant to Ephraim Hunt 1736. Originally called Huntstown. Renamed Ashfield 1765.	H, S	
Ashland	1846	Middlesex	**Framingham, Holliston, Hopkinton**	Hopkinton	Settled 1750.	H	
Athol	1762	Worcester	Gerry, Orange, **Payquage Plantation,** New Salem	Orange, Gerry, Royalston	Settled 1735. Originally Payquage Plantation.	H, S	
Attleboro	1694	Bristol	**Rehoboth**	Cumberland, R.I.; North Attleborough; Pawtucket, R.I.; Wrentham	Settled 1634. Originally North Purchase of Rehoboth.	H, S	F, K, W
Auburn	1778	Worcester	**Leicester, Oxford, Sutton, Worcester**	Millbury	Settled 1714. Called Ward to 1834.	H, S	
Avon	1888	Norfolk	Holbrook, Randolph, **Stoughton**		Settled 1700.		
Ayer	1871	Middlesex	**Groton, Shirley**		Settled 1668.	H	
Barnstable	1638	Barnstable			Settled 1637.	H, M, P	K, N, W
Barre	1774	Worcester	**Rutland**		Settled 1720. District of Rutland formed 1753. Town formed and renamed Hutchinson 1774. Renamed Barre 1776.	H, S	
Becket	1765	Berkshire	Loudon, **Plantation No. 4**	Middlefield	Settled 1740. Originally settled as Plantation No. 4.	H, S	
Bedford	1729	Middlesex	**Billerica, Concord,** Lexington		Settled 1640.	H, S	N
Belchertown	1761	Hampshire	**Cold Spring Plantation**	Greenwich, Pelham, Enfield	Settled 1731. Originally Cold Spring Plantation.	C, H	

Town	Inc.	County	Parent Town(s)	Daughter Town(s)	Notes	VR	CR
Bellingham	1719	Norfolk	**Dedham, Mendon, Wrentham**		Settled 1713.	H, S	
Belmont	1859	Middlesex	**Waltham, Watertown, West Cambridge**	Cambridge	Settled 1736.		
Berkley	1735	Bristol	**Dighton, Taunton**		Settled 1638.	H, N	
Berlin	1812	Worcester	**Bolton**, Lancaster, **Marlborough**	Northborough	Settled 1665. District formed from Bolton and Marlborough 1784.	P	
Bernardston	1762	Franklin	**Falltown Plantation**, Greenfield, Leyden	Colrain, Leyden	Settled 1738. Originally Falltown Plantation.	C, H	
Beverly	1668	Essex	**Salem**	Danvers	Settled 1626. Formerly part of Salem called "Basse River."	H, S	K
Billerica	1655	Middlesex		Bedford, Carlisle, Tewksbury, Wilmington	Settled 1637.	H, S	
Blackstone	1845	Worcester	**Mendon**	Millville	Settled 1662.	H	F
Blandford	1741	Hampden	**Glasgow**	Huntington (Norwich)	Settled 1735. Originally Suffield Equivalent Lands.	C, H	N
Bolton	1738	Worcester	**Lancaster**, Marlborough	Berlin, Hudson	Settled 1682.	H, S	
Boston	1630	Suffolk	Brighton, Charlestown, Dorchester, Hyde Park, Roxbury, West Roxbury	Braintree, Brookline, Chelsea	Settled 1625.	H, P	K, N, W
Bourne	1884	Barnstable	**Sandwich**		Settled 1640.		
Boxborough	1835	Middlesex	**Harvard, Littleton, Stow**		Settled 1680. District created 1783.	H, S	
Boxford	1685	Essex	Ipswich, **Rowley**	Groveland, Georgetown, Middleton	Settled 1645. Called Rowley Village to 1694.	H, S	
Boylston	1786	Worcester	**Shrewsbury**	West Boylston	Settled 1705.	H, S	
Braintree	1640	Norfolk	**Boston**	Milton, Quincy, Randolph	Settled 1634. Formed from part of Boston called Mount Wollaston.	P	
Brewster	1803	Barnstable	**Harwich**	Harwich	Settled 1656.	H, S	K

Town	Inc.	County	Parent Town(s)	Daughter Town(s)	Notes	VR	CR
Bridgewater	1656	Plymouth	**Duxbury**	Abington, Brockton, East Bridgewater, Halifax, North Bridgewater	Settled 1650. Originally Duxburrow New Plantation.	H, S	N
Brimfield	1731	Hampden		Palmer, Warren (Western)	Settled 1706.	H, S	N
Brockton	1821	Plymouth	**Bridgewater, East Bridgewater, West Bridgewater**	Whitman (South Abington)	Settled 1700. Called North Bridgewater to 1874.	H, S	
Brookfield	1718	Worcester		Ware, Warren (Western)	Settled 1664. Originally Quobauge.	H, S	
Brookline	1705	Norfolk	Boston, Roxbury		Settled 1638. Formed from part of Boston called Muddy River.	H, S	
Buckland	1779	Franklin	**No-Town Plantation, Charlemont,** Conway		Settled 1779. Originally No-Town Plantation.	H, S	
Burlington	1799	Middlesex	**Woburn**	Lexington	Settled 1641.	H, S	
Cambridge	1631	Middlesex	Arlington (West Cambridge), Belmont, Charlestown, Somerville, Watertown	Arlington (West Cambridge), Belmont, Brighton, Charlestown, Lexington, Somerville, Waltham	Settled 1630. Called New Town to 1636.	H, S	K, N
Canton	1797	Norfolk	**Stoughton**	Stoughton	Settled 1630.	S	T
Carlisle	1805	Middlesex	**Acton, Billerica, Chelmsford, Concord**	Concord, Chelmsford	Settled 1650. District incorporated 1785.	H, S	
Carver	1790	Plymouth	**Plympton**	Wareham	Settled 1660.	H, S	N
Charlemont	1765	Franklin	**Charlemont Plantation, Zoar Plantation**	Buckland, Heath	Settled 1742.	H, S	N
Charlton	1754/1755	Worcester	**Oxford, Country Gore**	Oxford, Southbridge, Sturbridge	Settled 1735.	H, S	
Chatham	1712	Barnstable			Settled 1665. Originally Manamoit.	H, P	
Chelmsford	1655	Middlesex	Carlisle, Wameset	Carlisle, Dunstable, Littleton, Lowell, Westford	Settled 1633.	H, S	

MA

Town	Inc.	County	Parent Town(s)	Daughter Town(s)	Notes	VR	CR
Chelsea	1739	Suffolk	**Boston**	Revere (North Chelsea), Saugus	Settled 1624. Formed from parts of Boston called Pullin Point, Rumney Marsh, and Winnissimet.	H, S	
Cheshire	1793	Berkshire	**Adams, Lanesborough, New Ashford District, Windsor**	Windsor	Settled 1766.	H	
Chester	1765	Hampden		Huntington (Norwich), Middlefield, Worthington	Settled 1760. Called Murrayfield to 1783.	H, S	N
Chesterfield	1762	Hampshire	Goshen, **New Hingham Plantation,** Huntington (Norwich)	Goshen	Settled 1760. Originally New Hingham Plantation.	C, H	
Chicopee	1848	Hampden	**Springfield**		Settled 1652.	H	
Chilmark	1714	Dukes	Tisbury	Tisbury, Gosnold	Settled 1671. Settled as Manor of Tisbury; Chilmark by 1694.	H, S	
Clarksburg	1798	Berkshire	**Bullock's Grant,** Florida	Florida	Settled 1764. Originally "a tract of land north of Adams."	H	
Clinton	1850	Worcester	**Lancaster**		Settled 1654.	H	
Cohasset	1775	Norfolk	**Hingham,** Scituate		Settled 1647. District formed 1770.	H, S	
Colrain	1761	Franklin	Bernardston, **Colrain Plantation**		Settled 1735.	H, S	
Concord	1635	Middlesex	Carlisle, Musketaquid	Acton, Bedford, Carlisle, Lincoln, Littleton	Settled 1635.	P	
Conway	1775	Franklin	**Deerfield,** Shelburne	Buckland, Goshen	Settled 1762. District formed 1767.	H, S	
Cummington	1779	Hampshire	**Plantation No. 5**	Plainfield	Settled 1762. Originally Plantation No. 5.	H, P	
Dalton	1784	Berkshire	**Ashuelot Equivalent,** Windsor	Hinsdale	Settled 1755. Originally Ashuelot Equivalent.	H, S	
Danvers	1775	Essex	Beverly, **Salem**	Peabody (South Danvers)	Settled 1636. District formed from Salem Village and Salem Middle Parish 1752.	H, S	K
Dartmouth	1664	Bristol		New Bedford; Westport; Little Compton, R.I.; Tiverton, R.I.	Settled 1650.	H, S	N, T

Town	Inc.	County	Parent Town(s)	Daughter Town(s)	Notes	VR	CR
Dedham	1636	Norfolk	Stoughton, Walpole	Bellingham, Dorchester, Dover, Hyde Park, Medfield, Needham, Norwood, Walpole, West Roxbury, Westwood	Settled 1635.	H, P	K, W
Deerfield	1677	Franklin	**Hatfield**	Conway, Greenfield, Shelburne, Whately	Settled 1673.	H, S	N
Dennis	1793	Barnstable	**Yarmouth**		Settled 1639.	H, P	
Dighton	1712	Bristol	**Taunton,** Wellington	Berkley, Somerset, Wellington	Settled 1678.	H	
Douglas	1775	Worcester		Uxbridge	Settled 1721. Called New Sherburn to 1746.	H, S	
Dover	1836	Norfolk	**Dedham**		Settled 1635. District created 1784.	H, S	N
Dracut	1701	Middlesex		Lowell	Settled 1664.	H, S	
Dudley	1732	Worcester	Middlesex Gore, **Oxford**	Southbridge, Webster	Settled 1714.	H, S	
Dunstable	1673	Middlesex	Chelmsford, Groton, Nottingham, N.H.	Groton; Litchfield, N.H.; Nashua, N.H.; Nottingham, N.H.; Tyngsborough	Settled 1656.	H, S	
Duxbury	1637	Plymouth		Bridgewater (Duxburrow New Plantation), Kingston, Pembroke	Settled 1624.	H, S	
East Bridgewater	1823	Plymouth	**Bridgewater,** Halifax	Brockton (North Bridgewater), Whitman (South Abington)	Settled 1649.	H, S	N
East Brookfield	1920	Worcester	**Brookfield**		Settled 1664.		
East Longmeadow	1894	Hampden	**Longmeadow**	Springfield	Settled 1740.		
Eastham	1646	Barnstable	Harwich	Orleans, Wellfleet	Settled 1644. Called Nawsett to 1651.	H, M, P	
Easthampton	1809	Hampshire	**Northampton, Southampton**		Settled 1664. District created 1785.	C, H	
Easton	1725	Bristol	Norton		Settled 1694. That part of Norton called the "Taunton North Purchase."	H, N	

MA

Town	Inc.	County	Parent Town(s)	Daughter Town(s)	Notes	VR	CR
Edgartown	1671	Dukes		Oak Bluffs (Cottage City)	Settled 1642. Originally Great Harbour.	H, S	N
Egremont	1775	Berkshire	Sheffield		Settled 1730. District created from lands west of Sheffield 1760.	H	
Erving	1838	Franklin	Northfield		Settled 1801. Originally Erving's Grant.	H	
Essex	1819	Essex	**Ipswich**		Settled 1634.	H, S	
Everett	1870	Middlesex	**Malden**	Medford	Settled 1630.		
Fairhaven	1812	Bristol	Freetown, **New Bedford,** Rochester	Acushnet	Settled 1670.	H	
Fall River	1803	Bristol	**Freetown,** Tiverton, R.I.		Settled 1656. Called Fall River to 1804. Called Troy to 1834.	D, H	F
Falmouth	1686	Barnstable	Mashpee		Settled 1660. Originally Suckanesset. Called Falmouth between 1686 and 1694.	H, P	N
Fitchburg	1764	Worcester	**Lunenburg**	Ashby, Westminster	Settled 1730.	H, P	K
Florida	1805	Berkshire	**Barnardston's Grant, Bullock's Grant,** Clarksburg, **King's Grant, Zoar**	Clarksburg	Settled 1783.	H	
Foxborough	1778	Norfolk	Sharon, **Stoughton, Stoughtonham, Walpole, Wrentham**	Walpole	Settled 1704.	H, S	
Framingham	1700	Middlesex	Holliston, Natick, Sherborn	Ashland, Marlborough, Southborough	Settled 1650.	H, S	
Franklin	1778	Norfolk	Medway, **Wrentham**	Medway, Norfolk	Settled 1660.	S	
Freetown	1683	Bristol	Tiverton	Fairhaven, R.I.; Fall River;Tiverton, R.I.	Settled 1675. Part of Freetown ceded to Tiverton. Parts of Tiverton remaining in Mass. after cession to R.I. annexed back to Freetown.	H, P	N
Gardner	1785	Worcester	**Ashburnham, Templeton, Westminster, Winchendon**	Ashburnham, Winchendon	Settled 1764.	H, S	

MA

Town	Inc.	County	Parent Town(s)	Daughter Town(s)	Notes	VR	CR
Georgetown	1838	Essex	Boxford, **Rowley**		Settled 1639.	H, S	
Gill	1793	Franklin	**Greenfield,** Northfield		Settled 1776.	H, S	
Gloucester	1642	Essex		Rockport	Settled 1623. Called Cape Ann to Gloucester 1642.	H, S	N
Goshen	1781	Hampshire	**Chesterfield, Chesterfield Gore Plantation,** Conway	Chesterfield	Settled 1761.	C, H	
Gosnold	1864	Dukes	**Chilmark**		Settled 1641. Formed from part of Chilmark called Elizabeth Islands.		
Grafton	1735	Worcester	**Hassanamisco Plantation,** Sutton, Shrewsbury		Settled 1718.	H, S	N
Granby	1768	Hampshire	**South Hadley**		Settled 1727.	C, H	N
Granville	1775	Hampden		Tolland	Settled 1736. District formed from tract of land called Bedford 1754.	H, S	N, T
Great Barrington	1761	Berkshire	**Sheffield, Stockbridge**	Alford, Lee	Settled 1726.	H, S	
Greenfield	1775	Franklin	**Deerfield**	Bernardston, Gill	Settled 1686. District formed from Deerfield 1753.	H, S	N
Groton	1655	Middlesex	Dunstable, Pepperell	Ayer, Dunstable, Harvard, Littleton, Pepperell, Shirley, Westford	Settled 1655. Formerly called Petapawoge.	H, S	
Groveland	1850	Essex	Boxford, **Bradford**		Settled 1639.		
Hadley	1661	Hampshire		Amherst, Hatfield, Northampton, South Hadley	Settled 1659. Formerly called "the new plantation near Northhampton."	C	
Halifax	1734	Plymouth	Bridgewater, **Middleborough, Pembroke, Plympton**	East Bridgewater	Settled 1670.	H, S	
Hamilton	1793	Essex	**Ipswich**		Settled 1638. Formed from part of Ipswich called Ipswich Hamlet.	H, S	
Hampden	1878	Hampden	**Wilbraham**		Settled 1741.	H, T	
Hancock	1776	Berkshire	**Jericho Plantation**	New Ashford	Settled 1767. Originally Jericho Plantation.	C, H	

Town	Inc.	County	Parent Town(s)	Daughter Town(s)	Notes	VR	CR
Hanover	1727	Plymouth	**Abington, Scituate**		Settled 1649.	H, S	K, N
Hanson	1820	Plymouth	**Pembroke**		Settled 1632.	H, S	N, W
Hardwick	1739	Worcester	Greenwich, Hardwick Gore, **Lambstown Plantation, New Braintree**	Dana, Greenwich, New Braintree	Settled 1737. Originally Lambstown Plantation.	H, S	
Harvard	1732	Worcester	**Groton, Lancaster, Stow**	Boxborough	Settled 1704.	H, S	N
Harwich	1694	Barnstable	Brewster	Brewster, Eastham	Settled 1670. Called Satucket to 1694. Annexed parts of Brewster 1848.	H, P	N
Hatfield	1670	Hampshire	**Hadley**	Whately, Williamsburg	Settled 1661.	C	
Haverhill	1641	Essex	Bradford	Methuen	Settled 1640. Annexed Bradford 1896.	H, S	
Hawley	1792	Franklin	**Plantation No. 7**	Plainfield	Settled 1760. Originally Plantation No. 7.	H, C	
Heath	1785	Franklin	**Charlemont**		Settled 1765.	H, S	
Hingham	1634	Plymouth		Cohasset	Settled 1633. Called Barecove to 1635.	H	
Hinsdale	1804	Berkshire	**Dalton, Peru (Partridgefield)**		Settled 1763.	H, S	
Holbrook	1872	Norfolk	**Randolph**	Avon	Settled 1710.	H	N
Holden	1741	Worcester	Paxton, **Worcester**	Paxton, West Boylston	Settled 1723. Formed from part of Worcester called North Worcester.	H, S	
Holland	1835	Hampden	**South Brimfield**		Settled 1725. District created from South Brimfield 1783.	H	
Holliston	1724	Middlesex	Hopkinton, **Sherborn**	Ashland, Framingham, Milford	Settled 1659.	H, S	
Holyoke	1850	Hampden	Northampton, **West Springfield**		Settled 1745.	H, T	F
Hopedale	1886	Worcester	**Milford**		Settled 1660.		
Hopkinton	1715	Middlesex	Ashland	Ashland, Holliston, Milford, Upton	Settled 1715. Originally Moguncoy.	H, S	
Hubbardston	1775	Worcester	**Rutland**	Princeton	Settled 1734. District formed 1767.	H, S	

MA

Town	Inc.	County	Parent Town(s)	Daughter Town(s)	Notes	VR	CR
Hudson	1866	Middlesex	**Bolton, Marlborough, Stow**		Settled 1699.	H	
Hull	1644	Plymouth			Settled 1624. Called Nantascot to 1644.	H, S	N
Huntington	1775	Hampshire	Clandford, Chester, **Murrayfield**	Chesterfield, Montgomery	Settled 1769. District of Norwich created from Murrayfield 1773. Called Norwich to 1855.	F	N
Ipswich	1634	Essex		Boxford, Essex, Hamilton, Rowley, Topsfield	Settled 1633.	H, S	
Kingston	1726	Plymouth	Duxbury, Pembroke, **Plymouth**		Settled 1620. Formed from North Precinct of Plymouth.	H, S	
Lakeville	1853	Plymouth	**Middleborough**		Settled 1717.	H	
Lancaster	1653	Worcester		Berlin, Bolton, Clinton, Harvard, Lancaster, Leominster, Shrewsbury, Sterling	Settled 1643. In 1653 the General Court ordered that Nashaway be called Prescott, that it be called West Towne, and finally that it be called Lancaster.	H, P	K, W
Lanesborough	1765	Berkshire			Settled 1753. Originally plantation of New Framingham.	C, H, P	D, N
Lawrence	1847	Essex	**Andover, Methuen,** North Andover	Methuen	Settled 1655.	H, S	
Lee	1777	Berkshire	**Glassworks Grant, Great Barrington, Washington, Williams Grant**		Settled 1760.	H, S	K
Leicester	1714	Worcester		Auburn (Ward), Paxton, Spencer, Worcester	Settled 1713.	H, S	
Lenox	1775	Berkshire	**Richmond,** Washington	Richmond (Richmont)	Settled 1750. District created from Richmond (Richmont) 1767.	B, H	N
Leominster	1740	Worcester	**Lancaster**		Settled 1653.	H, S	T
Leverett	1774	Franklin	**Sunderland**		Settled 1713.	C, H	
Lexington	1713	Middlesex	**Cambridge**		Settled 1640. Created from North Precinct of Cambridge.	H, S	D, N

MA

Town	Inc.	County	Parent Town(s)	Daughter Town(s)	Notes	VR	CR
Leyden	1809	Franklin	**Bernardston**	Bernardston	Settled 1738. District created from Bernardston 1784.	H	
Lincoln	1754	Middlesex	**Concord, Lexington, Weston**		Settled 1650.	H, S	
Littleton	1715	Middlesex	Chelmsford, Concord, Groton	Boxborough	Settled 1686. Called Nashoba to 1715.	H, S	
Longmeadow	1783	Hampden	**Springfield**	East Longmeadow, Springfield	Settled 1644.	H, R	
Lowell	1826	Middlesex	**Chelmsford**, Dracut, Tewksbury		Settled 1653.	H, S	K, N
Ludlow	1775	Hampden	**Springfield**		Settled 1751. District created from part of Springfield called Stony Hill 1774.	H	
Lunenburg	1728	Worcester	**Dorchester, Boardman's Farm, Turkey Hills, Woburn**	Fitchburg	Settled 1721.	H, P	N
Lynn	1635	Essex		Lynnfield, Nahant, Reading, Saugus, Swampscott	Settled 1629. Called Saugus to Lynn 1637.	H, S	
Lynnfield	1814	Essex	Lynn		Settled 1638. District established 1782.	H, S	N
Malden	1649	Middlesex	Charlestown, Medford	Everett, Malden, Medford, Melrose, Reading	Settled 1640.	H, S	
Manchester-by-the-Sea	1645	Essex	Salem		Settled 1629. Created from part of Salem called Jeffryes Creek. Called Manchester to 1990.	H, S	
Mansfield	1775	Bristol	**Norton**		Settled 1659. District created 1770.	H, S	
Marblehead	1649	Essex			Settled 1629. Called Marble Harbor to 1635.	H, P, S	
Marion	1852	Plymouth	**Rochester**		Settled 1679.	H	
Marlborough	1660	Middlesex	Framingham, Southborough	Berlin, Bolton, Hudson, Northborough, Southborough, Westborough	Settled 1657.	H, S	T

Town	Inc.	County	Parent Town(s)	Daughter Town(s)	Notes	VR	CR
Marshfield	1640	Plymouth	Scituate	Pembroke	Settled 1632. Called Rexhame as well as Marshfield. Renamed Marshfield 1643.	H, P	
Mashpee	1870	Barnstable	Sandwich	Falmouth, Sandwich	Settled 1660. District created from "lands belonging to the Indians" 1763. Plantation of Marshpee created 1788.	H	
Mattapoisett	1857	Plymouth	**Rochester**		Settled 1750.		N
Maynard	1871	Middlesex	**Stow, Sudbury**		Settled 1638.	H	
Medfield	1651	Norfolk	**Dedham**	Medway	Settled 1649. Established from Dedham Village 1650.	H, S	
Medford	1630	Middlesex	Charlestown, Everett, Malden	Malden, Winchester	Settled by 1630.	H, S	N
Medway	1713	Norfolk	Holliston, **Medfield,** Wrentham	Franklin, Holliston, Millis, Norfolk	Settled 1657.	H, S	
Melrose	1850	Middlesex	**Malden,** Stoneham		Settled 1629.		
Mendon	1667	Worcester	Uxbridge	Bellingham, Blackston, Milford, Upton, Uxbridge	Settled 1660. Originally Qunshapage. Parts of Uxbridge reannexed in 1770.	H, S	
Merrimac	1876	Essex	Amesbury		Settled 1638.		
Methuen	1725	Essex	**Haverhill,** Lawrence	Lawrence	Settled 1642.	H, S	N
Middleborough	1669	Plymouth		Halifax, Lakeville, Plympton	Settled 1660. Originally Namassaket. Renamed Middleborough 1669.	H, P	N
Middlefield	1783	Hampshire	**Becket, Chester, Partridgefield (Peru), Prescott's Grant, Washington, Worthington**		Settled 1780.	H, S	
Middleton	1728	Essex	**Andover, Boxford, Salem, Topsfield**		Settled 1659.	H, S	
Milford	1780	Worcester	**Mendon**	Hopedale	Settled 1662.	H, S	N
Millbury	1813	Worcester	Auburn (Ward), **Sutton**		Settled 1716.	H, S	
Millis	1885	Norfolk	**Medway**		Settled 1657.	H	

MA

Town	Inc.	County	Parent Town(s)	Daughter Town(s)	Notes	VR	CR
Millville	1916	Worcester	**Blackstone**		Settled 1662.		
Milton	1662	Norfolk	**Dorchester**	Hyde Park	Settled 1636. Created from part of Dorchester called Uncataguisset	S	
Monroe	1822	Franklin	**Rowe**		Settled 1800.	H, F	
Monson	1775	Hampden	**Brimfield**		Settled 1715. District created 1760.	C, F	
Montague	1775	Franklin	**Sunderland**	Wendell	Settled 1715. District created 1754.	H, S	
Monterey	1847	Berkshire	New Marlborough, Sandisfield, **Tyringham**		Settled 1739.	H, T	
Montgomery	1780	Hampden	**Westfield, Huntington (Norwich), Southampton**	Russell	Settled 1767. Created from part of Westfield called "New Addition" and parts of Norwich and Southampton.	H, S	
Mount Washington	1779	Berkshire			Settled 1692. Created from plantation called Tauconnuck Mountain.	H	
Nahant	1853	Essex	**Lynn**		Settled 1630.	H, T	
Nantucket	1671	Nantucket			Settled 1641. Originally called Sherburn and part of New York Province. Differs from Sherborn/ Sherburn, Middlesex County (q.v.). Island of Nantucket granted to Massachusetts Bay 1692. Renamed Nantucket 1795.	H, S	N
Natick	1781	Middlesex	Needham, Sherborn	Framingham	Settled by 1650 as Indian plantation. District created 1762.	H, S	
Needham	1711	Norfolk	**Dedham**	Natick, Wellesley	Settled 1680.	H, N, P	N, T
New Ashford	1835	Berkshire	Hancock	Cheshire	Settled 1762. District created 1781.	H, S	
New Bedford	1787	Bristol	Acushnet, **Dartmouth**	Fairhaven	Settled 1640.	H, S	N, T
New Braintree	1775	Worcester	**Brookfield, Hardwick**	Brookfield, Hardwick	Settled 1709. District created 1751.	H, S	
New Marlborough	1775	Berkshire		Monterey, Tyringham	Settled 1738. District created from plantation of New Marlborough 1759.	B, H	

Town	Inc.	County	Parent Town(s)	Daughter Town(s)	Notes	VR	CR
New Salem	1775	Franklin	Enfield, Greenwich, Prescott, Shutesbury	Athol, Orange, Prescott	Settled 1737. District created 1753.	H,S	
Newbury	1635	Essex		Newburyport, West Newbury (Parsons)	Settled 1635. Originally Wessacucuon. Renamed Newbury 1635.	S	N
Newburyport	1764	Essex	Newbury		Settled 1635.	H, S	
Newton	1691	Middlesex	Boston, **Cambridge**	Roxbury, Waltham	Settled 1639. Formed from parts of Cambridge called Cambridge Village and New Cambridge.	H, S	N
Norfolk	1870	Norfolk	**Franklin, Medway, Walpole, Wrentham**		Settled 1795.		
North Adams	1878	Berkshire	**Adams**		Settled 1737.		
North Andover	1855	Essex	**Andover**	Lawrence	Settled 1644.	H	
North Attleborough	1887	Bristol	**Attleborough**		Settled 1669.		F
North Brookfield	1812	Worcester	**Brookfield**	Brookfield	Settled 1664.	H	
North Reading	1853	Middlesex	**Reading**		Settled 1651.		
Northampton	1656	Hampshire	Hadley	Easthampton, Holyoke, Southampton, Westhampton	Settled 1654.	C,H	N
Northborough	1775	Worcester	Marlborough, **Westborough**		Settled 1672. District created 1766.	H, S	N
Northbridge	1775	Worcester	Sutton, **Uxbridge**	Sutton, Uxbridge	Settled 1704. District created 1772.	H, S	
Northfield	1723	Franklin		Erving, Gill	Settled 1673. Plantation at Squakeag granted 1714, to be called Northfield.	C, H	
Norton	1711	Bristol	Stoughton, **Taunton**	Easton, Mansfield	Settled 1669. Created from North Precinct of Taunton. Also called the North Purchase.	H, S	N
Norwell	1849	Plymouth	**Scituate**		Settled 1634. Called South Scituate to 1888.	H, T	
Norwood	1872	Norfolk	**Dedham, Walpole**		Settled 1678.	T	
Oak Bluffs	1880	Dukes	**Edgartown**		Settled 1642. Called Cottage City to 1907.	T	

Town	Inc.	County	Parent Town(s)	Daughter Town(s)	Notes	VR	CR
Oakham	1775	Worcester	**Rutland**		Settled 1749. District created 1762.	H, S	N
Orange	1810	Franklin	**Athol, Erving-shire Tract,** New Salem, **Royalston, Warwick**	Athol	Settled 1746. District created 1783.	H	
Orleans	1797	Barnstable	**Eastham**	Eastham	Settled 1693.	H, M, P	
Otis	1773	Berkshire	District of Bethleham, East Eleven Thousand Acres, **Tyringham Equivalent**	Becket	Settled 1735. Called Loudon to 1810.	H, S	
Oxford	1693	Worcester	Charlton, Oxford North Gore, Oxford South Gore, Sutton.	Auburn (Ward), Charlton, Dudley, Webster	Settled 1687.	H, S	
Palmer	1775	Hampden	Brimfield, The Elbows Plantation, Warren (Western)	Ware	Settled 1727. District created from plantation called "The Elbows" 1752. Also called Kingsfield.	H, S	
Paxton	1775	Worcester	Holden, **Leicester, Rutland**	Holden	Settled 1749. District created 1765.	C, H, P	
Peabody	1855	Essex	**Danvers**	Salem	Settled 1626. Called South Danvers to 1868.	H	
Pelham	1743	Hampshire	Belchertown, Enfield, **New Lisburn**	Prescott	Settled 1738. Originally tract of land called New Lisburn.	H,S	
Pembroke	1712	Plymouth	**Duxbury**	Halifax, Hanson, Kingston	Settled 1650. Formed from part of Duxbury called Mattakeeset.	H, S	N, W
Pepperell	1775	Middlesex	**Groton**	Groton	Settled 1720. District created 1753 formerly known as Second Precinct of Groton.	H, P	
Peru	1771	Berkshire	**Plantation No. 2**	Hinsdale, Middlefield	Settled 1767. Called Partridgefield to 1806.	H, S	
Petersham	1754	Worcester	Dana, Greenwich, **Nichewoag Plantation,** Prescott	Dana	Settled 1733.	H, S	
Phillipston	1786	Worcester	**Athol, Templeton**	Athol, Royalston, Templeton	Settled 1751. Called Gerry to 1814.	H, S	

Town	Inc.	County	Parent Town(s)	Daughter Town(s)	Notes	VR	CR
Pittsfield	1761	Berkshire	**Poontoosuck Plantation**		Settled 1752.	B,H	
Plainfield	1807	Hampshire	**Cummington,** Hawley		Settled 1770. District created from Cummington 1785.	B, H	
Plainville	1905	Norfolk	**Wrentham**		Settled 1661.		
Plymouth	1620	Plymouth		Kingston, Plympton, Wareham	Settled 1620.	H, P	K, W
Plympton	1707	Plymouth	Middleborough, **Plymouth**	Carver, Halifax, Kingston	Settled 1662.	H, S	N
Princeton	1771	Worcester	Hubbardston, **Rutland,** Westminster		Settled 1743. District created from Rutland 1759.	H, S	
Provincetown	1727	Barnstable	**Precinct of Cape Cod,** Truro		Settled 1700.	D, H	
Quincy	1792	Norfolk	**Braintree,** Dorchester, Milton	Milton	Settled 1625.	H, N	T
Randolph	1793	Norfolk	**Braintree**	Avon, Holbrook	Settled 1710.	H, N	N
Raynham	1731	Bristol	**Taunton**		Settled 1652.	H, R, P	N
Reading	1644	Middlesex	**Lynn,** Malden, Wakefield (South Reading)	North Reading, Stoneham, Wakefield (South Reading), Wilmington	Settled 1639. Created from part of Lynn called Lynn Village.	H, S	K
Rehoboth	1645	Bristol	Barrington	Attleborough, Seekonk, Swansea (Wannamoisett)	Settled 1636. Called Seacunck to 1645. The western part of Barrington that remained in Mass. after town was ceded to R.I. 1747 was annexed to Rehoboth.	P	N
Revere	1846	Suffolk	**Chelsea**	Winthrop	Settled 1630. Called North Chelsea to 1871.		K
Richmond	1765	Berkshire	Lenox, **Mount Ephraim, Yokum Town**	Lenox	Settled 1760. Called Richmont to 1785.	H, S	N
Rochester	1686	Plymouth		Fairhaven, Marion, Mattapoisett, Wareham	Settled 1638. Also called Scippian before 1686.	H, S	N, W
Rockland	1874	Plymouth	**Abington,** Hanover	Hanover	Settled 1673.		
Rockport	1840	Essex	**Gloucester**		Settled 1623.	H, S	N

MA

Town	Inc.	County	Parent Town(s)	Daughter Town(s)	Notes	VR	CR
Rowe	1785	Franklin	**Myrifield,** Zoar Plantation	Monroe	Settled 1762.	C, H	
Rowley	1639	Essex	Ipswich	Boxford, Georgetown	Settled 1638.	H, S	
Royalston	1765	Worcester	Athol, Gerry, **Royalshire**	Orange, Winchendon	Settled 1762.	H, S	
Russell	1792	Hampden	**Montgomery, Westfield**		Settled 1782.	C, H	
Rutland	1714	Worcester		Barre (Rutland District), Hubbardston, Oakham, Paxton, Princeton	Settled 1686.	H, S	
Salem	1626	Essex	Peabody (South Danvers)	Beverly, Danvers, Manchester-by-the-Sea (Manchester), Marblehead, Middleton, Swampscott	Settled 1626.	H, S	K, N
Salisbury	1639	Essex		Amesbury (Salisbury New Town)	Settled 1638. Called Colechester to 1640.	H, S	
Sandisfield	1762	Berkshire	East Eleven Thousand Acres, **Plantation No. Three,** District of Southfield		Settled 1750.	H, S	
Sandwich	1638	Barnstable	Mashpee	Barnstable, Bourne, Mashpee	Settled 1630.	H, P	N
Saugus	1815	Essex	Chelsea, **Lynn**	Wakefield	Settled 1630.	H, S	
Savoy	1797	Berkshire	**Plantation No. Six**		Settled 1777.	C, H	
Scituate	1633	Plymouth		Cohasset, Hanover, Marshfield, Norwell (South Scituate)	Settled 1630.	H, S	K
Seekonk	1812	Bristol	Pawtucket, R.I.; **Rehoboth**	East Providence, R.I.; Pawtucket, R.I.	Settled 1636.	A, H	A
Sharon	1765	Norfolk	Foxborough, **Stoughton**	Foxborough, Walpole	Settled 1650. Called Stoughtonham to 1783.	H, S	
Sheffield	1733	Berkshire	**Houssa-t[oa]nn[o]ck**	Egremont, Great Barrington, New Marlborough	Settled 1726.	B, H, N	N

Town	Inc.	County	Parent Town(s)	Daughter Town(s)	Notes	VR	CR
Shelburne	1775	Franklin	**Deerfield**	Conway	Settled 1756. District created 1768.	H, S	
Sherborn	1674	Middlesex	Natick	Framingham, Natick	Settled 1652. Also spelled Sherburn to 1852. Different from the Sherburn that became Nantucket 1795 (q.v.).	H, S	
Shirley	1775	Middlesex	**Groton**	Ayer	Settled 1720. District created 1753.	H, S	
Shrewsbury	1727	Worcester	Lancaster	Boylston, Grafton, Lancaster, Westborough	Settled 1722.	H, S	
Shutesbury	1761	Franklin	**Roadtown Plantation**	New Salem, Wendell	Settled 1735.	C, H	
Somerset	1790	Bristol	Dighton, **Swansea**		Settled 1677. Created from part of Swansea called Shewamet Purchase.	H	
Somerville	1842	Middlesex	**Charlestown**		Settled 1630.	H	N
South Hadley	1775	Hampshire	**Hadley**	Granby	Settled 1659. District created 1753.	C, H	
Southampton	1775	Hampshire	**Northampton**	Easthampton, Montgomery	Settled 1732. District created 1753.	C, H	D, N
South-borough	1727	Worcester	Framingham, **Marlborough**	Marlborough	Settled 1660.	H, S	
Southbridge	1816	Worcester	**Charlton, Dudley, Sturbridge**		Settled 1730.	H, P	
Southwick	1775	Hampden	**Westfield**		Settled 1770.	H	
Spencer	1775	Worcester	**Leicester**		Settled 1721. District created 1753.	H, S	
Springfield	1636	Hampden		Chicopee, Longmeadow, Ludlow, West Springfield, Westfield, Wilbraham	Settled 1636.	C, H P, R	K
Sterling	1781	Worcester	**Lancaster**	West Boylston	Settled 1720.	H, P	
Stockbridge	1739	Berkshire		Great Barrington, West Stockbridge	Settled 1734. Created from the "Indian Town on the Hoosatunnock River."	H, N	
Stoneham	1725	Middlesex	**Charlestown,** Malden, Reading, Woburn	Melrose, Wakefield	Settled 1645.	H, S	N

Town	Inc.	County	Parent Town(s)	Daughter Town(s)	Notes	VR	CR
Stoughton	1726	Norfolk	**Dorchester**	Avon, Bridgewater, Canton, Dedham, Norton, Sharon (Stoughtonham), Wrentham, Walpole	Settled 1713.	H, P	
Stow	1683	Middlesex	**Plantation of Pomposittlcut,** Sudbury	Boxborough, Harvard, Hudson, Maynard	Settled 1681.	H, S	
Sturbridge	1738	Worcester	Charlton, Middlesex Gore	Southbridge	Settled 1729. Created from tract of land called New Medfield.	H, P, S	N
Sudbury	1639	Middlesex		Maynard, Stow, Wayland (East Sudbury)	Settled 1638.	H, S	N
Sunderland	1714	Franklin		Leverett, Montague	Settled 1713. Originally settled by inhabitants of Hadley 1673. Called Swampfield to 1718.	C, H	
Sutton	1714	Worcester		Auburn (Ward), Grafton, Millbury, Northbridge, Oxford, Upton, Westborough	Settled 1704.	H, S	
Swampscott	1852	Essex	**Lynn**, Salem		Settled 1629.		
Swansea	1667	Bristol	Barrington, R.I.; **Rehoboth**	Barrington, R.I.	Settled 1667. Called Wannamoisett to 1668. The eastern part of Barrington that remained in Mass. after town was ceded to R.I. 1747 was annexed to Swansea.	P	F, N
Taunton	1639	Bristol		Berkley, Dighton, Norton, Raynham	Settled 1638.	H, S	F, N
Templeton	1762	Worcester	**Narragansett Plantation No. Six,** Phillipston	Gardner, Phillipston	Settled 1751.	H, S	
Tewksbury	1734	Middlesex	**Billerica**	Lowell	Settled 1637.	H, S	
Tisbury	1671	Dukes		West Tisbury	Settled 1660.	H, S	
Tolland	1810	Hampden	Granville		Settled 1750.	H, U	
Topsfield	1650	Essex	**Ipswich**	Middleton, Lawrence, North Andover	Settled 1635. Originally settled by 1648 as "the village at the new meadows at Ipswich."	H, S	

MA

Town	Inc.	County	Parent Town(s)	Daughter Town(s)	Notes	VR	CR
Townsend	1732	Middlesex	**Turkey Hills**	Ashby	Settled 1676.	H, P	
Truro	1709	Barnstable		Provincetown (Precinct of Cape Cod)	Settled 1700. Created from tract of land called Pawmett.	H, S	N
Tyngsbor-ough	1809	Middlesex	**Dunstable**		Settled 1661. District created 1789.	H, S	
Tyringham	1762	Berkshire	Plantation No. One		Settled 1735.	H, S	
Upton	1735	Worcester	**Hopkinton, Mendon. Sutton, Uxbridge**	Westborough	Settled 1728.	H, S	
Uxbridge	1727	Worcester	Douglas (New Sherburn), **Mendon**	Mendon, Upton, Uxbridge	Settled 1662.	H, S	
Wakefield	1812	Middlesex	**Reading**, Stoneham	Reading	Settled 1639. Called South Reading to 1868.	H, S	N
Wales	1775	Hampden	**Brimfield**	Holland	Settled 1726. District created 1762. Called South Brimfield to 1828.	C, H	
Walpole	1724	Norfolk	**Dedham**, Foxborough, Sharon, Stoughton	Dedham, Foxborough, Norfolk, Norwood	Settled 1659.	H, S	
Waltham	1738	Middlesex	Cambridge, Newton, **Watertown**	Belmont	Settled 1634.	H, S	
Ware	1775	Hampshire	Brookfield, Enfield, Greenwich, **Palmer, Ware River Parish**		Settled 1717. Ware River Parish created 1750. District created 1761.	C, H	
Wareham	1739	Plymouth	**Agawam Plantation**, Carver, Plymouth, Rochester		Settled 1678.	H, M, P	K
Warren	1742	Worcester	**Brimfield, Brookfield, Palmer (Kingsfield)**	Palmer, Ware	Settled 1664. Called Western to 1834.	H, S	
Warwick	1763	Franklin		Orange	Settled 1739. Formerly Roxbury-Canada plantation.	C, H	
Washington	1777	Berkshire		Lee, Lenox, Middlefield	Settled 1760. Formerly Hartwood plantation.	H, S	

Town	Inc.	County	Parent Town(s)	Daughter Town(s)	Notes	VR	CR
Watertown	1630	Middlesex		Belmont, Cambridge, Waltham, Weston	Settled 1630.	H, P	N
Wayland	1780	Middlesex	Sudbury		Settled 1638. Called East Sudbury to 1835.	H, S	
Webster	1832	Worcester	**Dudley, Oxford**		Settled 1713.	H, P	
Wellesley	1881	Norfolk	**Needham**		Settled 1660.		
Wellfleet	1763	Barnstable	**Eastham**		Settled 1724.	H, N	N
Wendell	1781	Franklin	**Ervingshire,** Montague, **Shutesbury**		Settled 1754.	H	
Wenham	1643	Essex			Settled 1635.	H, S	K, N
West Boylston	1808	Worcester	**Boylston, Holden, Sterling**		Settled 1642.	H, S	
West Bridgewater	1822	Plymouth	**Bridgewater**	Brockton (North Bridgewater)	Settled 1651.	H, S	
West Brookfield	1848	Worcester	**Brookfield**		Settled 1664.	H	
West Newbury	1819	Essex	**Newbury**		Settled 1635. Called Parsons to 1820.	H, S	
West Springfield	1774	Hampden	**Springfield,** Westfield	Agawam, Holyoke	Settled 1660.	H, S	K
West Stockbridge	1775	Berkshire	**Stockbridge**	Alford	Settled 1766. District created 1774.	H, S	N
West Tisbury	1892	Dukes	**Tisbury**		Settled 1669.	T	
Westborough	1717	Worcester	**Marlborough,** Shrewsbury, Sutton, Upton	Northborough	Settled 1675. Created from part of Marlborough called Chauncey.	H, S	
Westfield	1669	Hampden	**Springfield**	Montgomery, Russell, Southwick, West Springfield	Settled 1660. Created from part of Springfield called Woronoake.	C, H	N, W
Westford	1729	Middlesex	**Chelmsford,** Groton		Settled 1635.	H, S	
Westhampton	1778	Hampshire	**Northampton**		Settled 1762.	C, H	
Westminster	1770	Worcester	Fitchburg, **Narragansett Township No. 2**	Ashburnham, Fitchburg, Gardner, Princeton	Settled 1737. District created 1759.	H, S	

MA

Town	Inc.	County	Parent Town(s)	Daughter Town(s)	Notes	VR	CR
Weston	1713	Middlesex	**Watertown**	Lincoln	Settled 1642. Created from part of Watertown called The Farms.	S	
Westport	1787	Bristol	**Dartmouth**		Settled 1670.	H, S	T
Westwood	1897	Norfolk	**Dedham**		Settled 1640.		
Weymouth	1635	Norfolk			Settled 1630. Called Wessaguscus to 1635.	H, S	N
Whately	1771	Franklin	Deerfield, **Hatfield**		Settled 1672.	H, P	N
Whitman	1875	Plymouth	**Abington**, Brockton, **East Bridgewater**	Brockton	Settled 1670. Called South Abington to 1886.		
Wilbraham	1763	Hampden	**Springfield**	Hampden	Settled 1730.	C, D, H	T
Williamsburg	1775	Hampshire	**Hatfield**		Settled 1735. District created 1771.	H	
Williamstown	1765	Berkshire	West Hoosuck Plantation		Settled 1749.	H, S	
Wilmington	1730	Middlesex	Billerica, **Reading, Woburn**		Settled 1639.	S	
Winchendon	1764	Worcester	Gardner, **Ipswich-Canada,** Royalston	Gardner	Settled 1753. Created from Ipswich-Canada.	H, S	
Winchester	1850	Middlesex	**Medford, West Cambridge, Woburn**	Woburn	Settled 1640.	C	
Windsor	1771	Berkshire	Cheshire, **Plantation No. 4,** Plantation No. 5	Cheshire, Dalton	Settled 1767. Called Gageborough to 1778.	H, S	
Winthrop	1852	Suffolk	**Revere (North Chelsea)**		Settled 1635.	C	
Woburn	1642	Middlesex	**Charlestown**, Winchester	Burlington, Lunenburg, Stoneham, Wilmington, Winchester	Settled 1640. Originally Charlestown Village. Parts of Winchester annexed 1873.	P	
Worcester	1684	Worcester	Grafton Gore, Leicester	Auburn (Ward), Holden	Settled 1673. Created from Quansigamond plantation.	H, S	K, N, W

Town	Inc.	County	Parent Town(s)	Daughter Town(s)	Notes	VR	CR
Worthington	1768	Hampshire	Chester, **Plantation No. 3**	Middlefield	Settled 1764. Created from Plantation No. 3. Parts of Chester annexed 1799.	H, S	
Wrentham	1673	Norfolk	Stoughton	Bellingham, Foxborough, Franklin, Medway, Norfolk, Plainville	Settled 1669. Established from Wollonopaug 1673.	H, S	
Yarmouth	1639	Barnstable		Dennis	Settled 1639.	H, S	N

Ceded or Extinct Towns and Districts

The following towns were annexed to other towns or ceded to other states or are extinct because they were "drowned" by the Quabbin Reservoir. For more information about towns ceded to neighboring states, see the town lists in the relevant chapters.

Town	Inc.	County	Parent Town(s)	Daughter Town(s)	Notes	VR	CR
Barrington	1714	Bristol	**Swansea**	Rehoboth, Swansea	Part of Barrington ceded to R.I. 1747. Part that remained in Mass. annexed to Rehoboth and Swansea.	A	D, N
District of Bethlehem	1789	Berkshire	**North Eleven Thousand Acres**		Annexed to Loudon (Otis) 1809.	H	
Boston Corner District	1838	Berkshire			Ceded to New York 1853.		
Bradford	1675	Essex			Annexed to Haverhill 1897.	H, S	
Brighton	1807	Suffolk	**Cambridge**		Annexed to Boston 1874.	H	
Bristol	1681	Bristol			Originally settled as Mount Hope by 1679. Renamed Bristol by 1681. Ceded to Rhode Island 1747.	A	
Charlestown	1630	Middlesex	Cambridge, Medford	Abington (West Cambridge), Cambridge, Malden, Medford, Somerville, Stoneham	Settled 1630. Annexed to Boston 1873.	H, P	K, N
Dana	1801	Worcester	**Greenwich, Hardwick, Petersham**	Petersham	One of the "drowned towns" disbanded to form Quabbin Reservoir. Surviving area annexed to Petersham 1850.	H, S	

Town	Inc.	County	Parent	Daughter	Note	VR	CR
Dorchester	1630	Norfolk	Dedham	Boston, Hyde Park, Milton, Stoughton, Lunenburg, Quincy	Originally settled as Mattapan. Annexed to Boston 1870.	H, P	D, K, N
Enfield	1683	Worcester			Ceded to Connecticut 1749. Different from Enfield below.		
Enfield	1816	Hampshire	**Belchertown, Greenwich**	Greenwich	One of the "drowned towns" disbanded to form Quabbin Reservoir. Surviving area annexed to Belchertown, New Salem, Pelham, and Ware 1927 (amended 1938). Different from Enfield above.	C, H	
Greenwich	1754	Hampshire	Belchertown, Hardwick, **Quabin Plantation**	Dana, Enfield	Originally settled as Quabin Plantation. One of the "drowned towns" disbanded to form Quabbin Reservoir. Surviving area annexed to Hardwick, New Salem, Pelham, and Ware 1927 (amended 1938).	D, H, N	
Hyde Park	1868	Suffolk	**Dedham, Dorchester, Milton**		Settled 1630. Annexed to Boston 1911.	H	
Litchfield	1734	Middlesex	**Dunstable**		Ceded to New Hampshire 1740.		
Little Compton	1682	Bristol	**Dartmouth**		Established from part of Dartmouth called Saconnett/Sakonnett. Ceded to Rhode Island 1747.		
Nottingham	1733	Middlesex	**Dunstable**		Ceded to New Hampshire 1740.		
Pawtucket	1828	Bristol	Seekonk		Ceded to R.I. 1862.	A, W	A, T, W
Prescott	1822	Hampshire	**New Salem, Pelham**		One of the "drowned towns" disbanded to form Quabbin Reservoir. Surviving area annexed to New Salem and Petersham 1927 (amended 1938).	H, N	
Roxbury	1630	Norfolk	Newton	Boston, Brookline, West Roxbury	Settled 1630. Part of Roxbury annexed to Boston 1860. Remainder annexed to Boston 1868.	S	

MA

Town	Inc.	County	Parent	Daughter	Note	VR	CR
District of Southfield	1797	Berkshire	**South Eleven Thousand Acres**		Annexed to Sandisfield 1819.		
Suffield	1674	Worcester		Ceded to Connecticut 1749.			
Tiverton	1694	Bristol	**Dartmouth**, Freetown, Little Compton	Dartmouth	Ceded to Rhode Island 1747.	A	N
Wellington	1814	Bristol	**Dighton**	Dighton	Reannexed by Dighton 1828.		
West Roxbury	1851	Norfolk	Dedham, **Roxbury**		Settled 1630. Annexed to Boston 1874.	H	
Woodstock	1686	Worcester			Called New Roxbury to 1690. Ceded to Connecticut 1749.		
Zoar		Berkshire			Settled 1766. Unincorporated land tract. Portion west of Deerfield River incorporated as town of Florida 1805. Remaining portion annexed to Rowe and Charlemont, part of Franklin County 1838.		

"Glendale Woolen Mills." Sarah Cabot Sedgwick and Christina Sedgwick Marquand, *Stockbridge, 1739-1939: A Chronicle* (1939), facing p. 153.

New Hampshire

Introduction by David Curtis Dearborn

Since the first permanent settlement in 1623 at what is now Portsmouth, New Hampshire has been a crossroads for settlement and migration. For many years consisting of only four towns (Portsmouth, Dover, Exeter, and Hampton), New Hampshire had a small population and grew slowly.

Beginning around 1700, settlers began to trickle into the interior, augmented greatly by the migration of families from Essex and Middlesex Counties in Massachusetts. Later on, settlers from central and western Massachusetts and from Connecticut moved into southwestern New Hampshire and continued moving northward. In the 1710s and 1720s, groups of Ulster Scots arrived in New England, settling mainly in the hilly interior. In New Hampshire, their original settlement was at Londonderry, and from there they established other towns, chiefly in what are now Hillsborough and Cheshire Counties.

The boundary between Massachusetts and New Hampshire was undetermined and in dispute until it was finally surveyed and fixed in 1741. Then, between 1749 and 1764, New Hampshire Governor Benning Wentworth issued land grants for territory that was also claimed by the Province of New York—and which after the Revolution became the Republic (and later state) of Vermont. It's important for anyone with New England ancestry to be aware of these shifting state boundaries.

By the time of the American Revolution, most of New Hampshire south of the White Mountains had been settled, with descendants of the founders of the original four towns having moved north along and over the Maine border and into the Lakes Region and the Merrimack Valley. After the Revolution, migrants tended to move in four directions: many went west into Vermont, New York, or beyond; some removed to the Eastern Townships of Quebec; those in the eastern part of the state tended to move eastward into Maine; and people from all over the state (especially after the Civil War) moved to Greater Boston. Large numbers of French Canadians, from Quebec and, to a lesser extent, Acadians from the Maritime Provinces, moved south in the mid-nineteenth century to

The New Hampshire state seal.

work in the textile and lumber mills, their descendants today making up about a third of New Hampshire's population. They were joined by the Irish, Italians, and immigrants from many other countries.

New Hampshire has an undeserved reputation for being a "difficult" state in which to do research. In fact, a wealth of sources are available to the genealogist, with many now available online.

Vital Records

As in other New England states, records of births, marriages, and deaths are kept by town and city clerks, with records dating back to the earliest days of English settlement or to the establishment of the community. For a variety of reasons, records for a given town may not be complete, either because of destroyed or lost records (as in the case of those for Enfield), or laxness on the part of individual clerks or of families who failed to report vital events, especially births and deaths, that often took place at home. (New Durham is a good example.) When you cannot find a vital record, try exploring alternate or substitute records, such as church records, censuses, probate and land records, tax rolls, pensions, gravestones, and newspaper death notices.

In earlier times, it was common for vital records to be intermixed with other town business, such as selectmen's records, town meeting minutes, and tax rolls. In the absence of a sought-for vital record, examine these other town records for any mention of your ancestor's appearance or activity in the town.

Town records to about the 1840s, including vital records, have been microfilmed for most towns in the state. The New Hampshire State Library in Concord has a card index for these records; you can find copies of the films at the State Library and at NEHGS. The town of Exeter was overlooked when the index was prepared. Only a handful of New Hampshire towns have published vital records.

Beginning in the late nineteenth century, laws were passed requiring cities and towns to report vital events to the state,

STAFF PICKS

For New Hampshire Research

William Copeley, *Index to Genealogies in New Hampshire Town Histories* (Concord: New Hampshire Historical Society, 2000).

Sherry L. Gould, "New Hampshire," *A Guide to the Library of the New England Historic Genealogical Society,* Maureen A. Taylor and Henry B. Hoff, eds. (Boston: NEHGS, 2004), pp. 147–61.

John D. Haskell, Jr., and T. D. Seymour Bassett, eds., *New Hampshire: A Bibliography of Its History* (Boston: G. K. Hall, 1979).

Elmer M. Hunt, *New Hampshire Town Names and Whence They Came* (Peterborough, N.H.: Noone House, 1971).

Laird C. Towle and Ann N. Brown, *New Hampshire Genealogical Research Guide* (Bowie, Md.: Heritage Books, 1983).

but compliance was not total until the State Bureau of Vital Records was established in 1905. At that time, the state also required that town and city clerks transcribe older vital events onto cards, which were sent to Concord for central filing. Today, the cards recording births to 1900 and marriages and deaths to 1947, as well as a card index to New Hampshire divorces to 1947, can be viewed at the Division of Vital Records and Health Statistics. The cards are arranged in a peculiar and confusing manner: by the first and third letter of the last name. Thus the surname "Smith" would be filed in the "S–I" group near surnames such as Sainsbury, Shirley, Skidmore, Spinney, Stickney, and Swift. These cards have been microfilmed and made available by the Family History Library (FHL) and are also at NEHGS. Recently, the FHL digitized these cards; you can search them online at *www.Family Search.org*.

Civil unions for same-sex couples were allowed from January 1, 2008, to December 31, 2010. All civil unions not previously dissolved or annulled were converted to marriages on January 1, 2011, when same-sex marriages became legal. Births prior to 1911 and deaths, marriages, and divorces prior to 1961 have unrestricted access. Access to more recent New Hampshire births, marriages, and deaths is restricted, and you must demonstrate a direct interest in the event in order to see or purchase a copy of a record.

Since the late 1800s, each New Hampshire town has published an annual town report, with a summary of all official town business for the previous year. These reports also include somewhat abbreviated birth, marriage, and death records, although most of the state's larger cities stopped this practice many years ago and now simply publish statistical summaries. You can find copies of these town reports in local libraries and in town and city clerks' offices; a full set is at the State Library in Concord.

Probate Records

Probate records in New Hampshire are kept at the county level. For the most part, they consist of records of estates (wills and letters of administration) and guardianships. Prior to the establishment of the original five counties (Rockingham, Strafford, Hillsborough, Cheshire, and Grafton) in 1769 (with recordkeeping commencing in 1771), records were maintained at the province level. An 1887 fire destroyed all Coos County probate records up to that point.

Abstracts of all probate records from 1636 to 1771, including complete transcriptions of wills, are found in vols. 31–39 of the *New Hampshire State Papers*. NEHGS also has the original provincial probates on microfiche. Published abstracts of later records include Helen F. Evans, *Abstracts of the Probate Records of Rockingham County, NH 1771–1799* (2 vols.; Bowie, Md.: Heritage Books, 2000) and *Abstracts of the Probate Records of Strafford County, New Hampshire, 1771–1799* (Bowie, Md.: Heritage Books, 1983). There is an index to Hillsborough County probate records, 1771–1884, published by the county in 1974 (available at NEHGS).

Land Records

Although some early land conveyance records may be found in proprietors' records among town records, you will find most records of land transfer in the county registries of deeds. As with probate records, prior to the establishment of counties in New Hampshire in 1769 land conveyance records were kept on a province-wide basis. When the original five counties were created, Rockingham, being the area of the colony's original settlement, kept the earlier provincial deed books (100 volumes at that point), and continued numbering their volumes with 101, while the other four counties all commenced with volume 1. The 100 volumes of provincial deeds, along with a special card index to them that also indexes provincial probate records, is at the New Hampshire Records and Archives in Concord (microfilmed by the FHL and also available at NEHGS). Recently, Rockingham County completed the digitization of all its land records, including the provincial deeds and indexes, from the present back to 1643. You can view the indexes and images at *http://nhdeeds.com/rockingham/RoHome.html*.

In 1643, Massachusetts Bay created its original four counties, one of which was Norfolk County—not to be confused with the present–day Norfolk County, which is south of Boston. The original Norfolk County comprised the area north of the Merrimack River, including the Massachusetts towns of Salisbury and Haverhill, as well as the four New Hampshire towns of Portsmouth, Dover, Exeter, and Hampton. (See p. 194.) The latter two towns, having been settled only four years earlier by religious refugees from the Bay Colony, went along with this arrangement. Portsmouth and Dover, however, had existed as independent entities since the 1620s, having been established directly from England by private groups with their own patents; consequently, they ignored the new ruling. In 1679, New Hampshire was chartered as a royal colony to include the original four towns, and at that point Salisbury and Haverhill were absorbed into Essex County in Massachusetts. Despite this, deeds continued to be recorded in Norfolk County

sporadically until 1714, and anyone with ancestors in these towns should consult those deeds. The original four volumes of Norfolk County deeds are at the Essex County Registry of Deeds in Salem, Massachusetts, and have been microfilmed by the FHL (copies at NEHGS).

Deed books are organized by grantor and grantee volumes by time period (date of recording). For some counties, the index may include the name of the town where the land is located, as well as the type of deed (i.e., warranty, quitclaim, mortgage, agreement, or power of attorney). The 1887 fire that destroyed the Coos County probate records damaged but did not destroy the deeds; they have been recopied into 33 volumes. Additionally, the Coos County registry has seven volumes of records pertaining to land conveyances going back to 1772, copied from the registry in Grafton County, from which Coos was created in 1803. Similarly, Belknap County, created in 1840 out of Strafford, has 18 volumes of deeds copied from the parent county and covering the period 1771–1843.

Researchers with ancestors who lived along the present-day New Hampshire-Massachusetts border are advised to check land records for the Massachusetts counties of Essex, Middlesex, Worcester, and Hampshire, since the boundary between the two states was not accurately determined in colonial times.

Access to deeds (except Carroll County) for the past hundred years (start date varies by county) is available online at *www.nhdeeds.com*.

Court Records

The court system exercises judicial power. The courts interpret and apply the constitution and statutes and resolve disputes between parties. Parties are either plaintiffs (those bringing suit) or defendants (those accused of wrongdoing).

The provincial court records covering the period 1638–1771 (civil cases #1–30134), along with a card index, are available at the New Hampshire Records and Archives (microfilm at NEHGS). County records of the superior courts, inferior courts of common pleas, and courts of general sessions of the peace, dealing with civil and criminal matters, are found in the individual counties. Some of these records from the colonial period, into the nineteenth century, have been microfilmed by the FHL.

As mentioned earlier, the Division of Vital Records and Health Statistics has an index to New Hampshire divorces from the 1870s to 1947; the records themselves can be found in the county superior courts. For information on earlier records, see Sheldon S. Cohen, "What Man Hath Put Asunder: Divorce in New Hampshire, 1681–1784," *Historical New Hampshire* 41 (1986): 118–41.

Naturalizations prior to 1906 could take place in any court of record, including U.S. District and Superior Courts. Like other New England states, New Hampshire has a consolidated index to naturalizations, 1791–1906, arranged in Soundex order. Dexigraph copies of the original petitions and certificates are at the National Archives Northeast Region in Waltham, Massachusetts.

For name changes, see David Paul Davenport, "Name Changes in New Hampshire, 1679–1883," *Genealogical Journal* 15 (1986): 67–103, 213–48; and Richard P. Roberts, *New Hampshire Name Changes, 1768–1923* (Bowie, Md.: Heritage Books, 1996).

Compilations

William Copeley, *New Hampshire Family Records* (Bowie, Md.: Heritage Books, 1994).

The New Hampshire Genealogical Record (New Hampshire Society of Genealogists, 1903–10, 1990–present).

New Hampshire, *Provincial and State Papers. Miscellaneous Documents and Records Relating to New Hampshire*, 40 vols. (Concord, N.H.: G. E. Jenks, State Printer, 1867–1943).

Sybil Noyes, Charles Thornton Libby, and Walter Goodwin Davis, *Genealogical Dictionary of Maine and New Hampshire* (1928–39; rpt. Baltimore: Genealogical Publishing Co., 1976; rpt. Boston: NEHGS, 2012).

Charles Henry Pope, *The Pioneers of Maine and New Hampshire, 1623 to 1660: A Descriptive List, Drawn from Records of the Colonies, Towns, Churches, Courts, and Other Contemporary Sources* (Boston: C. H. Pope, 1908).

NH

Military Records

New Hampshire has extensive military records dating back to the seventeenth century, many of them published. Volumes 5, 6, 14, and 17 of the *State Papers* contain records of those who served in the French and Indian Wars. Volumes 14–17 contain documents relating to those who served in the Revolution. Although not a military record *per se*, the Association Test list published in volume 30 is important because it lists, town by town, those men who signed the oath in 1776 to support the Revolutionary cause— as well as those who refused to sign, either for religious or ethical reasons or because they supported the other side. Note that not all towns' lists survive. Volume 30 also contains records relating to the War of 1812 and lists of that war's pensioners for the first half of the nineteenth century. The New Hampshire Historical Society in Concord has a multivolume typescript abstract of all Revolutionary War pension applications from New Hampshire; this has been microfilmed and a copy is at NEHGS.

Other lists, especially for the colonial wars, War of 1812, and early nineteenth century, can be found in Chandler E. Potter, *The Military History of New-Hampshire* (Concord and Manchester, 1866–69; rpt. Baltimore: GPC, 1972).

For the Civil War, consult Augustus D. Ayling, *Revised Register of the Soldiers and Sailors of New Hampshire in the War of the Rebellion, 1861–1866* (Concord: Ira C. Evans, 1895).

Church Records

In many denominations ecclesiastical records were considered the property of the minister. Thus they would leave the church when the minister left, and they may be located far distant from the New Hampshire town in which the events occurred.

The Historical Records Survey published several useful guides to existing church records: *Guide to Church Vital Statistics Records in New Hampshire* (Manchester: Historical Records Survey, 1942); *Inventory of the Church Archives of New Hampshire: Protestant Episcopal* (Manchester: Historical Records Survey, 1942); and *Inventory of the Roman Catholic Church Records in New Hampshire* (Manchester: Historical Records Survey, 1938). A good overview of two of the state's major Protestant denominations is Robert F. Lawrence's *The New Hampshire Churches: Comprising Histories of the Congregational and Presbyterian Churches in the State, with Notices of Other Denominations* (Claremont, N.H., 1856).

The New Hampshire Historical Society's library has a large collection of original church records and transcriptions. For particulars, see William N. Copeley, "Church Records at the New Hampshire Historical Society," *Historical New Hampshire* 39 (1984): 152–59, or check the Society's online catalog at *http://nhhistory.library.net/* for the town of interest.

NEHGS continues to add church records to its lists of databases. As of this writing, church records for the towns of Boscawen (Second Church of Christ, 1804–83); Campton

(First Congregational Church, 1800–74); East Kingston, 1738–92; Kingston (Second Church of Christ); Lyme (Congregational Church); and Nottingham West [Hudson] (First Church of Christ, 1737–95) may be searched by members online at *AmericanAncestors.org*.

For those tracing New Hampshire–born ministers from colonial times to the mid-nineteenth century, an excellent source is Nathan F. Carter, *The Native Ministry of New Hampshire* (Concord: Rumford Printing, 1906), which contains thousands of short biographies, arranged by town of origin, with indexes by both name and denomination.

Above: "On the Death of Ambrose Abel of Goshen." Reminiscences of Alfred Abell (1772–1859), Selina Fletcher Little Collection (R. Stanton Avery Special Collections, NEHGS, Mss 935).

Other Records

Cemetery Records

The New Hampshire Historical Society's library has a good collection of copied New Hampshire cemetery records. Details are given in William N. Copeley, "A List of Cemetery Records in the New Hampshire Historical Society," *Historical New Hampshire* 30 (1975): 244–69, updated by his "Additional Cemetery Records in the New Hampshire Historical Society," *Historical New Hampshire* 35 (1980): 75–77; more recent additions will be listed in the Society's online catalog at *http://nhhistory.library.net/*.

NEHGS also has a good and growing collection of cemetery transcriptions. Many of these are being added to the Cemetery Transcriptions database from the NEHGS Manuscript Collection, online at *American Ancestors.org*.

The New Hampshire Old Graveyard Association (NHOGA) maintains a website (*www.rootsweb.ancestry.com/~nhoga/*) that lists all known burial sites in the state, arranged both by town and by name of cemetery, and listing for each its GPS coordinates and location on the USGS topographical quadrangle maps. It does not list the names of individuals buried in the cemeteries.

Photographs of gravestones for a number of cemeteries in the southeastern part of the state can be found in Glenn A. Knoblock, *Images of America: Historic Burial Grounds of the New Hampshire Seacoast* (Charleston, S.C.: Arcadia Publishing, 1999) and online at *http://gravematter.com*.

Maps

New Hampshire is well covered by both modern and historical maps and atlases. An indispensable guide to the earlier items is David A. Cobb, *New Hampshire Maps to 1900: An Annotated Checklist* (Hanover: New Hampshire Historical Society, 1981).

Town and City Atlas of the State of New Hampshire (Boston: D. H. Hurd, 1892) provides detailed maps of every town, showing the name of the owner of every dwelling, and includes detailed city maps. These were reprinted in the 1980s in paperback with reduced-size maps, with a separate volume for each county, by Saco Valley Printing of Fryeburg, Maine.

Historic USGS topographical maps of New Hampshire can be viewed online at *http://docs.unh.edu/nhtopos*. The NEHGS library has a large but incomplete collection of USGS sheet maps for New England, including some for New Hampshire; most were published in the late 1980s at a scale of 1:24,000.

Eighteenth-century maps of many New Hampshire towns, some showing the layout of lots and divisions with the names of their original owners, can be found sprinkled throughout the town volumes of the *State Papers*.

For anyone planning to drive New Hampshire's main streets and back roads, DeLorme's *New Hampshire Atlas & Gazetteer*, containing detailed color topographical maps of the entire state, is a must-have. You can find it in local bookstores or order it online from *http://delorme.com*.

Understanding county boundary changes is crucial for any researcher, but especially those using historical probate and land records. Gordon DenBoer with George E. Goodridge, comps., John H. Long, ed., *Atlas of Historical County Boundaries New Hampshire, Vermont* (New York: Simon & Schuster, 1993), contains detailed maps showing each such change and the date on which it occurred.

Together with maps and atlases, gazetteers should be consulted by those just learning New Hampshire's landscape. Three good gazetteers are John Hayward, *A Gazetteer of New Hampshire* ... (Boston, 1849; rpt. Bowie, Md.: Heritage Books, 1993); Eliphalet and Phinehas Merrill, *Gazetteer of the State of New–Hampshire* (Exeter, N.H.: C. Norris & Co., 1817; facsimile rpt. Bowie, Md.: Heritage Books, 1987); and Elmer M. Hunt, *New Hampshire Town Names and Whence They Came* (Peterborough, N.H.: Noone House, 1970).

Newspapers

The best collection of pre-1900 newspapers is at the New Hampshire Historical Society, while those for the period after 1900 (with some before) are available on microfilm at the New Hampshire State Library.

Marriage and death notices from a number of early New Hampshire newspapers have been collected and published. Among these are Otis G. Hammond, *Notices from the New Hampshire Gazette 1765–1800* (Lambertville, N.J.: Hunterdon House, 1970; also available online at *AmericanAncestors.org*), Scott Lee Chipman, *New England Vital Records from the Exeter News–Letter* [1831–65], 5 vols. (Camden, Me.: Picton Press, 1993–96 [N.H. Soc. of Genealogists Special Pub. Nos. 2–6]), and Scott Lee Chipman, *Genealogical Abstracts from Early New Hampshire Newspapers, Vol. 1* (Bowie, Md.: Heritage Books, 2000). This last collection includes records from six newspapers published in the late 1700s and early 1800s.

The Boston Public Library's Microtext Department has Manchester's *The Union Leader*, New Hampshire's major daily newspaper, on microfilm for the period 31 March 1863–2006.

City Directories

The best collection of New Hampshire city directories is at the New Hampshire State Library in Concord. The Boston Public Library's Microtext Department has some New Hampshire city directories on micro-film; consult the online catalog at *http://bostonpl.bibliocommons.com.*

Census Records

The U.S. Census for New Hampshire, 1790–1930, is mostly complete, with the following exceptions:

1800—*Rockingham County:* Atkinson, Greenland, Hampton, Hampton Falls, Londonderry, North Hampton, Pelham, Plaistow, Salem, Seabrook, Stratham, Windham. *Strafford County:* Alton, Barnstead, Brookfield, Effingham, Gilmanton, Middleton, New Durham, Ossipee, Tuftonboro, Wakefield, Wolfeborough. A substitute source for some of the missing Strafford County towns is John S. Fipphen, *1798 Direct Tax, New Hampshire District #13: Consisting of the Towns of Alton, Brookfield, Effingham, Middleton, New Durham, Ossipee, Tuftonboro, Wakefield, and Wolfeboro* (Bowie, Md.: Heritage Books, 1988).

1820—*Grafton County:* All. *Rockingham County:* Gosport, Greenland, New Castle, Newington, Portsmouth, Rye. *Strafford County:* All *except* Center Harbor, Gilford, Moultonborough, New Hampton, Sanbornton.

1890—All, except for the census of New Hampshire Union veterans.

As in some other New England states, the New Hampshire Society of Genealogists has begun compiling and publishing genealogical data on the families of the heads of household in the 1790 census. One volume has appeared so far: Diane Florence Gravel, CG, and David Watson Kruger, eds., *New Hampshire Families in 1790, Volume I* (Concord: New Hampshire Society of Genealogists, 2007).

Source Material and Guides

Essential for anyone researching New Hampshire history prior to 1800 is the 40-volume set known as the *State Papers*, more properly titled *Documents and Records*

Relating to New Hampshire (usually abbreviated by genealogists as *NHSP*), published by the state between 1867 and 1943. Although the volumes dealing with the Revolution (vols. 14–17 and 30) and the probate volumes (vols. 31–39) receive the most use by genealogists, the entire set is an invaluable resource for the state's early history. A volume-by-volume description is found in R. Stuart Wallace, "The State Papers? A Descriptive Guide," *Historical New Hampshire* 31 (1976): 119–28. The New Hampshire State Archives has placed these volumes online in pdf format, searchable at *www.sos.nh.gov/archives/nhstatepapers.html*. (*Warning:* each file is between 18 and 30 megabytes.) There is also a very handy every-name index (4.17 megabytes).

Sybil Noyes, Charles Thornton Libby, and Walter Goodwin Davis, *Genealogical Diction-ary of Maine and New Hampshire*, was originally published in five parts between 1928 and 1939 and has been reprinted numerous times in recent years by the Genealogical Publishing Company of Baltimore—and is now available in paperback format from NEHGS. It is an exhaustive, detailed genealogical and biographical dictionary of all known settlers in the area prior to 1699, with three generations of descendants. The *Genealogical Dictionary* may be searched online at *www.ancestry.com*.

William Copeley's *Index to Genealogies in New Hampshire Town Histories* (Concord: New Hampshire Historical Society, 1988) provides a surname index to the genealogies found in numerous town histories, mostly published in the late nineteenth or early twentieth centuries, in which families are treated for at least three generations.

"Littleton Cornet Band." James R. Jackson, *History of Littleton, New Hampshire* (1905), facing p. 454.

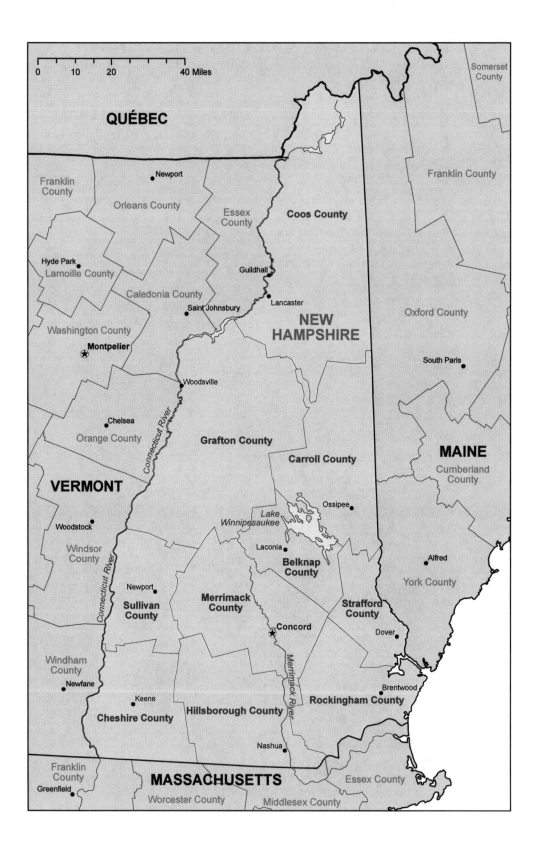

New Hampshire Repositories

The following are major repositories with large collections of materials of interest to genealogists. Check with each repository prior to visiting to obtain the most recent information about hours and access to materials in the collection.

New Hampshire Division of Archives and Records Management
71 South Fruit Street
Concord, NH 03301
www.sos.nh.gov/archives
(603) 271-2236; fax (603) 271-2272
archives@sos.state.nh.us
Hours: M–F 8:30–4

The New Hampshire Division of Archives and Records Management (NHARM) holds historical records for all branches of state government: executive, judicial, and legislative. Other materials in the collections include military records, land surveyors' records, provincial probate records, photographs, portraits, naturalizations, voter lists, and town records.

New Hampshire State Library
20 Park Street
Concord, NH 03301
www.nh.gov/nhsl
(603) 271-6823
See website for email addresses
Hours: M–F 8–4:30

With origins in 1717, the New Hampshire State Library is considered the oldest in the country. Among the resources of interest to genealogists are town and county histories, town reports, biographies, city directories, and military indexes. The New Hampshire Newspaper Project microfilmed hundreds of newspapers throughout the state.

Above: "Amoskeag Locomotive Works and 'Big Shop,' about 1855." L. Ashton Thorp, *Manchester of Yesterday* (1939), p. 84.

New Hampshire Department of State, Division of Vital Records Administration

71 South Fruit Street
Concord, NH 03301-2410
www.sos.nh.gov/vitalrecords
(603) 271-4650; fax (603) 271-3447
vitalrecords@sos.state.nh.us
Hours: M–F 8–4:30

The Division of Vital Records Administration (DVRA) houses records of births, marriages, civil unions, divorces, and deaths. On January 1, 2011, all civil unions not previously annulled or dissolved were converted to marriages. Current rules allow open access to births prior to 1911 and deaths, marriages, and divorces prior to 1961.

New Hampshire Historical Society

30 Park Street
Concord, NH 03301
www.nhhistory.org
(603) 228-6688
See website for email
Hours: Tu–Sat 9:30–5

The New Hampshire Historical Society (NHHS) was founded in 1823. Among the NHHS collections are 10,000 broadsides and ephemera items, 30,000 museum objects, 50,000 printed volumes, 200,000 photographic images, and 1.5 million pages of manuscripts. The Society has a research services team that can be hired.

New Hampshire Old Graveyard Association

PO Box 1016
Goshen, NH 03062
www.rootsweb.ancestry.com/~nhoga
See website for email

Portsmouth Athenaeum

Joseph P. Copley Research Library
6–8 Market Square
Portsmouth, NH 03801
www.portsmouthathenaeum.org
(603) 431-2538
info@portsmouthathenaeum.org
Hours: Tu, Th 1–4; Sat 10–4

The collections include both new and old books on a wide variety of subjects, including theology and local history. Special emphasis is placed on Portsmouth imprints and works related to the study of the history of the Portsmouth region. The museum presents many exhibits.

Above: "Ordway's Store, West Hampstead." Harriette Eliza Noyes, comp., *A Memorial of the Town of Hampstead, New Hampshire* (1899), after p. 32.

New Hampshire Counties

Name	Est.	Parent(s)	Probate District(s)	Deed District(s)	Note
Belknap	1840	Merrimack, Strafford	Belknap	Belknap	
Carroll	1840	Grafton, Strafford	Carroll	Carroll	
Cheshire	1769	Original County	Cheshire	Cheshire	
Coos	1803	Grafton	Coos	Coos	
Grafton	1769	Original County	Grafton	Grafton	
Hillsborough	1769	Original County	Hillsborough	Hillsborough	
Merrimack	1823	Grafton, Hillsborough, and Rockingham	Merrimack	Merrimack	
Rockingham	1769	Original County	Rockingham	Rockingham	Early provincial land and probate records filed at Rockingham.
Strafford	1769	Original County	Strafford	Strafford	
Sullivan	1827	Cheshire	Sullivan	Sullivan	

Extinct County

Name	Est.	Parent(s)	Probate District(s)	Deed District(s)	Note
Norfolk [Mass.]	1643	Original County	Norfolk	Norfolk	Abolished 1679, but recorded deeds through 1714. (See Old Norfolk County, Mass.)

Above: "The Old Man of the Mountain." Francis Chase, ed., *Gathered Sketches from the Early History of New Hampshire and Vermont* (1856), frontispiece.

NH

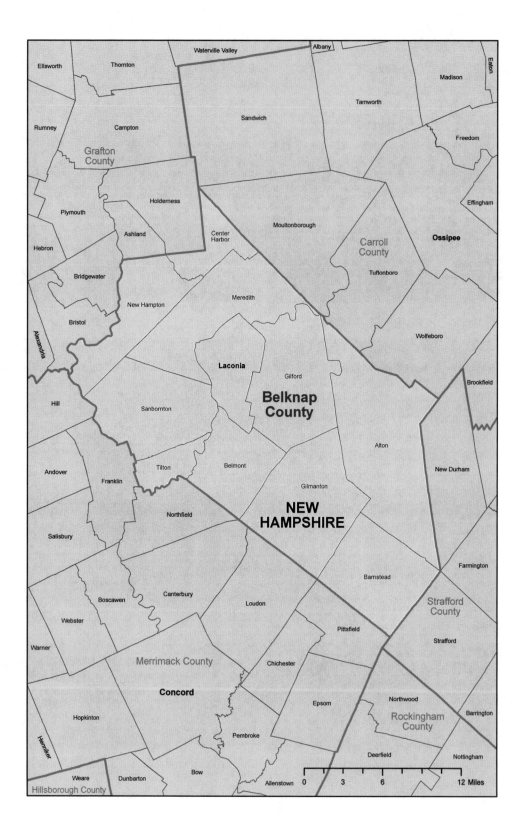

Ellsworth

Thornton

Waterville Valley

Albany

Eaton

Madison

Rumney

Campton

Sandwich

Tamworth

Grafton
County

Freedom

Plymouth

Holderness

Effingham

Hebron

Ashland

Center
Harbor

Moultonborough

Carroll
County

Ossipee

Bridgewater

Tuftonboro

New Hampton

Meredith

Bristol

Alexandria

Wolfeboro

Laconia

Gilford

Brookfield

Belknap
County

Hill

Sanbornton

Andover

Tilton

Belmont

Alton

New Durham

Franklin

Gilmanton

NEW
HAMPSHIRE

Salisbury

Northfield

Farmington

Barnstead

Strafford
County

Boscawen

Canterbury

Loudon

Webster

Pittsfield

Strafford

Warner

Merrimack County

Chichester

Concord

Northwood

Barrington

Hopkinton

Epsom

Rockingham
County

Henniker

Pembroke

Deerfield

Nottingham

Weare

Dunbarton

Bow

Allenstown

0   3   6   12 Miles

Hillsborough County

NH

Belknap County

Founded	1840
Parent Counties	Merrimack, Strafford
County Seat	Laconia

Towns

Alton, Barnstead, Belmont, Center Harbor, Gilford, Gilmanton, Laconia, Meredith, New Hampton, Sanbornton, Tilton

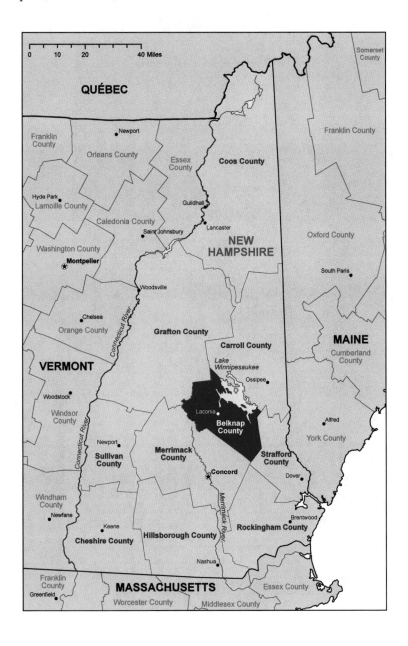

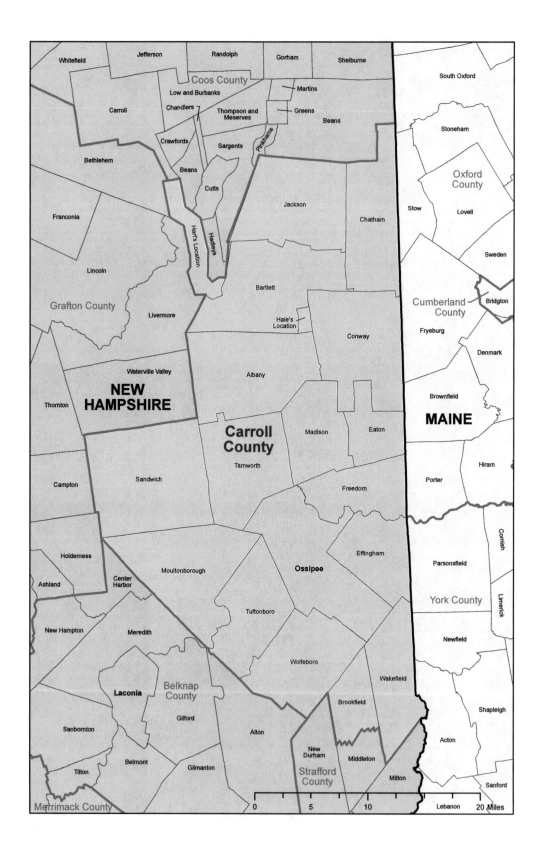

Carroll County

Founded	1840
Parent Counties	Grafton, Strafford
County Seat	Ossipee

Towns

Albany, Bartlett, Brookfield, Chatham, Conway, Eaton, Effingham, Freedom, Hart's Location, Jackson, Madison, Moultonborough, Ossipee, Sandwich, Tamworth, Tuftonboro, Wakefield, Wolfeboro

Unincorporated

Hales Location

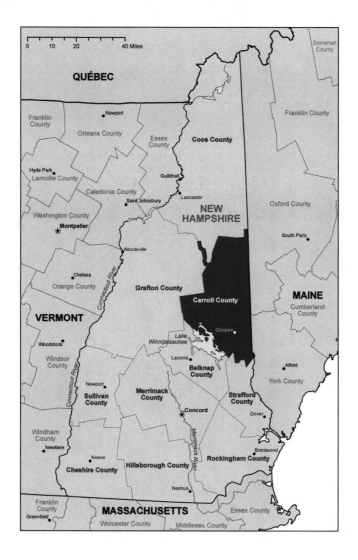

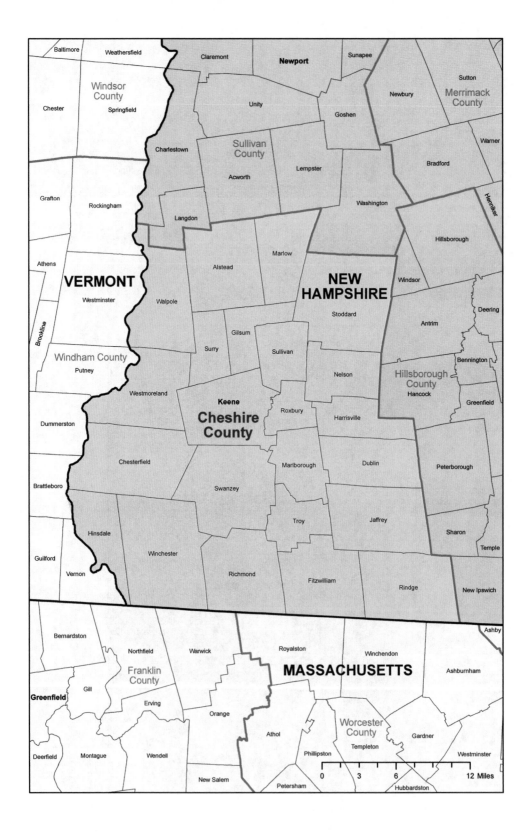

Cheshire County

Founded	1769
Original County	
County Seat	Keene

Towns

Alstead, Chesterfield, Dublin, Fitzwilliam, Gilsum, Harrisville, Hinsdale, Jaffrey, Keene, Marlborough, Marlow, Nelson, Richmond, Rindge, Roxbury, Stoddard, Sullivan, Surry, Swanzey, Troy, Walpole, Westmoreland, Winchester

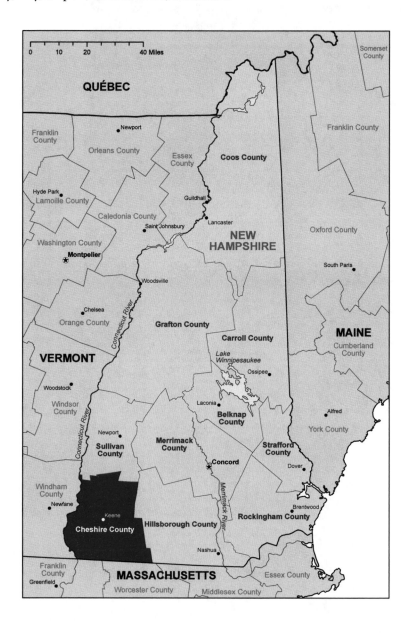

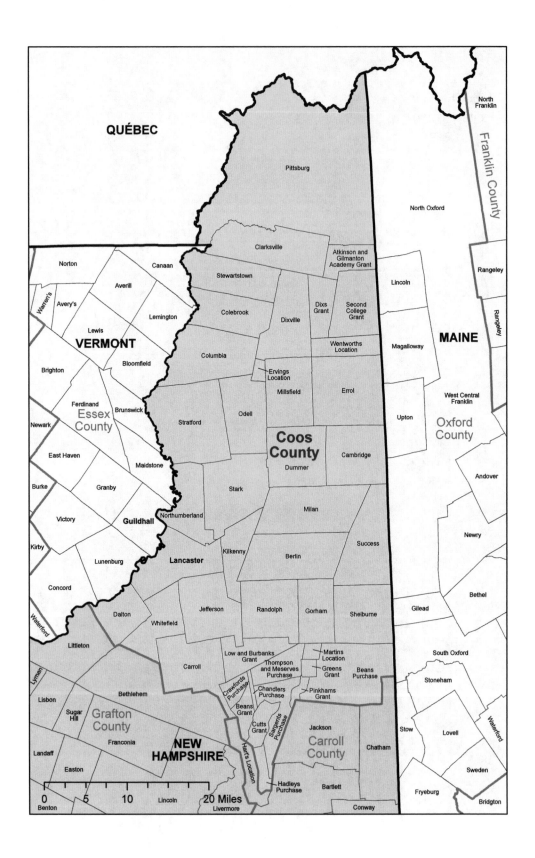

QUÉBEC

Pittsburg

North Franklin

Franklin County

Norton

Canaan

Clarksville

Atkinson and Gilmanton Academy Grant

North Oxford

Rangeley

Warren's

Avery's

Averill

Stewartstown

Lincoln

Rangeley

Lewis

Lemington

Colebrook

Dixville

Dixs Grant

Second College Grant

VERMONT

Bloomfield

Columbia

Wentworths Location

MAINE

Brighton

Magalloway

Ervings Location

West Central Franklin

Ferdinand

Brunswick

Millsfield

Errol

Newark

Essex County

Stratford

Odell

Coos County

Upton

Oxford County

East Haven

Maidstone

Cambridge

Andover

Burke

Granby

Stark

Dummer

Victory

Guildhall

Milan

Newry

Kirby

Northumberland

Success

Lunenburg

Kilkenny

Berlin

Concord

Lancaster

Bethel

Waterford

Dalton

Jefferson

Randolph

Gorham

Shelburne

Gilead

Lyman

Whitefield

Low and Burbanks Grant

Martins Location

Littleton

Carroll

Thompson and Meserves Purchase

Greens Grant

Beans Purchase

South Oxford

Lisbon

Bethlehem

Crawfords Purchase

Chandlers Purchase

Pinkhams Grant

Stoneham

Sugar Hill

Grafton County

Beans Grant

Stow

Lovell

Waterford

Landaff

Franconia

NEW HAMPSHIRE

Cutts Grant

Sargents Purchase

Jackson

Carroll County

Chatham

Easton

Hart's Location

Sweden

0   5   10   Lincoln   20 Miles

Hadleys Purchase

Bartlett

Fryeburg

Bridgton

Benton

Livermore

Conway

NH

Coos County

Founded	1803
Parent Counties	Grafton
County Seat	Lancaster

Towns

Berlin, Carroll, Clarksville, Colebrook, Columbia, Dalton, Dummer, Errol, Gorham, Jefferson, Lancaster, Milan, Northumberland, Pittsburg, Randolph, Shelburne, Stark, Stewartstown, Stratford, Whitefield

Unincorporated

Atkinson and Gilmanton Academy Grant, Beans Grant, Beans Purchase, Cambridge, Chandlers Purchase, Crawfords Purchase, Cutts Grant, Dixs Grant, Dixville, Ervings Location, Greens Grant, Hadleys Purchase, Kilkenny, Low and Burbanks Grant, Martins Location, Millsfield, Odell, Pinkhams Grant, Sargents Purchase, Second College Grant, Success, Thompson and Meserves Purchase, Wentworths Location

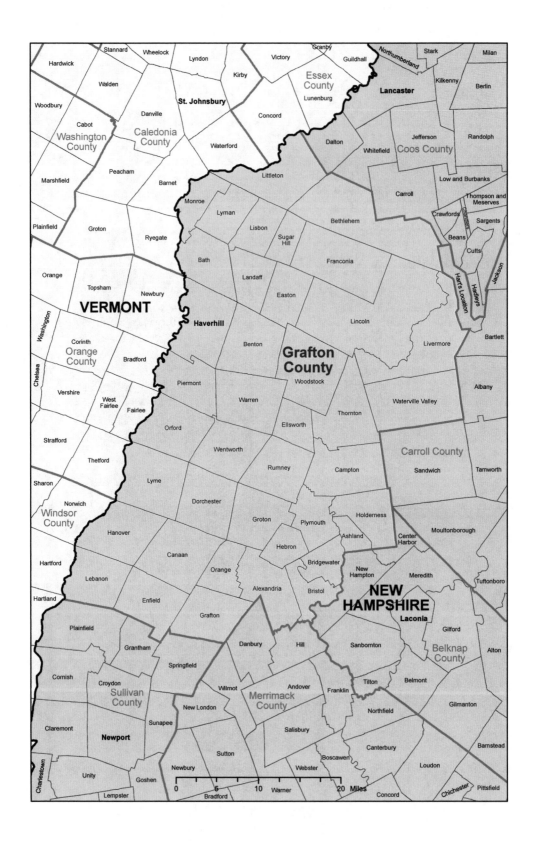

Grafton County

Founded	1769
Original County	
County Seat	Haverhill

Towns

Alexandria, Ashland, Bath, Benton, Bethlehem, Bridgewater, Bristol, Campton, Canaan, Dorchester, Easton, Ellsworth, Enfield, Franconia, Grafton, Groton, Hanover, Haverhill, Hebron, Holderness, Landaff, Lebanon, Lincoln, Lisbon, Littleton, Lyman, Lyme, Monroe, Orange, Orford, Piermont, Plymouth, Rumney, Sugar Hill, Thornton, Warren, Waterville Valley, Wentworth, Woodstock

Unincorporated

Livermore

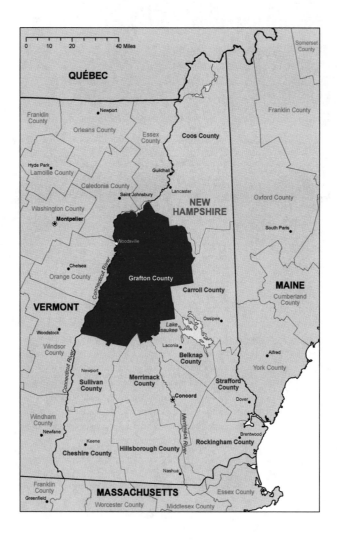

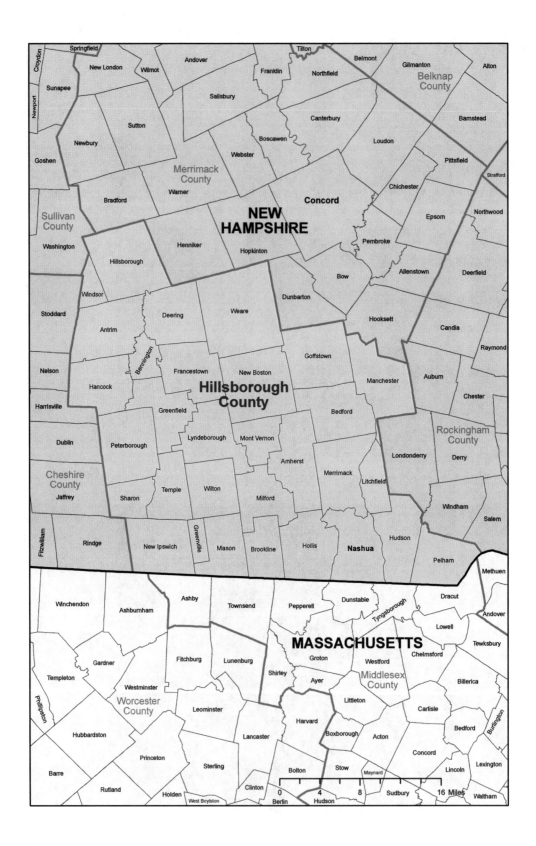

Hillsborough County

Founded	1769
Original County	
County Seat	Nashua

Towns

Amherst, Antrim, Bedford, Bennington, Brookline, Deering, Francestown, Goffstown, Greenfield, Greenville, Hancock, Hillsborough, Hollis, Hudson, Litchfield, Lyndeborough, Manchester, Mason, Merrimack, Milford, Mont Vernon, Nashua, New Boston, New Ipswich, Pelham, Peterborough, Sharon, Temple, Weare, Wilton, Windsor

Extinct

Nashville

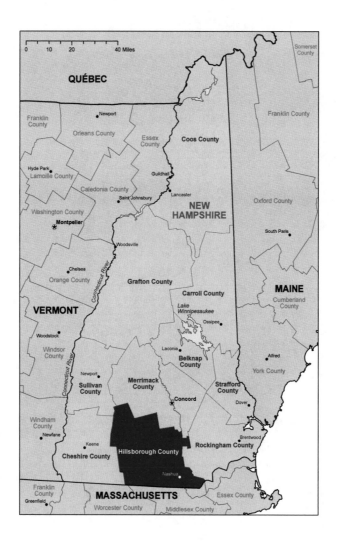

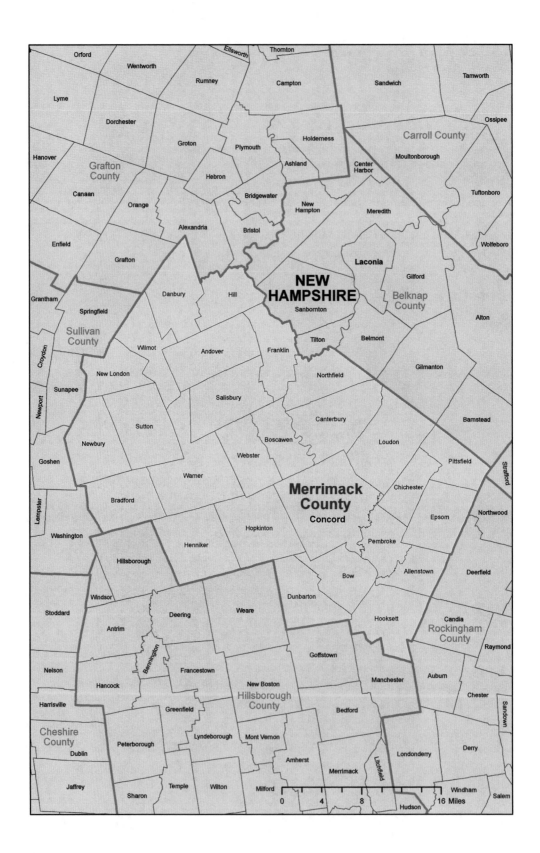

Merrimack County

Founded	1823
Parent Counties	Grafton, Hillsborough, Rockingham
County Seat	Concord

Towns

Allenstown, Andover, Boscawen, Bow, Bradford, Canterbury, Chichester, Concord, Danbury, Dunbarton, Epsom, Franklin, Henniker, Hill, Hooksett, Hopkinton, Loudon, New London, Newbury, Northfield, Pembroke, Pittsfield, Salisbury, Sutton, Warner, Webster, Wilmot

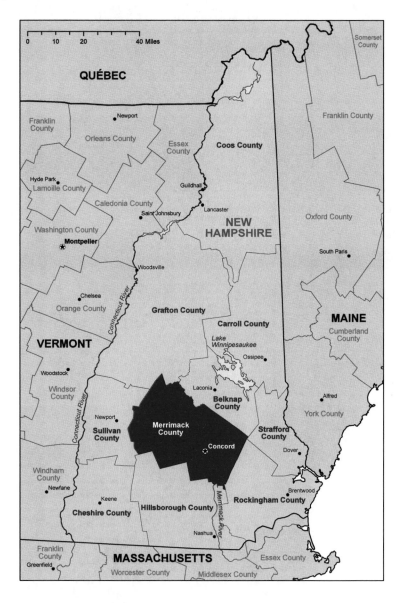

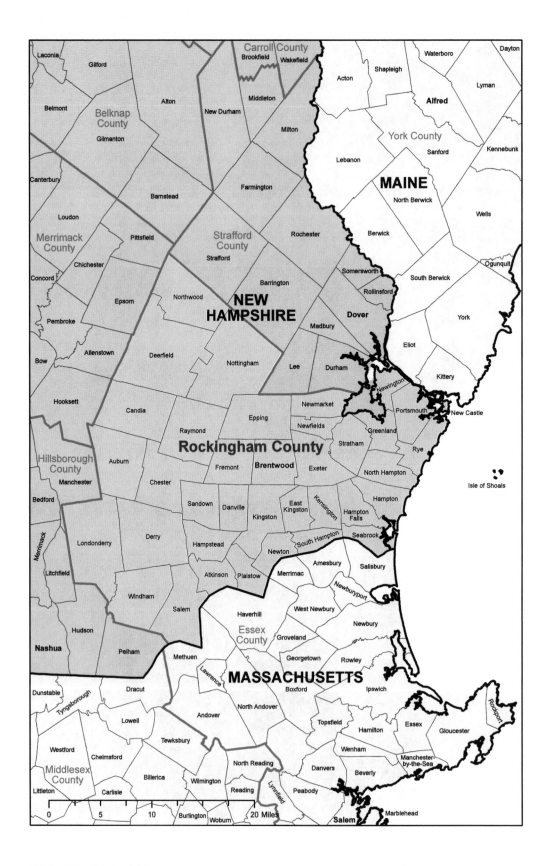

Rockingham County

Founded	1769
Original County	
County Seat	Brentwood

Towns

Atkinson, Auburn, Brentwood, Candia, Chester, Danville, Deerfield, Derry, East Kingston, Epping, Exeter, Fremont, Greenland, Hampstead, Hampton, Hampton Falls, Kensington, Kingston, Londonderry, New Castle, Newfields, Newington, Newmarket, Newton, North Hampton, Northwood, Nottingham, Plaistow, Portsmouth, Raymond, Rye, Salem, Sandown, Seabrook, South Hampton, Stratham, Windham

Extinct

Gosport, Monson

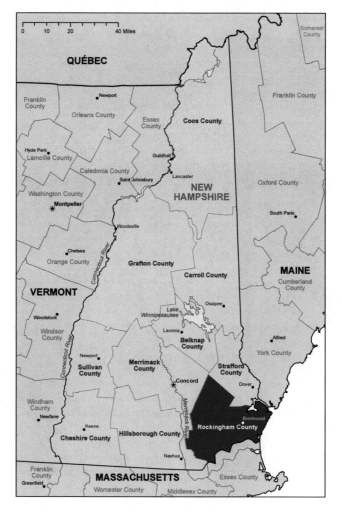

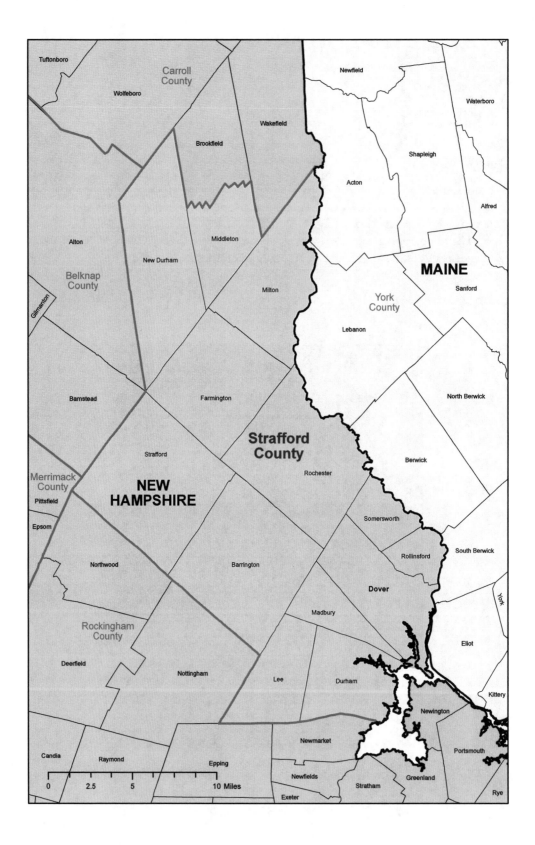

Strafford County

Founded	1769
Original County	
County Seat	Dover

Towns

Barrington, Dover, Durham, Farmington, Lee, Madbury, Middleton, Milton, New Durham, Rochester, Rollinsford, Somersworth, Strafford

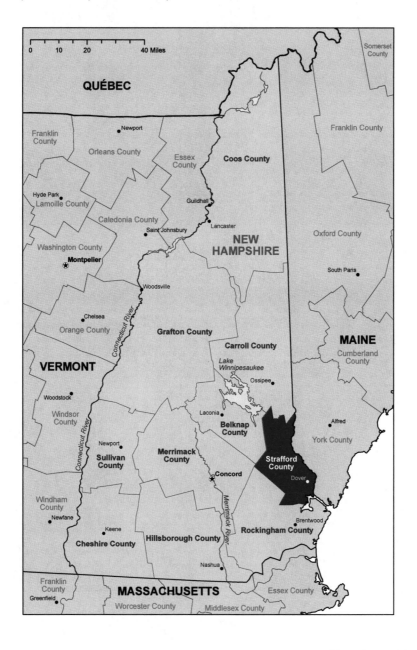

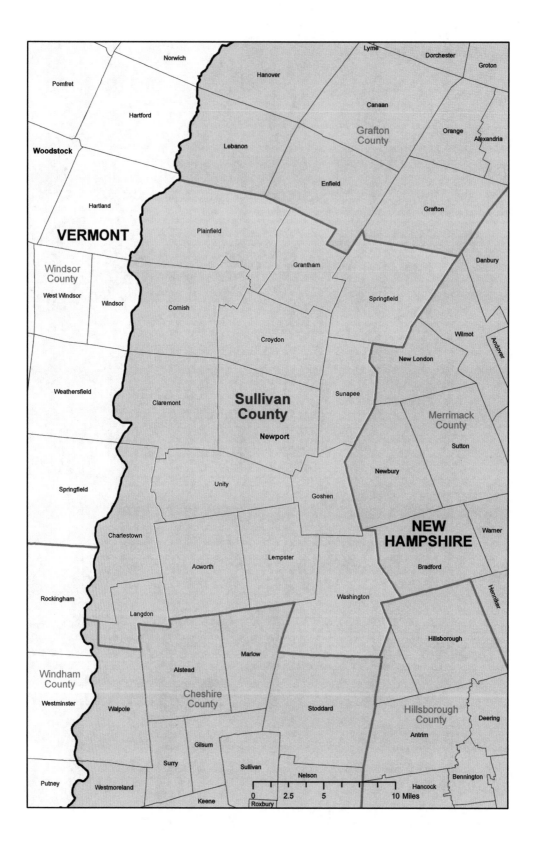

Sullivan County

Founded	1827
Parent County	Cheshire
County Seat	Newport

Towns

Acworth, Charlestown, Claremont, Cornish, Croydon, Goshen, Grantham, Langdon, Lempster, Newport, Plainfield, Springfield, Sunapee, Unity, Washington

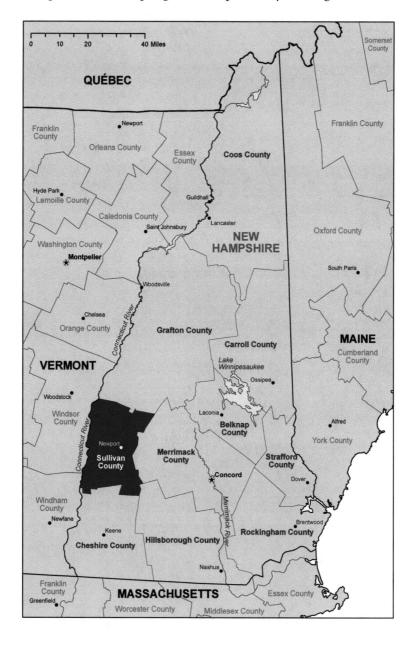

Probate Records

Probate in New Hampshire is handled on the county level. Each county has a probate court to handle estate matters, guardianships, adoptions, name changes, etc. You can find general information about the probate system at *www.courts.state.nh.us/probate/index.htm*.

Belknap County
Belknap Probate Court
64 Court Street
Laconia, NH 03247

Mailing Address
PO Box 1343
Laconia, NH 03247-1343

www.courts.state.nh.us/courtlocations/
belkprobdir.htm
(603) 524-0903
Belknap.Probate@courts.state.nh.us
Hours: M–F 8–4

Carroll County
Carroll Probate Court
Carroll County Courthouse
96 Water Village Road, Box 1
Ossipee, NH 03864
www.courts.state.nh.us/courtlocations/
carrprobdir.htm
(603) 539-4123
Carroll.Probate@courts.state.nh.us
Hours: M–F 8–4

Cheshire County
Cheshire Probate Court
12 Court Street
Keene, NH 03431
www.courts.state.nh.us/courtlocations/
cheshprobdir.htm
(603) 357-7786
Cheshire.Probate@courts.state.nh.us
Hours: M–F 8–4

Coos County
Coos Probate Court
55 School Street, Suite 104
Lancaster, NH 03584

www.courts.state.nh.us/courtlocations/
coosprobdir.htm
(603) 788-2001
Coos.Probate@courts.state.nh.us
Hours: M–F 8–4

Grafton County
Grafton Probate Court
3785 Dartmouth College Highway, Box 3
North Haverhill, NH 03774
www.courts.state.nh.us/courtlocations/
grafprobdir.htm
(603) 787-6931
Grafton.Probate@courts.state.nh.us
Hours: M–F 8–4

Hillsborough County
Hillsborough Probate Court
30 Spring Street, Suite 103
Nashua, NH 03060

Mailing Address
PO Box 387
Nashua, NH 03061-0387

www.courts.state.nh.us/courtlocations/
hillsprobdir.htm
(603) 882-1231
Hillsborough.Probate@courts.state.nh.us
Hours: M–F 8–4

Merrimack County
Merrimack Probate Court
163 North Main Street
Concord, NH 03301
www.courts.state.nh.us/courtlocations/
merrprobdir.htm
(603) 224-9589
Merrimack.Probate@courts.state.nh.us
Hours: M–F 8–4

Rockingham County

Rockingham Probate Court
10 Route 125
Brentwood, NH 03833

Mailing Address
PO Box 789
Kingston, NH 03848

www.courts.state.nh.us/courtlocations/
rockprobdir.htm
(603) 642-7117
Rockingham.Probate@courts.state.nh.us
Hours: M–F 8–4

Strafford County

Strafford Probate Court
County Farm Road
Dover, NH 03820

Mailing Address
PO Box 799
Dover, NH 03820

www.courts.state.nh.us/courtlocations/
straffprobdir.htm
(603) 742-2550
Strafford.Probate@courts.state.nh.us
Hours: M–F 8–4

Sullivan County

Sullivan Probate Court
14 Main Street
Newport, NH 03773

Mailing Address
PO Box 417
Newport, NH 03773

www.courts.state.nh.us/courtlocations/
sullprobdir.htm
(603) 863-3150
Sullivan.Probate@courts.state.nh.us
Hours: M–F 8–4

Land Records

In New Hampshire, land transfers—like probate—are handled at the county level, by registries of deeds.

Belknap County Registry of Deeds

64 Court Street
Laconia, NH 03247

Mailing Address
PO Box 1343
Laconia, NH 03247-1343

www.nhdeeds.com/belknap/BeHome.html
(603) 527-5420, (603) 527-5421; fax
    (603) 527-5429
belkcopies@nhdeeds.com
Hours: M–F 8–4

Carroll County Registry of Deeds

Route 171
Ossipee, NH 03864

Mailing Address
PO Box 163
Ossipee, NH 03864

http://sites.google.com/site/
carrollcountynhregistryofdeeds/home

(603) 539-4872, (603) 539-7511;
    fax (603) 539-5239
Hours: M–F 9–5

Cheshire County Registry of Deeds

33 West Street
Keene, NH 03431

Mailing Address
PO Box 584
Keene, NH 03431

www.nhdeeds.com/cheshire/ChHome.html
(603) 352-0403; fax (603) 352-7678
See website for email
Hours: M–F 8:30–4:30

Coos County Registry of Deeds
55 School Street, Suite 103
Lancaster, NH 03584
www.nhdeeds.com/coos/CoHome.html
(603) 788-2392; fax (603) 788-4291
See website for email
Hours: M–F 8–4

Grafton County Registry of Deeds
3855 Dartmouth College Highway, Box 4
North Haverhill, NH 03774
www.nhdeeds.com/grafton/GrHome.htm
(603) 787-6921; fax (603) 787-2363
graftoncopies@nhdeeds.com
Hours: M–F 7:30–4:30

Hillsborough County Registry of Deeds
19 Temple Street
Nashua, NH 03061
Mailing Address
PO Box 370
Nashua, NH 03061-0370
www.nhdeeds.com/hillsborough/HiHome.html
(603) 882-6933; fax (603) 882-7527
hilscopies@nhdeeds.com
Hours: M–F 8–4

Merrimack County Registry of Deeds
163 North Main Street
Concord, NH 03302
Mailing Address
PO Box 248
Concord, NH 03302-0248
https://gov.propertyinfo.com/NH-Merrimack
(603) 228-0101; fax (603) 226-0868
merctydeed@aol.com
Hours: M–F 8–4

Rockingham County Registry of Deeds
10 Route 125
Brentwood, NH 03833-6248
Mailing Address
PO Box 896
Kingston, NH 03848
www.nhdeeds.com/rockingham/RoHome.html
(603) 642-5526; fax (603) 642-8548
See website for email
Hours: M–F 8–4

Strafford County Registry of Deeds
259 County Farm Road
Dover, NH 03820
Mailing Address
PO Box 799
Dover, NH 03820
www.nhdeeds.com/strafford/StHome.html
(603)742-1741; fax (603) 749-5130
See website for email
Hours: M–F 8:30–4:30

Sullivan County Registry of Deeds
14 Main Street
Newport, NH 03773
Mailing Address
PO Box 448
Newport, NH 03773-0448
www.nhdeeds.com/sullivan/SuHome.html
(603) 863-2110; fax (603) 863-0013
See website for email
Hours: M–F 8–4

The Earl of Halifax Inn (Portsmouth, N.H.), later known as the William Pitt Tavern or Stavers Tavern. Mary Caroline Crawford, *Little Pilgrimages Among Old New England Inns* (1907), facing p. 296.

New Hampshire Towns

There are 221 towns and 13 cities in New Hampshire, as well as 24 unincorporated grants, locations, purchases, and townships (different from towns). Between 1778 and 1781, thirty-two New Hampshire towns joined Vermont. They were ceded back to New Hampshire in 1782:

Acworth	Chesterfield	Hanover	Lincoln	Saville
Alstead	Claremont	Haverhill	Lyman	Surry
Althorp	Cornish	Hinsdale	Lyme	Walpole
Bath	Enfield	Lancaster	Morristown	
Canaan	Gilsum	Landaff	Orford	
Cardigan	Grafton	Lebanon	Piermont	
Charlestown	Gunthwaite	Leicester	Richmond	

Current cities and towns appear in the first table. Extinct towns appear in the second table. Unincorporated territory appears in the third table. Bold names in the parent town column indicate original parent towns. Names that are not bold indicate towns from which additional territory was annexed after the formation of the town.

VR and CR codes

F   Catholic Church records and other records published by French–Canadian societies
N   Manuscript or typescript at NEHGS
P   Published volume
S   Published substitute records (e.g., newspapers, vital records, etc.)
W   Database available on *AmericanAncestors.org*

Above: "Old Concord Coach." Mary Caroline Crawford, *Little Pilgrimages Among Old New England Inns* (1907), facing p. 312.

Town	Inc.	County	Parent	Daughter	Comment	VR	CR
Acworth	1766	Sullivan			Original grant for town of Barnet in 1752, but never settled. Regranted 1766.		
Albany	1766	Carroll			Called Burton to 1833. Ceded by Grafton Co. and annexed to Strafford Co. 1800.		
Alexandria	1782	Grafton	Orange	Hill, Danbury, Bridgewater	First granted 1753.		N
Allenstown	1831	Merrimack	Bow		First granted 1721.		F
Alstead	1763	Cheshire			Settled as a fort against Indian attacks 1735.		
Alton	1796	Belknap		Barnstead, Wolfeboro	Settled 1770. Called New Durham Gore to 1796. Territory original part of paper town of Kingswood.	P	
Amherst	1760	Hillsborough	Milford, Monson, Mont Vernon		Granted by Mass. as Narragansett No. 3, 1728. Settled 1735. Part of Mass. to 1741. Called Souhegan West to 1760.		
Andover	1779	Merrimack			Granted 1746. Settled 1761. Called New Breton to 1779.		
Antrim	1777	Hillsborough			Originally called Cumberland, then Society Land. Renamed Antrim at incorporation.		
Ashland	1868	Grafton	**Holderness**				
Atkinson	1767	Rockingham	**Plaistow**				W
Auburn	1845	Rockingham	**Chester**		First settled 1720.		
Barnstead	1727	Belknap	Alton (New Durham Gore)			P	
Barrington	1722	Strafford		Strafford		P	
Bartlett	1790	Carroll	Chatham, Jackson		Settled 1717.		
Bath	1761	Grafton			Settled 1765. Regranted 1769.	W	
Bedford	1750	Hillsborough			Granted by Mass. as Narragansett No. 5, 1730. Part of Mass. to 1741. Called Souhegan East to 1750.		
Belmont	1859	Belknap	**Gilmanton**		First chartered 1727. Called Upper Gilmanton to 1869.		
Bennington	1842	Hillsborough	**Deering, Francestown, Greenfield, Hancock**				
Benton	1764	Grafton			Called Coventry to 1840.		N

Town	Inc.	County	Parent	Daughter	Note	VR	CR
Berlin	1829	Coos			Granted 1771. Called Maynesborough to 1829.		
Bethlehem	1799	Grafton			Established as Lloyd's Hills 1774.	N	
Boscawen	1760	Merrimack		Bristol, Webster	Granted by Mass. 1732. Called Contoocook to 1760.		N, W
Bow	1727	Merrimack		Allenstown, Concord, Pembroke (Suncook)	Original grant in territory claimed by both Mass. and N.H.		
Bradford	1787	Merrimack	**New Bradford,** Newbury (Fishersfield), **Washington, Washington Gore**		Granted as New Bradford 1771. See also Orange.		
Brentwood	1742	Rockingham	**Exeter**	Fremont (Poplin)	Called Brintwood to 1742.		
Bridgewater	1788	Grafton	**Hill (New Chester)**	Bristol			
Bristol	1819	Grafton	**Hill (New Chester)**				
Brookfield	1794	Carroll	**Middleton**		Settled 1726.	P	
Brookline	1769	Hillsborough	**Hollis**		Part of 1637 grant. Called Raby to 1798.		
Campton	1761	Grafton		Plymouth	Originally granted 1761. Settled 1765. Regranted 1767. Ceded by Strafford Co., annexed to Grafton Co. 1782.		N, W
Canaan	1761	Grafton	Dame's Gore, Gate's/State's Gore		Settled 1767.		
Candia	1763	Rockingham	**Chester**		Created from section of Chester called Charmingfare.		
Canterbury	1741	Merrimack		Concord (Rumford), Loudon, Northfield	Granted 1727.	N	
Carroll	1832	Coos			Granted 1772. Called Bretton Woods to 1832.		
Center Harbor	1797	Belknap	**New Hampton**	Meredith			
Charlestown	1753	Sullivan	Unity (Buckingham)	Langdon	Granted by Mass. as No. 4 1735. Regranted by N.H. as Charlestown 1753.		
Chatham	1767	Carroll	Conway		Settled 1781. Ceded by Coos Co. and annexed to Strafford Co. 1823.		

Town	Inc.	County	Parent	Daughter	Note	VR	CR
Chester	1722	Rocking-ham		Auburn, Candia, Hooksett, Manchester (Derryfield)	Granted 1720. Called Cheshire to 1722.		
Chesterfield	1752	Cheshire			Established 1735. Called No. 1 to 1752.		
Chichester	1727	Merrimack		Pittsfield		P	
Claremont	1764	Sullivan	Unity (Buckingham)		Settled 1762.		
Clarksville	1853	Coos			Granted 1789. Called Dartmouth College Grant to 1872.		
Colebrook	1796	Coos			Granted 1762 as Dryden. Regranted 1770. Called Colebrooke Town to 1796.		
Columbia	1797	Coos	Hales Location		Granted as Preston 1762. Regranted 1770. Called Cockburntown to 1811.		
Concord	1733	Merrimack	Bow		Settled 1659. Granted 1725. Called Penacook to 1733. Called Rumford to 1765. Incorporated by Mass. 1733. Incorporated by N.H. 1765.	S	F
Conway	1765	Carroll			Ceded by Grafton Co. and annexed to Strafford Co. 1778.	P	
Cornish	1765	Sullivan	Croydon, Grantham		Established 1763.		
Croydon	1763	Sullivan		Cornish, Grantham		P	
Dalton	1784	Coos			Granted 1764 as Chiswick. Settled by 1773. Called Apthorp to 1784.		
Danbury	1795	Merrimack	**Alexandria**, Hill, Wilmot		Ceded by Grafton Co. and annexed to Merrimack Co. 1874.		
Danville	1760	Rocking-ham			Settled 1694. Called Hawke to 1836.	P	
Deerfield	1766	Rocking-ham	**Nottingham**				
Deering	1774	Hills-borough			Settled 1765.		
Derry	1827	Rocking-ham	Londonberry		Settled 1719.		
Dorchester	1761	Grafton			Regranted 1766 and 1772.		

Town	Inc.	County	Parent	Daughter	Note	VR	CR
Dover	1623	Strafford		Durham, Newington (Bloody Point), Somersworth	Earlier called Hiltons Point, Newichwannock, Cocheco, Bristol, Northam.	P, S, W	P
Dublin	1771	Cheshire			Granted 1749. Settled 1762. Called Monadnock No. 3 or North Monadnock to 1771.		
Dummer	1848	Coos			Granted 1773.		
Dunbarton	1765	Merrimack		Hooksett	Granted and settled as Gorham's-town 1735. Regranted as Starks-town 1748. Called Starkstown to 1765.		
Durham	1732	Strafford	**Dover**	Lee, Newmarket	Settled 1669. Created from section of Dover called Oyster River Plantation.		
East Kingston	1738	Rocking-ham	**Kingston**	Newton (Newtown), South Hampton	Called Kingston East Parish to 1779.	W	N
Easton	1876	Grafton	**Landaff**		Created from part of Landaff called Eastern Landaff.		
Eaton	1766	Carroll		Madison			
Effingham	1778	Carroll	Wakefield	Freedom (North Effingham)	Granted 1749. Called Leavittstown to 1778.	P	
Ellsworth	1802	Grafton			Granted 1769. Called Trecothick to 1802.		
Enfield	1778	Grafton			Granted as Endfield 1761. Regranted as Relhan 1766. Incorporated as Relhan 1778. Renamed Enfield 1781.	N, W	
Epping	1741	Rocking-ham	**Exeter**				
Epsom	1727	Merrimack				P	P
Errol	1836	Coos			Granted 1774.		
Exeter	1638	Rocking-ham	Hampton	Brentwood, Epping, Newmarket, Stratham	Area of Stratham, originally settled as Squamscott and Winnicutt, was part of Hampton, then annexed to Exeter 1695.		
Farmington	1798	Strafford	**Rochester**		Settled as West Parish, portion of Rochester.	P	
Fitzwilliam	1773	Cheshire		Troy	Granted 1752. Called Monadnock No. 4 and Stoddard's Town to 1773.		

Town	Inc.	County	Parent	Daughter	Note	VR	CR
Francestown	1772	Hills-borough	Greenfield, New Boston Addition, Society Land				
Franconia	1764	Grafton			Granted 1764. Regranted 1772. Sometimes called Indian Head Town after the Old Man of the Mountain.		
Franklin	1828	Merrimack	**Andover, Northfield, Salisbury, Sanbornton**		Originally known as Pemigewasset Village.		F
Freedom	1831	Carroll	**Effingham**		Called North Effingham to 1832.		
Fremont	1764	Rocking-ham	**Brentwood**	Danville	Called Poplin to 1854.	P	
Gilford	1812	Belknap	**Gilmanton**		Created from section of Gilmanton called Gunstock Parish.		
Gilmanton	1727	Belknap	Governor's Island	Belmont (Upper Gilmanton), Gilford	Settled 1761.	P	N
Gilsum	1763	Cheshire		Keene, Nelson (Pac-kersfield), Stoddard, Sullivan, Surry	Originally granted as Boyle 1752. Regranted 1763.		
Goffstown	1761	Hills-borough	New Boston	Hooksett, Manchester (Derryfield)	Granted by Mass. as Narragansett No. 4, Piscataquog Village, and Shovestown. Granted by N.H. 1748.	W	
Gorham	1836	Coos	**Shelburne**		Created from part of Shelburne called Shelburne Addition 1770.		
Goshen	1791	Sullivan	**Lempster, Newbury (Fishersfield), Newport, Sunapee (Wendell), Unity**		Settled as part of Saville (Sunapee) 1768. Incorporated as part of Wendell (Sunapee) 1781.		
Grafton	1778	Grafton			Granted 1761. Grant surrendered 1762. Regranted 1769. Settled 1772.		
Grantham	1761	Sullivan		Cornish, Enfield (Relhan), Meriden	Granted 1761. Regranted as New Grantham 1767. Called New Grantham to 1818.		

NH

Town	Inc.	County	Parent	Daughter	Note	VR	CR
Greenfield	1791	Hills-borough	**Society Land, Peterborough, Lynde-borough,** Lyndeborough Gore	Francestown	Settled 1753.		
Greenland	1721	Rocking-ham	**Portsmouth,** Stratham		Created as a parish of Portsmouth 1638. Became separate parish 1705. Also called Piscataqua and Strawberry Banke.		P
Greenville	1872	Hills-borough	**Mason**		Created from part of Mason known at various times as Mason Harbor, Mason Village, and Slipton.		
Groton	1761	Grafton			Granted 1761. Regranted 1766. Called Cockermouth to 1796.		
Hampstead	1749	Rocking-ham	**Amesbury, Mass.;** Atkin-son; **Haverhill, Mass.**	Danville	Settled 1728. Ceded by Mass. to N.H. 1739. Called Timberlane to 1749.		P
Hampton	1639	Rocking-ham		Danville, East Kings-ton, Hamp-ton Falls, Kensington, Kingston, North Hampton, Sandown, Seabrook, South Hampton	Originally called Winnacunnet or Winnicumet. Settled 1638.	N, P, W	P
Hampton Falls	1726	Rocking-ham	Hampton		Created from section of Hampton called Fall Side and Fall Parish.	P	N
Hancock	1779	Hills-borough	Antrim, Society Land		Settled 1764. Part of terri-tory called Society Land or Cumberland.		
Hanover	1761	Grafton					
Harrisville	1870	Cheshire	Dublin, Hancock, Marlborough, Nelson, Roxbury		Called Twitcheville or Cheshire Mills prior to incorporation. Settled 1760.		
Hart's Location	2001	Carroll			Granted 1772. Township until 2001.		
Haverhill	1763	Grafton			Originally called Lower Coos.		
Hebron	1792	Grafton	Cockermouth (Groton), Plymouth				

Town	Inc.	County	Parent	Daughter	Note	VR	CR
Henniker	1768	Merrimack			Granted by Mass. 1735 as No. 6. Also called New Marlborough; Ceded from Mass. 1741. Granted as Todd's-town 1752.		
Hill	1778	Merrimack	Alexandria	Bristol, Wilmot	Granted 1753. Called New Chester to 1837.		
Hillsborough	1772	Hillsborough			Granted by Mass. 1735 as No. 7.		
Hinsdale	1753	Cheshire	**Northfield, Mass.**	Vernon, Vt.	Originally spelled Hindsdale.		N
Holderness	1761	Grafton			Granted 1751. Regranted 1761 as New Holderness. Called New Holderness to 1816.		
Hollis	1746	Hillsborough	Dunstable		Originally granted as West Dunstable or Nittisset 1739.		
Hooksett	1822	Merrimack	Chester, Dunbarton, Goffstown		First known as Chester Woods and Rowe's Corner.		
Hopkinton	1765	Merrimack		Londonderry	Mass. grant 1735. Called No. 5, then New Hopkinton to 1765.		N
Hudson	1746	Hillsborough	Dunstable, Mass.		Called Nottingham West 1741–1830.	P, W	N
Jackson	1800	Carroll	Bartlett	Bartlett	Called New Madbury to 1800. Called Adams to 1829.	P	F
Jaffrey	1773	Cheshire			Granted 1749. Called Monadnock No. 2, Middle Monadnock, and Middletown to 1773.		
Jefferson	1796	Coos			Granted as Dartmouth 1765. Called Dartmouth to 1796.		
Keene	1753	Cheshire			Granted as Upper Ashuelot 1735. Renamed Keene at incorporation.	P	
Kensington	1737	Rockingham	Hampton Falls				
Kingston	1694	Rockingham	Hampton	East Kingston	Often spelled Kingstown in early records.	P, W	N
Laconia	1855	Belknap	Meredith, Gilford		Created form portion of Meredith and Gilford called Meredith Bridge.	P	F
Lancaster	1763	Coos			Granted 1764.		
Landaff	1774	Grafton			Incorporated 1774.		
Langdon	1787	Sullivan	Charlestown, Walpole				
Lebanon	1761	Grafton			Incorporated as city 1957.		
Lee	1766	Strafford	Durham				

Town	Inc.	County	Parent	Daughter	Note	VR	CR
Lempster	1761	Sullivan			Granted by Mass. 1735 as No. 9. Regranted as Dupplin 1753.		
Lincoln	1764	Grafton					
Lisbon	1763	Grafton			Chartered as Concord 1763, as Chiswick 1764, and as Gunthwaite 1768.		
Litchfield	1734	Hills-borough	**Dunstable, Mass.**		Called Naticook to 1729. Called Brenton's Farm to 1734.		
Littleton	1784	Grafton	Dalton (Ap-thorp), Lisbon, Sugar Hill	Dalton (Apthorp)	Part of 1764 charter called Chiswick. Chartered as Apthorp 1770. Incorporated 1784.		
Londonderry	1722	Rocking-ham		Derry, Manchester (Derryfield), Windham	Settled 1718. Called Nutfield to 1722.	N, P, W	
Loudon	1773	Merrimack	Canterbury, Northfield		Part of 1727 grant that included Canterbury and Northfield.	N	
Lyman	1761	Grafton		Monroe			
Lyme	1761	Grafton			Settled 1764. Also spelled Lime.	P, W	P, N
Lynde-borough	1764	Hills-borough		Greenfield, Milford, Mount Ver-non, Temple (Peterbor-ough Slip)	Settled 1735. Called Salem-Canada to 1763, when regranted by N.H.		
Madbury	1768	Strafford	Dover, Durham		Granted 1755.		
Madison	1852	Carroll	**Albany, Eaton**			P	
Manchester	1751	Hills-borough	Bedford, **Ches-ter,** Goffstown, **Harrytown, Londonderry**		First known as Harrytown. Granted as Tyng's Town 1735. Called Derryfield to 1810.		F
Marlborough	1776	Cheshire	Dublin, Swanzey	Roxbury, Troy	Granted as Monadnock No. 5 1752 (different from Monadnock No. 5 Grant in what is today Vermont). Unofficially called New Marlborough to 1776.		
Marlow	1761	Cheshire		Stoddard	Granted as Addison 1753. Regranted as Marlow 1761.		
Mason	1768	Hills-borough	**Townsend, Mass.**	Greenville	Granted 1749. Called No. 1 to 1768.		N
Meredith	1768	Belknap	Bear Island, Stone-dam	Center Har-bor, Laconia	Granted 1748. First called Palmerstown or Second Township, then called New Salem to 1768.		
Merrimack	1746	Hills-borough	**Dunstable**		Settled in 1720s.		

Town	Inc.	County	Parent	Daughter	Note	VR	CR
Middleton	1778	Strafford		Brookfield	Granted 1749.		
Milan	1824	Coos			Granted as Paulsbourg 1771.		
Milford	1794	Hills-borough	**Amherst, Duxbury School Farm, Hollis,** Lyndeborough, **Mile Slip**				
Milton	1802	Strafford	**Rochester**		Originally part of Rochester known as Three Ponds or Milton Mills.	P	N
Monroe	1854	Grafton	**Lyman**		First known as Hurd's Location or West Lyman. Granted 1769.		
Mont Vernon	1803	Hills-borough	**Amherst**				
Moultonbor-ough	1777	Carroll	Long Island		Granted 1763.	P	
Nashua	1746	Hillsbor-ough	**Dunstable, Mass.,** Nashville	Hollis, Nashville	Called Dunstable to 1836.	P	F
Nelson	1774	Cheshire		Roxbury, Sullivan	Granted 1752. Called Monadnock No. 6 to 1774. Called Packersfield to 1814.		
New Boston	1763	Hills-borough		Goffstown	Granted by Mass. 1736.		
New Castle	1693	Rocking-ham	**Portsmouth**		Granted 1679. Originally called Great Island.	P, W	
New Durham	1762	Strafford		Alton (New Durham Gore)	Granted 1749. Called Cocheco to 1762.	P	
New Hampton	1777	Belknap		Center Harbor	Granted 1765. Called Moultonbor-ough Addition to 1777.		
New Ipswich	1762	Hills-borough			Granted by Mass. 1735. Granted by N.H. 1750. Called Ipswich 1762–66.		
New London	1779	Merrimack	Kearsarge Gore, Sunapee (Saville)	Wilmot	Granted 1753 as Heidelberg. Granted as Alexandria Addition 1773.		
Newbury	1778	Merrimack	**Dantzic, Fisherfield**		Granted 1753 as Dantzic. Regranted 1754 as Hereford. Called Fishersfield 1772–1837.		
Newfields	1849	Rocking-ham	**Newmarket**		First called Newfield Village. Called South Newmarket to 1895.		
Newington	1764	Rocking-ham	**Dover**	Portsmouth	Called Bloody Point to 1714.	P	
Newmarket	1727	Rocking-ham	Durham, **Exeter**	Newfields (South Newmarket)			N

Town	Inc.	County	Parent	Daughter	Note	VR	CR
Newport	1761	Sullivan			Granted 1753. Called Grenville to 1761. Regranted 1761.		N
Newton	1749	Rocking-ham	**South Hampton**		Called Newtown to 1846.	P	
North Hampton	1742	Rocking-ham	**Hampton**		First settled 1639. Created from section of Hampton called North Hill Parish.	P	
Northfield	1780	Merrimack	**Canterbury, Franklin**	Franklin	Created from north section of Canterbury.		
North-umberland	1779	Coos			Granted 1761 as Stonington. Regranted 1771 as Northumberland.		
Northwood	1773	Rocking-ham	Nottingham		Settled 1763, known as North Woods.		
Nottingham	1722	Rocking-ham		Deerfield, Northwood		N, W	
Orange	1790	Grafton	Hebron	Hebron	Granted 1769. Called Cardigan to 1790.		
Orford	1761	Grafton		Wentworth	Granted 1761. Settled 1765.		
Ossipee	1785	Carroll	Tamworth	Tamworth	Known as Wigwam Village then New Garden. Called Ossipee Gore to 1785.	P	
Pelham	1746	Hills-borough	**Dunstable, Mass.; Dracut, Mass.**		Settled 1722. Ceded by Rockingham Co. and annexed by Hillsborough Co. 1824.		
Pembroke	1759	Merrimack	Bow		Granted by Mass. 1728. Called Lovewell's Town or Suncook to 1759.		N
Peterbor-ough	1760	Hills-borough		Greenfield, Temple (Peterbor-ough Slip)	Granted by Mass. 1737. Settled 1739.		F, N
Piermont	1764	Grafton	Wentworth	Wentworth	Settled 1768.		
Pittsburg	1840	Coos			Section on U.S./Canada border declared itself the sovereign nation of Indian Stream Republic 1832–40, until border dispute was resolved. Indian Stream Re-public annexed by Pittsburg 1840.		
Pittsfield	1782	Merrimack	**Chichester**				
Plainfield	1761	Sullivan		Grantham			
Plaistow	1749	Rocking-ham	**Haverhill, Mass., Kingston**	Atkinson	Called Haverhill District 1741–49.	P, W	N
Plymouth	1763	Grafton	Campton, Hebron	Hebron			

Town	Inc.	County	Parent	Daughter	Note	VR	CR
Portsmouth	1631	Rocking-ham		Greenland, New Castle (Great Island)	Granted 1622. Called Piscataqua and Strawberry Banke to 1653.		N
Randolph	1824	Coos			Granted 1772 as Durand.		
Raymond	1764	Rocking-ham	**Chester**		Created from section of Chester called Freetown.		
Richmond	1752	Cheshire		Swanzey, Troy	Granted by Mass. 1735. Called Sylvester-Canada to 1752.		
Rindge	1768	Cheshire			Granted by Mass. 1736. Called Rowley-Canada to 1749. Called Monadnock No. 1 to 1768.		
Rochester	1722	Strafford		Farmington, Milton	Granted by Mass. 1722. Settled 1728.		
Rollinsford	1849	Strafford	**Somersworth**		Part of Dover when incorporated 1641; became part of Somers-worth when it separated from Dover 1729.		
Roxbury	1812	Cheshire	**Keene, Nelson (Packersfield), Marlborough**		One part of Monadnock No. 5 (Marlborough).		
Rumney	1761	Grafton			Regranted 1767.		
Rye	1726	Rocking-ham	**Hampton, Gosport, Newcastle, Portsmouth (Piscataqua, Strawberry Bank)**		Site of first settlement in N.H. 1623. Originally part of Ports-mouth called Sandy Beach.		
Salem	1750	Rocking-ham	**Dracut, Mass.; Haver-hill, Mass.; Methuen, Mass.**		Known as North Parish of Methuen or Methuen District. Named Salem 1741.		F
Salisbury	1768	Merrimack			Granted by Mass. 1736. Called Baker's Town to 1749. Regranted 1749 as Stevenstown.		
Sanbornton	1770	Belknap	Tilton	Tilton	Originally known as First Township. Granted 1748.		N
Sandown	1756	Rocking-ham	**Kingston**				
Sandwich	1763	Carroll	Sandwich Addition			P	N
Seabrook	1768	Rocking-ham	**Hampton Falls,** South Hampton		Settled 1638.	P	

Town	Inc.	County	Parent	Daughter	Note	VR	CR
Sharon	1791	Hills-borough	**Jaffrey, Peterborough, Temple**		Settled 1638. Known as Peterborough Slip or Sliptown.		
Shelburne	1820	Coos	Shelburne Addition	Gorham	Granted 1769.		
Somers-worth	1754	Strafford	**Dover**	Rollinsford	First settled ca. 1650. Became Summersworth parish 1729.		
South Hampton	1742	Rocking-ham	**Amesbury, Mass.; Salisbury, Mass.**	Hampton Falls, Newton (Newtown)			
Springfield	1794	Sullivan	Heath's Gore		Granted 1769. Called Protectworth to 1794.		
Stark	1795	Coos	Stratford	Dummer, Lancaster	Granted 1774. Called Percy to 1795. Called Piercy to 1832.		
Stewarts-town	1795	Coos			Granted 1770. Called Stuart Town to 1795. Incorporated as Stuart 1795. Reincorporated as Stewart-stown 1799.		
Stoddard	1774	Cheshire		Nelson (Packers-field), Sullivan	Granted 1752. Called Monadnock No. 7 or Limerick to 1774.		
Strafford	1820	Strafford	**Barrington**				
Stratford	1773	Coos		Stark (Percy)	Granted 1762.		
Stratham	1716	Rocking-ham	**Exeter**	Greenland	Originally settled 1631 as Squamscott or Winnicutt. Ceded by Hampton and annexed to Exeter 1695.	N	N
Sugar Hill	1962	Grafton	**Lisbon (Gunthwaite)**		Settled ca. 1789.		
Sullivan	1787	Cheshire	**Gilsum, Keene, Nelson (Packersfield), Stoddard**	Gilsum			
Sunapee	1781	Sullivan		Goshen, New London	Called Corey's Town to 1768. Called Saville to 1781. Called Wendell to 1850.		
Surry	1769	Cheshire	**Gilsum, Westmoreland**				
Sutton	1784	Merrimack			Granted 1748. Called Parrystown to 1784.		
Swanzey	1753	Cheshire			Granted by Mass. 1734. Called Lower Ashuelot to 1753. Regranted by N.H. 1753.		
Tamworth	1766	Carroll	Ossipee (Ossipee Gore)	Ossipee (Os-sipee Gore)	Settled 1771.	P	

Town	Inc.	County	Parent	Daughter	Note	VR	CR
Temple	1768	Hills-borough	Lyndeborough (Salem-Canada), Peterborough	Sharon	Granted by Mass. 1750. Regranted by N.H. 1750. Called Peterborough Slip to 1768.		
Thornton	1763	Grafton	Blanchard's Gore, Waterville		Granted 1763. Regranted 1768. Settled 1770.		N
Tilton	1869	Belknap	**Sanbornton**		Settled as southern part of Sanbornton known as Sanbornton Bridge or Bridge Village.		
Troy	1815	Cheshire	**Fitzwilliam, Marlborough, Richmond, Swanzey**				
Tuftonboro	1795	Carroll	Birch Island, Cow Island, Farm Island, Little Bear Island, Whortleberry Island	Wolfe-borough	Granted 1750. Settled after the Revolutionary War.		
Unity	1764	Sullivan		Charlestown, Claremont, Goshen	Granted 1753. Called Buckingham to 1764.		
Wakefield	1774	Carroll	Milton	Effingham (Leavitt's Town)	Granted 1749. Called Ham's-town, East-town, or Watertown to 1774.		
Walpole	1752	Cheshire		Langdon	Granted by Mass. 1736. Called No. 3 to 1752.		
Warner	1774	Merrimack	Kearsarge Gore		Granted by Mass. 1735. Called No. 1, and New Amesbury to 1749.		
Warren	1763	Grafton			Settled 1767.		
Washington	1776	Sullivan			Granted by Mass. 1735 as Monadnock No. 8. Granted by N.H. 1752. Called New Concord to 1768. Regranted 1768. Called Camden to 1776.		
Waterville Valley	1829	Grafton	Gills and Foss Grant, John Raymond Grant		Called Waterville to 1967.		
Weare	1764	Hills-borough			Granted by Mass. 1735 as Beverly-Canada or Halestown to 1748. Granted by New Hampshire 1748. Called Robiestown or Wearestown to 1764.		
Webster	1860	Merrimack	**Boscawen**				
Wentworth	1766	Grafton	Orford, Piermont		Regranted 1772.		

Town	Inc.	County	Parent	Daughter	Note	VR	CR
Westmore-land	1752	Cheshire		Surry	Granted by Mass. 1735. Called No. 2 or Great Meadows to 1752.		
Whitefield	1804	Coos			Granted 1774. Settled 1801. Called Whitefields to 1804.		
Wilmot	1807	Merrimack	**Kearsarge Gore, New London**		Part of 1775 grant.		
Wilton	1762	Hills-borough	Lyndeborough		Settled 1738. Granted by Mass. 1749. Called No. 2 to 1762.	P	
Winchester	1753	Cheshire	Richmond		Settled by 1732. Granted by Mass. 1733. Called Arlington to 1740. Granted by N.H. 1753.		
Windham	1742	Rocking-ham	**Londonderry**	Salem	Settled as part of Londonderry 1719.		N
Windsor	1798	Hills-borough	Wheeler's Gore		Granted 1748. Called Campbell's Gore to 1798.		
Wolfeboro	1770	Carroll	Alton (New Durham Gore), Tuftonboro		Granted 1759.	P	
Woodstock	1763	Grafton			Granted 1763 as Peeling. Regranted 1771 as Fairfield. Renamed 1840.		

Extinct Towns

The following areas have never had large populations. In many instances they exist only on paper. Few, if any, records exist for these locations.

Town	Inc.	County	Parent	Daughter	Note	VR	CR
Appledore	1661				Also called Hog Island. Population left in 1680s for Star Island, which became Gosport.		
Gosport	1715	Rocking-ham		Rye	Also called Star Island. Annexed to Rye 1876.		
Monson	1746	Rocking-ham	**Dunstable, Mass.**	Amherst (Souhegan West), Hollis	Annexed by Amherst and Hollis 1770.		
Nashville	1842	Hills-borough	**Nashua**	Nashua	Annexed by Nashua 1853.		

Unincorporated Territory

Town	Inc.	County	Parent	Daughter	Note
Atkinson and Gilmanton Academy Grant	1809	Coos			
Beans Grant	1855	Coos			
Beans Purchase	1812	Coos			
Cambridge	1773	Coos			
Chandlers Purchase	1835	Coos			
Crawfords Purchase	1834	Coos			
Cutts Grant	1810	Coos			
Dixs Grant		Coos	**Dixville**		
Dixville	1805	Coos		Dix's Grant	
Ervings Location		Coos			
Greens Grant		Coos			
Hadleys Purchase		Coos			
Hales Location		Carroll			
Kilkenny	1774	Coos			
Livermore		Grafton			
Low and Burbanks Grant		Coos			
Martins Location		Coos			
Millsfield	1774	Coos			
Odell	1834	Coos			
Pinkhams Grant		Coos			
Sargents Purchase		Coos			
Second College Grant		Coos			Owned and controlled by Dartmouth College.
Success	1779	Coos			
Thompson & Meserves Purchase	1855	Coos			
Wentworths Location	1797	Coos			Incorporated 1881–1966; now an organized township.

Rhode Island

Introduction by Maureen A. Taylor

The State of Rhode Island and Providence Plantations is the smallest state, and the one with the longest name, in the United States. Between 1636 and 1642 there were four settlements: Aquidneck Island, home to Newport and Portsmouth, was early called Rhode Island, and the settlements on the northern end of Narragansett Bay at Providence and Warwick were the Providence Plantations. The four towns received a charter in 1644. The Royal Charter of 1663 guaranteed religious toleration in the province.

Newport flourished because of its excellent harbor and defensible island location. The political influence of the merchant trade there caused it to become the wealthiest of the towns. With only one exception, every governor from 1663 to 1743 was from Newport. In 1731, when the Old State House in Providence was built, Newport and Providence became co-capitals. Newport was considered the primary capital; business was conducted at its Colony House, built in 1739. Important events were held in Newport except during the Revolutionary War, when the town was occupied by the British.

The legislative branch, called the General Assembly, was elected by the freemen. In addition to their judicial duties, the county courthouses in Newport, Providence, and South Kingstown served as meeting places for the General Assembly on a rotating basis. There was no fixed place for the state government in the early national period. In 1854, the General Assembly voted to meet only in Providence. Ceremonial inaugurations of governors were held at Newport until 1901. Providence became the sole capital of the state with the opening of its current State House in 1901.

Although Rhode Island is the smallest state, it packs a genealogical wallop. Records from Rhode Island's four original towns—Newport, Portsmouth, Providence, and Warwick—are extensive and readily available, with record-keeping from the 1630s on. Most genealogically based records are kept on the town level, with the exception of court documents, which are organized by

The Rhode Island seal.

RI

county. A great deal of material is online, in print, or on microfilm.

Several things about Rhode Island research mislead genealogists. First, the state has more than one hundred post offices and place names, but records are kept only at the town and city level. A second potential source of confusion comes from the constant subdivision of the original towns to create new towns. This has led to some records being in a location different than one might expect (for example, North Smithfield's early records can be found in Central Falls, which was separated from Lincoln, which was separated from Smithfield).

In addition, border conflicts in the colonial period and shifting state boundaries can create confusion. In colonial times the western border with Connecticut was in constant turmoil, especially during the seventeenth century. The border with Massachusetts also experienced changes. In 1746, the territory that is today Barrington, Bristol, Cumberland, Little Compton, Tiverton, and Warren was transferred to Rhode Island from Massachusetts. Part of Seekonk, Massachusetts, was ceded in 1828 and joined with part of North Providence to form Pawtucket. The western area of Seekonk was transferred to Rhode Island in 1862 and became East Providence. Therefore, it is a good idea to search records of surrounding towns (and counties in Massachusetts) even if they are over state lines.

Vital Records

Early vital records can be found amid colonial town documents and occasionally within religious records. By 1647 the colonial government required all marriage banns (but not birth or death records) to be entered in the records of the town clerk. In reality, compliance was less than 50 percent. It's not unusual to see colonial births recorded at the town level organized by family group rather than by the date of the event. Vital records are available in city and town halls (as well as online and on microfilm), except for the majority of Newport's colonial records. They were taken by the British during the American Revolution and were on a ship sunk in New York Harbor, but retrieved several hours later. Surviving fragments were stabilized with silk and are at the Newport Historical Society.

An 1853 law required statewide civil registration of births, marriages, and deaths, but once again compliance was an issue. There are duplications and omissions in these records on the state and town levels. It is important to check all available sources of vital records, since an event may be transcribed on the city level, the state level, or in both places with variations.

The twenty-one-volume *Vital Record of Rhode Island* by James N. Arnold was the first large-scale publication of the state's early vital records to 1850. The transcriptions include references to the volumes and page numbers of the original record books from which the information was taken. Arnold also included church records and newspaper notices.[1] Alden Beaman's *Rhode Island Vital Records, New Series* attempted to fill in missing entries using vital record substitutes. Beaman analyzed evidence found in land and cemetery records.[2]

Beaman's works generally end in 1850 or 1860, but cemetery records from Newport Common Burial Ground include births

---

[1] James N. Arnold, *Vital Record of Rhode Island 1636-1850*, 21 vols. (Providence: Narragansett Historical Publishing Company, 1891-1912).

[2] Alden Beaman, *Vital Records of Rhode Island, New Series*, vol. 1 (Princeton, Mass.: privately printed, 1976-).

through 1930. As Arnold provides records only to 1850, there is a gap between the published records and those required by the 1853 law. The Rhode Island State Archive has an index to records that predate the 1853 law and are not included in the published volumes for earlier years, including those from 1851 and 1852. Records from Arnold and Beaman are indexed separately.

The Office of Vital Records maintains all birth and marriage records for 101 years and death records for 51 years. Access is restricted to direct relatives only. This is the only office that can issue certified copies. Currently, birth and marriage records more than 101 years old are accessible to the public at various repositories—including the Rhode Island State Archives, Rhode Island Historical Society, and NEHGS. Death records older than 51 years are also open to the public and available at RISA and NEHGS.

Probate Records

Probate records include administrations, adoptions, guardianships, inventories, petitions, and wills. In Rhode Island, these are kept on the town level, since probate courts were overseen by town councils. The completeness of a probate record depends on when it was created and the size of the estate. For instance, until 1818, the city of Providence ordered an inventory of a deceased person's belongings regardless of the size and worth of the estate. After 1818 inventories were prepared only when a person died intestate. Probate records for the period 1667 to 1813 were also kept by the Rhode Island General Council and are available on microfilm. The *Rhode Island Genealogical Register* published abstracts of wills; Volume 8 includes an index to wills published in this series.

The ease of accessing probate documents varies from town to town, but locating Providence records from 1646 to 1899 requires a three-step process: consult the published

For Rhode Island Research

Cherry Fletcher Bamberg, "Rhode Island," pp. 162–181 of *A Guide to the Library of the New England Historic Genealogical Society,* Maureen A. Taylor and Henry B. Hoff, eds. (Boston: NEHGS, 2004).

Christine Lamar. *A Guide to Genealogical Materials in the Rhode Island Historical Society Library* (Providence, R.I.: Rhode Island Historical Society, 1985).

Roger N. Parks, ed. *Rhode Island: A Bibliography of Its History* (Hanover, N.H.: University Press of New England, 1983).

Helen Schatvet Ullmann, *A Finding Aid for Rhode Island Town Records in Arnold's* Vital Record of Rhode Island, *Beaman's* Rhode Island Vital Records: New Series, *and the* Rhode Island Genealogical Register (Acton, Mass., 2000).

index to the records to locate a docket number, identify the volume and page of the documents, then find the probate records using that reference.[3] Documents dating from 1646 to 1870 can be examined on microfilm. For material after 1870, researchers must go to Providence City Hall.

Adoption Records

Informal adoptions were the norm from the colonial period to the mid-nineteenth century and were often cited as apprenticeships, guardianships, or indentures. As of 1866, all adoption records were kept by the probate courts. The General Assembly also processed

---

[3] Edward Fields, *Index to the Probate Records for the City of Providence* (Providence: Snow and Farnum, 1902). This is also available as a searchable database at *www.AmericanAncestors.org.*

adoptions, and the names of the parties appear in the annual reports of the General Assembly with the records kept by the State Archives. In the early twentieth century, adoption records began to be filed in the Juvenile Division of the Superior Court.

Today all adoption records for the twentieth century, including those filed with the Superior Court, are sealed and are the responsibility of the Family Court (22 Hayes Street, Providence, RI 02908), which was founded in 1962.

Church Records

Religious toleration was one of the founding tenets of Rhode Island, meaning that a wide variety of religious dissenters settled in the colony. In the seventeenth century, Roger Williams brought his group of followers from Salem, Massachusetts, to Providence. The first Baptist church in America was formed in Rhode Island. Members of the Society of Friends (Quakers), Huguenots, Jews, and others also found safe haven in Rhode Island. With so many and varied sects, early Rhode Island church records are less standardized than those of Massachusetts or Connecticut. For genealogical research, Congregational and Episcopal records are the richest source, since these denominations baptized children. Seventh Day Baptist churches and Quakers kept excellent records, and it is often possible to trace migrations to and from New York State, New Jersey, Wisconsin, and even West Virginia through these records.

In many denominations the ecclesiastical records were considered the property of the minister. Thus they would leave the church when the minister left, and they may be located far distant from the Rhode Island town in which the events occurred.

Both the Rhode Island Historical Society and the Newport Historical Society have church records in their manuscripts department. If you are unable to locate the records for a defunct parish, try contacting one of these repositories to see if the missing records might be in their collections. RIHS has miscellaneous church records for Protestant

"Cliff Walk [Newport]." Samuel Adams Drake, *Nooks and Corners of the New England Coast* (1875), p. 375.

churches while NHS has a comprehensive collection of records for Newport's churches, including Trinity Church. Records pertaining to the Society of Friends have been deposited at the RIHS; early Huguenot records were published in the *New York Genealogical and Biographical Record*; Congregational records can be found at the Congregational Library in Boston, Massachusetts; Episcopal diocese records are in the Special Collections Department at the University of Rhode Island; and Roman Catholic church records are held at the Diocesan Archives in Providence. There are no genealogically significant records from the very early years of the First Baptist Church. Later records have been published.

Land and Property Records

While the earliest colonial charters for the area are held either in the Massachusetts State Archives or in the National Archives (U.K.), many colonial land grants and charters are at the Rhode Island State Archives. Plots in the four original towns—Providence, Portsmouth, Newport, and Warwick (Shawomet)—were purchased by the settlers directly from the Narragansett Indians. Land claims were disputed by the first settlers and by the governing bodies of the bordering colonies of Massachusetts and Connecticut; as noted above, these controversies continued into the mid-nineteenth century. Individual disputes over land were managed by the towns in different ways. In Providence, for example, Roger Williams decided that everyone who was admitted to the town should have the same amount of property. RISA houses a card index of land transactions from 1648 to 1776.

The vast majority of individual land transactions are recorded on the town level. A fire damaged or destroyed some of the record books for North Kingstown in the 1870s, but some have been reconstructed. Records for the Commonwealth Land Title Insurance Company (1850-1905) contain abstracts of deeds recorded during the period covered by the firm. The material is indexed by location and is part of the collections of the RIHS.

Court Records

The court system exercises judicial power. The courts interpret and apply the constitution and statutes and resolve disputes between parties. Parties are either plaintiffs (the party bringing suit) or defendants (the party accused of wrongdoing).

From 1647 to 1729, the colony-wide General Court (later the General Court of Trials) heard both criminal and civil cases. This court was replaced by the county-based Courts of Common Pleas and a Superior Court of Judicature. The Rhode Island Supreme Court Judicial Records Center maintains records for civil and criminal cases (1671–1900), divorces (1749–1900), and naturalization papers (1793–1974). Court documents are organized by county. The documents for Bristol, Kent, and Washington Counties are in poor condition and may not be available to researchers. Only the earliest court records have been transcribed and published.

Civil court records date from 1671 but exist only as abstracts in record books. Beginning in 1700, the record books are supplemented by actual court documents. Divorce petitions from 1749 and later are part of the civil court documents. Before that date they were handled by the General Assembly. Naturalizations were first handled by the civil court in 1793. RISA has a ten-volume set of law cases from 1729 to 1741.

The Judicial Records Center is also the repository for all criminal cases as well as any proceedings of the Rhode Island Superior Court. These documents date from 1729, when the formation of the county system created the criminal, civil and Superior courts.

Military Records

Manuscript service records for the state guard, militia units, and other branches of service up to the end of World War II reside at the RISA and RIHS. The majority of service records for the colonial period exist as rosters or as part of correspondence in the manuscript collections of the RISA and RIHS. Printed sources for King George's War (1740–48), the French and Indian War (1755–62), the American Revolution (1775–83), and the Civil War (1861–65) are available at various repositories. Unfortunately, no comprehensive list of Rhode Island individuals who participated in the American Revolution exists. Researchers interested in the Revolution should also consult the holdings of the John Carter Brown Library at Brown University and the National Archives. Pension files are online at www.fold3.com.

The RISA has enlistment papers, regimental descriptive books, and compiled military records for the Civil War. After the war, the Adjutant General issued an *Annual Report* that lists all the Rhode Island regiments and brief biographies of those who served.[4]

The state's only surviving Federal Census Schedule for the 1890 census is the Special Schedules of the Eleventh Census Enumerating Union Veterans and Widows of Union Veterans of the Civil War, which enumerates all soldiers or their widows living in Rhode Island at the time of the census. It is available on microfilm through the National Archives and has been indexed.[5] The 1865 and 1905 state censuses also identify veterans and in-service personnel.

Records for the three Rhode Island militia units that served in the Spanish American War are held by the RISA, as are the draft registrations for World War I (also available on www.Ancestry.com) and casualty lists for World War II, Korea, and Vietnam.

The RISA maintains material in its collection from the late nineteenth and twentieth centuries relating to the military service of Rhode Islanders in the state guard, the National Guard, and the militia. The information on WWI soldiers, while incomplete, is a valuable replacement for the federal records lost in the 1973 fire at the Military Personnel Records Center in St. Louis.

---

[4] Rhode Island Adjutant General, *Annual Report of the State of Rhode Island and Providence Plantations for the Year 1865*, 2 vols. (Providence: E. L. Freeman, 1893-95).

[5] Rhode Island Special Census of Veterans (Utah: Accelerated Indexing Systems, 1986)

Other Records

Immigration Records

In the nineteenth century, there were three main ports of entry into Rhode Island: Bristol/Warren, Providence, and Newport. Passenger lists for the ports of Bristol and Warren and Providence are part of the United States Custom House Papers, located at the Rhode Island Historical Society; those for Newport are at the National Archives. Passenger lists for the port of Providence in the twentieth century are available as a microfilm publication from the National Archives and can be accessed by researchers at the RIHS and the Family History Library.[6]

Immigrants filed a Declaration of Intention no sooner than two years after arrival and a petition for citizenship five years after arriving, or two years after filing their declaration. These papers were kept in town, county, or district courts. Some records (most 1791–1906, some later) were copied and indexed

by the Works Progress Administration. Both the copies and the index are at the National Archives. Naturalization records for Rhode Island for the period 1894–1916 are missing.

The Judicial Records Center has naturalization records for the period 1793 to 1974 (with gaps from 1894 to 1916) for the state courts. The National Archives holds federal court records from 1793 to 1904; United States District Court records from 1842 to 1844 and 1888 to 1945; and United States Circuit Court records from 1846 to 1884 and 1893 to 1906. For records after 1906, contact the National Archives or the United States Customs and Immigration Service (USCIS).

Another source for information on immigrant ancestors is the American Citizenship Campaign records manuscript collection. This organization was formed in the state during World War I, probably in 1917, to encourage new immigrants to seek citizenship. Records list all foreign males over the age of 18 by ethnic group, with a street address and

---

[6] *Index to Passengers Arriving at Providence June 18, 1911 to October 5, 1954* (NARA T518). Passenger lists from 1911 to 1943 exist on microfilm.

Above: "Graves on the Bluff, Fort Road [Newport]" Samuel Adams Drake, *Nooks and Corners of the New England Coast* (1875), p. 398.

length of time in the country. These are available at the Manuscripts Department of RIHS.

Census Records

At least five colonial population lists exist for the eighteenth century—1730, 1747 (actually a list of freemen), 1774, 1777, and 1782. Originals are at the RISA or the RIHS and all have been transcribed and published. State censuses were taken at ten-year intervals between 1865 and 1935, but the 1895 returns are missing (save for Bristol). Card indexes exist for 1865 and 1875, while the 1885, 1905, and 1935 censuses are self-indexed alphabetically by town. 1915 and 1925 are arranged by street. State censuses are available online at *FamilySearch.org*. There are four known local enumerations for Providence—1776, 1791, 1825, and 1845 (for this last year, records for only half of the second ward survive).

All existing federal population census records for Rhode Island are indexed, with the exception of those for 1910 (which is searchable at *Ancestry.com* and *FamilySearch.org*). An individual can be located by using city directories in conjunction with the census. Of note are the Special Schedules for Rhode Island, which can be found at either the RISA or the RIHS: agricultural and mortality schedules exist for 1850–1880 and manufacturing schedules for 1850, 1860, and 1880. In the absence of the population schedules for 1890, researchers can sometimes refer to veterans and widows schedules.

Rhode Island Historical Cemeteries Database

Since 1990 this project has documented almost a half million inscriptions in cemeteries throughout Rhode Island. More than 600 previously forgotten cemeteries were recorded. The database includes information on the cemetery transcriptions as well as the gravestones within them. Some of these cemeteries have been published in book form.

STAFF PICKS

Compilations

John O. Austin. *The Genealogical Dictionary of New England: Comprising Three Generations of Settlers Who Came Before 1690, with Many Families Carried to the Fourth Generation*, rev. ed. (Baltimore: Genealogical Publishing Co., 1969).

Gleanings from Rhode Island Town Records (Rhode Island Genealogical Society, annual special bonus issue of *Rhode Island Roots,* 2006–present).

Rhode Island Roots (Rhode Island Genealogical Society, 1975–present).

Joseph Jencks Smith. *Civil and Military List of Rhode Island, 1647-1850* (Providence: J. J. Smith, 1900).

Maureen Taylor, ed. *Rhode Island Passenger Lists: Port of Providence 1798–1808; 1820–1872; Port of Bristol and Warren, 1820–1871* (Baltimore: Genealogical Publishing Co., 1995).

An index to the inscriptions is available on *AmericanAncestors.org* and *RIGenWeb.org*. The index includes only names and dates from inscriptions. The full database includes much additional information.

The full database can be accessed at the American-French Genealogical Society in Woonsocket, the Rhode Island Historical Society Library, and the public libraries of Coventry, East Greenwich, Warwick, and West Warwick. An updated version of the database that includes photographs of 400,000 stones can be accessed at the RIHS Library and the Langworthy Library in Hopkinton.

Newspapers

Rhode Island has a fascinating history of newspaper publishing. The first paper in the colony was the *Rhode Island Gazette*, published from 1732 to 1733. The longest-running newspaper is the *Providence Journal*, established in 1833 and still printed today. The *Newport Mercury* (1755–1876), started by James Franklin, and the *Providence Gazette* (1762–1825), are both critical research tools. Searching in the Early American Newspaper Database through *AmericanAncestors.org* is an excellent use of the researcher's time. Under the auspices of the United States Newspaper Project, the RIHS microfilmed all known Rhode Island newspapers including foreign-language papers. These reels can be accessed at the RIHS.

Genealogical Manuscript Collections

Manuscripts relating to the history of the state and the genealogy of its families can be found at the RIHS, NHS, RISA, and the John Hay Library at Brown University.[7] These include the DAR transcriptions of Bible, cemetery, death, marriage, and probate records; the Sidney S. Rider Collection of correspondence, newspaper clippings, church histories, and published materials on Rhode Island; the Louise Prosser Bates collection of deed abstracts, land grants, probate records, genealogies, town records, and cemetery records; and the Anthony Tarbox Briggs collection of transcripts of cemetery records, family records, vital records, and wills.

---

[7] RIHS also has a large number of unpublished genealogies of Rhode Island families.

Above: Bull Dog Tavern, Providence. Mary Caroline Crawford, *Little Pilgrimages among Old New England Inns* (1907), facing p. 28.

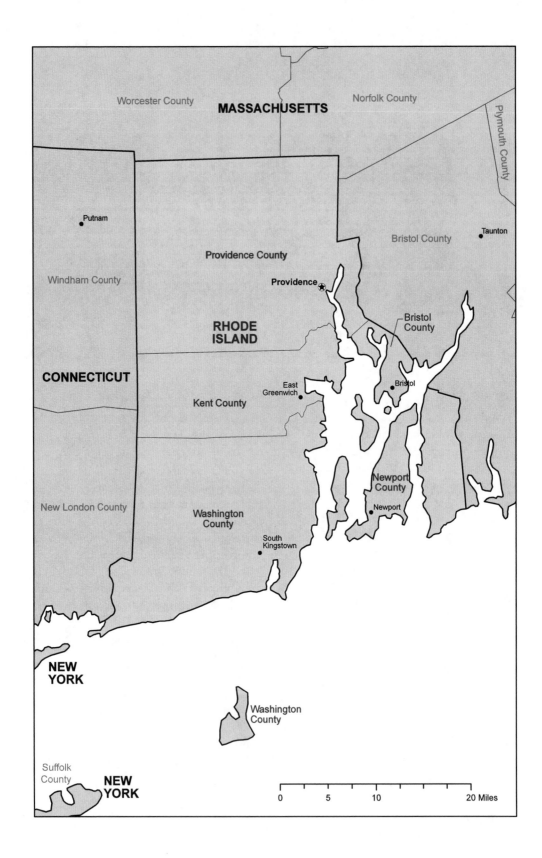

Rhode Island Repositories

These are major repositories with large collections of materials of interest to genealogists. Check with each repository prior to visiting to obtain the most recent information about hours and access to materials in the collection.

Rhode Island State Archives

337 Westminster Street
Providence, RI 02903
http://sos.ri.gov/archives
(401) 222-2353; fax (401) 222-3199
statearchives@sos.ri.gov
Hours: M–F 8:30–4:30

The Rhode Island State Archives (RISA) preserves the historical records of the State of Rhode Island and Providence Plantations. These records date from 1638 to the present. RISA holds statewide records of birth and marriage more than 101 years old; records of death more than 51 years old; and original state census records, tax lists, and other state records. RISA also offers "temporary" storage space to towns for their records. Portsmouth and Little Compton, for example, currently have some materials stored at RISA. This storage can last any-where from years to decades, and materials can be returned to the town at any time. If you cannot find records at the town level, check with RISA to determine if they have been deposited there. RISA also administers the State Records Center, which hold inactive records of state agencies. Access to materials at the Records Center requires permission from the originating state agency.

Rhode Island State Library

State House, 2nd floor
Providence, RI 02903
http://sos.ri.gov/library
(401) 222-2473; fax (401) 222-3034
statelibrary@sos.ri.gov
Hours: M–F 8:30–4:30

cont. on next page

Above: Patrick Kiernan family register, 1845–1852 (R. Stanton Avery Special Collections, NEHGS, Mss 486).

Rhode Island State Library *(cont.)*

The Rhode Island State Library has more than 155,000 volumes in its collections. Among these items are local histories of Rhode Island towns, military histories, town annual reports, records of the executive and legislative branches of state government, and publications of the United States government.

Rhode Island Supreme Judicial Court Records Center

5 Hill Street
Pawtucket, RI 02860
www.courts.ri.gov/JudicialRecordsCenter
(401) 721-2641; fax (401) 721-2653
judicialrecordscenter@courts.ri.gov
Hours: M–F 8:30–4:30

The Rhode Island Supreme Judicial Court Records Center (JRC) is the central repository for semi-active, inactive, and archival records of the court system. Current records are maintained at the respective courts. Archival records date from 1671 to 1900. These records include civil and criminal court records, and divorce records. Naturalization records from 1793 to 1874 are also available at JRC.

Office of Vital Records, Rhode Island Department of Health

3 Capitol Hill, Rm. 101
Providence, RI 02908-5097
www.health.ri.gov/records
(401) 222-2811
See website for email
Hours: M–F 12:30–4

Rhode Island Historical Society

Research Library
121 Hope Street
Providence, RI 02906
www.rihs.org/libraryhome.htm
(401) 273-8107; fax (401) 751-7930

See website for email
Hours: W–F, 2nd Sat 10–5

The Rhode Island Historical Society, founded in 1822, is the fourth-oldest state historical society in the United States. The collections include 100,000 books and printed materials; 400,000 photographs and maps; 5,000 manuscripts; and 9 million feet of motion-picture film. The Museum Division holds another 25,000 objects. Printed collections date to 1589; they include local histories, genealogies, and the largest collection of Rhode Island newspapers and pre-1800 imprints available anywhere.

City Archives, City of Providence

25 Dorrance Street, 5th floor
Providence, RI 02903
http://cityof.providenceri.com/archives
(401) 421-7740 ext. 314
See website for email
Hours: M–F 8:30–4:30

Newport Historical Society

Headquarters and Resource Center
82 Touro Street
Newport, RI 02840
www.newporthistorical.org
(401) 846-0813; fax (401) 846-1853
See website for email
Hours by appointment

City Archives, City of Warwick

Warwick City Hall, 2nd floor
3275 Post Road
Warwick, RI 02886
www.warwickri.gov
(401) 738-2000 ext 6220
vital.records@warwickri.com
Hours: M–F 8:30–4:30

Counties

Name	Est.	Parent(s)	Probate District(s)	Deed District(s)	Note
Bristol	1746	Bristol Co., Mass.	Towns	Towns	Originally part of Plymouth Colony. Transferred to Rhode Island as part of border settlement with Massachusetts.
Kent	1750	Providence	Towns	Towns	
Newport	1703	Original County	Towns	Towns	
Providence	1703	Original County	Towns	Towns	
Washington	1729	Newport	Towns	Towns	Called Kings County to the Revolution. Unofficially called South County.

Above: Timothy Whiting gravestone. Harriette Merrifield Forbes, "New England Gravestones, 1653–1800" (R. Stanton Avery Special Collections, NEHGS, Mss 936).

RI

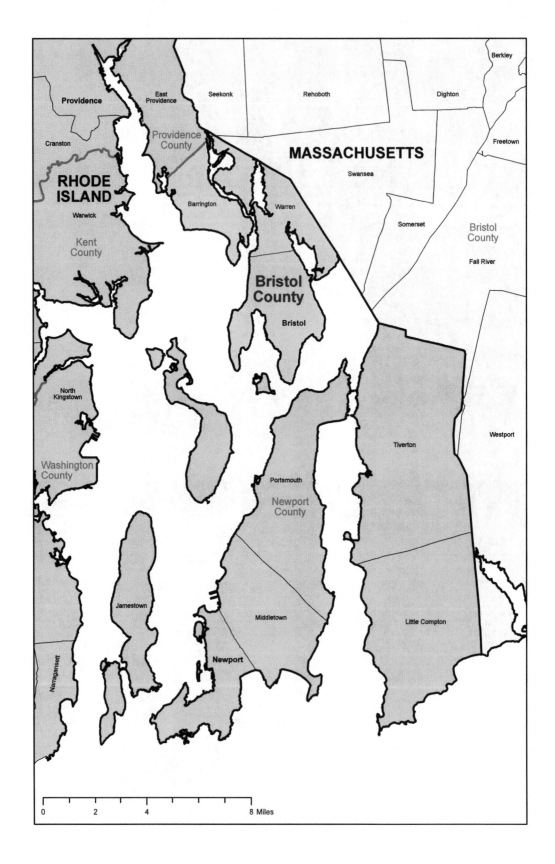

Bristol County

Founded	1747
Parent County	Bristol County, Massachusetts
County Seat	Bristol

Towns

Barrington, Bristol, Warren

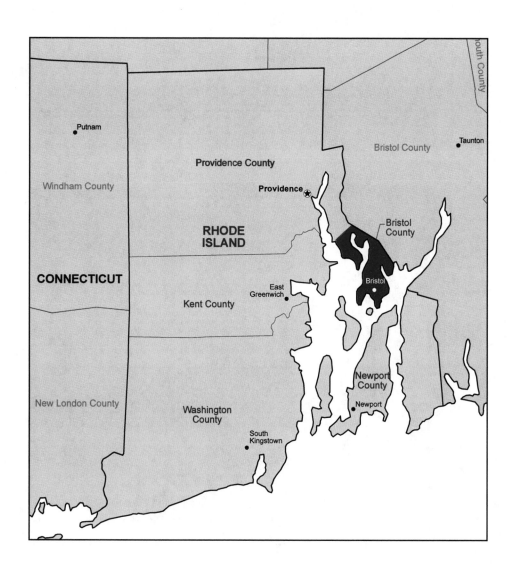

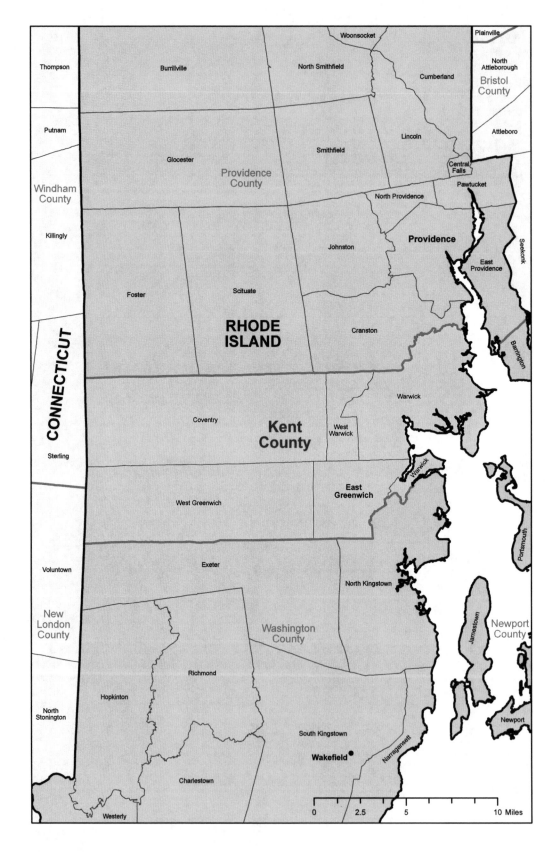

Kent County

Founded	1750
Parent County	Providence
County Seat	East Greenwich

Towns

Coventry, East Greenwich, Warwick, West Greenwich, West Warwick

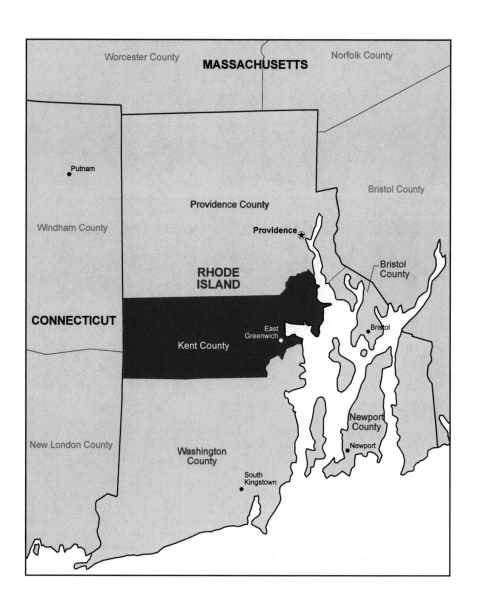

RI

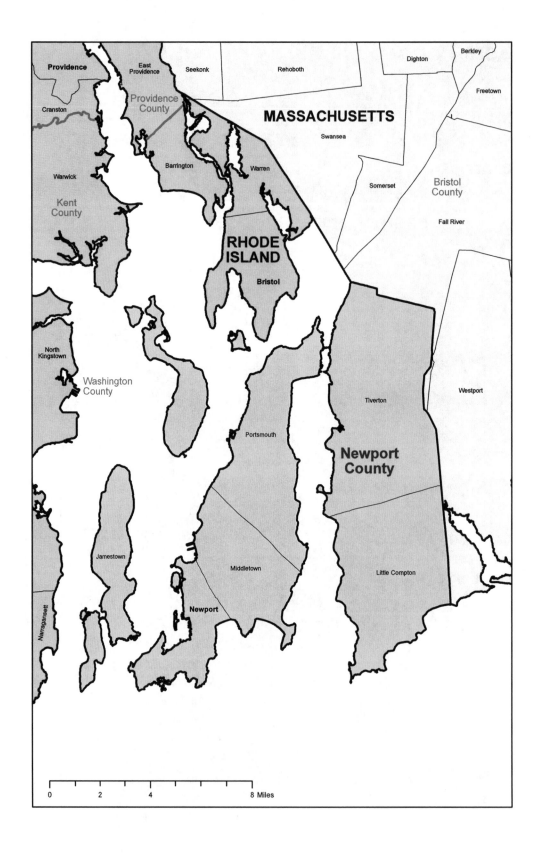

Newport County

Founded	1703
Original County	
County Seat	Newport

Towns

Jamestown, Little Compton, Middletown, Newport, Portsmouth, Tiverton

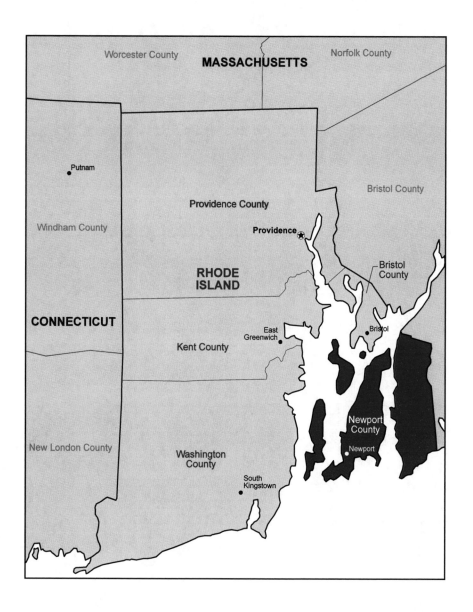

RI

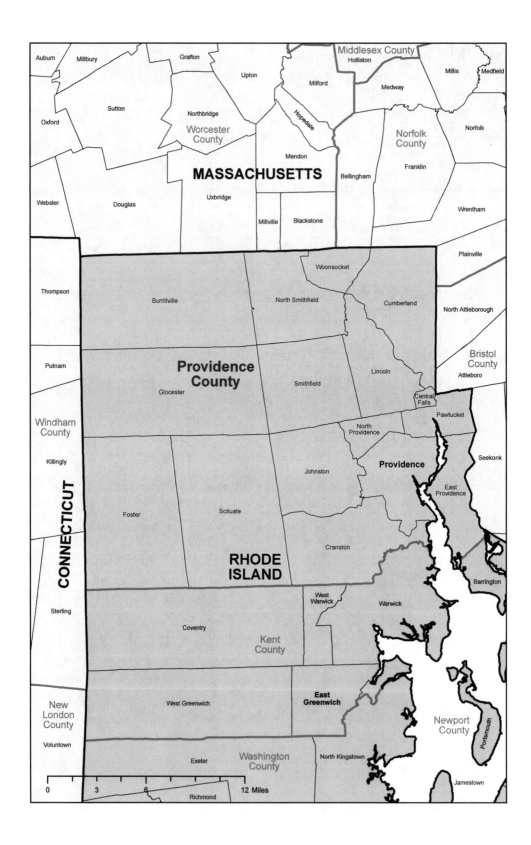

Providence County

Founded	1703
Original County	
County Seat	Providence

Towns

Burrillville, Central Falls, Cranston, Cumberland, East Providence, Foster, Glocester, Johnston, Lincoln, North Providence, North Smithfield, Pawtucket, Providence, Scituate, Smithfield, Woonsocket

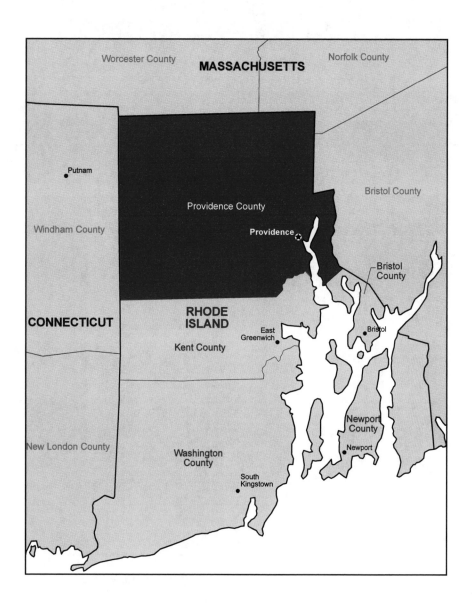

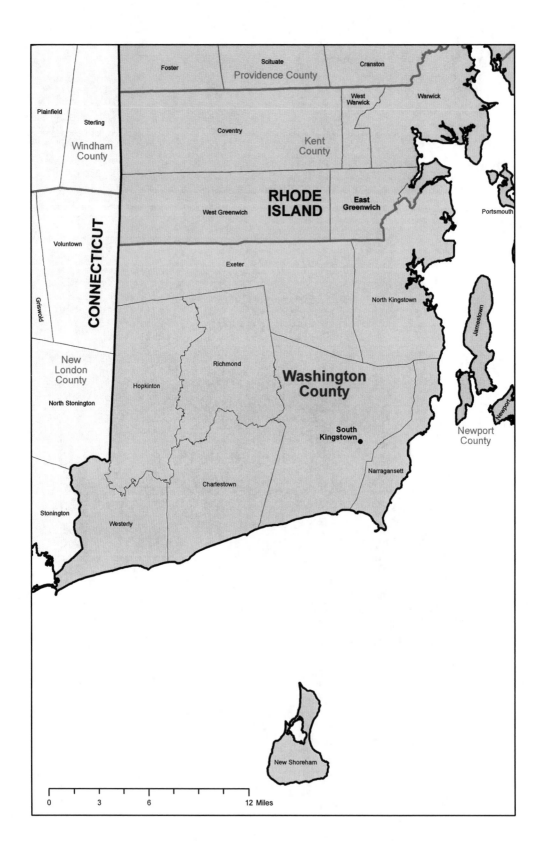

Washington County

Founded	1729
Parent County	Newport
County Seat	South Kingstown

Towns

Charlestown, Exeter, Hopkinton, Narragansett, New Shoreham, North Kingstown, Richmond, South Kingstown, Westerly

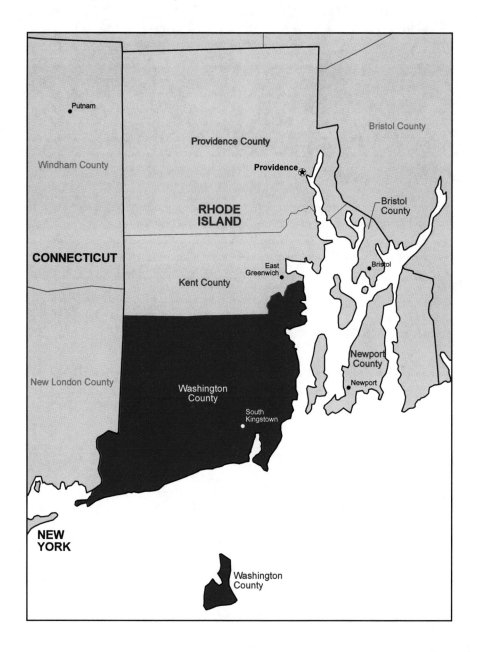

Probate and Land Records

Unlike other states, both probate and land transactions are recorded on the town level in Rhode Island. Land records are maintained by the town clerk. In some towns probate matters are a duty of the board of selectmen. Other localities have separate probate courts to handle estate matters. In all cases, the town or city clerk's office oversees the records.

Barrington
Town Clerk
283 County Road
Barrington, RI 02806-2406
www.ci.barrington.ri.us
(401) 247-1900
See website for email
Hours: M–F 8:30–4:30

Bristol
Town Clerk
10 Court Street
Bristol, RI 02809
www.bristolri.us
(401) 253-7000; fax (401) 253-2647
See website for email
Hours: M–F 8:30–4:30

Burrillville
Town Clerk
105 Harrisville Main Street
Harrisville, RI 02830
www.burrillville.org
(401) 568-4300; fax (401) 568-0490
See website for email
Hours: M–W 8:30–4:30; Th 8:30–7;
F 8:30–12:30

Central Falls
City Clerk
580 Broad Street, 1st floor
Central Falls, RI 02863
www.centralfallsri.us
(401) 727-7400; fax (401) 727-7406
See website for email
Hours: M–Th 8:30–4:30; F 8:30–12

Above: "Market Square [Providence]." *Handbook of Historical Sites in Rhode Island* (1936), p. 4.

RI

Charlestown

Town Clerk
4540 South County Trail
Charlestown, RI 02813
www.charlestownri.org
(401) 364–1200; fax (401) 364–1238
See website for email
Hours: M–F 8:30–4:30

Coventry

Town Clerk
1670 Flat River Road
Coventry, RI 02816
www.town.coventry.ri.us
(401) 822–9173; fax (401) 822–9132
See website for email
Hours: M–F 8:30–4:30

Cranston

City Clerk
869 Park Avenue
Cranston, RI 02910
www.cranstonri.com
(401) 461–1000
See website for email
Hours: M–F 8:30–4:30

Cumberland

Town Clerk
45 Broad Street
Cumberland, RI 02864
www.cumberlandri.org
(401) 728–2400 ext 138
See website for email
Hours: M–F 8:30–4:30; summer 9–4

East Greenwich

Town Clerk
125 Main Street, 2nd floor
East Greenwich, RI 02818

Mailing Address
Box 111
East Greenwich, RI 02818

www.eastgreenwichri.com
(401) 886–8606; fax (401) 886–8625
See website for email
Hours: M–F 8:30–4:30

East Providence

City Clerk
145 Taunton Avenue
East Providence, RI 02914–4505
www.eastprovidence.com
(401) 435–7592
See website for email
Hours: M–F 8–4

Exeter

Town Clerk
675 Ten Rod Road
Exeter, RI 02822
www.town.exeter.ri.us
(401) 295–7500; (401) 294–3891;
    fax (401) 295–1248
clerk@town.exeter.ri.us
Hours: M–F 9–4

Foster

Town Clerk
181 Howard Hill Road
Foster, RI 02825
www.townoffoster.com
(401) 392–9200; fax (401)702–5010
See website for email
Hours: M–F 8:30–5:30

Glocester

Town Clerk
1145 Putnam Pike
Glocester, RI 02814
www.glocesterri.org
(401) 568–6206 ext 0; fax (401) 568–5850
townclerk@GlocesterRhodeIsland.org
Hours: M–F 8–4:30

Hopkinton

Town Clerk
One Town House Road
Hopkinton, RI 02833
www.hopkintonri.org
(401) 377–7777; fax (401) 377–7788
See website for email
Hours: M–F 8:30–4:30

Jamestown

Town Clerk
93 Narragansett Avenue
Jamestown, RI 02835
www.jamestownri.net
(401) 423–7200; fax (401) 423–7230
Hours: M–F 8–4:30

Johnston

Town Clerk
1385 Hartford Avenue
Johnston, RI 02919
www.townofjohnsonri.com
(401) 351–6618; fax (401) 423–7230
See website for email
Hours: M–F 8–4:30

Lincoln

Town Clerk
100 Old River Road
Lincoln, RI 02865
www.lincolnri.org
(401) 333–1100 ext 8005; fax (401) 423–7230
See website for email
Hours: M–F 8:30–4:30

Little Compton

Town Clerk
40 Commons
Little Compton, RI 02837

Mailing Address
PO Box 226
Little Compton, RI 02837

www.little-compton.com
(401) 635–4400; fax (401) 635–2470
See website for email
Hours: M–F 8–4

Middletown

Town Clerk
350 East Main Road
Middletown, RI 02842
www.middletownri.com
(401) 847–0009
See website for email
Hours: M–F 8–4

Narragansett

Town Clerk
25 Fifth Avenue
Narragansett, RI 02882
www.narragansettri.gov
(401) 782–0624; fax (401) 783–9367
See website for email
Hours: M–F 8:30–4:30

New Shoreham

Town Clerk
16 Old Town Road
Block Island, RI 02807

Mailing Address
PO Box 220
Block Island, RI 02807

www.new-shoreham.com
(401) 466–3200; fax (401) 466–3219
townclerk@new-shoreham.com
Hours: M–F 9–3

Newport

City Clerk
43 Broadway
Newport, RI 02840
www.cityofnewport.com
(401) 845–5300
See website for email
Hours: M–F 8:30–4:30

North Kingstown

Town Clerk
80 Boston Neck Road
North Kingstown, RI 02852
www.northkingstown.org
(401) 294–3331; fax (401) 294–2437
probatecourt@northkingstown.org (probate
    only; for other areas, see website)
Hours: M–F 8:30–4:30

North Providence

Town Clerk
2000 Smith Street
North Providence, RI 02911
www.northprovidenceri.gov
(401) 232–0900, ext 205
See website for email
Hours: M–F 8:30–4:30; summer 8:30–4

North Smithfield

Town Clerk
575 Smithfield Road
North Smithfield, RI 02911
www.smithfieldri.com
(401) 233–1000; fax (401) 233–1080
See website for email
Hours: M–F 8:30–4:30

Pawtucket

City Clerk
137 Roosevelt Avenue
Pawtucket, RI 02860
www.pawtucketri.com
(401) 728–0500; fax (401) 728–8932
See website for email
Hours: M–F 8:30–4:30

Portsmouth

Town Clerk
2200 East Main Road
Portsmouth, RI 02871
www.portsmouthri.com
(401) 683–2101; fax (401) 683–6804
See website for email
Hours: M–F 8:30–4:30

Providence

Vital Records and Deeds
City Registrar
25 Dorrance Street, Room 104
Providence, RI 02903

Probate Records
Probate Court
25 Dorrance Street, Room 311
Providence, RI 02903

www.providenceri.com
(401) 421–7740; fax for probate court
    (401) 861–6208
See website for email
Hours: M–F 8:30–4:30; summer 8:30–4

See Providence City Archives on page 290
for information on older records.

Richmond

Town Clerk
5 Richmond Townhouse Road
Wyoming, RI 02898
www.richmondri.com
(401) 539–9000
townclerk@richmondri.com
Hours: M–F 9–4

Scituate

Town Clerk
195 Danielson Pike
Scituate, RI 02857
www.scituateri.org
(401) 647–2822; fax (401) 647–7220
See website for email
Hours: M–F 8:30–4

Smithfield

Town Clerk
64 Farnum Pike
Smithfield, RI 02917
www.smithfieldri.com
(401) 233–1000; fax (401)232–7244
See website for email
Hours: M–F 8:30–4:30

South Kingstown

Town Clerk
180 High Street
Wakefield, RI 02879
www.southkingstownri.com
(401) 789–9331; fax (401)789–5280
See website for email
Hours: M–F 8:30–4:30

Tiverton

Town Clerk
343 Highland Road
Tiverton, RI 02878
www.tiverton.ri.gov
(401) 625–6703; fax (401) 625–6711
See website for email
Hours: M–F 8:30–4

Warren

Town Clerk
514 Main Street
Warren, RI 02885
www.townofwarren-ri.com
(401) 245–7340; fax (401) 245–7421
See website for email
Hours: M–F 9–4

Warwick

Town Clerk
3275 Post Road, Second Floor
Warwick, RI 02886
www.warwickri.gov

Probate Records
(401) 738–2000 x 6213
probate.court@warwickri.com
Hours: M–F 8:30–4:30

Land Records
(401) 738–2000 x 6029
land.evidence@warwickri.com
Hours: M–F 8:30–4:30

Vital Records
(401) 738–2000 x 6033
vital.records@warwickri.com
Hours: M–F 8:30–4:30

See City of Warwick Archives on p. 290 for information on older records.

West Greenwich

Town Clerk
280 Victory Highway
West Greenwich, RI 02817
www.wgtownri.org
(401) 392–3800
Hours: M–F 8:30–4

West Warwick

Town Clerk
1170 Main Street
West Warwick, RI 02893
www.westerly.govoffice.com
(401) 822-9201; fax (401) 822-9266
See website for email
Hours: M–F 8:30–4:30; summer 8:30–4

Westerly

Town Clerk
45 Broad Street
Westerly, RI 02891
www.westerly.govoffice.com
(401) 348–2509
See website for email
Hours: M–F 8:30–4:30

Woonsocket

Town Clerk
169 Main Street
Woonsocket, RI 02895
www.ci.woonsocket.ri.us
(401) 767–8875
See website for email
Hours: M–F 8:30–4

Towns

There are currently 8 cities and 31 towns in the state of Rhode Island and Providence Plantations. The following chart lists the name of each town, the date of its incorporation as a town, the county, towns from which it was formed (or from which land was later added to the town), towns that were formed from it (or to which land was added from it), and notes about the town. **Bold** names in the parent column indicate original parent towns. Names that are not bold indicate towns from which additional territory was annexed after the formation of the town.

The chart also shows which vital records and church records are available as manuscripts, typescripts, published books, or online.

VR and CR codes

A   James N. Arnold, *Vital Record of Rhode Island, 1636–1850* (first seven vols.)
B   Alden Beaman, *Rhode Island Vital Records, New Series*
F   Catholic Church records and other records published by French-Canadian societies
R   *Rhode Island Genealogical Register*
P   Published volume
W   Database available on *AmericanAncestors.org*

Town	Inc.	County	Parent	Daughter	Note	VR	CR
Barrington	1770	Bristol	**Warren, Swansea, Mass.**		Established 1653.	A, W	A, W
Bristol	1746	Bristol			Established 1680. Ceded by Mass. 1747.	A, P, W	A, W
Burrillville	1806	Providence	**Glocester**		Established 1730.	A, W	F
Central Falls	1895	Providence	**Lincoln**		Established 1730.		F
Charlestown	1738	Washington	**Westerly**		Established 1669.	A, B, W	A, W
Coventry	1743	Kent	**Warwick**		Established 1639.	A, W	A, W
Cranston	1910	Providence	**Providence**		Established 1754.	A, P, W	
Cumberland	1746	Providence	**Attleboro, Mass.**	Woonsocket	Ceded from Mass. 1747. Created from Attleboro Gore.	A, W	F
East Greenwich	1677	Kent		West Greenwich	Called Dedford from 1678 to 1689.	A, B, W	A, B, W
East Providence	1958	Providence	**Seekonk, Mass.**		Established 1812. Ceded from Mass. 1862.	A, W	A, W
Exeter	1743	Washington	**North Kingstown**		Established 1641.	A, B, W	A, R, W
Foster	1781	Providence	**Scituate**		Established 1636.	A, W	
Glocester	1731	Providence	**Providence**	Burrillville	Established 1639.	A, W	
Hopkinton	1757	Washington	**Westerly**		Established 1639.	A, B, W	A, W
Jamestown	1678	Newport			Established 1639.	A, B, W	
Johnston	1759	Providence	**Providence**		Established 1636.	A, W	
Lincoln	1871	Providence	**Smithfield**	Central Falls	Established 1650.		F
Little Compton	1746	Newport			Established 1682. Ceded from Mass. 1747.	A, B, W	A, W
Middletown	1743	Newport	**Newport**		Established 1639.	A, B, W	

RI

Town	Inc.	County	Parent	Daughter	Note	VR	CR
Narragansett	1901	Washington	**South Kingstown**		Established 1888.		
New Shoreham	1672	Washington			Established 1664. Called Block Island to 1672.	A, W	
Newport	1784	Newport		Middletown	Established 1639.	A, B, W	A, W
North Kingstown	1674	Washington		Exeter	Established 1641. Called Rochester 1678–89. Called Kingstown to 1723.	A, B, W	A, W
North Providence	1765	Providence	**Providence**	Pawtucket	Established 1636.	A, W	
North Smithfield	1871	Providence	**Smithfield**		Established 1730. Called Slater briefly in March 1871.		
Pawtucket	1862	Providence	**Seekonk, Mass.;** North Providence		Established 1671.	A, W	A, F, W
Portsmouth	1639	Newport			Established 1638. Called Pocasset by natives prior to European settlement.	A, B, W	
Providence	1831	Providence		Cranston, Glocester, Johnston, North Providence, Smithfield	Established 1636.	A, W	A, P, W
Richmond	1747	Washington	**Westerly**		Established 1669.	A, B, W	A, W
Scituate	1731	Providence	**Providence**		Established 1636.	A, W	
Smithfield	1731	Providence	**Providence**		Established 1636.	A, W	A, W
South Kingstown	1723	Washington	**North Kingstown (Kingstown)**	Narragansett	Established 1657.	A, B, W	A, W
Tiverton	1747	Newport			Established 1694. Ceded from Mass. 1747.	A, B, W	A, W
Warren	1747	Bristol	**Barrington**		Established 1620. Ceded from Mass. 1747.	A, W	A, W
Warwick	1931	Kent		Coventry, West Warwick	Established 1642. Chartered 1648.	A, W	A, F, W

Town	Inc.	County	Parent	Daughter	Note	VR	CR
West Greenwich	1741	Kent	**East Greenwich**		Established 1639.	A, B, W	A, B, W
West Warwick	1913	Kent	**Warwick**		Established 1648.		F
Westerly	1669	Washington		Charlestown, Hopkinton, Richmond	Established 1661. Called Haversham 1686–89.	A, B, W	A, W
Woonsocket	1888	Providence	**Cumberland, Smithfield**		Established 1867.		F

"Main Street Bridge and Falls [Pawtucket] during the Freshet of 1886." John W. Haley, *The Lower Blackstone River Valley* (1937), facing p. 56.

Vermont

Introduction by Scott Andrew Bartley

Vermont was the last frontier of New England. Part or all of the state was claimed at various times by Massachusetts, New Hampshire, and New York before Vermont asserted its independence from the original thirteen colonies in 1777. It remained a separate country until its admission as the fourteenth state of the United States in 1791.

In 1749, New Hampshire Governor Benning Wentworth made the first New Hampshire grant, for the town of Bennington. The state of Vermont began to grow in earnest near the end of the French and Indian War (1754-1763).

Between 1749 and 1764 Governor Wentworth issued 135 grants for territory that is now in Vermont. Most of these towns still exist today. Between 1765 and 1776, New York started issuing patents for territory now in Vermont. Of the eighty-three town patents with names, only twenty were con-firmations of New Hampshire grants. Fifty-eight existed in name only; no settlements were made in their territory. Only five New York patents survive as towns today.

While pioneers poured into the region after the Revolution, within twenty years many residents picked up and moved to New York and points westward. Most small towns in Vermont saw their populations peak in the early 1800s.

Towns are the primary locale for record-keeping. Here you will find the customary New England-style vital records, town meeting minutes, tax records, and land records. These are the true "original" records. All facets of the court system, including civil, criminal, divorce, and probate matters, are handled at the county level. The state's Supreme Court settles appealed cases from the counties.

Vital Records

Though not required until the passage of a state law in 1779, vital records were widely recorded long before that. However, do expect gaps in all records. Until the 1840s it was common practice to record the births of children by family group rather than by date. Such a set of records might include births that occurred before the family arrived in town. Beginning in 1857, towns were required to send a copy of their records to the state on an annual basis, which greatly improved the recording of all events; by 1900, participa-

The Vermont state seal.

tion in the annual reporting of records was considered nearly complete.

Vermont is one of a handful of states in which an early attempt was made to create a statewide index of vital records amassed prior to the registration requirement. This card index was initiated in 1919 and finished in 1920. The state encouraged town clerks to copy each vital record in their books and paid them per entry submitted. Realizing that deaths were greatly underreported, the state also paid clerks to transcribe the inscriptions of all pre-1870 gravestones in town. These transciptions were included in the first set of index cards as a fourth category. The cards are arranged alphabetically within the following periods: 1760–1870, 1871–1908, 1909–41, 1942–54, 1955–79, then yearly from 1980 to the present. (This last group contains copies of full certificates.) State copies of vital records for the last five years are held at the Vermont Department of Health; state copies of older records are held at the Vermont State Archives and Records Administration.

Many repositories hold the microfilmed version of this state card index, and genealogical websites have recently begun to offer the information online. The fee-based *www.Ancestry.com* provides access to vital records from 1909 to 2008, though they have omitted any non-standard index cards. *www.FamilySearch.org* offers the index from 1760 to 1954. NEHGS holds microfilmed records through 1990.

This state index is the likely reason why only a few Vermont town vital records have been published in journals or stand-alone publications. The following were published in *Vermont Genealogy,* the journal of the Genealogical Society of Vermont:

- Scott Andrew Bartley, "Vital Records of Springfield, Vt." [Special Publication Number 13] in 16, No. 1 [Spring 2011] — with index.
- Jonathan W. Stevens and Elizabeth W. Stevens, "Vital Records in Volume 1

STAFF PICKS

For Vermont Research

Scott Andrew Bartley, "Vermont," pp. 182–196 of *A Guide to the Library of the New England Historic Genealogical Society,* Maureen A. Taylor and Henry B. Hoff, eds. (Boston: NEHGS, 2004).

T. D. Seymour Bassett, *Vermont: A Bibliography of Its History* (Boston: G. K. Hall, 1981).

Matt Bushnell Jones, *Vermont in the Making* (Cambridge, Mass.: Harvard University Press, 1939).

John A. Leppmann, *Bibliography for Vermont Genealogy,* 2nd ed., Genealogical Society of Vermont, Special Publication No. 11 (St. Albans, Vt., 2005).

Lewis D. Stilwell, *Migration from Vermont* (Montpelier: Vermont Historical Society, 1948).

of the Andover Town Records" in 15 [2010]: 112-32.
- Margaret R. Jenks, "Vital Records of Castleton" in 14 [2009]: 97-171.
- Jonathan W. Stevens and Elizabeth W. Stevens, "Vital Records in Book A of the Chester Town Records" in 13 [2008]: 53-65.
- Eric G. Grundset, "Brookline, Vermont, Vital Records Prior to 1857" in 9 [2004]: 122-33, 179-92.
- Joann H. Nichols, "Vital Records of Somerset, Vermont" in 1 [1996]: 165-72; 2 [1997]: 32-37.

Civil unions for same-sex couples were recorded from 1 July 2000 to 1 September 2009, when same-sex marriage was legalized in Vermont. Divorce records are held in the county family courts. There is a statewide divorce index from 1861 to 1968, and alphabetically arranged summaries from 1968 to 1979 at the state archives. *Ancestry.com* offers an online divorce index that covers 1981 to 1984 and 1989 to 2001 (subscription required).

Land Records

In Vermont, it can be difficult to locate land records if your ancestor lived in multiple locations. Land records are created at the town level, and there is no master index on either the county or state level. Each town has a master grantor and grantee index. There can be an index card system with all cards arranged in a single alphabetical index or ledger book indexes with separate columns for grantors and grantees.

It should be noted that *some* early land records were registered at the county level when the land did not lie in a jurisdiction with an established government (i.e. gores, unorganized towns, etc.). Not every county had land records, but the following list shows the deeds on microfilm at the Vermont State Archives and Records Administration:

- Addison Co. land deeds, 1784–1870, 7 volumes
- Addison Co. land deeds, index, 1774–1926
- Bennington Co. land deeds, 1782–1832, 5 volumes (individually indexed)
- Bennington Co. land deeds, index, [1782–1891], volumes A–E
- Bennington Co. land deeds, index, 1891–1984, volumes F–I
- Caledonia Co. land deeds, 1796–1971, 6 volumes (includes Harris Gore proprietor's records)
- Caledonia Co. land deeds, index, 1796–1971
- Chittenden Co. land deeds, 1785–1970, 14 volumes
- Chittenden Co. land deeds, index, 1785–1944 (through volume 12)
- Cumberland Co. land deeds, 1766–77, 2 volumes (individually indexed)
- Essex Co. land deeds, 1793–1971, 21 volumes
- Essex Co. land deeds, index, 1793–1871

STAFF PICKS

Compilations

Scott Andrew Bartley, "Name Changes in Vermont, 1778–1900," *Vermont Genealogy* 9 [2004], no. 1.

_____, "Genealogies Found in Vermont Histories," *Vermont Genealogy* 10 [2005], no. 1.

Abby Maria Hemenway, *The Vermont Historical Gazetteer: A Magazine, Embracing a History of Each Town, Civil, Ecclesiastical, Biographical and Military*, 5 vols. (Burlington, Vt., 1868–91).

Alden M. Rollins, *Vermont Religious Certificates* (Rockport, Me.: Picton Press, 2003).

_____, *Vermont Warnings Out*, 2 vols. (Camden, Me.: Picton Press, 1995, 1997).

- Essex Co. land deeds, index, 1871-1971
- Franklin Co. land deeds, 1797–1883, 7 volumes (individually indexed)
- Orange Co. land deeds, 1771–1832, volumes A–I
- Orange Co. land deeds, index, 1771–1952 [included in above films]
- Orleans Co. land deeds, 1799–1849, 4 volumes (individually indexed)
- Rutland Co. land deeds, 1773–1849, 9 volumes
- Rutland Co. land deeds, index [note: volume 8 missing]
- Windsor Co. land deeds, 1784–94, 1 volume (indexed)

New York was the last state to claim control over the region before Vermont declared its independence. At various times, New York established the counties of Charlotte (upstate New York and western Vermont), Cumberland (eastern Vermont), Gloucester (northeastern Vermont), and Albany (once all of Vermont, then western Vermont, and lastly the southwestern corner). New York kept land records at the county level. The deeds for Cumberland County survive and were published in their entirety in the following volumes:

- Scott Andrew Bartley, "Cumberland County, New York, Land Deeds, Volume 1, 1761-1774," *Vermont Genealogy* 13 (2008): 1-52.

- Scott Andrew Bartley, "Cumberland County, New York, Land Deeds, Volume 2, 1767-1774," *Vermont Genealogy* 14 (2009): 1-17.

- Scott Andrew Bartley, "Cumberland County, New York, Land Deeds, Volume 3, 1772-1775," *Vermont Genealogy* 15 (2010): 155-57.

Probate Records

Probates are recorded in probate districts. Each county either represents one complete district or is divided into two districts. Historically, there were twenty districts (the southern six counties having two districts per county), but as of 2012 there are fourteen districts representing the fourteen counties. The last dual districts were eliminated in 2011. Probate records up to 1850 and in some cases to 1900 have been microfilmed. The Genealogical Society of Utah is presently scanning the records of several counties up to 1915 and the original file papers, where they survive. The docket books usually have an index in each volume. The card index to the estate and guardianship records can be found only at the probate court itself (and at the Family History Library). The time frames of these indexes vary, but most go to the 1960s. Some of the indexes are closed as they contain cards for adoption cases. In Vermont, adoption cases are open to researchers after 99 years.

If you are using the probate records at the Vermont State Archives and Records Administration, however, you will encounter a problem. The office is currently interpreting the Homeland Security Act guidelines such that only their staff can look at the microfilm indexes. If your request is deemed acceptable, they consult the index, write down the corresponding volume and pages, and hand you the secured film. This policy prevents you from searching the index for other estates that might be important for your research. Going to the court itself or the Family History Library in Salt Lake City allows you to bypass this procedure. NEHGS does not hold any of these probate index films.

The only major loss of probate records is for Addison District, whose records burned in an 1852 fire. Before 1824, this district included the entire county. Some burnt records were recovered for 1801–51 and filmed. The next worst loss is Fair Haven District, which is missing record books 1-2, 7, 9, and 12-18.

Probate records are just beginning to be published. Volumes available to date (2012) include the following:

- Scott Andrew Bartley, "Abstracts of Bennington District Probate Records, Book 1, 1778-1792," *Vermont Genealogy* 12 (2007): 1-60.

- Scott Andrew Bartley and Marjorie J. Bartley, comp., *Windsor County, Vermont, Probate Index, 1778-1899* (St. Albans, Vt.: Genealogical Society of Vermont, 2000), which covers both the Hartford and Windsor Districts of the county.

- Margaret R. Jenks and Danielle L. Robert, *Rutland County, Vermont, Probate Extracts, Rutland District* [parts 1-5, covering 1781-1849], ed. by Dawn D. Hance (Granville, N.Y., 2007).

- _____, *Rutland County, Vermont, Probate Extracts, Fair Haven District* [parts 1-3 covering 1797-1855], ed. by Dawn D. Hance (Granville, N.Y., 2007-2008).
- Indexed images of the filed papers for Chittenden and Essex Counties, 1791-1919 on *www.FamilySearch.org*.

No probate records have been found for the years prior to independence (1777), though the researcher is urged to check the appropriate records for New Hampshire and New York for this period.

Court Records

The court system exercises judicial power. The courts interpret and apply the constitution and statutes and resolve disputes between parties. Parties are either plaintiffs (the party bringing suit) or defendants (the party accused of wrongdoing).

Vermont modeled its judicial system and state law on Connecticut. Its first constitution, established by convention on 2 July 1777, provided that the people had a right to trial by jury; that courts of justice would be established in every county; and that the Supreme Court and the several courts of common pleas would have the usual powers of such courts and the power of chancery. Between the end of the New York courts' sessions in June of 1775 and the 1778 legislation enacted by the General Assembly, there was effectively no legal court system in Vermont. Temporary courts were created by the General Assembly on 24 March 1778 with five judges for the "shires" of Newbury, Westminster, Benning-ton, and Rutland. The nature of these courts was clarified on 5 June of that year, when it was stated that these courts were not county courts. The courts created later that year were the Supreme Court of Judicature, Court of Chancery, County Court, Probate Court, Justices' Court, and Court of Confiscation.

The best guide to these records is Diane Rapaport, *New England Court Records: A Research Guide for Genealogists and Historians* (Burlington, Mass.: Quill Pen Press, 2006). The only published court records are for the pre-statehood New York jurisdiction of Charlotte County: Scott Andrew Bartley, "Court of General Sessions of the Peace for Charlotte County, New York, Volume 1, 19 Oct. 1773 to 20 June 1775," *Vermont Genealogy* 14 [2009]: 18-31, and Scott Andrew Bartley, "Court of General Sessions of the Peace for Charlotte County, New York, Volume 2, 13 Apr. 1779 to 24 Feb. 1784," *Vermont Genealogy* 14 [2009]: 18-31.

Anna Frances Gardner with doll buggy, Springfield, Vermont. Bertrand A. Chapman Family Papers (R. Stanton Avery Special Collections, NEHGS, Mss H 20).

Church Records

Unlike southern New England, the town church in Vermont could be any denomination. The most common groups before 1900 were Baptist, Congregational, Episcopal, Methodist, and Roman Catholic. All households were taxed to support the town church unless they could prove their support of another church in town. "Religious certificates" were recorded in the town books and are useful for identifying the religious minorities of the town. Certificates for the entire state have been published in *Vermont Religious Certificates* by Alden M. Rollins (Rockport, Me.: Picton Press, 2003).

Churches generally house their own records. In smaller towns, some of the earliest records have occasionally been deposited in the town clerk's safe. You might also check the major manuscript repositories in the state. For a listing of churches extant in 1939, see the WPA's *Directory of Churches and Religious Organizations in the State of Vermont* (Montpelier, Vt.: Historical Records Survey, 1939). For an overview of religious issues in the state, see the articles "Cabin Religion in Vermont, 1724-1791" by T. D. Seymour Bassett in *Vermont History*, 62: 2 [Spring 1994]: 69-87, and the "Formation of Town Churches" by John C. DeBoer and Clara Merritt DeBoer in *Vermont History*, 64: 2 [Spring 1996]: 69-88.

In many denominations the ecclesiastical records were considered the property of the minister. Thus they would leave the church when the minister left, and they may be located far distant from the Vermont town in which the events occurred.

Military Records

While the many soldiers traveling across the region during the French and Indian War (1754-63) spurred settlement in Vermont, records from this war are of little use for genealogical research in Vermont. Not until the Revolutionary War does the researcher begin to benefit from the records created by the military. The State Arsenal that housed military records was struck by lightning on 31 August 1945 and burned. Fortunately, many of their holdings for the Revolutionary War, War of 1812, Civil War, Spanish American War, and World War I had already been published.

Original records that survived are part of the Records of the Adjutant and Inspector General's Office. The collection includes the Revolutionary War, War of 1812, Vermont Militia (most of 1838-44), Civil War (the bulk of the collection), Vermont National Guard, and the Spanish-American War. These records are all housed at the Vermont State Archives, though their condition necessitates that the public use the microfilms. A guide to these records is available at *http://vermont-archives.org/collect/pdf/A-315.pdf.* The Privacy Act of 1974 restricts access to twentieth-century military records to the veteran or anyone the soldier designates. The records can be accessed at Vermont Veterans Affairs (118 State St., Montpelier, VT, 05620-4401, (802) 828-3379/(888) 666-9844). A bibliography of published military history and records through World War I can be found in the "Vermont" chapter by Scott Andrew Bartley in *A Guide to the Library of the New England Historic Genealogical Society* edited by Maureen A. Taylor and Henry B. Hoff (Boston: NEHGS, 2004), page 194, and to Desert Storm in "And there I was — : The Vermont Army National Guard in Operation Desert Storm, 1990–1991" (1991).

Cemetery Records

Other than the pre-1870 gravestone inscriptions from the vital records card file mentioned above, cemetery records were not widely available until the Vermont Old Cemetery Association (V.O.C.A.) began inventorying each town in 1972. The group identified nearly 1,900 cemeteries and used their survey to publish *Burial Grounds in Vermont* (Bradford, Vt.: V.O.C.A., 1991). The best guide for published transcriptions is Joann H. Nichols, Patricia L. Haslam, and Robert M. Murphy, *Index to Known Cemetery Listings in Vermont* (Montpelier, Vt.: Vermont Hist. Soc., 4th ed., 1999). There is an annotated list of more than fifty towns with published cemetery transcriptions in the NEHGS manuscript collections. (See *A Guide to the Library of the New England Historic Genealogical Society,* edited by Maureen A. Taylor and Henry B. Hoff [Boston: NEHGS, 2004].) Addison and Rutland County towns are best represented.

Special Sources

The following list of sources addresses a variety of topics of interest to genealogists:

- Scott Andrew Bartley, ed., *Vermont Families in 1791,* 2 vols. (Vol. 1, Camden, Me.: Picton Press, 1992; Vol. 2, St. Albans: Genealogical Society of Vermont, 1997).
- Scott Andrew Bartley, "Vermont Vital Records: A First Stop for Genealogists" (1999), online at *www.AmericanAncestors. org/vermont-vital-records.*
- Scott Andrew Bartley, "Migration: A Story of Vermont Before 1850" (2000) online at *www.AmericanAncestors.org/migration-a-story-of-vermont-before-1850.*
- Scott Andrew Bartley, "Vermont Research Facilities" (2002-2003), in three parts online at *www.AmericanAncestors.org/ articles-authors/#bartley.* This three-part article is among a score of articles on Vermont by Bartley at *AmericanAncestors.org.*
- Scott Andrew Bartley, "Name Changes in Vermont, 1778-1900," *Vermont Genealogy* 9, no. 1 [Jan. 2004].
- Scott Andrew Bartley, "Declarations of Aliens, Lower Canada, 1794-1811," *Vermont Genealogy,* 12, nos. 1-2 [Jan.-Apr. 2006].

- John J. Duffy, Samuel B. Hand, and Ralph H. Orth, *The Vermont Encyclopedia* (Hanover, N.H.: University Press of New England, 2003).
- Carleton Edward Fisher and Sue Gray Fisher, comps., *Soldiers, Sailors, and Patriots of the Revolutionary War—Vermont* (Camden, Me.: Picton Press, 1992).
- Eric G. Grundset, ed., "Chapter Two: New Hampshire and Vermont," in *Forgotten Patriots: African American and American Indian Patriots in the Revolutionary War* (Washington, D.C.: National Society Daughters of the American Revolution, 2008), 39–76.
- Andrew E. Nuquist and Edith W. Nuquist, *Vermont State Government and Administration: An Historical and Descriptive Study of the Living Past* (Burlington, Vt., 1966), 644 pp. Not necessarily for the average genealogist, this volume is a source for information on how the government has functioned.
- Michael Sherman, Gene Sessions, and P. Jeffrey Potash, *Freedom and Unity: A History of Vermont* (Barre: Vermont Historical Society, 2004).

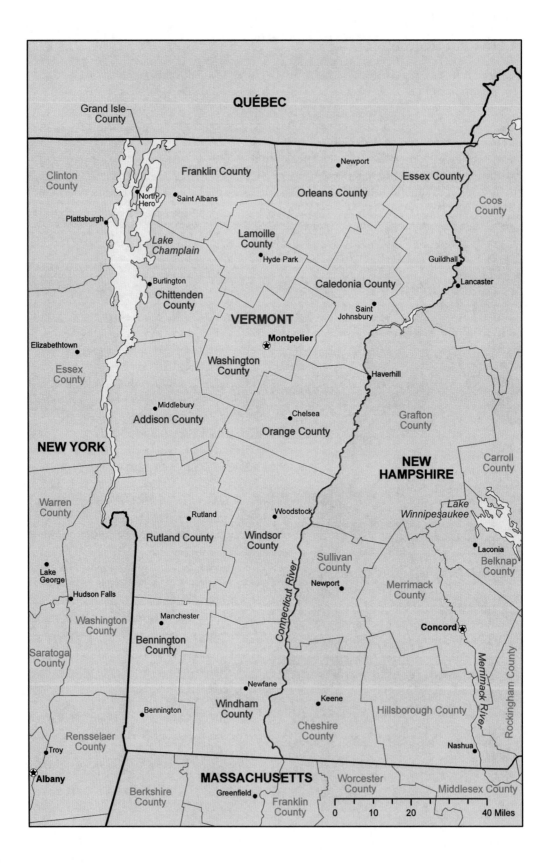

Vermont Repositories

The following are major repositories with large collections of materials of interest to genealogists. Check with each repository prior to visiting to obtain the most current information about hours and access to materials in the collection.

Vermont State Archives and Records Administration

Office of the Secretary of State
1078 U.S. Route 2, Middlesex
Montpelier, VT 05633-7701
www.vermont-archives.org
(802) 828-3700; fax (802) 828-3710
See website for email
Hours: Office, M–F 7:45–4:30; Reference
Room, M–F 9–4

Records of birth, marriage, civil union, divorce, dissolution, and death more than five
years old are held by VSARA. (For vital records less than five years old, see the Vital
Records Division, at right.) Other holdings include military records, naturalizations, and the Nye Index to eighteenth- and
nineteenth-century Vermont state records.
A number of indexes are available online.
VSARA also houses historical records from
courts around the state.

Vermont Department of Health, Division of Vital Records

108 Cherry Street
Burlington, VT 05402
http://healthvermont.gov/research/records/
vital_records.aspx
(802) 863-7200; fax (802) 863-7275
See website for email
Hours: M–F 7:45–4:30

Records of birth, marriage, civil union, divorce, dissolution, and death less than five
years old are held at the Division of Vital
Records. (Civil unions were discontinued
on September 1, 2009, when same-sex marriage was legalized in Vermont.) For records
more than five years old, see the Vermont
State Archives and Records Administration,
at left.

Above: Chapman family photograph, 1924, Springfield, Vermont. Bertrand A. Chapman Family Papers (R. Stanton Avery Special Collections, NEHGS, Mss H 20).

Vermont State Library

Division of Reference, Law and
Information Services
109 State Street
Montpelier, VT 05609-0601
www.libraries.vermont.gov
(802) 828-3268; fax (802) 828-1481
dol_ill_mail@dol.state.vt.us
Hours: M–F 7:45–4:30

The Vermont State Library has numerous genealogies, county and town histories, statistical reports, and other published sources. It houses about 1,000 newspapers from around the state dating from the 1780s. It also is the state repository for NHPRC (National Historic Publications and Record Commission) filming of all Vermont newspapers.

Vermont Historical Society

Leahy Library
Vermont History Center
60 Washington Street
Barre, VT 05641-4209
www.vermonthistory.org
(802) 479-8500; fax (802) 479-8510
vhs-info@state.vt.us
Hours: Tu, Th, F, 2nd Sat 9–4; W 9–8

The Leahy Library holds books and pamphlets dating from the 1770s, and broadsides, maps, and photographs in addition to its manuscript collections. Only a small por-

tion of the manuscript collections appear in the online catalog. The library also has microfilms (including vital records), videotapes, records, and audiotapes, which include oral histories.

Bennington Museum

75 Main Street
Bennington, VT 05201-2885
www.benningtonmuseum.org
(802) 447-1571
info@benningtonmuseum.org
Hours: M–Tu, Th–Sat 1–5

The Bennington Museum has the second largest genealogical collection in the state.

University of Vermont Bailey/Howe Library

538 Main Street
Burlington, VT 05405-0036
www.library.uvm.edu
(802) 656-2023; fax (802) 656-4038
See website for email
Hours: M–Th, 8–10; F 8–5

The Special Collections Department houses the Wilbur Collection of Vermontiana.

Vermont Old Cemetery Association

PO Box 266
Weston, VT 05161
www.voca58.org

Vermont Counties

There are currently fourteen counties in Vermont. Bennington was the original county. The most recent, Lamoille, was created in 1835. The second table shows the only extinct Vermont county. The third table shows the four New York counties that originally contained territory in Vermont.

Name	Est.	Parent(s)	Probate District(s)	Deed District(s)*	Note
Addison	1785	Rutland	Addison, New Haven	Towns	
Bennington	1778	Original County	Bennington, Manchester	Towns	
Caledonia	1792	Orange	Caledonia	Towns	
Chittenden	1787	Addison	Chittenden	Towns	
Essex	1792	Orange	Essex	Towns	
Franklin	1792	Chittenden	Franklin	Towns	
Grand Isle	1802	Franklin	Grand Isle	Towns	
Lamoille	1835	Chittenden, Franklin, Orleans, and Washington	Lamoille	Towns	
Orange	1781	Cumberland	Bradford, Randolph (through 1994); Orange (1994 to present)	Towns	
Orleans	1792	Orange	Orleans	Towns	
Rutland	1781	Bennington	Rutland and Fair Haven	Towns	
Washington	1810	Addison, Caledonia, Chittenden, and Orange	Washington	Towns	Called Jefferson to 1814.
Windham	1781	Cumberland	Marlboro and Westminster	Towns	
Windsor	1781	Cumberland	Windsor and Hartford	Towns	

Extinct Vermont County

Name	Est.	Parent(s)	Probate District(s)	Deed District(s)	Note
Cumberland	1772	Albany, N.Y.	Cumberland	Towns	Abolished when Orange, Windham, and Windsor were formed 1781.

New York Counties

Name	Est.	Parent(s)	Probate District(s)	Deed District(s)	Note
Albany	1764		Albany		Abolished by Vt. 1777.
Charlotte	1772	Albany			Abolished by Vt. 1777.
Cumberland	1772	Albany		County	Abolished by Vt. 1777.
Gloucester	1766	Albany		County	Abolished by Vt. 1777.

* Some county deeds exist for land that was sold prior to the formation of some towns.

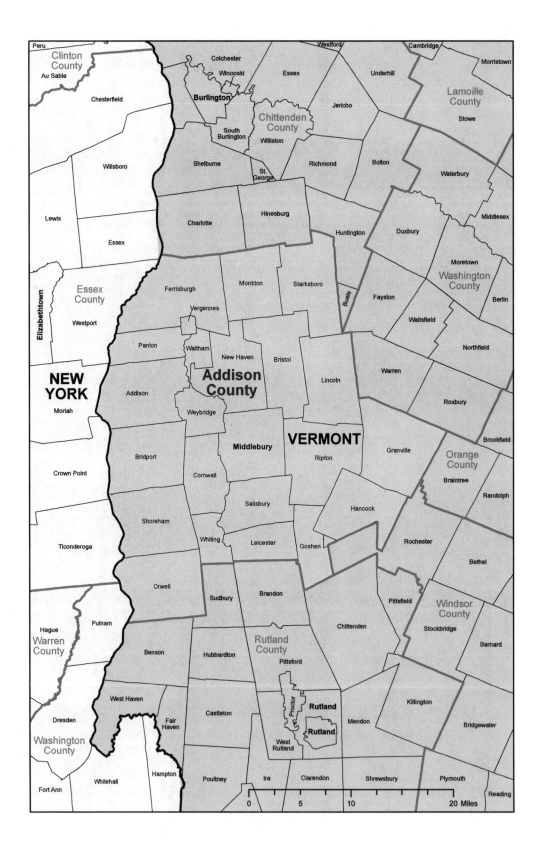

VT

Addison County

Founded	1785
Parent County	Rutland
County Seat	Middlebury

Towns

Addison, Bridport, Bristol, Cornwall, Ferrisburgh, Goshen, Granville, Hancock, Leicester, Lincoln, Middlebury, Monkton, New Haven, Orwell, Panton, Ripton, Salisbury, Shoreham, Starksboro, Vergennes, Waltham, Weybridge, Whiting

Extinct

Goshen Gore No. 2

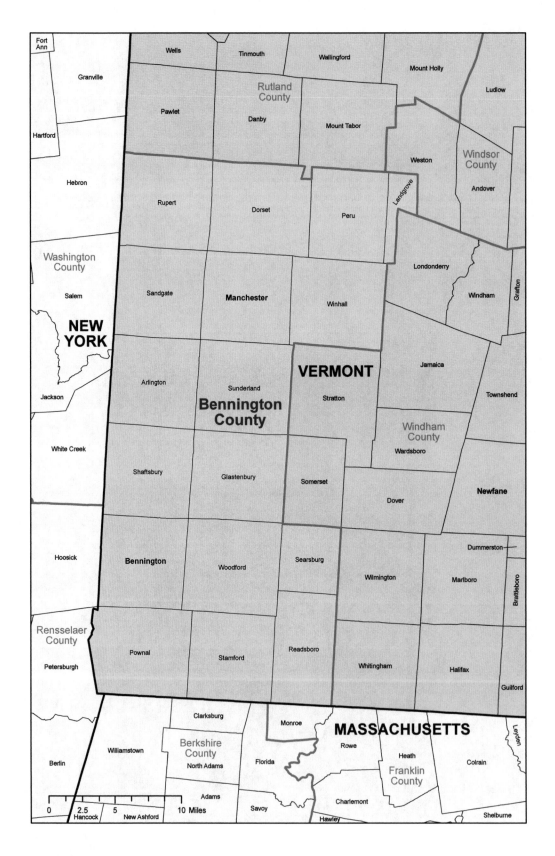

VT

Bennington County

Founded 1779
Original County
County Seats Bennington, Manchester

Towns

Arlington, Bennington, Dorset, Landgrove, Manchester, Peru, Pownal, Readsboro, Rupert, Sandgate, Searsburg, Shaftsbury, Stamford, Sunderland, Winhall, Woodford

Unincorporated

Glastenbury

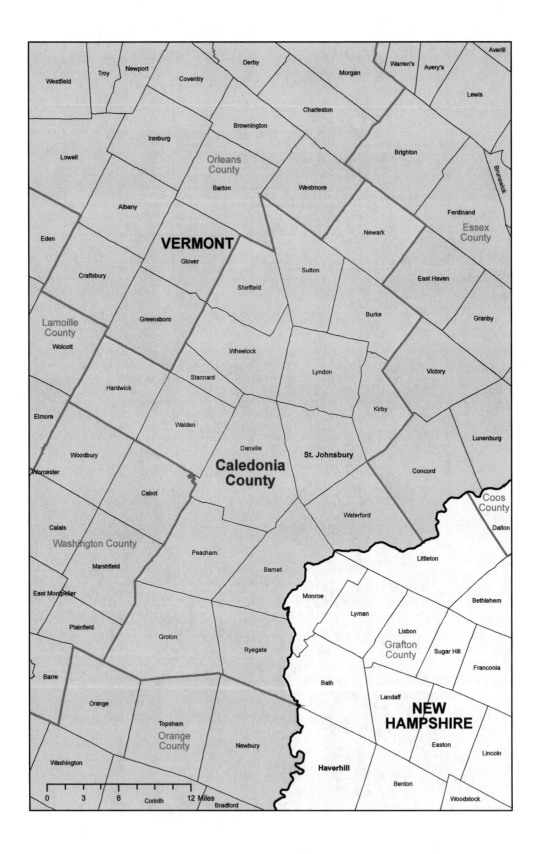

VT

Caledonia County

Founded	1792
Parent County	Orange
County Seat	Saint Johnsbury

Towns

Barnet, Burke, Danville, Groton, Hardwick, Kirby, Lyndon, Newark, Peacham, Ryegate, Saint Johnsbury, Sheffield, Stannard, Sutton, Walden, Waterford, Wheelock

Extinct

Bradleyvale, Deweysburgh, Harris Gore, Hopkinsville

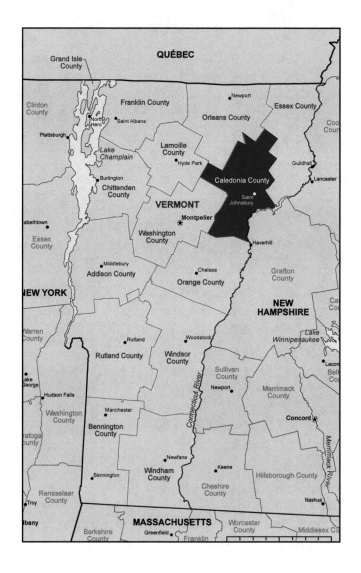

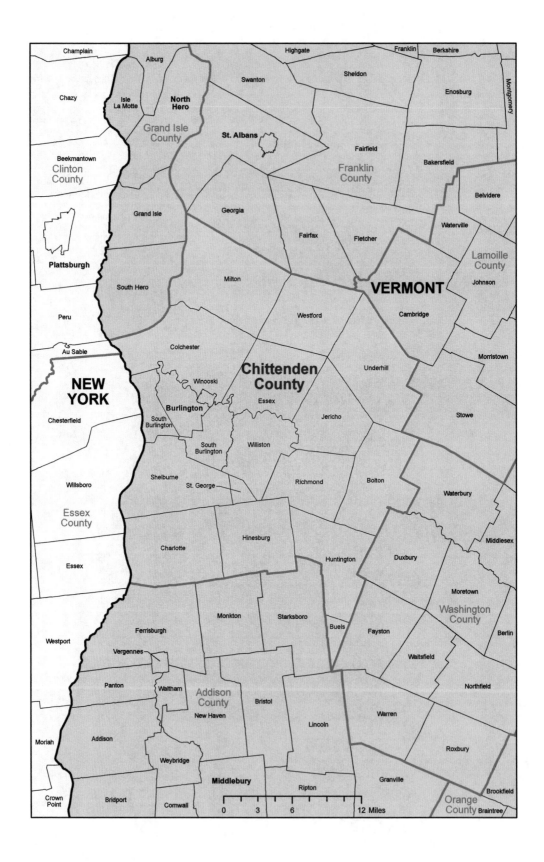

VT

Chittenden County

Founded	1787
Parent County	Addison
County Seat	Burlington

Towns

Bolton, Burlington, Charlotte, Colchester, Essex, Hinesburg, Huntington, Jericho, Milton, Richmond, Saint George, Shelburne, South Burlington, Underhill, Westford, Williston, Winooski

Unincorporated

Buel's Gore

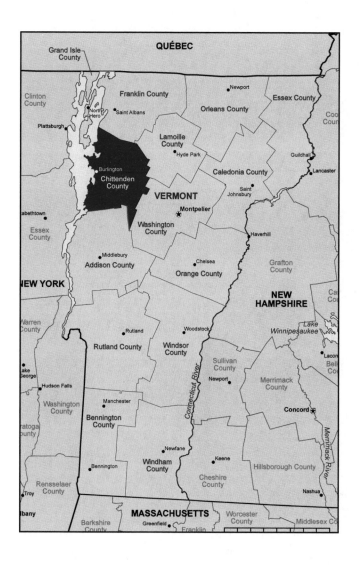

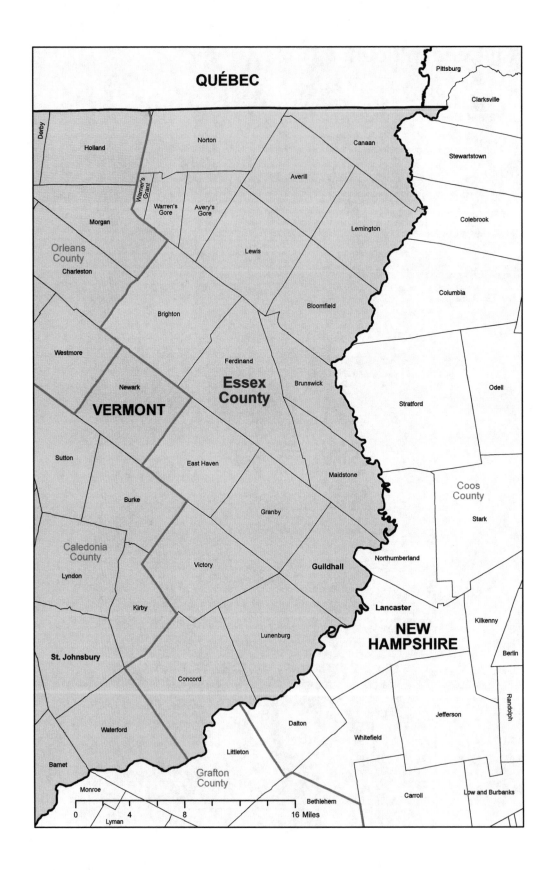

QUÉBEC

Pittsburg

Clarksville

Derby

Holland

Norton

Canaan

Stewartstown

Warner's Grant

Warren's Gore

Avery's Gore

Averill

Morgan

Lemington

Colebrook

Orleans County

Charleston

Lewis

Brighton

Bloomfield

Columbia

Westmore

Ferdinand

Brunswick

Newark

Essex County

Odell

VERMONT

Stratford

Sutton

East Haven

Maidstone

Burke

Granby

Coos County

Stark

Caledonia County

Victory

Guildhall

Northumberland

Lyndon

Kirby

Lancaster

Kilkenny

NEW HAMPSHIRE

Berlin

Lunenburg

St. Johnsbury

Randolph

Concord

Waterford

Dalton

Jefferson

Littleton

Whitefield

Barnet

Grafton County

Monroe

Carroll

Low and Burbanks

Bethlehem

0   4   8   16 Miles

Lyman

VT

Essex County

Founded	1792
Parent County	Orange
County Seat	Guildhall

Towns

Bloomfield, Brighton, Brunswick, Canaan, Concord, East Haven, Granby, Guildhall, Lemington, Lunenberg, Maidstone, Norton, Victory

Extinct or Unincorporated

Averill, Avery's Gore, Ferdinand, Lewis, Warner's Grant, Warren Gore, Wenlock

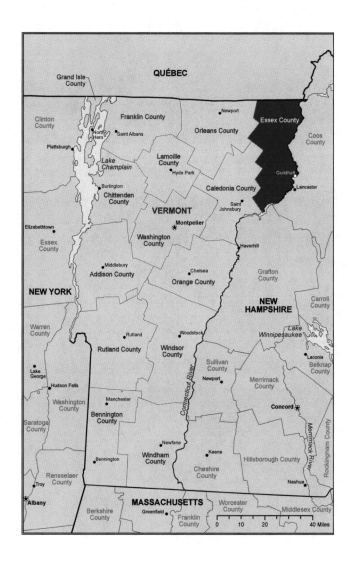

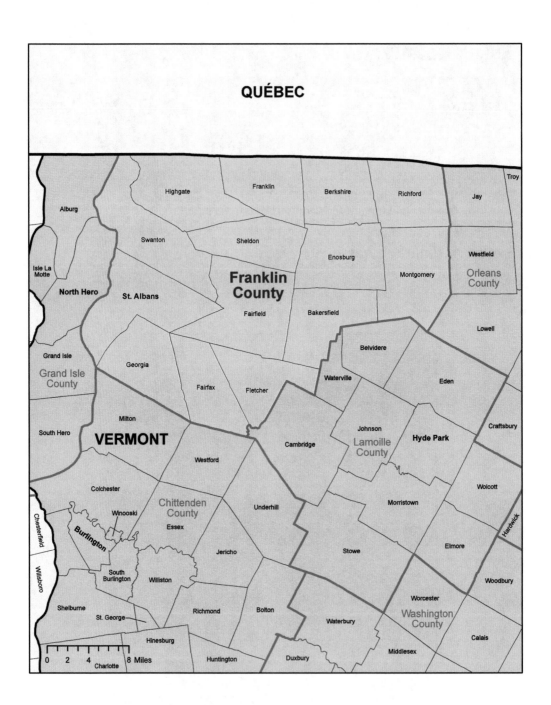

QUÉBEC

Troy

Highgate   Franklin   Berkshire   Richford   Jay

Alburg

Swanton   Sheldon   Enosburg   Montgomery   Westfield

Isle La
Motte

North Hero   St. Albans   **Franklin**   Orleans
County   County

Fairfield   Bakersfield   Lowell

Grand Isle   Belvidere

Georgia   Eden
Grand Isle   Waterville
County   Fairfax   Fletcher

Milton   Johnson   Craftsbury
South Hero   **VERMONT**   Lamoille   **Hyde Park**
County
Westford   Cambridge

Colchester   Wolcott

Winooski   Underhill   Morristown   Hardwick
Chittenden
County
Burlington   Essex
Chesterfield
Jericho   Stowe   Elmore   Woodbury
South
Burlington   Williston
Willsboro
Shelburne   Worcester
St. George   Richmond   Bolton   Washington   Calais
County
Waterbury
Hinesburg
Middlesex
0   2   4   8 Miles   Huntington   Duxbury
Charlotte

Franklin County

Founded	1792
Parent County	Chittenden
County Seat	Saint Albans

Towns

Bakersfield, Berkshire, Enosburgh, Fairfax, Fairfield, Fletcher, Franklin, Georgia, Highgate, Montgomery, Richford, Saint Albans, Sheldon, Swanton

Extinct

Knowlton's Gore, Marvin's Gore, Smithfield

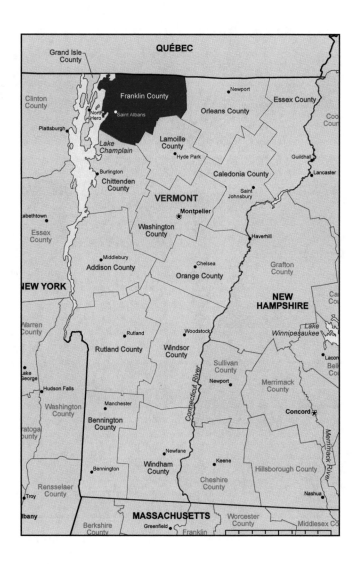

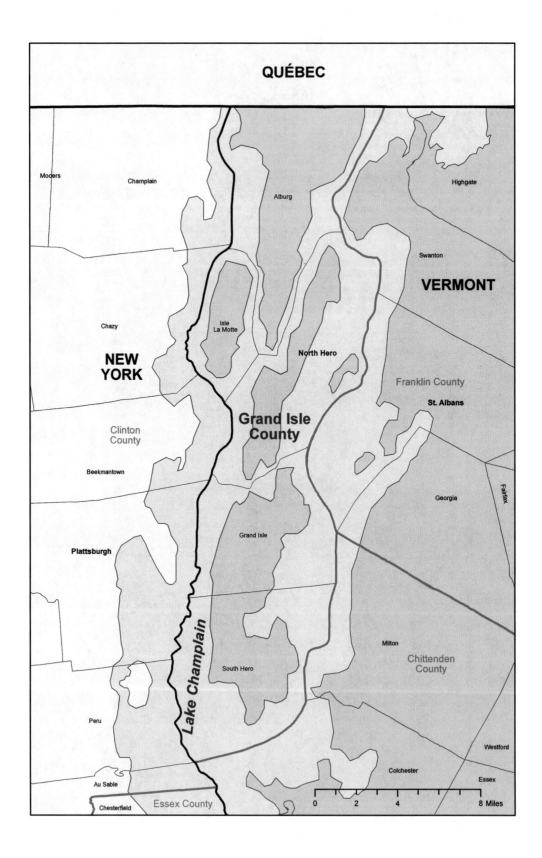

QUÉBEC

Moders

Champlain

Alburg

Highgate

Swanton

VERMONT

Isle
La Motte

Chazy

North Hero

**NEW
YORK**

Franklin County

St. Albans

**Grand Isle
County**

Clinton
County

Beekmantown

Fairfax

Georgia

Grand Isle

Plattsburgh

Milton

Lake Champlain

Peru

Chittenden
County

South Hero

Westford

Au Sable

Colchester

Essex

Chesterfield

Essex County

| 0 | 2 | 4 | 8 Miles |

Grand Isle County

Founded	1802
Parent Counties	Chittenden, Franklin
County Seat	North Hero

Towns

Alburgh, Grand Isle, Isle La Motte, North Hero, South Hero

Extinct

Two Heroes

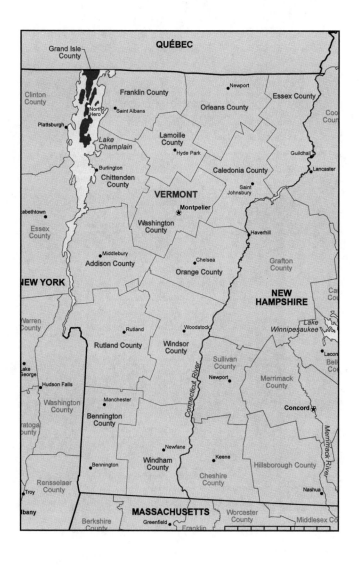

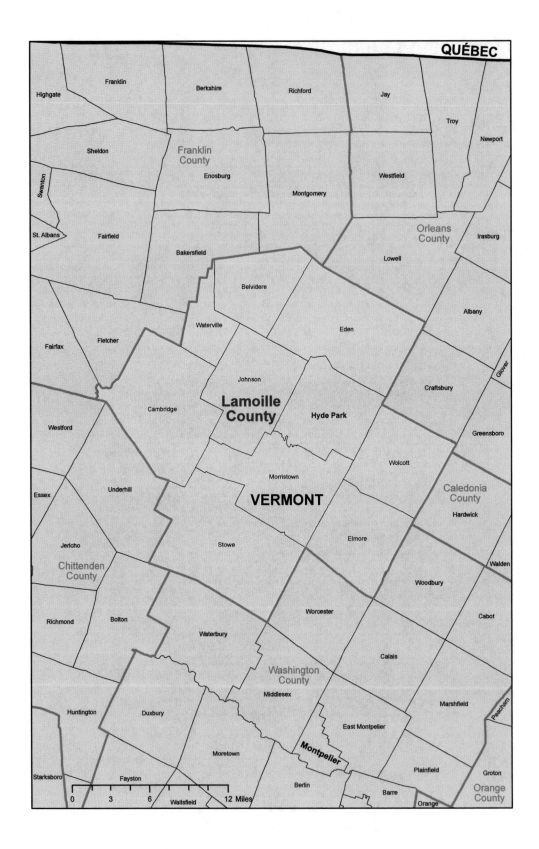

QUÉBEC

Franklin
Highgate
Berkshire
Richford
Jay
Troy
Newport

Sheldon
Franklin
County
Westfield
Enosburg
Montgomery

Swanton

St. Albans
Fairfield
Orleans
County
Irasburg
Bakersfield
Lowell

Belvidere
Albany

Waterville
Eden

Fairfax
Fletcher
Glover

Johnson
Craftsbury

Lamoille
County
Cambridge
Hyde Park
Greensboro

Westford

Wolcott

Essex
Underhill
VERMONT
Caledonia
County
Hardwick

Morristown

Jericho
Stowe
Elmore
Walden

Chittenden
County
Woodbury

Richmond
Bolton
Worcester
Cabot

Waterbury
Calais

Washington
County
Middlesex
Marshfield

Huntington
Duxbury
East Montpelier
Peacham

Moretown
Montpelier
Plainfield
Groton

Starksboro
Fayston
Berlin
Orange
County
Barre

0   3   6   12 Miles
Waitsfield
Orange

Lamoille County

Founded	1835
Parent Counties	Chittenden, Franklin, Orleans, Washington
County Seat	Hyde Park

Towns

Belvidere, Cambridge, Eden, Elmore, Hyde Park, Johnson, Morristown, Stowe, Waterville, Wolcott

Extinct

Mansfield, Sterling

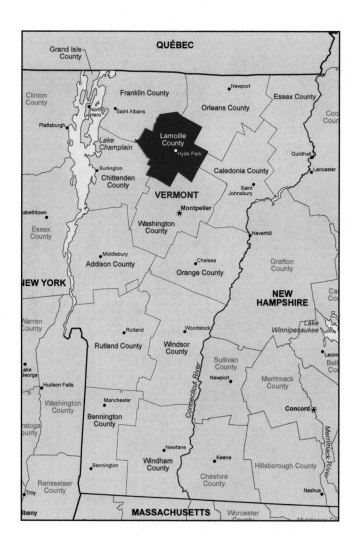

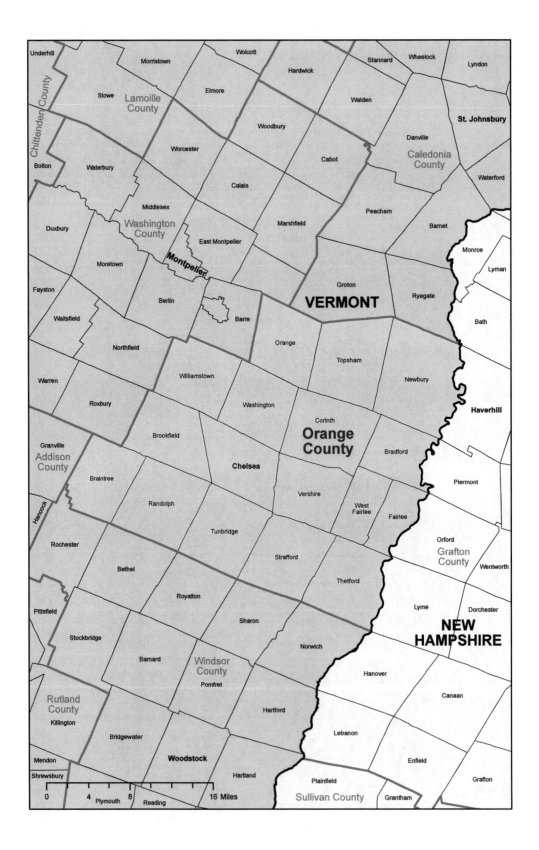

Orange County

Founded	1781
Parent County	Cumberland
County Seat	Chelsea

Towns

Bradford, Braintree, Brookfield, Chelsea, Corinth, Fairlee, Newbury, Orange, Randolph, Strafford, Thetford, Topsham, Tunbridge, Vershire, Washington, West Fairlee, Williamstown

Extinct

Norfolk, Walden Gore

VT

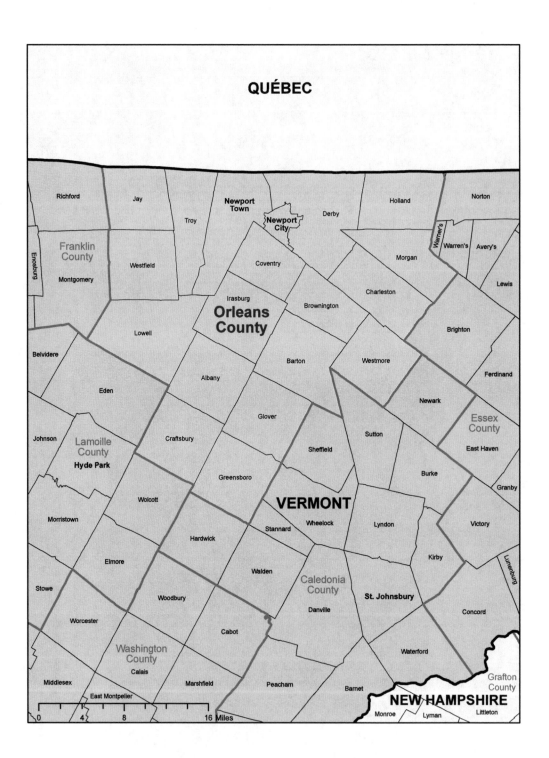

QUÉBEC

Richford | Jay | Newport Town | Derby | Holland | Norton

Troy | Newport City | Warren's | Avery's

Franklin County | Westfield | Coventry | Morgan | Lewis

Montgomery | Charleston

Irasburg | Brownington | Brighton

Orleans County | Lowell | Barton | Westmore | Ferdinand

Belvidere

Albany | Newark | Essex County

Eden | Glover | Sutton | East Haven

Johnson | Craftsbury | Sheffield | Burke | Granby

Lamoille County | Hyde Park | Greensboro | VERMONT

Wolcott | Lyndon | Victory

Morristown | Wheelock | Stannard | Kirby | Lunenburg

Hardwick | Caledonia County

Elmore | Walden | St. Johnsbury | Concord

Stowe | Danville

Worcester | Woodbury | Waterford

Cabot | Washington County | Calais | Grafton County

Middlesex | Marshfield | Peacham | Barnet | NEW HAMPSHIRE

East Montpelier | Monroe | Lyman | Littleton

0   4   8   16 Miles

Orleans County

Founded	1792
Parent Counties	Chittenden, Orange
County Seat	Newport

Towns

Albany, Barton, Brownington, Charleston, Coventry, Craftsbury, Derby, Glover, Greensboro, Holland, Irasburg, Jay, Lowell, Morgan, Newport, Troy, Westfield, Westmore

Extinct or Unincorporated

Coventry Gore, Kelly's Grant, Kelly's Grant No. 2, Woodbridge

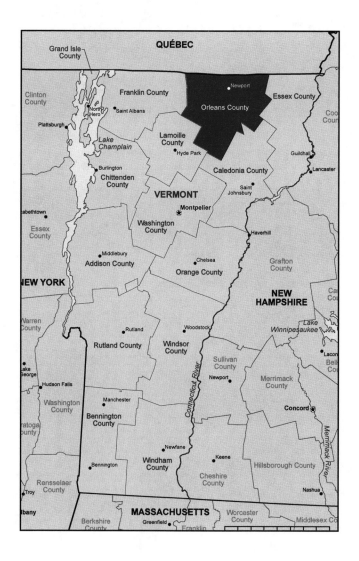

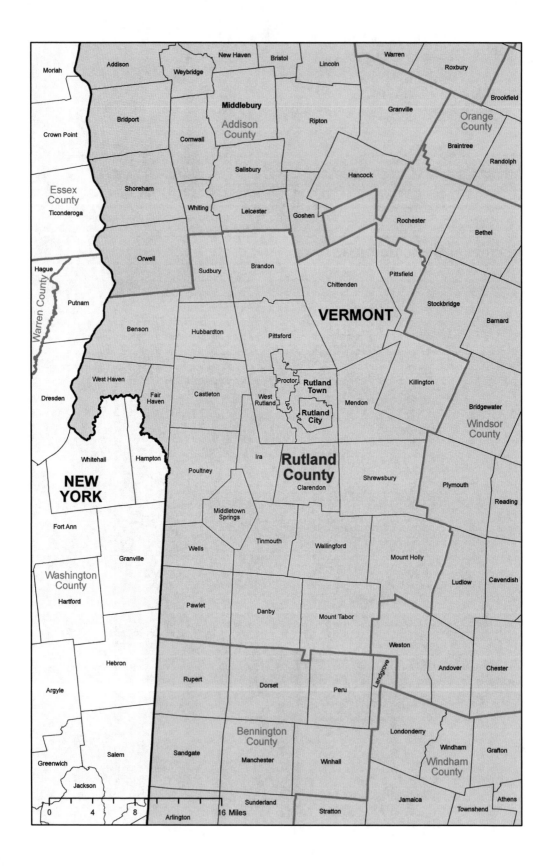

Moriah

Addison

Weybridge

New Haven

Bristol

Lincoln

Warren

Roxbury

Brookfield

Middlebury

Bridport

Cornwall

*Addison
County*

Ripton

Granville

*Orange
County*

Braintree

Randolph

Crown Point

Salisbury

Hancock

*Essex
County*

Shoreham

Ticonderoga

Whiting

Leicester

Goshen

Rochester

Bethel

Orwell

Sudbury

Brandon

Chittenden

Pittsfield

Hague

Putnam

Stockbridge

Warren County

Benson

Hubbardton

Pittsford

VERMONT

Barnard

West Haven

Fair
Haven

Castleton

Proctor

**Rutland
Town**

Mendon

Killington

Dresden

West
Rutland

**Rutland
City**

Bridgewater

*Windsor
County*

Whitehall

Hampton

Poultney

Ira

**Rutland
County**

Shrewsbury

Plymouth

Reading

**NEW
YORK**

Clarendon

Fort Ann

Middletown
Springs

Tinmouth

Wallingford

Mount Holly

Ludlow

Cavendish

Granville

Wells

*Washington
County*

Pawlet

Danby

Mount Tabor

Hartford

Weston

Hebron

Rupert

Dorset

Peru

Landgrove

Andover

Chester

Argyle

Salem

*Bennington
County*

Londonderry

Windham

Grafton

Greenwich

Sandgate

Manchester

Winhall

*Windham
County*

Jackson

0   4   8   16 Miles

Sunderland

Jamaica

Athens

Arlington

Stratton

Townshend

Rutland County

Founded	1781
Parent County	Bennington
County Seat	Rutland

Towns

Benson, Brandon, Castleton, Chittenden, Clarendon, Danby, Fair Haven, Hubbardton, Ira, Killington, Mendon, Middletown Springs, Mount Holly, Mount Tabor, Pawlet, Pittsfield, Pittsford, Poultney, Proctor, Rutland, Shrewsbury, Sudbury, Tinmouth, Wallingford, Wells, West Haven, West Rutland

Extinct

Jackson's Gore, Parker's Gore, Philadelphia

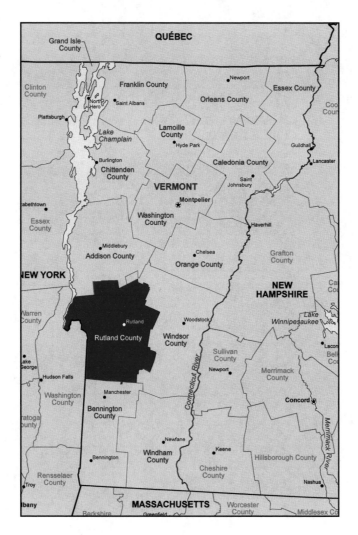

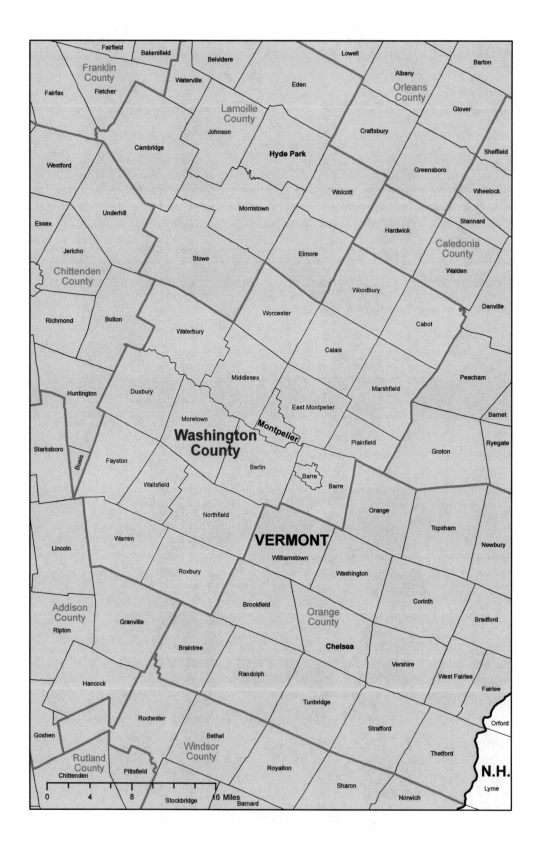

VT

Washington County

Founded	1810
Parent Counties	Caledonia, Chittenden, Orange
Original County	Called Jefferson to 1814
County Seat	Montpelier

Towns

Barre, Berlin, Cabot, Calais, Duxbury, East Montpelier, Fayston, Marshfield, Middlesex, Montpelier, Moretown, Northfield, Plainfield, Roxbury, Waitsfield, Warren, Waterbury, Woodbury, Worcester

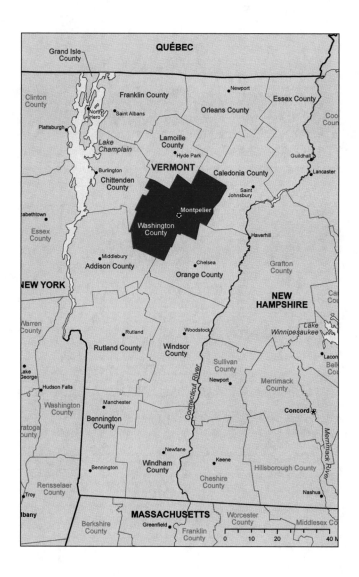

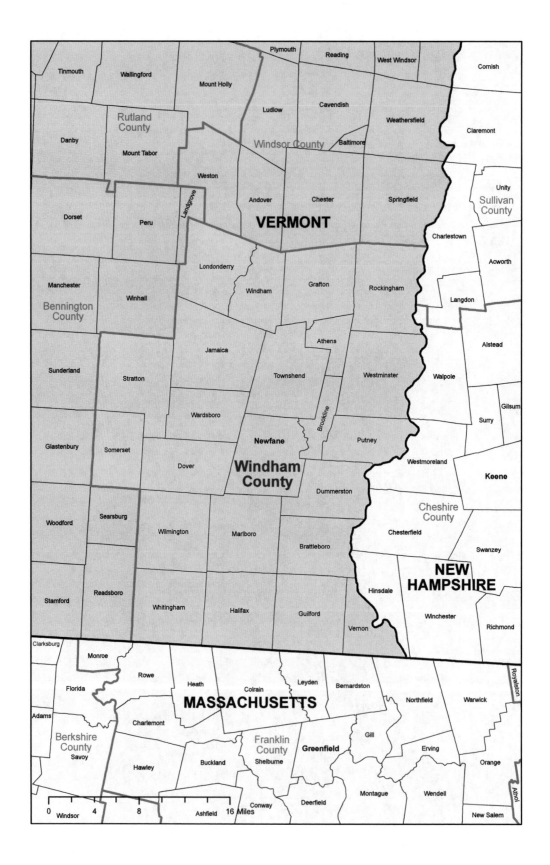

Windham County

Founded	1779 (as Cumberland); renamed 1781
Parent County	Cumberland
County Seat	Newfane

Towns

Athens, Brattleboro, Brookline, Dover, Dummerston, Grafton, Guilford, Halifax, Jamaica, Londonderry, Marlboro, Newfane, Putney, Rockingham, Stratton, Townshend, Vernon, Wardsboro, Westminster, Whitingham, Wilmington, Windham

Extinct or Unincorporated

Acton, Aiken's Gore, Hitchcock's Gore, Johnson's Gore, Somerset

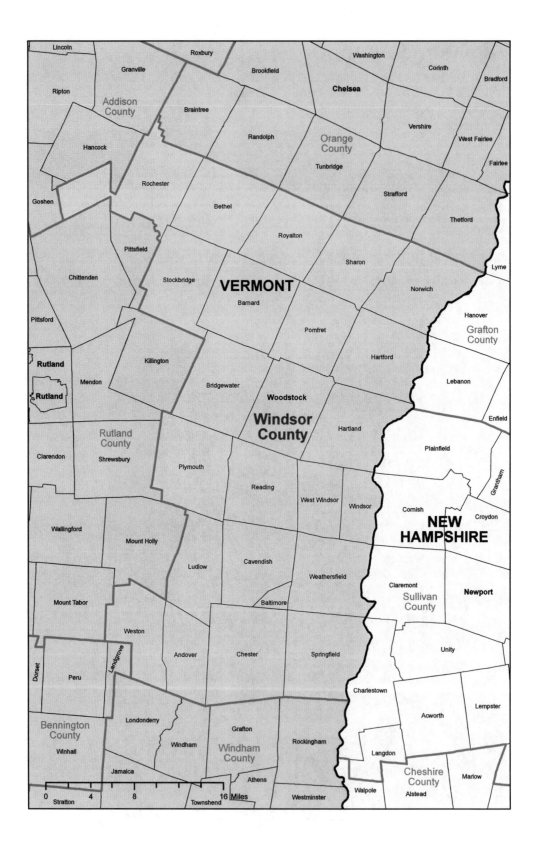

Windsor County

Founded	1781
Parent County	Cumberland
County Seat	Woodstock

Towns

Andover, Baltimore, Barnard, Bethel, Bridgewater, Cavendish, Chester, Hartford, Hartland, Ludlow, Norwich, Plymouth, Pomfret, Reading, Rochester, Royalton, Sharon, Springfield, Stockbridge, Weathersfield, West Windsor, Weston, Windsor, Woodstock

Extinct

Benton's Gore

Probate Records

Probate in Vermont is recorded on the county level; today there is one court for one county. Older records will usually be found at the primary county probate court. Access to originals may be restricted for those records that are available on microfilm.

Addison County

Addison Probate Court
7 Mahady Court
Middlebury, VT 05753
www.vermontjudiciary.org/gtc/probate
(802) 388-2612
Hours: M–F 8–4:30

Extinct Districts

Addison
Towns served: Bridport, Cornwall, Goshen, Granville, Hancock, Leicester, Middlebury, Orwell, Ripton, Salisbury, Shoreham, Weybridge, Whiting

New Haven
Towns served: Addison, Bristol, Ferrisburg, Lincoln, Monkton, New Haven, Panton, Starksboro, Waltham, Vergennes

Bennington County

Bennington Probate Court
207 South Street
Bennington, VT 05201

Mailing Address
PO Box 65
Bennington, VT 05201-0065

www.vermontjudiciary.org/gtc/probate
(802) 447-2705
Hours: M–F 8–4:30

Extinct Districts

Bennington
Towns served: Bennington, Glastenbury, Pownal, Readsboro, Searsburg, Shaftsbury, Stamford, Woodford

Manchester
Towns served: Arlington, Dorset, Landgrove, Manchester, Peru, Rupert, Sandgate, Sunderland, Winhall

Above: Workers at box factory, Springfield, Vermont. Bertrand A. Chapman Family Papers (R. Stanton Avery Special Colelctions, NEHGS, Mss H 20).

Caledonia County

Caledonia Probate Court
1126 Main St
St. Johnsbury, VT 05819

Mailing Address
PO Box 406
St. Johnsbury, VT 05819-0406
www.vermontjudiciary.org/gtc/probate
(802) 748-6605; fax (802) 748–6603
Hours: M–F 8–4:30

Chittenden County

Chittenden Probate Court
175 Main Street
Burlington, VT 05401

Mailing Address
PO Box 511
Burlington, VT 05402

www.vermontjudiciary.org/gtc/probate
(802) 651-1518
Hours: M–F 8–4:30

Essex County

Essex Probate Court
49 Mill Street Extension
Island Pond, VT 05846

Mailing Address
PO Box 426
Island Pond, VT 05846-0426

www.vermontjudiciary.org/gtc/probate
(802) 723-4770
Hours: M–W 8–4:30

Franklin County

Franklin Probate Court
17 Church Street
St. Albans, VT 05478
www.vermontjudiciary.org/gtc/probate
(802) 524-4112
Hours: M–F 8–4:30

Grand Isle County

Called Alburgh Probate District to 1805.
Grand Isle Probate Court
3677 Route 2
North Hero, VT 05474

Mailing Address
PO Box 7
North Hero, VT 05474-0007

www.vermontjudiciary.org/gtc/probate
(802) 372-8350
Hours: M–F 8–4:30

Lamoille County

Lamoille Probate Court
154 Main Street
Hyde Park, VT 05655

Mailing Address
PO Box 102
Hyde Park, VT 05655-0102

www.vermontjudiciary.org/gtc/probate
(802) 888-3306
Hours: M–F 8–4:30

Orange County

Orange Probate Court
5 Court Street
Chelsea, VT 05038-9746
www.vermontjudiciary.org/gtc/probate
(802) 685-4610
Hours: M–F 8–4:30

Extinct Districts

Bradford District
Towns served: Bradford, Corinth, Fairlee,
Newbury, Strafford, Thetford, Topsham,
Vershire, West Fairlee

Randolph District
Towns served: Braintree, Brookfield,
Chelsea, Orange, Randolph, Tunbridge,
Washington, Williamstown

Orleans County

Orleans Probate Court
247 Main Street
Newport, VT 05855
www.vermontjudiciary.org/gtc/probate
(802) 334-3366
Hours: M–F 8–4:30

Rutland County

Rutland Probate Court
83 Center Street
Rutland, VT 05701
www.vermontjudiciary.org/gtc/probate
(802) 775-0114
Hours: M–F 8–4:30

Extinct Districts

Fair Haven
Towns served: Benson, Castleton, Fair Haven, Hubbardton, Pawlet, Poultney, Sudbury, Wells, West Haven

Rutland
Towns served: Brandon, Chittenden, Clarendon, Danby, Ira, Mendon, Middletown Springs, Mount Holly, Mount Tabor, Pittsfield, Pittsford, Proctor, Rutland, Sherburne, Shrewsbury, Tinmouth, Wallingford, West Rutland

Washington County

Washington Probate Court
10 Elm Street, Unit 2
Montpelier, VT 05602
www.vermontjudiciary.org/gtc/probate
(802) 828-3405
Hours: M–F 8–4:30

Windham County

Windham Probate Court
80 Flat Street, Suite 104
Brattleboro, VT 05301
www.vermontjudiciary.org/gtc/probate
(802) 257-2898
Hours: M–F 8–4:30

Extinct Districts

Marlboro
Towns served: Brattleboro, Dover, Dummerston, Guilford, Halifax, Marlboro, Newfane, Somerset, Stratton, Vernon, Wardsboro, Whitingham, Wilmington

Westminster
Towns served: Athens, Brookline, Grafton, Jamaica, Londonderry, Putney, Rockingham, Townshend, Westminster, Windham

Windsor County

Windsor Probate Court
62 Pleasant Street
Woodstock, VT 05091-0275
www.vermontjudiciary.org/gtc/probate
(802) 457-1503
Hours: M–F 8–12, 1–4:30

Extinct Districts

Hartford
Towns served: Barnard, Bethel, Bridgewater, Hartford, Hartland, Norwich, Pomfret, Rochester, Royalton, Sharon, Stockbridge, Woodstock

Windsor
Towns served: Andover, Baltimore, Cavendish, Chester, Ludlow, Plymouth, Reading, Springfield, Weathersfield, Weston, West Windsor, Windsor

Land Records

Land records in Vermont are usually found at the town level. The town clerk serves as the register of deeds. Counties hold some very early land records for areas outside jurisdictions with an established government. See p. 313 for a discussion of county land records. For more information, see *www.vermont.gov* or *http://vermont-elections.org/2012TCGuide1.2012.pdf.*

Addison
Town Clerk
65 Vermont Route 17W
Addison, VT 05491

Mailing Address
7099 Vermont Route 22A
Addison, VT 05491

(802) 759–2020; fax (802) 759–2233
addisontown@gmavt.net
Hours: M–F 8:30–12, 1–4:30

Albany
Town Clerk
827 Main Street
Albany, VT 05820

Mailing Address
PO Box 284
Albany, VT 05820

(802) 755–6100
albany@gaw.com
Hours: Tu, Th, 9–4; W, 9–7

Alburgh
Town Clerk
1 North Main Street
Alburgh, VT 05440
www.alburghvt.org
(802) 796–3468; fax (802) 796–3939
village@fairpoint.net
Hours: M–F 9–5

Andover
Town Clerk
953 Weston–Andover Road
Andover, VT 05143
(802) 875–2765; fax (802) 875–6647
clerk@vermontel.net
Hours: M, Tu, Th, F 9–1; W 11–3

Arlington
Town Clerk
3828 Vermont Route 7A
Arlington, VT 05250

Mailing Address
PO Box 304
Arlington, VT 05250

(802) 375–2332; fax (802) 375–2332
arltc@comcast.net
Hours: M–F 9 –2

Athens
Town Clerk
56 Brookline Road
Athens, VT 05143
(802) 869–3370; fax (802) 869–3370
townofathens@hotmail.com
Hours: M 9–1 or by appt.

Bakersfield
Town Clerk
40 East Bakersfield Road
Bakersfield, VT 05441

Mailing Address
PO Box 203
Bakersfield, VT 05441

(802) 827–4495; fax (802) 827–3106
townclerk_bakersfield@comcast.net
Hours: M–F 9–12

Baltimore
Town Clerk
1902 Baltimore Road
Baltimore, VT 05143
(802) 263–5274; fax (802) 263–5274
baltimorevt@tds.net
Hours: W 4–6; Th 9–11; and by appt.

Barnard

Town Clerk
115 North Road
Barnard, VT 05031–0274

Mailing Address
PO Box 274
Barnard, VT 05031–0274

(802) 234–9211
barnardto@gmail.com
Hours: M–W 8–3:30

Barnet

Town Clerk
1743 US Route 5 South
Barnet, VT 05821

Mailing Address
PO Box 15
Barnet, VT 05821

www.barnetvt.org
(802) 633–2256; fax (802) 633–4315
townclerk@barnetvt.org
Hours: M–F 9–12, 1–4:30

Barre, City of

City Clerk
6 N. Main Street, Suite 6
Barre, VT 05641

Mailing Address
PO Box 418
Barre, VT 05641

www.barrecity.org
(802) 476–0242; fax (802) 476–0264
Hours: M–F 7:30–4:30

Barre, Town of

Clerk–Treasurer
149 Websterville Road
Websterville, VT 05678

Mailing Address
PO Box 124
Websterville, VT 05678

www.barretown.org
(802) 479–9391; fax (802) 479–9332
Hours: M–F 8–4:30

Barton

Town Clerk
34 Main Street
Barton, VT 05822
(802) 525–6222; fax (802) 525–8856
bartontown@comcast.net
Hours: M–Th 7:30–4; F 7:30–12

Belvidere

Town Clerk
3996 Vermont Route 109
Belvidere, VT 05442
(802) 644–6621; fax (802) 644–6621
beltc@pshift.net
Hours: Tu–Th 8:30–3:30

Bennington

Town Clerk
205 South Street
Bennington, VT 05201
www.bennington.com
(802) 442–1043; fax (802) 442–1068
Hours: M–F 8–5

Benson

Town Clerk
2760 Stage Road
Benson, VT 05731

Mailing Address
PO Box 163
Benson, VT 05731

www.benson–vt.com
(802) 537–2611; fax (802) 537–2612
mail@benson–vt.com
Hours: M, Tu, Th, F 9–3; W 3–7

Berkshire

Clerk–Treasurer
4454 Watertower Road
Enosburg Falls, VT 05450
(802) 933–2335; fax (802) 933–5913
berkshire_clerk@surfglobal.net
Hours: M, Tu 8–5; W, Th 8–4

Berlin
Town Clerk
108 Shed Road
Berlin, VT 05602
www.berlinvt.org
(802) 229–9298; fax (802) 229–9530
townclerk@berlinvt.org
Hours: Tu–Th 8:30–3:30

Bethel
Town Clerk
134 South Main Street
Bethel, VT 05032

Mailing Address
PO Box 404
Bethel, VT 05032
http://bethelvt.com

(802) 234–9722; fax (802) 234–6840
betheltownclerk@comcast.net
Hours: M, Th 8–12:30, 1–4; Tu, F 8–12

Bloomfield
Clerk–Treasurer
27 Schoolhouse Road
Bloomfield, VT 05905

Mailing Address
PO Box 336
North Stratford, NH 03590

(802) 962–5191; fax (802) 962–5191
bloomfieldtown@wildblue.net
Hours: Tu, Th 9–3 and by appt.

Bolton
Clerk–Treasurer
3045 Roosevelt Hwy.
Waterbury, VT 05676
www.boltonvt.com
(802) 434–3064; fax (802) 434–6404
Hours: M–Th 8–4

Bradford
Town Clerk
172 North Main Street
Bradford, VT 05033

Mailing Address
PO Box 339
Bradford, VT 05033

www.bradford–vt.us
(802) 222–4727; fax (802) 222–3520
clerk@bradford–vt.us
Hours: M–Th 8:30–4:30; F 9–12

Braintree
Town Clerk
932 Vermont Route 12A
Braintree, VT 05060
www.braintreevt.com
(802) 728–9787; fax (802) 728–9787
braintreetownclerk@comcast.net
Hours: Tu 9–12, 1–4; W–Th 9–12, 1–4; and
by appt.

Brandon
Town Clerk
49 Center Street
Brandon, VT 05733
www.townofbrandon.com
(802) 247–5721; fax (802) 247–5481
Hours: M–F 8:30–4

Brattleboro
Town Clerk
230 Main Street, Suite 108
Brattleboro, VT 05301
www.brattleboro.org
(802) 251–8157; fax (802) 257–2312
Hours: M–F 8:30–5

Bridgewater

Town Clerk
7335 US Route 4
Bridgewater, VT 05034
(802) 672–3334; fax (802) 672–5395
twnbridg@comcast.net
Hours: M–Th 8–4

Bridport

Town Clerk
82 Crown Point Road
Bridport, VT 05734

Mailing Address
PO Box 27
Bridport, VT 05734

(802) 758–2483; fax (802) 758–2483
bridporttown@gmavt.net
Hours: M, Tu, F 9–4; Th 9–12

Brighton

Clerk–Treasurer
49 Mill Street Ext.
Island Pond, VT 05846

Mailing Address
PO Box 377
Island Pond, VT 05846

(802) 723–4405; fax (802) 723–4405
brightonclerk@comcast.net
Hours: M–F 8–3:30

Bristol

Town Clerk
1 South Street
Bristol, VT 05443

Mailing Address
PO Box 249
Bristol, VT 05443

www.bristolvt.net
(802) 453–2486; fax (802) 453–5188
bristoltown@gmavt.net
Hours: M–F 8–4:30

Brookfield

Town Clerk
40 Ralph Road
Brookfield, VT 05036

Mailing Address
PO Box 463
Brookfield, VT 05036

www.brookfieldvt.org
(802) 276–3352; fax (802) 376–3926
btownhall@aol.com
Hours: Tu–Th 8:30–12, 1–4:30

Brookline

Clerk–Treasurer
736 Grassy Brook Road
Brookline, VT 05345

Mailing Address
PO Box 403
Newfane, VT 05345

www.brooklinevt.com
(802) 365–4648; fax (802) 365–4092
brook763@comcast.net
Hours: Tu, Th 9–2; 1st Sat. of month 9–12

Brownington

Clerk–Treasurer
622 Schoolhouse Road
Brownington, VT 05860

Mailing Address
PO Box 66
Orleans, VT 05860

(802) 754–8401; fax (802) 754–8401
browningtontc@comcast.net
Hours: M, W, Th 9–4; and by appt.

Brunswick

Town Clerk
994 Vermont Route 102
Brunswick, VT 05905
(802) 962–5514; fax (802) 962–5522
bruns321@sover.net
Hours: Th 4–6; 1st Sat. of month 9–12; and
    by appt.

Burke
Clerk–Treasurer
212 School Street
West Burke, VT 05871
www.burkevermont.org
(802) 467–3717; fax (802) 467–8623
burke@burkevermont.com
Hours: M–F 8–4

Burlington
Town Clerk
149 Church Street
Burlington, VT 05401
www.ci.burlington.vt.us
(802) 865–7019; fax (802) 865–7000
Hours: M–F 8–4:30

Cabot
Town Clerk
3084 Main Street
Cabot, VT 05647

Mailing Address
PO Box 36
Cabot, VT 05647

www.cabotvt.us
(802) 563–2279; fax (802) 563–2623
tcocabot@fairpoint.net
Hours: M–Th 9–5

Calais
Clerk–Treasurer
3120 Pekin Brook Road
East Calais, VT 05650
www.calaisvermont.gov
(802) 456–8720; fax (802) 456–8720
calais.townclerk@gmail.com
Hours: M, Tu, Th 8–5; Sat 8–12

Cambridge
Clerk–Treasurer
85 Church Street, Suite 201
Jeffersonville, VT 05464

Mailing Address
PO Box 143
Jeffersonville, VT 05464

www.townofcambridgevt.org
(802) 644–2251; fax (802) 644–8348
See website for email
Hours: M–F 8–4

Canaan
Town Clerk
318 Christian Hill
Canaan, VT 05903

Mailing Address
PO Box 159
Canaan, VT 05903

www.canaanvt.org
(802) 266–3370; fax (802) 266–8253
Hours: M–F 9–3

Castleton
Town Clerk
556 Main Street
Castleton, VT 05735

Mailing Address
PO Box 727
Castleton, VT 05735

www.bsi-vt.com
(802) 468–2212 ext 214; fax (802) 468–5482
casclerk@shoreham.net
Hours: M, Tu, Th 8:30–12:30, 1:30–5;
      W 8:30–12:30, 1:30–6

Cavendish
Town Clerk
37 High St
Cavendish, VT 05142

Mailing Address
PO Box 126
Cavendish, VT 05142

(802) 226–7291 or (802) 226–7292;
      fax (802) 226–7290
Hours: M, Tu, Th, F 9–12, 1–4:30;
      W 9–12, 1–6

Charleston

Clerk–Treasurer
5063 Vermont Route 105
West Charleston, VT 05872
www.charlestonvt.org
(802) 895–2814; fax (802) 895–2814
townofcharlestonvt@comcast.net
Hours: M, Tu, Th 8–3

Charlotte

Town Clerk
159 Ferry Road
Charlotte, VT 05445

Mailing Address
PO Box 119
Charlotte, VT 05445

www.charlottevt.org
(802) 425–3071; fax (802) 425–4713
See website for email
Hours: M–F 8–4

Chelsea

Town Clerk
296 Vermont Route 110
Chelsea, VT 05038

Mailing Address
PO Box 266
Chelsea, VT 05038

www.chelseavt.org
(802) 685–4460; fax (802) 685–4460
town.clerk@chelseavt.us
Hours: M 8:30–2:30, 4:30–6:30;
    Tu–F 8:30–2:30

Chester

Town Clerk
556 Elm Street
Chester, VT 05143

Mailing Address
PO Box 370
Chester, VT 05143

www.chester.govoffice.com
(802) 875–2173; fax (802) 875–2237
tcchester@vermontel.net
Hours: M–F 8–5

Chittenden

Town Clerk
337 Holden Road
Chittenden, VT 05737

Mailing Address
PO Box 89
Chittenden, VT 05737

(802) 483–6647; fax (802) 483–2504
chittendenvt@comcast.net
Hours: M, Tu, Th, F 1:30–5; W 1:30–7

Clarendon

Town Clerk
279 Middle Road
Clarendon, VT 05759

Mailing Address
PO Box 30
Clarendon, VT 05759

www.clarendonvt.org
(802) 775–4274; fax (802) 775–4274
clarendonclerk@comcast.net
Hours: M–Th 10–4

Colchester

Town Clerk
781 Blakely Road
Colchester, VT 05446

Mailing Address
PO Box 55
Colchester, VT 05446

http://colchestervt.gov
(802) 264–5520; fax (802) 264–5503
See website for email
Hours: M–F 8–4

Concord

Town Clerk
374 Main Street
Concord, VT 05824

Mailing Address
PO Box 317
Concord, VT 05824

www.concordvt.com
(802) 695–2220; fax (802) 695–2552
conclerk@charterinternet.com
Hours: M, Th, F 9–3; Tu 12–6

Corinth

Town Clerk
1387 Cookeville Rd
Corinth, VT 05039

Mailing Address
PO Box 461
Corinth, VT 05039

www.corinthvt.org
(802) 439–5850; fax (802) 439–5850
corino@tops–tele.com
Hours: M 8–4; Tu 8–6; Th 9–3; 1st Sat 10–12

Cornwall

Town Clerk
2629 Route 30
Cornwall, VT 05753
www.cornwall.govoffice2.com
(802) 462–2775; fax (802) 462–2606
cornwallvt@shoreham.net
Hours: Tu–F 9–5

Coventry

Town Clerk
168 Main Street
Coventry, VT 05825

Mailing Address
PO Box 104
Coventry, VT 05825

(802) 754–2288; fax (802) 754–6274
covtc@sover.net
Hours: M, Tu, Th, F 8–12; W 4–7; 3rd Sat 9–2

Craftsbury

Town Clerk
85 South Craftsbury Rd
Craftsbury, VT 05826

Mailing Address
PO Box 55
Craftsbury, VT 05826

www.townofcraftsbury.com
(802) 586–2823; fax (802) 586–2323
craftsbury@gmail.com
Hours: Tu–F 8:30–4; M and Sat by appt.

Danby

Town Clerk
130 Brook Road
Danby, VT 05739

Mailing Address
PO Box 231
Danby, VT 05739

(802) 293–5136; fax (802) 293–5311
danbytownclerk@vermontel.net
Hours: M–Th 9–12, 1–4

Danville

Town Clerk
36 Route 2 W
Danville, VT 05828–0183

Mailing Address
PO Box 183
Danville, VT 05828–0183

www.danvillevt.com
(802) 684–3352; fax (802) 684–9606
danvtc36@yahoo.com
Hours: M–F 8–4

Derby

Clerk–Treasurer
124 Main Street
Derby, VT 05829

Mailing Address
PO Box 25
Derby, VT 05829

www.derbyvt.org
(802) 766–4906; fax (802) 766–2027
derbytc@derbyvt.org
Hours: M–Th 7–5

Dorset

Clerk
112 Mad Tom Road
East Dorset, VT 05253

Mailing Address
PO Box 24
East Dorset, VT 05253

cont. on next page

Dorset cont.
www.dorsetvt.com
(802) 362–1178 ext 2; fax (802) 362–5156
dorsetclerk@gmail.com
Hours: M–Th 8:30–3:30; F 8:30–12:30

Dover
Clerk
102 Route 100
West Dover, VT 05356

Mailing Address
PO Box 527
West Dover, VT 05356

www.doververmont.com
(802) 464–8000; fax (802) 464–8721
dvrclerk@sover.net
Hours: M–F 9–5

Dummerston
Clerk
1523 Middle Road
East Dummerston, VT 05346
www.dummerston.org
(802) 257–1496; fax (802) 257–4671
townclerk@dummerston.org
Hours: M, Tu, Th, F 9–3; W 11–5

Duxbury
Clerk–Treasurer
5421 Vermont Route 100
Duxbury, VT 05676
www.duxburyvermont.org
(802) 244–6660; fax (802) 244–5442
duxbury1@myfairpoint.net
Hours: M 8–4; W 10–6; Tu, Th, F
     7:30–3:30

East Haven
Clerk–Treasurer
64 Community Building Road
East Haven, VT 05837

Mailing Address
PO Box 10
East Haven, VT 05837

(802) 467–3772
tclerk1790@kingcon.com
Hours: Tu 1–6; Th 8–1; and by appt.

East Montpelier
Town Clerk
40 Kelton Road
East Montpelier, VT 05651

Mailing Address
PO Box 157
East Montpelier, VT 05651

(802) 223–3313; fax (802) 223–4467
eastmonttct@comcast.net
Hours: M–Th 9–5; F 9–12

Eden
Town Clerk
71 Old Schoolhouse Road
Eden Mills, VT 05653
www.edenvt.org
(802) 635–2528; fax (802) 635–1724
See website for email
Hours: M–Th 8–4

Elmore
Town Clerk
1175 Vermont Route 12
Elmore, VT 05657

Mailing Address
PO Box 123
Lake Elmore, VT 05657

www.elmorevt.org
(802) 888–2637; fax (802) 888–2637
Hours: Tu, W, Th 9–3; and by appt.

Enosburgh
Town Clerk
239 Main Street
Enosburg Falls, VT 05450

Mailing Address
PO Box 465
Enosburg Falls, VT 05450

www.enosburghvermont.org
(802) 933–4421; fax (802) 933–4832
enostown@myfairpoint.net
Hours: M–F 8–3

Essex
Town Clerk
81 Main Street
Essex Junction, VT 05452
http://essexjunction.org
(802) 878–6944; fax (802) 878–6946
See website for email
Hours: M–F 7:30–4:30

Fair Haven
Town Clerk
3 North Park Place
Fair Haven, VT 05743
http://fairhavenvt.org
(802) 265–3610 ext 4; fax (802) 265–3176
See website for email
Hours: M–F 8–4

Fairfax
Town Clerk
67 Hunt St
Fairfax, VT 05454

Mailing Address
PO Box 27
Fairfax, VT 05454

(802) 849–6111 ext 2; fax (802) 849–6276
fairfaxtownclerk@live.com
Hours: 1st & 3rd M 9–4, 6–8; Tu–F 9–4

Fairfield
Town Clerk
25 North Rd
Fairfield, VT 05455

Mailing Address
PO Box 5
Fairfield, VT 05455

www.fairfieldvermont.us
(802) 827–3261; fax (802) 827–3653
See website for email
Hours: M, Tu, Th, F 8–3; W 10:30–5:30

Fairlee
Town Clerk
75 Town Common
Fairlee, VT 05045

Mailing Address
PO Box 95
Fairlee, VT 05045

www.fairleevt.org
(802) 333–4363; fax (802) 333–9214
townclerk@fairleevt.org
Hours: M–Th 8:30–3:30; and by appt.

Fayston
Town Clerk
866 North Fayston Road
Fayston, VT 05660
www.faystonvt.com
(802) 496–2454; fax (802) 496–9850
faystontc@madriver.com
Hours: M–Th 9–3:30; F 9–3

Ferrisburgh
Town Clerk
3279 Route 7
Ferrisburgh, VT 05456

Mailing Address
PO Box 6
Ferrisburgh, VT 05456

http://twp.ferrisburgh.vt.us
(802) 877–3429; fax (802) 877–6942
ferrisburghclerk@comcast.net
Hours: M–F 8–4

Fletcher
Town Clerk
215 Cambridge Rd
Fletcher, VT 05444
fletchervt.net
(802) 849–6616; fax (802) 849–2500
townfletcher@surfglobal.net
Hours: M–Th 8–3:30; M 6:30–8:30

Franklin
Town Clerk
5167 Main St
Franklin, VT 05457

Mailing Address
PO Box 82
Franklin, VT 05457

www.franklinvermont.com
(802) 285–2101; fax (802) 285–2181
townoff@franklinvt.net
Hours: M, Tu, F 8:30–3:30; W 8:30–12;
    Th 8:30–6

Georgia
Town Clerk
47 Town Common Road North
Georgia Center, VT 05478
http://townofgeorgia.com
(802) 524–3524; fax (802) 524–3543
georgia_clerk@comcast.net
Hours: M–F 8–4

Glover
Town Clerk
51 Bean Hill
Glover, VT 05839
http://townofglover.com
(802) 525–6227; fax (802) 525–4115
glovertc@comcast.net
Hours: M–Th 8–4

Goshen
Town Clerk
50 Carlisle Hill Road
Goshen, VT 05733
www.goshenvt.org
(802) 247–6455; fax (802) 247–6740
townclerk@goshenvt.org
Hours: Tu 9–1

Grafton
Town Clerk
117 Main Street
Grafton, VT 05146

Mailing Address
PO Box 180
Grafton, VT 05146

www.graftonvermont.org
(802) 843–2419; fax (802) 843–6100
gtclerk@vermontel.net
Hours: M, Tu, Th, F 9–12, 1–4

Granby
Town Clerk
9005 Granby Road
Granby, VT 05840

Mailing Address
PO Box 56
Granby, VT 05840

(802) 328–3611; fax (802) 328–2200
granby@wildblue.net
Hours: by appt.

Grand Isle
Town Clerk
9 Hyde Road
Grand Isle, VT 05458

Mailing Address
PO Box 49
Grand Isle, VT 05458

www.grandislevt.org
(802) 372–8830; fax (802) 372–8815
clerk@town.grand–isle.vt.us
Hours: M–F 8:30–3:30; M 5–7; Sat 10–12

Granville
Town Clerk
4801 Vermont Route 100
Granville, VT 05747

Mailing Address
PO Box 66
Granville, VT 05747

www.granvillevermont.org
(802) 767–4403; fax (802) 767–3968
granvilletown@gmavt.net
Hours: M–Th 9–3

Greensboro

Town Clerk
81 Lauredon Ave
Greensboro, VT 05841

Mailing Address
PO Box 119
Greensboro, VT 05841

http://greensboro.govoffice.com
(802) 533–2911; fax (802) 533–2191
greensborovt@yahoo.com
Hours: M–Th 9–4:30

Groton

Town Clerk
1476 Scott Hwy
Groton, VT 05046
www.grotonvt.com
(802) 584–3276; fax (802) 584–3276
grotonclerk@fairpoint.net
Hours: M, Tu, Th 8:30–12:30, 1–5; W, F
8:30–12:30

Guildhall

Town Clerk
13 Courthouse Dr.
Guildhall, VT 05905

Mailing Address
PO Box 10
Guildhall, VT 05905

www.guildhallvt.org
(802) 676–3797; fax (802) 676–3518
townclerk@guildhallvt.org
Hours: Tu 9–6; Th 9–12, 5–7

Guilford

Town Clerk
236 School Road
Guilford, VT 05301
www.guilfordvt.org
(802) 254–6857; fax (802) 257–5764
guilfordtc@yahoo.com
Hours: M 7–6; Tu, W, Th 7–5

Halifax

Town Clerk
246 Branch Road
West Halifax, VT 05358

Mailing Address
PO Box 127
West Halifax, VT 05358

www.halifaxvermont.com
(802) 368–7390; fax (802) 368–7390
townclerk@halifaxvermont.com
Hours: M, Tu, F 8–3; Sat 9–12

Hancock

Town Clerk
48 Vermont Route 125
Hancock, VT 05748

Mailing Address
PO Box 100
Hancock, VT 05748

(802) 767–3660; fax (802) 767–3660
hancocktwnclerk@yahoo.com
Hours: M–Th 10–4

Hardwick

Town Clerk
20 Church Street
Hardwick, VT 05843

Mailing Address
PO Box 523
Hardwick, VT 05843

www.hardwickvt.org
(802) 472–5971; fax (802) 472–3793
hardwicktc@vtlink.net
Hours: M–F 8–4

Hartford

Town Clerk
171 Bridge Street
White River Junction, VT 05001
www.hartford-vt.org
(802) 295–2785; fax (802) 295–6382
See website for email
Hours: M–F 8–5

Hartland

Town Clerk
1 Quechee Road
Hartland, VT 05048

Mailing Address
PO Box 349
Hartland, VT 05048

www.hartland.govoffice.com
(802) 436–2444; fax (802) 436–2464
hartlandvtclerk@vermontel.com
Hours: M–F 7–7

Highgate

Town Clerk
2996 Vermont Route 78
Highgate, VT 05459

Mailing Address
PO Box 189
Highgate, VT 05459

highgate.weebly.com
(802) 868–4697; fax (802) 868–3064
hgtownclerk@gmail.com
Hours: M–F 8:30–12, 1–4:30

Hinesburg

Town Clerk
10632 Route 116
Hinesburg, VT 05461
www.hinesburg.org
(802) 482–2281; fax (802) 482–5404
hinesburgclerk@gmavt.net
Hours: M, Tu, Th, F 8–4; W 10–6

Holland

Town Clerk
120 School Road
Holland, VT 05830
(802) 895–4440; fax (802) 895–4440
holland1805@hotmail.com
Hours: M, Tu, Th 8–4:30; Sat by appt.

Hubbardton

Town Clerk
1831 Monument Hill Rd.
Hubbardton, VT 05735
http://hubbardtonvt.com
(802) 273–2951; fax (802) 273–3729
clrkhubb@shoreham.net
Hours: M, W, F 9–2

Huntington

Town Clerk
4930 Main Road
Huntington, VT 05462
http://huntingtonvt.org
(802) 434–2032
huntingtonclerk@gmavt.net
Hours: M 7–7; Tu, W, Th 8–3

Hyde Park

Town Clerk
344 Vermont Route 15 West
Hyde Park, VT 05655

Mailing Address
PO Box 98
Hyde Park, VT 05655

www.hydeparkvt.com
(802) 888–2300; fax (802) 888–6878
See website for email
Hours: M–F 8–4

Ira

Town Clerk
53 West Road
Ira, VT 05777

Mailing Address
PO Box 870
West Rutland, VT 05777

(802) 235–2745; fax (802) 235–1045
iraclerk@vermontel.net
Hours: M 9:30–2:30; Tu 2:15–7:15

Irasburg

Town Clerk
161 Route 58 East
Irasburg, VT 05845

Mailing Address
PO Box 51
Irasburg, VT 05845

(802) 754–2242; fax (802) 754–2242
irasburgtc@comcast.net
Hours: M–Th 9–3

Isle La Motte

Town Clerk
2272 Main Street
Isle La Motte, VT 05463

Mailing Address
PO Box 250
Isle La Motte, VT 05463

www.islelamotte.us
(802) 928–3434; fax (802) 928–3002
islemott@fairpoint.net
Hours: Tu, Th 7:30–3:30; W, F 1–5; Sat
   8–12

Jamaica

Town Clerk
28 Town Office Road
Jamaica, VT 05343

Mailing Address
PO Box 173
Jamaica, VT 05343

www.jamaicavermont.org
(802) 874–4681; fax (802) 874–4681
jamaica_vt@svcable.net
Hours: Tu–F 9–4; Sat by appt.

Jay

Town Clerk
1036 Vermont Route 242
Jay, VT 05859
www.jayvt.com
(802) 988–2996; fax (802) 988–2996
townofjay@comcast.net
Hours: M–Th 7–4

Jericho

Town Clerk
67 Vermont Route 15
Jericho, VT 05465

Mailing Address
PO Box 67
Jericho, VT 05465

www.jerichovt.gov
(802) 899–4936 ext 1; fax (802) 899–5549
jerichovermont@yahoo.com
Hours: M–Th 8–4; F 8–3; Sat by appt.

Johnson

Town Clerk
293 Lower Main West
Johnson, VT 05656

Mailing Address
PO Box 383
Johnson, VT 05656

www.townofjohnson.com
(802) 635–2611; fax (802) 635–2393
Hours: M–F 7:30–4

Killington

Town Clerk
2706 River Road
Killington, VT 05751

Mailing Address
PO Box 429
Killington, VT 05751

www.killingtontown.com
(802) 422–3243; fax (802) 422–3030
See website for email
Hours: M–F 9–3

Kirby

Town Clerk
346 Town Hall Road
Kirby, VT 05851
(802) 626–9386; fax (802) 626–9386
kirbytc@kingcon.com
Hours: Tu, Th 8–3

Landgrove

Town Clerk
88 Landgrove Road
Landgrove, VT 05148

Mailing Address
PO Box 508
Londonderry, VT 05148

(802) 824–3716; fax (802) 824–4677
townoflandgrove@gmail.com
Hours: Th 9–1

Leicester

Town Clerk
44 Schoolhouse Road
Leicester, VT 05733
www.leicestervt.org
(802) 247–5961 ext 3; fax (802) 247–6501
leicestervt@comcast.net
Hours: M, Tu, Th 9–2

Lemington

Town Clerk
2549 River Road
Vermont Route 102
Lemington, VT 05903
(802) 277–4814; fax (802) 277–4091
lemitown@localnet.com
Hours: W 2:30–5:30

Lincoln

Town Clerk
62 Quaker Street
Lincoln, VT 05443
www.lincolnvermont.org
(802) 453–2980; fax (802) 453–2975
clerk@lincolnvermont.org
Hours: M, Tu, Th 8–2; W 8–2, 4–7;
    Sat by appt.

Londonderry

Town Clerk
100 Old School Street
South Londonderry, VT 05155

Mailing Address
PO Box 118
South Londonderry, VT 05155

www.londonderryvt.org
(802) 824–3356; fax (802) 824–4259
londontown@vermontel.net
Hours: Tu–F 9–3; Sat 9–12

Lowell

Town Clerk
2170 Vermont Route 100
Lowell, VT 05847
(802) 744–6559; fax (802) 744–2357
Hours: M, Th 9–2:30

Ludlow

Town Clerk
37 Depot Street
Ludlow, VT 05149

Mailing Address
PO Box 307
Ludlow, VT 05149

www.ludlow.vt.us
(802) 228–3232; fax (802) 228–8399
treasure@ludlow.vt.us
Hours: M–F 8:30–4:30

Lunenburg

Town Clerk
9 West Main Street
Lunenburg, VT 05906

Mailing Address
PO Box 54
Lunenburg, VT 05906

(802) 892 5959; fax (802) 892 5100
lunenburg01@live.com
Hours: M–Th 8:30–12, 1–3; F 8:30–12

Lyndon

Town Clerk
119 Park Avenue
Lyndonville, VT 05851

Mailing Address
PO Box 167
Lyndonville, VT 05851–0167

www.lyndonvt.org
(802) 626–5785; fax (802) 626–1265
ltc@kingcon.com
Hours: M–F 7:30–4:30

Maidstone

Town Clerk
508 Vermont Route 102
Maidstone, VT 05905

Mailing Address
PO Box 118
Guildhall, VT 05905

(802) 676–3210; fax (802) 676–3210
townclerk@hughes.net
Hours: M, Th 9–3

Manchester

Town Clerk
6039 Main St
Manchester Center, VT 05255

Mailing Address
PO Box 830
Manchester Center, VT 05255

www.manchester-vt.gov
(802) 362–1313; fax (802) 362–1314
See website for email
Hours: M, Tu, F 8–5:45; W 8–6

Marlboro

Town Clerk
510 South Road
Marlboro, VT 05344

Mailing Address
PO Box E
Marlboro, VT 05344

www.marlboro.vt.us
(802) 254–2181; fax (802) 257–2447
marlboroclerk@myfairpoint.net
Hours: M, W, Th 9–4

Marshfield

Town Clerk
122 School Street, Room 1
Marshfield, VT 05658
http://town.marshfield.vt.us
(802) 426–3305; fax (802) 426–3045
clerk@town.marshfield.vt.us
Hours: Tu–F 8–12, 12:30–4

Mendon

Town Clerk
2282 US Route 4
Mendon, VT 05701
www.mendonvt.org
(802) 775–1662; fax (802) 773–9682
mendonclerk@comcast.net
Hours: M, W, Th 8–5; Tu 8–4

Middlebury

Town Clerk
94 Main Street
Middlebury, VT 05753
www.middlebury.govoffice.com
(802) 388–8100 ext 211, 212, 213;
 fax (802) 388–4261
See website for email
Hours: M–Th 7:30–5:30

Middlesex

Town Clerk
5 Church Street
Middlesex, VT 05602
www.middlesexvermont.org
(802) 223–5915; fax (802) 223–1298
middlesxtwnclrk@comcast.net
Hours: M–Th 8:30–12, 1–4:30; F 8:30–12

Middletown Springs

Town Clerk
10 Park Avenue
Middletown Springs, VT 05757

Mailing Address
PO Box 1232
Middletown Springs, VT 05757

(802) 235–2220; fax (802) 235–2066
middletown@vermontel.net
Hours: M, Tu 9–12, 1–4; F 1–4; Sat 9–12

Milton

Town Clerk
43 Bombardier Rd
Milton, VT 05468

Mailing Address
PO Box 18
Milton, VT 05468

www.milton.govoffice2.com
(802) 893–4111; fax (802) 893–1005
See website for email
Hours: M–F 8–5

Monkton

Town Clerk
280 Monkton Ridge
Monkton, VT 05473

Mailing Address
PO Box 12
Monkton, VT 05469

www.monktonvt.com
(802) 453 3800; fax (802) 453–3612
monktontc@comcast.net
Hours: M, Tu, F 8–1; Th 8–1, 5–7

Montgomery

Town Clerk
98 Main Street
Montgomery Center, VT 05471

Mailing Address
PO Box 356
Montgomery Center, VT 05471

www.montgomeryvt.us
(802) 326–4719; fax (802) 326–5053
montgomerytc@fairpoint.net
Hours: M 8–12, 1–6; Tu, Th, F 8–12, 1–4

Montpelier

City Clerk
39 Main Street–City Hall
Montpelier, VT 05602
www.montpelier-vt.org
(802) 223–9500; fax (802) 223–9523
See website for email
Hours: M–F 8–4:30

Moretown

Town Clerk
994 Route 100B
Moretown, VT 05660

Mailing Address
PO Box 666
Moretown, VT 05660

(802) 496–3645; fax (802) 329–2221
moretownclerk@gmavt.net
Hours: M–F 7–3

Morgan

Town Clerk
41 Meade Hill Road
Morgan, VT 05853

Mailing Address
PO Box 45
Morgan, VT 05853

(802) 895–2927; fax (802) 895–4204
tmorganvt@comcast.net
Hours: M, Th 8–4; Tu, W 8–3

Morristown

Town Clerk
43 Portland Street
Morrisville, VT 05661

Mailing Address
P O Box 748
Morrisville, VT 05661

www.morristownvt.org
(802) 888–6370; fax (802) 888–6375
Hours: M, Tu, Th, F 8:30–4:30;
    W 8:30–12:30

Mount Holly

Town Clerk
50 School St
Mount Holly, VT 05758

Mailing Address
PO Box 248
Mount Holly, VT 05758

www.mounthollyvt.org
(802) 259–2391
mthollytc@yahoo.com
Hours: M–Th 8:30–4

Mount Tabor

Town Clerk
522 Brooklyn Road
Mount Tabor, VT 05739

Mailing Address
PO Box 245
Mount Tabor, VT 05739

(802) 293–5282; fax (802) 293–5287
mttabor@vermontel.net
Hours: Tu, W 9–12; Sat by appt.

New Haven

Town Clerk
78 North Street
New Haven, VT 05472
www.newhavenvt.com
(802) 453–3516; fax (802) 453–7552
newhavenclerk@gmavt.net
Hours: M–F 9–3

Newark

Town Clerk
1336 Newark Street
Newark, VT 05871
(802) 467–3336
tclerknewark@kingcon.com
Hours: M, W, Th 9–4

Newbury

Town Clerk
4982 Main Street South
Newbury, VT 05051

Mailing Address
PO Box 126
Newbury, VT 05051

(802) 866–5521; fax (802) 866–5301
clerk@newburyvt.org
Hours: M, W, Th, F 8:30–2:30; Tu 8:30–6

Newfane

Town Clerk
555 Vermont Route 30
Newfane, VT 05345

Mailing Address
PO Box 36
Newfane, VT 05345

www.newfanevt.com
(802) 365–7772 ext 10; fax (802) 365–7692
tclerknewfane@svcable.net
Hours: M–Th 8–6; Sat by appt.

Newport, City of

City Clerk
222 Main St
Newport, VT 05855
www.newportvermont.org
(802) 334–2112; fax (802) 334–5632
newportcityclerkjim@comcast.net
Hours: M–F 8–4:30

Newport, Town of

Town Clerk
102 Vance Hill Road
Newport Center, VT 05857

Mailing Address
PO Box 85
Newport Center, VT 05857

(802) 334–6442; fax (802) 334–6442
nctownclerk@comcast.net
Hours: M–Th 7–4:30

North Hero
Town Clerk
6441 US Route 2
North Hero, VT 05474

Mailing Address
PO Box 38
North Hero, VT 05474

www.northherovt.com
(802) 372–6926; fax (802) 372–3806
townclerk@northherovt.com
Hours: M, Tu, Th 8–4:30; W, F, Sat 8–12

Northfield
Town Clerk
51 South Main Street
Northfield, VT 05663
www.northfield-vt.gov
(802) 485–5421; fax (802) 485–8426
See website for email
Hours: M–F 8–4:30

Norton
Town Clerk
12 Vermont Route 114E
Norton, VT 05907
(802) 822–9935; fax (802) 822–9965
townofnorton@myfairpoint.net
Hours: Tu, Th 10–4; last Sat of month 10–12

Norwich
Town Clerk
300 Main Street
Norwich, VT 05055

Mailing Address
PO Box 376
Norwich, VT 05055

www.norwich.vt.us
(802) 649–1419 ext.103; fax (802) 649–0123
clerk@norwich.vt.us
Hours: M, Tu, W, F 8:30–4:30; Th 8:30–5

Orange
Town Clerk
392 US Route 302
Orange, VT 05649

Mailing Address
PO Box 233
East Barre, VT 05649

www.orangevt.org
(802) 479–2673; fax (802) 479–2673
See website for email
Hours: M–F 8–12, 1–4

Orwell
Town Clerk
436 Main Street
Orwell, VT 05760

Mailing Address
PO Box 32
Orwell, VT 05760

www.town-of-orwell.org
(802) 948–2032
tckorwel@sover.net
Hours: M, Tu, Th 9:30–12, 1–3:30;
    F 9:30–12, 1–6

Panton
Town Clerk
3176 Jersey Street
Panton, VT 05491
www.pantonvt.us
(802) 475–2333; fax (802) 475–2785
panton@gmavt.net
Hours: M, Tu, 9–3; W, Th 8–3

Pawlet
Town Clerk
122 School Street
Pawlet, VT 05761

Mailing Address
PO Box 128
Pawlet, VT 05761

http://pawlet.vt.gov
(802) 325–3309; fax (802) 325–6109
pawletclerk@vermontel.net
Hours: M, W 8:30–3:30; Tu 11–6; Th 9–12

Peacham

Town Clerk
79 Church Street
Peacham, VT 05862

Mailing Address
PO Box 244
Peacham, VT 05862

www.peacham.net/townclerk
(802) 592–3218; fax (802) 592–3218
townclerk@peacham.net
Hours: M, Tu, Th, F 8:30–12:30; W 8:30–
   12:30, 3–6:30

Peru

Town Clerk
402 Main St
Peru, VT 05152

Mailing Address
PO Box 127
Peru, VT 05152

(802) 824–3065; fax (802) 824–5596
perutown@myfairpoint.net
Hours: Tu, Th 8:30–4

Pittsfield

Town Clerk
40 Village Green
Pittsfield, VT 05762–0556

Mailing Address
PO Box 556
Pittsfield, VT 05762–0556

www.pittsfieldvt.org/townclerk.php
(802) 746–8170
townofpittsfield@myfairpoint.net
Hours: Tu 12–6; W, Th 9–3

Pittsford

Town Clerk
426 Plains Road
Pittsford, VT 05763

Mailing Address
PO Box 10
Pittsford, VT 05763

http://pittsfordvermont.com
(802) 483–6500 ext 13; fax (802) 483–6612
clerktreasurer@pittsfordvermont.com
Hours: M–W, 8–4:30; Th 8–6; F, 8–3; and
   by appt.

Plainfield

Town Clerk
149 Main Street
Plainfield, VT 05667

Mailing Address
PO Box 217
Plainfield, VT 05667

www.plainfieldvt.us
(802) 454–8461; fax (802) 454–8467
plainfieldtc@gmail.com
Hours: M, W, F 7:30–12, 12:30–4

Plymouth

Town Clerk
68 Town Office Road
Plymouth, VT 05056
www.plymouthvt.org
(802) 672–3655; fax (802) 672–5466
clerk@plymouthvt.org
Hours: M–Th 8–4:30

Pomfret

Town Clerk
5218 Pomfret Road
North Pomfret, VT 05053
www.pomfretvt.us
(802) 457–3861
clerk@pomfretvt.us
Hours: M, W, F 8:30–2:30

Poultney

Town Clerk
98 Depot Street
Poultney, VT 05764
(802) 287– 4003
poultneytownclerk@comcast.net
Hours: M–F 8:30–12:30, 1:30–4

Pownal

Town Clerk
467 Center Street
Pownal, VT 05261

Mailing Address
PO Box 411
Pownal, VT 05261

www.pownal.org/TownOffice/TownOffice.html
(802) 823–7757; fax (802) 823–0116
powclerk@sover.net
Hours: M, W, Th, F 9–2; Tu 9–4

Proctor

Town Clerk
45 Main Street
Proctor, VT 05765
www.proctorvermont.com/townclerk.htm
(802) 459–3333; fax (802) 459–2356
proctor_tc@comcast.net
Hours: M–F 8–4

Putney

Town Clerk
127 Main Street
Putney, VT 05346

Mailing Address
PO Box 233
Putney, VT 05346

www.putneyvt.org
(802) 387–5862; fax (802) 387–4708
putneytc@putneyvt.org
Hours: M, Th, F 9–2; W 9–2, 7–9; Sat 9–12

Randolph

Town Clerk
7 Summer Street
Randolph, VT 05060

Mailing Address
Drawer B
Randolph, VT 05060

randolphvt.govoffice2.com
(802) 728–5433, ext 11; fax (802) 728–5818
clerk@municipaloffice.randolph.vt.us
Hours: M–F 8–4:30

Reading

Town Clerk
799 Route 106
Reading, VT 05062

Mailing Address
PO Box 72
Reading, VT 05062

www.readingvt.govoffice.com
(802) 484–7250; fax (802) 484–7250
readingvermont@comcast.net
Hours: M–Th 8–4

Readsboro

Town Clerk
301 Phelps Lane
Readsboro, VT 05350

Mailing Address
PO Box 187
Readsboro, VT 05350

http://officialtownofreadsboro.org/townclerk.php
(802) 423–5405; fax (802) 423–5423
readsto@gmail.com
Hours: M, Tu, Th, F 8–12, 12:30–3:30;
    W 4:30–8:30; 1st Sat 8 –11

Richford

Town Clerk
94 Main Street
Richford, VT 05476

Mailing Address
PO Box 236
Richford, VT 05476

www.richfordvt.org/townclerk.php
(802) 848–7751; fax (802) 848–7752
townclerk@richfordvt.org
Hours: M–F 8:30–4

Richmond

Town Clerk
203 Bridge Street
Richmond, VT 05477

Mailing Address
PO Box 285
Richmond, VT 05477–0285

www.richmondvt.com/town/town_clerk.php
(802) 434–2221; fax (802) 434–5570
townclerk@richmondvt.com
Hours: M 8–5; Tu–Th 8–4; F 8–12; Sat by
    appt.

Ripton

Town Clerk
1311 Route 125
Ripton, VT 05766

Mailing Address
PO Box 10
Ripton, VT 05766

www.riptonvt.org/town-clerk
(802) 388–2266; fax (802) 388–0012
townoffice@riptonvt.org
Hours: M 2–6; Tu–Th 9–1; and by appt.

Rochester

Town Clerk
67 School Street
Rochester, VT 05767

Mailing Address
PO Box 238
Rochester, VT 05767

www.rochestervermont.org
(802) 767–3631; fax (802) 767–6028
rochestertown@comcast.net
Hours: Tu–F 8–4

Rockingham

Town Clerk
7 Village Square
Bellows Falls, VT 05101

Mailing Address
PO Box 370
Bellows Falls, VT 05101

www.rockbf.org/
(802) 463–3964; fax (802) 463–1228
See website for email
Hours: M–F 8:30–4:30

Roxbury

Town Clerk
1664 Roxbury Road
Roxbury, VT 05669

Mailing Address
PO Box 53
Roxbury, VT 05669

www.roxbury.govoffice2.com
(802) 485–7840; fax (802) 485–9160
townrox@tds.net
Hours: Tu–F 9–12, 1–4

Royalton

Town Clerk
23 Alexander Place #1
South Royalton, VT 05068

Mailing Address
PO Box 680
South Royalton, VT 05068

http://royaltonvt.com/residents-information/
    town-officials
(802) 763–7207; fax (802) 763–7207
royalclerk@bluemoo.net
Hours: M–Th 8–3

Rupert

Town Clerk
187 East Street
West Rupert, VT 05776

Mailing Address
PO Box 140
West Rupert, VT 05776

(802) 394–7728; fax (802) 394–2524
rupert187@myfairpoint.net
Hours: M 11–7; Tu, W 12–5; Th 8:30–3:30

Rutland, City of
City Clerk
1 Strongs Avenue
Rutland, VT 05701

Mailing Address
PO Box 969
Rutland, VT 05701

http://rutland.govoffice.com
(802) 773–1800 ext 9; fax (802) 773–1846
See website for email
Hours: M–F 8:30–5

Rutland, Town of
Town Clerk
181 Business Route 4
Center Rutland, VT 05736

Mailing Address
PO Box 225
Center Rutland, VT 05736

www.rutlandtown.com
(802) 773–2528; fax (802) 773–7295
See website for email
Hours: M–F 8–4:30

Ryegate
Town Clerk
18 South Bayley–Hazen Road
Ryegate, VT 05042

Mailing Address
PO Box 332
Ryegate, VT 05042

http://ryegatevt.com
(802) 584–3880; fax (802) 584–3880
ryegateclerk@yahoo.com
Hours: M, Tu, W 1–5; F 9–1; Sat by appt.

Saint Albans, City of
City Clerk
100 North Main Street
St. Albans, VT 05478

Mailing Address
PO Box 867
St. Albans, VT 05478

www.stalbansvt.com
(802) 524–1500 ext 264; fax (802) 524–1516

See website for email
Hours: M–F 7:30–4

Saint Albans, Town of
Town Clerk
579 Lake Road
St. Albans Bay, VT 05478

Mailing Address
PO Box 37
St. Albans Bay, VT 05481

www.stalbanstown.com
(802) 524–2415; fax (802) 524–9609
stalbtwn@comcast.net
Hours: M–F 8–4

Saint George
Town Clerk
One Barber Road
St. George, VT 05495
www.stgeorgevt.com
(802) 482–5272; fax (802) 482–5548
stgeorgevtclerk@comcast.net
Hours: M, W, F 8–12; Tu 9–12; Th 9–12,
    4:30–6

Saint Johnsbury
Town Clerk
1187 Main Street, Suite 2
St. Johnsbury, VT 05819
www.town.st-johnsbury.vt.us
(802) 748–4331; fax (802) 748–1267
See website for email
Hours: M–F 7:30–4:30

Salisbury
Town Clerk
25 Schoolhouse Road
Salisbury, VT 05769

Mailing Address
PO Box 66
Salisbury, VT 05769

www.townofsalisbury.org
(802) 352–4228; fax (802) 352–9832
town.clerk@comcast.net
Hours: M 11–5; Tu 10–2; Th 12–7

Sandgate

Town Clerk
3266 Sandgate Road
Sandgate, VT 05250
www.sandgatevermont.com
(802) 375.9075; fax (802) 375.8350
townclerk@sandgatevermont.com
Hours: Tu, W 9:30–12:30; and by appt.

Searsburg

Town Clerk
18 Town Garage Road
Searsburg, VT 05363

Mailing Address
PO Box 157
Wilmington, VT 05363

(802) 464–8081; fax (802) 464–8081
Hours: M 8–4; Tu, F 8–12

Shaftsbury

Town Clerk
61 Buck Hill Rd
Shaftsbury, VT 05262

Mailing Address
PO Box 409
Shaftsbury, VT 05262

www.shaftsbury.net
(802) 442–4038; fax (802) 442–0955
shaftsburyclerk@comcast.net
Hours: M 9–5; Tu–F 9–3

Sharon

Town Clerk
69 Vermont Route 132
Sharon, VT 05065

Mailing Address
PO Box 250
Sharon, VT 05065

www.sharonvt.net
(802) 763–8268 ext 1; fax (802) 763–7392
clerk@sharonvt.net
Hours: M–Th 7–4:30

Sheffield

Town Clerk
37 Dane Road
Sheffield, VT 05866

Mailing Address
PO Box 165
Sheffield, VT 05866

(802) 626–8862; fax (802) 626–8862
maplequeen@surfglobal.net
Hours: M, F 8–2; W 8–2, 5–8

Shelburne

Town Clerk
5420 Shelburne Road
Shelburne, VT 05482

Mailing Address
PO Box 88
Shelburne, VT 05482

www.shelburnevt.org/departments/21.html
(802) 985–5036; fax (802) 985–9550
See website for email
Hours: M–F 8:30–5

Sheldon

Town Clerk
1640 Main Street
Sheldon, VT 05483

Mailing Address
PO Box 66
Sheldon, VT 05483

(802) 933–2524; fax (802) 933–4951
tc@sheldonvt.com
Hours: M 8–6; Tu, W, Th, F 8–3

Shoreham

Town Clerk
297 Main St
Shoreham, VT 05770
www.shorehamvt.org/town/clerk/index.shtml
(802) 897–5841; fax (802) 897–2545
clerk@shorehamvt.org
Hours: M, Tu, Th, F 9–12, 1–4

Shrewsbury

Town Clerk
9823 Cold River Road
Shrewsbury, VT 05738
www.shrewsburyvt.org/townclerk.php
(802) 492–3511; fax (802) 492–3511
shrewsburyclerk@vermontel.net
Hours: M–Th 9–3; and by appt.

South Burlington

Town Clerk
575 Dorset St
South Burlington, VT 05403
www.sburl.com
(802) 846–4105
See website for email
Hours: M–F 8–4:30

South Hero

Town Clerk
333 Route 2
South Hero, VT 05486–0175

Mailing Address
PO Box 175
South Hero, VT 05486–0175

www.southherovt.org/townclerk.php
(802) 372–5552; fax (802) 372–3809
southherotc@aol.com
Hours: M–W 8:30–12, 1–4:30; Th 8:30–12, 1–5

Springfield

Town Clerk
96 Main Street
Springfield, VT 05156
http://springfieldvt.govoffice2.com/
(802) 885–2104; fax (802) 885–1617
tosclerk@vermontel.net
Hours: M–F 8–4:30

Stamford

Town Clerk
986 Main Road
Stamford, VT 05352

www.stamfordvt.org/officeofthetownclerk.html
(802) 694–1361; fax (802) 694–1636
stamfdvt@sover.net
Hours: Tu 11–4; W 12–4; Th 12–4, 7–9;
 F 12–4

Stannard

Town Clerk
615 Stannard Mountain Road
Stannard, VT 05842

Mailing Address
PO Box 94
Greensboro Bend, VT 05842

(802) 533–2577; fax (802) 533–2577 (call
 first)
townofstannard@vtlink.net
Hours: W 8–12

Starksboro

Town Clerk
2849 Vermont Route 116
Starksboro, VT 05487

Mailing Address
PO Box 91
Starksboro, VT 05487

www.starksboro.org/directory.asp
(802) 453–2639; fax (802) 453–7293
starksboro@madriver.com
Hours: M–Th 8:30–4:30

Stockbridge

Town Clerk
1722 Vermont Route 100
Stockbridge, VT 05772

Mailing Address
PO Box 39
Stockbridge, VT 05772

(802) 746–8400; fax (802) 746–8400
townofstockbridge@myfairpoint.net
Hours: Tu–Th 8–4:30; F 8–12

Stowe

Town Clerk
67 Main Street
Stowe, VT 05672

Mailing Address
PO Box 248
Stowe, VT 05672

www.townofstowevt.org/townclerk/index.html
(802) 253–6133; fax (802) 253–6143
See website for email
Hours: M–F 8–4:30

Strafford

Town Clerk
227 Justin Morrill Highway
Strafford, VT 05072

Mailing Address
PO Box 27
Strafford, VT 05072

www.townofstraffordvt.com/TownClerk.html
(802) 765–4411; fax (802) 765–9621
townofstrafford@wavecomm.com
Hours: M–Th 7:30–4:30

Stratton

Town Clerk
9 West Jamaica Road
Stratton, VT 05360
http://townofstrattonvt.com/Town_Clerk.html
(802) 896–6184; fax (802) 896–6630
townclerk@townofstrattonvt.com
Hours: M–Th 9–3

Sudbury

Town Clerk
Route 30 & Huff Pond Road
Sudbury, VT 05733

Mailing Address
36 Blacksmith Lane
Sudbury, VT 05733

(802) 623–7296; fax (802) 623–7296
Hours: M 9–4; W 7–9; F 9–3; and by appt.

Sunderland

Town Clerk
181 South Road
Sunderland, VT 05252

Mailing Address
PO Box 295
East Arlington, VT 05252–0295

www.sunderlandvt.org
(802) 375–6106; fax (802) 375–6106
sunderlandvt@comcast.net
Hours: M, Tu, Th 8–2; W 8–12, 6–8;
     F by appt.

Sutton

Town Clerk
167 Underpass Road
Sutton, VT 05867

Mailing Address
PO Box 106
Sutton, VT 05867

(802) 467–3377; fax (802) 467–1052
Hours: M, Tu, Th, F 9–5; W 9–12

Swanton

Town Clerk
1 Academy Street
Swanton, VT 05488

Mailing Address
PO Box 711
Swanton, VT 05488

www.swantonvermont.org/townclerk.php
(802) 868–4421; fax (802) 868–4957
townclerk@swantonvermont.org
Hours: M–F 7–5

Thetford

Town Clerk
3910 Vermont Route 113
Thetford Center, VT 05075

Mailing Address
PO Box 126
Thetford Center, VT 05075

cont. on next page

Thetford *(cont.)*
www.thetfordvermont.us/departments/clerk-office
(802) 785–2922; fax (802) 785–2031
townclerk@thetfordvermont.us
Hours: M 6–8; Tu–Th 8–4; and by appt.
  (closed Fri in summer months)

Tinmouth
Town Clerk
9 Mountain View Road
Tinmouth, VT 05773

Mailing Address
515 North End Road
Tinmouth, VT 05773

http://tinmouthvt.org/contact.php
(802) 446–2498; fax (802) 446–2498
tinmouthtown@vermontel.net
Hours: M, Th 8–12, 1–5; some Saturdays
  9–12; and by appt.

Topsham
Town Clerk
6 Harts Road
Topsham, VT 05076

Mailing Address
PO Box 69
Topsham, VT 05076

www.topshamvt.org/townoffice.php
(802) 439–5505; fax (802) 439–5505
topsham@tops–tele.com
Hours: M 1–6; Tu, Th, F 9–4

Townshend
Town Clerk
2006 Vermont Route 30
Townshend, VT 05353

Mailing Address
PO Box 223
Townshend, VT 05353

www.townshendvt.net/clerk/Contact.htm
(802) 365–7300; fax (802) 365–7309
tnclk@svcable.net
Hours: M–W, F 9–4

Troy
Town Clerk
142 Main Street
North Troy, VT 05859
www.troyvt.org/townclerk.php
(802) 988–2663; fax (802) 988–4692
townoftroy@comcast.net
Hours: M–Th 9–12, 1–5

Tunbridge
Town Clerk
271 Vermont Route 110
Tunbridge, VT 05077

Mailing Address
PO Box 6
Tunbridge, VT 05077

www.tunbridgevt.com/contact
(802) 889–5521; fax (802) 889–3744
townclerk@tunbridge.biz
Hours: M–Th 7:30–3; and by appt.

Underhill
Town Clerk
12 Pleasant Valley Rd
Underhill, VT 05489

Mailing Address
PO Box 32
Underhill Center, VT 05490

www.underhillvt.gov
(802) 899–4434 ext 101; fax (802) 899–2137
underhillclerk@comcast.net
Hours: M–F 8–4

Vergennes
Town Clerk
120 Main Street
Vergennes, VT 05491

Mailing Address
PO Box 35
Vergennes, VT 05491

http://vergennes.org/departments-page/#tabs-27
(802) 877–2841; fax (802) 877–1160
clerk@vergennes.org
Hours: M–F 8–4:30

Vernon
Town Clerk
567 Governor Hunt Road
Vernon, VT 05354
www.vernon-vt.org/home.html
(802) 257–0292; fax (802) 254–3561
vernontc@sover.net
Hours: M–Th 7–5; F and Sat by appt.

Vershire
Town Clerk
6894 Vermont Route 113
Vershire, VT 05079
www.vershirevt.org/2.html
(802) 685–2227; fax (802) 685–2224
clerk–treasurer@vershirevt.org
Hours: Tu–Th 9–4; 1st Sat 10–12

Victory
Town Clerk
102 Radar Road
Victory, VT 05858

Mailing Address
PO Box 609
North Concord, VT 05858

(802) 328–2400
townofvictory@wildblue.net
Hours: Th 9–4; and by appt.

Waitsfield
Town Clerk
Nine Bridge Street
Waitsfield, VT 05673
www.waitsfieldvt.us/clerk/index.cfm
(802) 496–2218; fax (802) 496–9284
waitsfld@madriver.com
Hours: M–F 8–4:30

Walden
Town Clerk
12 Vermont Route 215
Walden, VT 05873
(802) 563–2220; fax (802) 563–3008
waldentc@pivot.net
Hours: M–W 9–4; Th 9–5

Wallingford
Town Clerk
75 School Street
Wallingford, VT 05773
www.wallingfordvt.com/town_clerk.htm
(802) 446–2336; fax (802) 446–3174
townclerk@wallingfordvt.com
Hours: M–Th 8–4:30; F 8–12

Waltham
Town Clerk
2053 Maple Street
Waltham, VT 05491

Mailing Address
PO Box 175
Vergennes, VT 05491

(802) 877–3641; fax (802) 877–3641
waltham@gmwireless.net
Hours: Tu, F 9–3

Wardsboro
Town Clerk
71 Main Street
Wardsboro, VT 05355

Mailing Address
PO Box 48
Wardsboro, VT 05355

(802) 896–6055; fax (802) 896–1000
wardsborotownoffice@myfairpoint.net
Hours: M–Th 9–12, 1–4:30

Warren
Town Clerk
42 Cemetery Road
Warren, VT 05674

Mailing Address
PO Box 337
Warren, VT 05674

www.warrenvt.org/depts/clerk.htm
(802) 496–2709; fax (802) 496–2418
clerk@warrenvt.org
Hours: M–F 9–4:30

Washington

Town Clerk
2895 Vermont Route 110
Washington, VT 05675
(802) 883–2218; fax (802) 883–2218
washingtontownclerk@gmail.com
Hours: M, Tu 8:30–4; W–F by appt.

Waterbury

Town Clerk
51 South Main Street
Waterbury, VT 05676
www.waterburyvt.com/clerk
(802) 244–8447; fax (802) 244–1014
See website for email
Hours: M–F 8–4:30

Waterford

Town Clerk
532 Maple Street
Waterford, VT 05848

Mailing Address
PO Box 56
Lower Waterford, VT 05848

(802) 748–2122; fax (802) 748–8196
townofwaterford@gmail.com
Hours: M, Th, F 8:30–3:30; Tu 12–6

Waterville

Town Clerk
850 Vermont Route 109
Waterville, VT 05492

Mailing Address
PO Box 31
Waterville, VT 05492

www.watervillevt.com
(802) 644–8865; fax (802) 644–8865
townofwaterville@myfairpoint.net
Hours: M, Tu, Th 9–1:30

Weathersfield

Town Clerk
5259 Route 5
Ascutney, VT 05030

Mailing Address
PO Box 550
Ascutney, VT 05030

www.weathersfieldvt.org/town-clerk
(802) 674–9500; fax (802) 674–2117
tclerk@weathersfield.org
Hours: M–W 9–4; Th 9–5:30; and by appt.

Wells

Town Clerk
108 Route 30
Wells, VT 05774

Mailing Address
PO Box 585
Wells, VT 05774

*www.wellsvermont.com/gov_town_clerk_*
newcomer_msg.htm
(802) 645.0486; fax (802) 645.0464
wellstownclerk@comcast.net
Hours: M, W, Th 7:30–3:30; Tu 11–6; and
by appt.

West Fairlee

Town Clerk
870 Route 113
West Fairlee, VT 05083
www.westfairleevt.com
(802) 333–9696; fax (802) 333–9611
westfairleetc@hotmail.com
Hours: M, Tu, W 9:30–12, 1–3:30

West Haven

Town Clerk
2919 Main Road
West Haven, VT 05743
(802) 265–4880; fax (802) 265–3828
whavenoffice2919@aol.com
Hours: M, W 1–3:30; and by appt.

West Rutland

Town Clerk
35 Marble Street
West Rutland, VT 05777
www.westrutlandtown.com/tdtownclerk.php
(802) 438–2204; fax (802) 438–5133
Hours: M–Th 9–12, 1–4; F by appt.

West Windsor

Town Clerk
22 Brownsville–Hartland Road
West Windsor, VT 05089

Mailing Address
PO Box 6
Brownsville, VT 05037

www.westwindsorvt.govoffice2.com
(802) 484–7212; fax (802) 484–3518
west.windsor.townclerk@valley.net
Hours: M–F 9–12, 1:30–4:30

Westfield

Town Clerk
38 School Street
Westfield, VT 05874
(802) 744–2484; fax (802) 744–6224
townofwestfield@comcast.net
Hours: M–W 8–4; Th 8–12

Westford

Town Clerk
1713 Vermont Route 128
Westford, VT 05494
www.westfordvt.us/clerk.php
(802) 878–4587; fax (802) 879–6503
townclerk@westfordvt.us
Hours: M–F 8:30–4:30; (July–Aug)
    F 8:30–1

Westminster

Town Clerk
3651 US Route 5
Westminster, VT 05158

Mailing Address
PO Box 147
Westminster, VT 05158

http://westminster.govoffice.com
(802) 722–4091; fax (802) 722–9816
westmntc@comcast.net
Hours: M–F 8:30–4; evenings by appt.

Westmore

Town Clerk
54 Hinton Hill Road
Westmore, VT 05860
www.westmoreonline.org/main
(802) 525–3007; fax (802) 525–1131
clerk@westmoreonline.org
Hours: M–Th 8–12, 1-4; and by appt.

Weston

Town Clerk
12 Lawrence Hill Road
Weston, VT 05161

Mailing Address
PO Box 98
Weston, VT 05161

www.westonvt.org
(802) 824–6645; fax (802) 824–4121
clerk@westonvt.org
Hours: M–F 8–1

Weybridge

Town Clerk
1727 Quaker Village Road
Weybridge, VT 05752
http://weybridge.govoffice.com
(802) 545–2450; fax (802) 545–2624
info@weybridge.govoffice.com
Hours: M, Tu, Th, F 9–2

Wheelock

Town Clerk
1192 Route 122
Wheelock, VT 05851

Mailing Address
PO Box 1328
Lyndonville, VT 05851

(802) 626–9094; fax (802) 626–9094
wheelocktc@yahoo.com
Hours: M–Th 7:45–3

Whiting
Town Clerk
29 South Main Street
Whiting, VT 05778
(802) 623–7813; fax (802) 623–7813
townofwhiting@shoreham.net
Hours: M, W 9–12, 4–6; F 9–12; and by appt.

Whitingham
Town Clerk
2948 Vermont Route 100
Jacksonville, VT 0542

Mailing Address
PO Box 529
Jacksonville, VT 05342

(802) 368–7887; fax (802) 368–7519
whitinghamtownclerk@yahoo.com
Hours: M, Tu, Th, F 9–2; W 9–2, 5–7;
     1st Sat. 9–12

Williamstown
Town Clerk
2470 Vermont Route 14
Williamstown, VT 05679

Mailing Address
PO Box 646
Williamstown, VT 05679

www.williamstownvt.org/clerk.html
(802) 433–5455/2168; fax (802) 433–2160
clerk@williamstownvt.org
Hours: M, Tu, Th 8–4:30; F 8–2

Williston
Town Clerk
7900 Williston Road
Williston, VT 05495
http://town.williston.vt.us
(802) 878–5121; fax (802) 764–1140
See website for email
Hours: M–F 8:30–5

Wilmington
Town Clerk
2 East Main Street
Wilmington, VT 05363

Mailing Address
PO Box 217
Wilmington, VT 05363

www.wilmingtonvermont.us
(802) 464–5836; fax (802) 464–1238
wilmclrk@sover.net
Hours: M–W 8:30–12, 1–4; Th–F 8:30–4

Windham
Town Clerk
5976 Windham Hill Road
Windham, VT 05359
(802) 874–4211; fax (802) 874–4144
clerk@windham–vt.us
Hours: Tu, Th, F 10–3

Windsor
Town Clerk
29 Union Street
Windsor, VT 05089

Mailing Address
PO Box 47
Windsor, VT 05089

www.windsorvt.org/government/offices/clerk
(802) 674–5610; fax (802) 674–1017
See website for email
Hours: M–W 8–5; Th 8–4

Winhall
Town Clerk
3 River Road
Bondville, VT 05340

Mailing Address
PO Box 389
Bondville, VT 05340

http://winhall.govoffice2.com
(802) 297–2122; fax (802) 297–2582
winclerk@comcast.net
Hours: M–Th 9–12; and by appt.

Winooski

Town Clerk
27 West Allen Street
Winooski, VT 05404
http://onioncity.com
(802) 655–6419; fax (802) 655–6414
See website for email
Hours: M–F 7:30–5:30

Wolcott

Town Clerk
28 Railroad Street
Wolcott, VT 05680

Mailing Address
PO Box 100
Wolcott, VT 05680

www.wolcottvt.org
(802) 888–2746; fax (802) 888–2669
wolcott@pshift.com
Hours: M by appt.; Tu 8–6; W–F 8–4

Woodbury

Town Clerk
1672 Route 14
Woodbury, VT 05681

Mailing Address
PO Box 10
Woodbury, VT 05681

(802) 456 7051; fax (802) 456 8834
towoodbury@comcast.net
Hours: M 9–1, 6–8; Tu–Th 9–1

Woodford

Town Clerk
1391 Vermont Route 9
Woodford, VT 05201
(802) 442–4895; fax (802) 442–4816
woodfordvt@comcast.net
Hours: M, W, F 8:30–11, 12:30–4; Tu, Th
  8:30–4; and by appt.

Woodstock

Town Clerk
31 The Green
Woodstock, VT 05091
www.townofwoodstock.org
(802) 457–3611; fax (802) 457–2329
See website for email
Hours: M–F 8–12; 1–4:30

Worcester

Town Clerk
20 Worcester Village Road
Worcester, VT 05682

Mailing Address
PO Box 161
Worcester, VT 05682

www.worcestervt.org
(802) 223–6942, ext 1; fax (802) 229–5216
worcesterclerk@comcast.net
Hours: M, Tu, Th 9–3; W 9–5

Towns

The state of Vermont includes 255 locations. There are 237 towns, 9 cities, 5 unincorporated areas, and 4 gores. Gores and unincorporated towns have no local government. Their affairs are managed by a supervisor appointed by the state.

The following chart lists the name of each town, the date of its incorporation as a town, the county, towns from which it was formed (or from which land was later added to the town), towns that were formed from it (or to which land was added from it), and notes about the town. In the Parent Towns column, towns from which other towns were formed are indicated in **bold** type. Parts of other towns later annexed are in regular type.

The chart also shows vital records and church records that are available as manuscript, typescript, published books, or online. Extinct towns (those that are no longer extant or that were annexed by other towns) and unincorporated towns and gores are listed in the second table. For more information, good sources are *Vermont Municipalities*, State Papers of Vermont, Vol. 19 (Montpelier, 1986), and *Vermont Place-Names* by Esther Munroe Swift (Brattleboro, Vt.: Stephen Greene Press, 1977).

VR and CR codes

F   Catholic Church records and other records published by French–Canadian societies
N   Manuscript or typescript at NEHGS
P   Miscellaneous published volumes.
V   *Vermont Genealogy*
W   Pre-1850 vital records available on *AmericanAncestors.org*

Town	Inc.	County	Parent	Daughter	Note	VR	CR
Addison	1761	Addison		Waltham, Weybridge	N.H. Grant 1761.	V	
Albany	1815	Orleans	Lowell		Chartered 1782. Called Lutterloh to 1815.		V
Alburgh	1781	Grand Isle		Highgate			
Andover	1761	Windsor		Weston	N.H. grant 1761.	V	
Arlington	1761	Bennington			N.H. grant 1761.		
Athens	1780	Windham	Avery's Gore, Grafton (Tomlinson), Rockingham	Brookline			
Bakersfield	1791	Franklin	Avery's Gore, Coit's Gore, Fairfield, Knoulton's Gore, Knight's Gore	Enosburgh, Waterville			
Baltimore	1793	Windsor	**Cavendish**				
Barnard	1761	Windsor			N.H. grant 1761.	N	
Barnet	1763	Caledonia			N.H. grant 1763.		
Barre	1793	Washington			Chartered 1781. Called Wildersburg to 1793.		
Barton	1789	Orleans	Sheffield				

Town	Inc.	County	Parent	Daughter	Note	VR	CR
Belvidere	1791	Lamoille	Avery's Gore (Franklin Co.)	Eden, Waterville			
Bennington	1749	Bennington			N.H. grant 1749.		
Benson	1780	Rutland		Orwell			
Berkshire	1781	Franklin					
Berlin	1763	Washington		Montpelier	N.H. grant 1763.		
Bethel	1779	Windsor					
Bloomfield	1830	Essex			N.H. grant 1762. Called Minehead to 1830.		
Bolton	1763	Chittenden			N.H. grant 1763.		
Bradford	1788	Orange			N.Y. patent 1770. Called Mooretown to 1788.		
Braintree	1781	Orange		Rochester			
Brandon	1784	Rutland			N.H. grant 1761. Called Neshobe to 1784.		
Brattleboro	1753	Windham			N.H. grant 1753.	N, W	V
Bridgewater	1761	Windsor			N.H. grant 1761.		
Bridport	1761	Addison			N.H. grant 1761.		
Brighton	1832	Essex	Wenlock	Ferdinand	Chartered 1781. Called Random to 1832.		F
Bristol	1789	Addison	Ripton	Lincoln	N.H. grant as Pocock 1762. Called Pocock to 1789.	N, W	
Brookfield	1781	Orange		Chelsea	Ceded from Rutland Co. and annexed to Orange Co. 1783.		
Brookline	1794	Windham	**Athens**, Newfane, **Poultney**	Athens		V	
Brownington	1790	Orleans				P	
Brunswick	1761	Essex			N.H. grant 1761.		
Burke	1782	Caledonia		Hopkinsville, Kirby			
Burlington	1763	Chittenden		South Burlington	N.H. grant 1761.	S	F
Cabot	1781	Washington		Danville	Ceded from Caledonia Co. and annexed to Washington Co. 1855.		
Calais	1781	Washington					
Cambridge	1781	Lamoille	Fairfax, Fletcher, Sterling				
Canaan	1782	Essex	Lemington, Norfolk	Lemington			
Castleton	1761	Rutland			N.H. grant 1761.	V	

Town	Inc.	County	Parent	Daughter	Note	VR	CR
Cavendish	1761	Windsor			N.H. grant 1761.		
Charleston	1825	Orleans			Chartered 1780. Called Navy to 1825.		
Charlotte	1762	Chittenden			N.H. grant 1762.		
Chelsea	1788	Orange	Brookfield		Chartered 1781. Called Turnersburg to 1788.		
Chester	1766	Windsor			N.H. grant 1754. Called Flamstead to 1761. Regranted 1761. Called New Flamstead to 1766. Granted by N.Y. 1766.	V	
Chittenden	1780	Rutland	Brandon, Philadelphia	Sherburne			
Clarendon	1761	Rutland		Ira	N.H. grant 1761.		
Colchester	1763	Chittenden	Loomis Island	Milton	N.H. grant 1763.		F
Concord	1780	Essex	Bradleyvale		Ceded from Essex Co. and annexed by Caledonia Co. 1826.		
Corinth	1764	Orange	Vershire		N.H. grant 1764.		
Cornwall	1761	Addison		Middlebury	N.H. grant 1761.		
Coventry	1780	Orleans		Newport (Duncansborough)	Called Orleans 1841–1843.		
Craftsbury	1781	Orleans			Chartered 1781. Called Minden to 1781.		
Danby	1761	Rutland		Mount Tabor (Harwick)	N.H. grant 1761.		
Danville	1782	Caledonia	Cabot, Deweysburgh, Walden Gore			V	
Derby	1779	Orleans	Bell Island, Black Island, Salem			V	
Dorset	1761	Bennington	Mount Tabor (Harwick)		N.H. grant 1761.	V	
Dover	1810	Windham	Marlboro, Somerset, **Wardsboro**		Created from South Wardsboro district.	W	
Dummerston	1753	Windham		Putney	N.H. grant 1753. Called Fullam to 1937. Unofficially called Dummerston from 1753.		
Duxbury	1763	Washington			N.H. grant 1763.		
East Haven	1790	Essex					
East Montpelier	1848	Washington	**Montpelier**				

Town	Inc.	County	Parent	Daughter	Note	VR	CR
Eden	1781	Lamoille	Belvidere				
Elmore	1781	Lamoille			Ceded from Lamoille Co. and annexed to Washington Co. 1821.		
Enosburgh	1780	Franklin	Bakersfield				
Essex	1763	Chittenden			N.H. grant.		F
Fair Haven	1779	Rutland		West Haven			
Fairfax	1763	Franklin		Cambridge	N.H. grant 1763.	N, W	V
Fairfield	1763	Franklin	Smithfield	Bakersfield, Sheldon (Hungerford)	N.H. grant 1763.		V
Fairlee	1761	Orange		West Fairlee	N.H. grant 1761.		
Fayston	1782	Washington					
Ferrisburgh	1762	Addison		Vergennes	N.H. grant 1762.		
Fletcher	1781	Franklin		Cambridge			
Franklin	1817	Franklin			Chartered 1789. Called Huntsburg to 1817.		
Georgia	1763	Franklin			N.H. grant 1763.	P	
Glover	1783	Orleans					
Goshen	1792	Addison	Brandon, Philadelphia	Goshen Gore No. 1, Goshen Gore No. 2, Ripton, Rochester			
Grafton	1792	Windham	Athens, Avery's Gore	Athens	N.H. grant 1754. Called T(h)omlinson to 1792.		
Granby	1761	Essex			N.H. grant 1761.		
Grand Isle	1810	Grand Isle	South Hero		Chartered as Two Heroes 1779. Two Heroes split into North and South Hero 1788. Middle Hero divided from South Hero 1798. Renamed Grand Isle 1810.		
Granville	1834	Addison	Avery's Gore		Chartered 1769. Called Kingston to 1834. Ceded from Orange Co. and annexed to Addison Co. 1787.		
Greensboro	1781	Orleans					
Groton	1789	Caledonia	Harris Gore				
Guildhall	1761	Essex			N.H. grant 1761.		
Guilford	1754	Windham			N.H. grant 1754.		
Halifax	1750	Windham			N.H. grant 1750.		
Hancock	1781	Addison		Rochester	Annexed to Addison Co. 1791.		

Town	Inc.	County	Parent	Daughter	Note	VR	CR
Hardwick	1781	Caledonia				W	
Hartford	1761	Windsor	Woodstock	Woodstock	N.H. grant 1761.	P, V	
Hartland	1761	Windsor			N.H. grant 1761. Called Hertford to 1782.		
Highgate	1763	Franklin	Alburgh, Marvin's Gore	Swanton	N.H. grant 1763.		
Hinesburg	1762	Chittenden			N.H. grant 1762.		
Holland	1779	Orleans					
Hubbardton	1764	Rutland		Sudbury	N.H. grant 1764.		
Huntington	1763	Chittenden		Bolton	N.H. grant 1763. Called New Huntington to 1795.		
Hyde Park	1781	Lamoille	Morristown			N	
Ira	1781	Rutland	Clarendon	Castleton, Middletown	No official record of grant, but granting fee was ordered with date due for payment of 1 June 1781.		
Irasburg	1781	Orleans	Lowell				
Isle La Motte	1779	Grand Isle			Called Isle La Motte to 1802. Called Vineyard to 1830.		
Jamaica	1780	Windham				N. W	
Jay	1792	Orleans					
Jericho	1763	Chittenden			N.H. grant 1763.		
Johnson	1792	Lamoille	Sterling			N	
Killington	1761	Rutland	Chittenden, Parker's Gore, Pittsfield	Pittfield	N.H. grant 1761. Called Sherburne 1800–1999.		
Kirby	1807	Caledonia	**Burke,** Hopkinsville				
Landgrove	1780	Bennington					
Leicester	1761	Addison			N.H. grant 1761.		
Lemington	1761	Essex		Canaan	N.H. grant 1761.		
Lincoln	1780	Addison	Avery's Gore (Addison Co.), Bristol, Ripton	Warren			
Londonderry	1781	Windham	Windham	Windham			
Lowell	1831	Orleans	Kelly's Grant No. 2	Albany (Lutter-loh), Irasburg, Montgomery	Chartered 1791. Called Kellyvale to 1831.		
Ludlow	1761	Windsor		Middletown, Mount Holly	N.H. grant 1761.	P	
Lunenburg	1763	Essex			N.H. grant 1763.		

Town	Inc.	County	Parent	Daughter	Note	VR	CR
Lyndon	1780	Caledonia					
Maidstone	1761	Essex			N.H. grant 1761.		
Manchester	1761	Bennington	Winhall		N.H. grant 1761.		V
Marlboro	1761	Windham			N.H. grant 1761.		
Marshfield	1790	Washington					
Mendon	1827	Rutland	**Medway, Parker's Gore,** Rutland		Chartered as Parker's Gore 1796. Called Parkerstown to 1827.		
Middlebury	1761	Addison	Cornwall, Ripton, Weybridge		N.H. grant 1761.		
Middlesex	1763	Washington	Waterbury		N.H. grant 1763.		
Middletown Springs	1784	Rutland	**Ira, Poultney, Tinmouth, Wells**		Called Middletown to 1884.		
Milton	1763	Chittenden	Colchester		N.H. grant 1763.		V
Monkton	1762	Addison		Starksboro	N.H. grant 1762.		
Montgomery	1799	Franklin	Avery's Gore (Franklin Co.), Lowell (Kellyvale)				
Montpelier	1781	Washington					
Moretown	1763	Washington		Duxbury	N.H. grant 1763.		
Morgan	1801	Orleans	Brownington Gore, Whitelaw's Gore	Wenlock	Chartered 1780. Called Caldersburgh to 1801.	W	
Morristown	1780	Lamoille	Sterling	Hyde Park		N	
Mount Holly	1792	Rutland	**Jackson's Gore, Ludlow,** Weston				
Mount Tabor	1803	Rutland	Danby, Peru (Bromley)	Dorset	N.H. grant 1761. Called Harwick to 1803.		
New Haven	1761	Addison	New Haven Gore, Vergennes	Vergennes, Waltham	N.H. grant 1761. The part of New Haven ceded to Vergennes was annexed back, then ceded to form Waltham.		
Newark	1781	Caledonia			Ceded from Essex Co. and annexed by Caledonia Co. 1824. Annexed to Caledonia Probate District 1826.		
Newbury	1763	Orange			N.H. grant 1763.	V	
Newfane	1753	Windham		Brookline	N.H. grant 1753.		

Town	Inc.	County	Parent	Daughter	Note	VR	CR
Newport	1816	Orleans	Coventry, Coventry Gore, Derby, Province Island, Salem		Chartered 1802. Called Duncansborough to 1816.		
North Hero	1779	Grand Isle	Butler's Island, Knight's Island	Hyde Island			
Northfield	1781	Washington	Waitsfield				
Norton	1779	Essex					F
Norwich	1761	Windsor		Thetford	N.H. grant 1761.		
Orange	1781	Orange					
Orwell	1763	Addison	Benson	Whiting	N.H. grant 1763. Ceded from Rutland Co. and annexed to Addison Co. 1847.	N	
Panton	1761	Addison	Ferrisburgh	Vergennes, Weybridge	N.H. grant 1761.		
Pawlet	1761	Rutland			N.H. grant 1761.		
Peacham	1763	Caledonia	Deweysburgh		N.H. grant 1763.		N
Peru	1804	Bennington		Mount Tabor (Harwick)	N.H. grant 1761. Called Bromley to 1804.		
Pittsfield	1781	Rutland					
Pittsford	1761	Rutland		Proctor	N.H. grant 1761.		
Plainfield	1797	Washington	Goshen Gore No. 2		Called St. Andrew's Gore 1764–1797.		
Plymouth	1797	Windsor		Shrewsbury	N.H. grant 1761. Called Saltash to 1797.		
Pomfret	1761	Windsor		Sharon	N.H. grant 1761.	W	
Poultney	1761	Rutland		Middletown, Wells	N.H. grant 1761.		
Pownal	1760	Bennington			N.H. grant 1760.		
Proctor	1886	Rutland	**Pittsford, Rutland**				
Putney	1753	Windham	Dummerston (Fullam)	Brookline	N.H. grant 1753.	N, P, W	
Randolph	1781	Orange					
Reading	1761	Windsor			N.H. grant 1761.		
Readsboro	1770	Bennington			N.Y. patent 1770.		
Richford	1780	Franklin					
Richmond	1794	Chittenden	Bolton, **Jericho, Williston, Huntington**				
Ripton	1781	Addison	Goshen, Middlebury, Salisbury	Bristol, Lincoln			

Town	Inc.	County	Parent	Daughter	Note	VR	CR
Rochester	1781	Windsor	Braintree, Goshen, Hancock, Pittsfield				
Rockingham	1752	Windham		Athens	N.H. grant 1752.	P	P, W
Roxbury	1781	Washington			Ceded from Orange Co. and annexed to Washington Co. 1820.		
Royalton	1781	Windsor			N.Y. patent 1769.		
Rupert	1761	Bennington		Proctor, West Rutland	N.H. grant 1761.		
Rutland	1761	Rutland			N.H. grant 1761.	S	
Ryegate	1763	Caledonia			N.H. grant 1763.		
St. Albans	1763	Franklin	Johnson's Island, Wood's Island		N.H. grant 1763.		
St. George	1763	Chittenden	Shelburne		N.H. grant 1763.		
St. Johnsbury	1786	Caledonia					S
Salisbury	1761	Addison			N.H. grant 1761.		
Sandgate	1761	Bennington			N.H. grant 1761.		
Searsburg	1781	Bennington					
Shaftsbury	1761	Bennington			N.H. grant 1761.		
Sharon	1761	Windsor	Pomfret		N.H. grant 1761.		
Sheffield	1793	Caledonia		Barton			
Shelburne	1763	Chittenden		Saint George	N.H. grant 1763.	N, W	
Sheldon	1792	Franklin	Fairfield		N.H. grant 1763. Called Hungerford to 1792.		
Shoreham	1761	Addison			N.H. grant 1761.		
Shrewsbury	1761	Rutland	Plymouth (Saltash)		N.H. grant 1761.		
South Burlington	1864	Chittenden	**Burlington**				
South Hero	1788	Grand Isle	Savage Island		Created with North Hero from Two Heroes.		
Springfield	1761	Windsor			N.H. grant 1761.	V	W
Stamford	1753	Bennington			N.H. grant 1753.		
Stannard	1867	Caledonia	**Goshen**		Ceded from Goshen 1854. Called Goshen Gore No. 1 to 1867.		
Starksboro	1780	Addison	Monkton		Ceded from Chittenden Co. and annexed to Addison Co. 1794.		N
Stockbridge	1761	Windsor	Parker's Gore	Pittsfield	N.H. grant 1761.		

Town	Inc.	County	Parent	Daughter	Note	VR	CR
Stowe	1763	Lamoille	Mansfield, Sterling			V	
Strafford	1761	Orange			N.H. grant 1761.		
Stratton	1761	Windham	Stratton Gore, Somerset		N.H. grant 1761.		
Sudbury	1763	Rutland	Hubbardton		N.H. grant 1763.	P	
Sunderland	1761	Bennington			N.H. grant 1761.		
Sutton	1812	Caledonia			Chartered 1782. Called Billymead to 1812.		
Swanton	1763	Franklin	Highgate		N.H. grant 1763.		
Thetford	1761	Orange	Norwich		N.H. grant 1761.		
Tinmouth	1761	Rutland		Middletown, Wallingford	N.H. grant 1761.		
Topsham	1763	Orange			N.H. grant 1763.		
Townshend	1753	Windham	Acton		N.H. grant 1753.		
Troy	1801	Orleans	Kelly's Grant, Woodbridge		Called Missisquoi to 1803.		
Tunbridge	1761	Orange			N.H. grant 1761.		
Underhill	1763	Chittenden	Mansfield		N.H. grant 1763.		F
Vergennes	1788	Addison	**Ferrisburg, New Haven, Panton**	New Haven			
Vernon	1802	Windham			Chartered 1753. Called Hinsdale 1753–1802.	V	
Vershire	1781	Orange	Corinth		Called Ely 1878–82.		
Victory	1781	Essex	Bradleyvale				
Waitsfield	1782	Washington	Northfield			N	
Walden	1781	Caledonia	Monroe				
Wallingford	1761	Rutland	Tinmouth		N.H. grant 1761.		
Waltham	1796	Addison	**New Haven**		Incorporated from that part of New Haven that annexed to Vergennes, then ceded back to New Haven.		
Wardsboro	1780	Windham	Somerset	Dover		V	
Warren	1789	Washington	Lincoln		Annexed to Washington Co. 1829.		
Washington	1781	Orange					
Waterbury	1763	Washington	Bolton, Middlesex		N.H. grant 1763.		
Waterford	1797	Caledonia			Chartered 1780. Called Littleton to 1797.		

Town	Inc.	County	Parent	Daughter	Note	VR	CR
Waterville	1824	Lamoille	**Bakersfield, Belvidere, Coits Gore**			N	
Weathersfield	1761	Windsor			N.H. grant 1763.		
Wells	1761	Rutland		Middletown, Poultney	N.H. grant 1761.		
West Fairlee	1797	Orange	**Fairlee**		Chartered as part of Fairlee 1761.		
West Haven	1792	Rutland	Fair Haven				
West Rutland	1886	Rutland	**Rutland**				
West Windsor	1814	Windsor	**Windsor**		Windsor divided 1783. Chartered 1799. Incorporated out of Windsor 1814. Separate incorporation repealed 1815. Reincorporated out of Windsor 1848.		
Westfield	1780	Orleans				N, W	
Westford	1763	Chittenden			N.H. grant 1763.		
Westminster	1752	Windham			N.H. grant 1752.		
Westmore	1787	Orleans			Chartered 1781. Called Westford to 1787.		
Weston	1799	Windsor	**Andover, Benton's Gore**	Mount Holly			
Weybridge	1761	Addison	Addison, New Haven, Panton	Middlebury	N.H. grant 1761.	W	W
Wheelock	1785	Caledonia					
Whiting	1763	Addison			N.H. grant 1763.		
Whitingham	1770	Windham			N.Y. patent 1770.		
Williamstown	1781	Orange					
Williston	1763	Chittenden			N.H. grant 1763.		
Wilmington	1751	Windham	Somerset	Dover	N.H. grant 1751.		
Windham	1795	Windham	**Londonderry, Mack's Leg**	Londonderry			
Windsor	1761	Windsor		West Windsor	N.H. grant 1761.		
Winhall	1761	Bennington		Manchester	N.H. grant 1761.		
Winooski	1921	Chittenden	Colchester		Created from part of Colchester called Winooski Village.		F
Wolcott	1781	Lamoille					
Woodbury	1781	Washington			Annexed to Washington Co. 1835. Called Monroe 1838–43.		

Town	Inc.	County	Parent	Daughter	Note	VR	CR
Woodford	1753	Bennington			N.H. grant 1753. Grant renewed 1762.		
Woodstock	1761	Windsor	Hartford, Hartland	Hartford	N.H. grant 1761.		
Worcester	1763	Washington			N.H. grant 1763.	W	

Extinct or Unincorporated Towns and Gores

The following areas have never had large populations. In many instances they exist only on paper. Few, if any, records exist for these locations.

Town	Est.	County	Parent	Daughter	Note	VR	CR
Acton	1800	Windham	Johnson's Gore	Townshend	Annexed to Townshend 1840.		
Aiken's Gore	1781	Windham		Grafton (Tomlinson)	Annexed to Grafton 1816.		
Averill	1762	Essex			N.H. grant 1762. Unincorporated.		
Avery's Gore	1791	Essex			Unincorporated.		
Benton's Gore	1787	Windsor		Weston	Annexed to Weston 1799.		
Bradleyvale	1803	Caledonia	Pearsall's Gore	Concord, Victory	Annexed to Concord and Victory 1856.		
Buel's Gore	1780	Chittenden			Unincorporated. Attempted annexation to Huntington 1937, but refused by Huntington.		
Coventry Gore	1781	Orleans		Newport	Annexed to Newport 1894.		
Deweysburgh	1782	Caledonia		Danville, Peacham	Annexed to Danville and Peacham 1810.		
Ferdinand	1761	Essex	Brighton (Random), Wenlock		Unincorporated.		
Glastenbury	1761	Bennington			Incorporation ended 1937.		
Goshen Gore No. 2	1798	Addison	Goshen	Plainfield	Annexed to Plainfield 1874.		
Harris Gore	1801	Caledonia		Groton, Marshfield	Annexed to Groton and Marshfield 1890.		
Hitchcock's Gore	1783			Putney	Annexed to Putney.		
Hopkinsville	1790	Caledonia		Kirby	Joined with Burke Tongue to create Kirby.		
Jackson's Gore	1781	Rutland		Mount Holly	Joined with part of Ludlow to create Mount Holly.		

Town	Inc.	County	Parent	Daughter	Note	VR	CR
Johnson's Gore	1782	Windham		Acton	Annexed to Acton 1800.		
Kelly's Grant	1792	Orleans		Missisquoi	Annexed to Troy (Missisquoi) 1801.		
Kelly's Grant No. 2	1791	Orleans		Kellyvale	Annexed to Lowell (Kellyvale) 1825.		
Knowlton's Gore	1791	Franklin		Bakersfield	Annexed to Bakersfield 1792.		
Lewis	1762	Essex			N.H. grant 1762. Unincorporated.		
Mansfield	1763	Lamoille		Underhill, Stowe	Annexed to Stowe 1848.		
Marvin's Gore	1793	Franklin		Highgate	Annexed to Highgate 1806.		
Norfolk	1782	Orange		Canaan	Annexed to Canaan 1801.		
Parker's Gore	1793			Medway	Merged with Medway to form Mendon (Parkerstown) 1804.		
Philadelphia	1780	Rutland	Brandon, Chittenden, Pittsford	Brandon, Chittenden	Annexed to Chittenden 1816.		
Smithfield	1763	Franklin		Fairfield	Annexed to Fairfield 1792.		
Somerset	1761	Windham		Dover, Stratton, Wartsboro, Wilmington	N.H. grant. Unincorporated 1937.	V	
Sterling	1805	Lamoille		Cambridge, Johnson, Morristown, Stowe	Annexed to Johnston, Morristown, Stowe, 1855.		
Two Heroes	1779	Grand Isle		North Hero, South Hero	Divided into North Hero and South Hero 1791.		
Walden Gore	1782	Orange		Danville	Annexed to Danville 1792.		
Warner's Grant	1791	Essex			Unincorporated.		
Warren Gore	1789	Essex			Unincorporated. Charter to credit the town of Warren, Washington Co., "with enough acreage to have a town."		
Wenlock	1761	Essex	Caldersburgh	Brighton (Random), Ferdinand	Annexed to Brighton and Ferdinand 1853.		
Woodbridge	1781	Orleans		Troy	Annexed to Troy.		

The following towns were annexed from New York, but ceded to Vermont in 1781. All were then ceded back to New York. The established date is the date of the town's establishment in Vermont. The town itself may have been founded earlier in New York.

Town	Est.	County	Parent	Daughter	Note
Black Creek	1781	Rutland			Ceded back to N.Y. 1790.
Cambridge	1781	Bennington			Ceded back to N.Y. 1790.
Eastborough	1781	Rutland			Ceded back to N.Y. 1790.
East Saratoga	1781	Bennington			Ceded back to N.Y. 1790.
Granville	1781	Rutland			Ceded back to N.Y. 1790.
Greenfield	1781				Ceded back to N.Y. 1790.
Hoosack	1781	Bennington			Ceded back to N.Y. 1790.
Kingsbury	1781	Rutland			Ceded back to N.Y. 1790.
Little Hoosack	1781	Bennington			Ceded back to N.Y. 1790.
North Granville	1781	Rutland			Ceded back to N.Y. 1790.
Saratoga	1781	Bennington			Ceded back to N.Y. 1790.
Scorticook	1781	Bennington			Ceded back to N.Y. 1790.
Scotch Patent	1781	Rutland			Ceded back to N.Y. 1790. Also called Argyle.
Skeensboro	1781	Rutland			Ceded back to N.Y. 1790.
South Granville	1781	Rutland			Ceded back to N.Y. 1790.
White Creek	1781	Rutland			Ceded back to N.Y. 1790. Also called New Perth.

In 1778, thirty-two towns were annexed to Vermont from New Hampshire. They were ceded back to New Hampshire in 1782:

Acworth	Charlestown	Grafton	Lancaster	Lyme	Surry
Alstead	Chesterfield	Grantham	Landaff	Morristown	Walpole
Althorp	Claremont	Gunthwaite	Lebanon	Orford	
Bath	Cornish	Hanover	Leicester	Piermont	
Canaan	Enfield	Haverhill	Lincoln	Richmond	
Cardigan	Gilsum	Hinsdale	Lyman	Saville	

Subject Index

See the Index of Places for specific counties, cities, and towns, including select extinct, ceded, unorganized, and unincorporated towns and territories.

Boldface page numbers indicate maps.

B

Bailey/Howe Library, University of Vermont, 320
Bennington [Vt.] Museum, 320
Berkshire Family History Association, 12
Boston Athenaeum, 164
Boston, Archdiocese of, Archives, 164
Boston, City of, Archives, 163

C

Cape Cod Genealogical Society, 13
Cemetery records
  Connecticut, 22
  Maine, 85
  New Hampshire, 233
  Rhode Island, 286
  Vermont, 317
Census records. *See also* State census records
  Connecticut, 22
  Maine, 84, 85
  Massachusetts, 161
  New Hampshire, 234
  Rhode Island, 286
Central Massachusetts Genealogical Society, 13
Church records, 6
  Connecticut, 23
  Maine, 81
  Massachusetts, 158
  New Hampshire, 232
  Rhode Island, 282–83
  Vermont, 316
City of Boston Archives, 163
City directories, New Hampshire, 234
Congregational Christian Historical Society (Boston), 164
Congregational Library (Boston), 164
Connecticut Ancestry Society, 13
Connecticut Archives, 22
Connecticut Historical Society, 26
Connecticut Professional Genealogists Council, 13
Connecticut Society of Genealogists, 13
Connecticut State Library, 25
Connecticut Valley Historical Museum, 164
Connecticut, 17–78
  adoptions, 19
  Archives, 22
  cemetery lists, 22
  church records, 23
  Collections of the Connecticut Archives, 21

counties, 27–43
court records, 20
Department of Public Health, State Office of Vital Records, 26
land records, 20, 52
map of, **24**
Military Census of 1917, 22
military records, 21–22
newspaper records, 22
passenger lists, 22
probate districts, **44**–51
probate records, 19, 45
repositories in, 25–26
State Archives, 21, 25
state census records, 22
State Library, 25
towns, 70–78
vital records, 17–19
Counties
  Connecticut, 27–43
  Maine, 89–121
  Massachusetts, 165–94
  New Hampshire, 239–59
  New York, 321
  Rhode Island, 291–301
  Vermont, 321–49
Court records, 3
  Connecticut, 20
  Maine, 83
  Massachusetts, 159–60
  New Hampshire, 230–31
  Rhode Island, 283–84
  Vermont, 315

D

Descendants of the Founders of Ancient Windsor, 13
Dubois Library, University of Massachusetts, 164

E

Essex Society of Genealogists, 13

F

Falmouth Genealogical Society, 13
Franco-American Genealogical Society of York County, 13
Freemen, lists of, 3
French-Canadian Genealogical Society of Connecticut, 13

New Hampshire Historical Society, 238
New Hampshire Old Graveyard Association, 238
New Hampshire Society of Genealogists, 14
New Haven Colony Historical Society, 26
New York, counties, 321
Newport [RI] Historical Society, 290
Newspaper records
  Connecticut, 22
  New Hampshire, 234
  Rhode Island, 287
Notarial records, 3–4

O

Old Broad Bay Family History Association, 14
Old Colony Historical Society [MA], 164

P

Passenger lists, 2–3. *See also* Immigration records
  Connecticut, 22
  Massachusetts, 161
Peabody-Essex Museum, Phillips Library, 165
Phillips Library, Peabody-Essex Museum, 165
Polish Genealogical Society of Connecticut and the Northeast, 15
Portsmouth [N.H.] Athenaeum, 238
Probate districts, of Connecticut, **44**–51
Probate records
  Connecticut, 19, 45
  Maine, 81–82, 122
  Massachusetts, 157–58, 195
  New Hampshire, 229, 260
  Rhode Island, 282–82, 302
  Vermont, 314–15, 350
Providence [RI], City of, Archives, 290

R

Records, types used in New England research, 2–6. *See also specific types of records; specific states*
Registries of deeds. *See* Land records
Repositories
  Connecticut, 25–26
  Maine, 87–88
  Massachusetts, 163–65
  New England, 11
  New Hampshire, 237–38
  Rhode Island, 289–90
  Vermont, 319–20

Rhode Island, 279–310
  adoption records, 281–82
  cemetery records, 286
  census records, 286
  church records, 282–83
  counties, 291–301
  court records, 283–84
  Department of Health, Office of Vital Records, 290
  immigration records, 285–86
  land and property records, 283, 302
  manuscript collections, 287
  map of, **288**
  military records, 284
  newspapers, 287
  probate records, 281–82, 302
  repositories, 289–90
  State Archives, 289
  State Library, 289
  Supreme Judicial Court Records Center, 290
  towns, 307–10
  vital records, 280–81
Rhode Island Black Heritage Society, 14
Rhode Island Genealogical Society, 15
Rhode Island Historical Cemeteries Database, 286
Rhode Island Historical Society, 290

S

Sons and Daughters of the First Settlers of Newbury, Mass., 15
South Shore Genealogical Soicety, 15
State census records. *See also* Census records
  Connecticut, 22
  Maine, 85
  Massachusetts, 161
Strafford County Genealogical Society, 15
Swedish Ancestry Research Association (SARA), 15

T

Town records, 4–5
Towns
  Connecticut, 70–78
  Maine, 164–54
  Massachusetts, 201–26
  New Hampshire, 263–78
  Rhode Island, 307–10
  Vermont, 384–96

Index of Places

This index of places directs the reader to page numbers where specific counties, cities, and towns are mentioned in the book.

- *Nearly every county is mentioned in at least two places: in the county table, and on the relevant two-page spread for the county.*
- *Most towns are mentioned in at least two places: on the relevant county page, and in a town table.*
- *We have provided page numbers for probate and/or town clerk offices for states where probate and/ or land records are handled by the county or town.*

The index does include select extinct, unincorporated, or unorganized towns or territories. It also includes archaic names, with cross-references to current county, city, or town names.

Other mentions of place names (e.g., in narrative text or in addresses of repositories) are not indexed. Villages are not indexed. When a town and a county have the same name, the town is listed first. Towns with the same name are listed alphabetically by ZIP abbreviation.

Boldface page numbers indicate maps.

Argyle, ME, 109, 151
Arlington, NH. *See* Winchester, NH
Arlington, MA, 183, 203
Arlington, VT, 325, 353, 384
Aroostook Co., ME, 89, **92,** 93, 122, 124
Arrowsic, ME, 113, 127
Arundel, ME, 121, 127. *See also* Kennebunkport, ME
Ashburnham, MA, 193, 203
Ashby, MA, 183, 203
Ashfield, MA, 177, 203
Ashford, CT, 43, 52, 71
Ashland, MA, 183, 203
Ashland, ME, 93, 127
Ashland, NH, 249, 264
Ashuelot Equivalent. *See* Dalton, MA
Athens, ME, 115, 127
Athens, VT, 347, 353, 384
Athol, MA, 193, 203
Atkinson, ME, 111
Atkinson, NH, 255, 264
Atkinson and Gilmanton Academy Grant, NH, 247, 278
Attleboro, MA, 171, 203
Auburn, MA, 193, 203
Auburn, ME, 91, 127
Auburn, NH, 255, 264
Augusta, ME, 101, 128
Aurora, ME, 99, 128
Averill, VT, 331, 384, 394
Avery's Gore, VT, 331, 394
Avon, CT, 31, 52, 71
Avon, MA, 187, 203
Avon, ME, 97, 128
Ayer, MA, 183, 203

B
Baileyville, ME, 119, 128
Baker's Town, MA. *See* Salisbury, NH
Bakersfield, VT, 333, 353, 384
Baldwin, ME, 95, 128
Ballstown, ME. *See* Jefferson, ME
Baltimore, VT, 349, 353, 384
Bancroft, ME, 93, 128
Bangor, ME, 109, 128
Bar Harbor, ME, 99, 128
Barecove, MA. *See* Hingham, MA
Baring, ME, 119
Baring [Plantation], ME, 119, 151
Barkhamsted, CT, 33, 52, 71
Barnard, ME, 111, 151
Barnard, VT, 349, 354, 384
Barnet, VT, 327, 354, 384
Barnstable, MA, 167, 203
Barnstable Co., MA, 165, **166,** 167, 195, 198
Barnstead, NH, 241, 264
Barre, MA, 193, 203

Barre, VT, 345, 354, 384
Barrington, MA, 171, 224. *See also* Barrington, RI
Barrington, NH, 257, 264
Barrington, RI, 293, 302, 308
Bartlett, NH, 243, 264
Barton, VT, 341, 354, 384
Basse River, MA. *See* Beverly, MA
Bath, ME, 113, 128
Bath, NH, 249, 263, 264
Bath, VT, 396. *See also* Bath, NH
Beacon Falls, CT, 37, 53, 71
Beals, ME, 119, 128
Beans Grant, NH, 247, 278
Beans Purchase, NH, 247, 278
Beaver Cove, ME, 111, 128
Becket, MA, 169, 203
Beddington, ME, 119, 128
Bedford, MA, 183, 203. *See also* Granville, MA
Bedford, NH, 251, 264
Belchertown, MA, 181, 203
Belfast, ME, 117, 128
Belgrade, ME, 101, 128
Belknap Co., NH, 239, **240,** 241, 260, 261
Bellingham, MA, 187, 204
Belmont, MA, 183, 204
Belmont, ME, 117, 128
Belmont, NH, 241, 264
Belvidere, VT, 337, 354, 385
Benedicta, ME, 93, 151
Bennington, NH, 251, 264
Bennington, VT, 325, 354, 385
Bennington Co., VT, 321, **324,** 325, 350
Benson, VT, 343, 354, 385
Benton, ME, 101, 128
Benton, NH, 249, 264
Benton's Gore VT, 349, 394
Berkley, MA, 171, 204
Berkshire, VT, 333, 354, 385
Berkshire Co., MA, 165, **168,** 169, 195, 198
Berlin, CT, 31, 53, 71
Berlin, MA, 193, 204
Berlin, ME, 97, 151
Berlin, NH, 247, 265
Berlin, VT, 345, 355, 385
Bernardston, MA, 177, 204
Berwick, ME, 121, 128
Bethany, CT, 37, 53, 71
Bethel, CT, 29, 53, 71
Bethel, ME, 107, 128
Bethel, VT, 349, 355, 385
Bethlehem, CT, 33, 53, 71
Bethlehem, District of [MA], 169, 224
Bethlehem, NH, 249, 265
Beverly, MA, 175, 204

Beverly-Canada. *See* Weare, NH
Biddeford, ME, 121, 128
Billerica, MA, 183, 204
Billymead, VT. *See* Sutton, VT
Bingham, ME, 115, 128
Black Creek, VT/NY, 396
Blackstone, MA, 193, 204
Blaine, ME, 93, 128
Blanchard, ME, 111, 152
Blandford, MA, 179, 204
Block Island, RI. *See* New Shoreham, RI
Bloody Point, NH. *See* Newington, NH
Bloomfield, CT, 31, 53, 71
Bloomfield, VT, 331, 355, 385
Blue Hill, ME, 99, 128
Bolton, CT, 41, 53, 71
Bolton, MA, 193, 204
Bolton, VT, 329, 355, 385
Boothbay, ME, 105, 129
Boothbay Harbor, ME, 105, 129
Boscawen, NH, 253, 265
Boston, MA, 191, 204
Boston Corner District, MA, 169, 224
Bourne, MA, 167, 204
Bow, NH, 253, 265
Bowdoin, ME, 113, 129
Bowdoinham, ME, 113, 129
Bowerbank, ME, 111, 129
Boxborough, MA, 183, 204
Boxford, MA, 175, 204
Boyle, NH. *See* Gilsum, NH
Boylston, MA, 193, 204
Bozrah, CT, 39, 53, 71
Bradford, MA, 175, 224
Bradford, ME, 109, 129
Bradford, NH, 253, 265
Bradford, VT, 339, 355, 385
Bradley, ME, 109, 129
Bradleyvale, VT, 327, 394
Braintree, MA, 187, 204
Braintree, VT, 339, 355, 385
Brandon, VT, 343, 355, 385
Branford, CT, 37, 53, 71
Brattleboro, VT, 347, 355, 385
Bremen, ME, 105, 129
Brenton's Farm, NH. *See* Litchfield, NH
Brentwood, NH, 255, 265
Bretton Woods, NH. *See* Carroll, NH
Brewer, ME, 109, 129
Brewster, MA, 167, 204
Bridge Village, NH. *See* Tilton, NH
Bridgeport, CT, 29, 54, 71
Bridgewater, CT, 33, 54, 71
Bridgewater, MA, 189, 205
Bridgewater, ME, 93, 129
Bridgewater, NH, 249, 265

Bridgewater,VT, 349, 356, 385
Bridgton, ME, 95, 129
Bridport,VT, 323, 356, 385
Brighton, MA, 183, 224
Brighton,VT, 331, 356, 385
Brighton Plantation, ME, 115, 129
Brimfield, MA, 179, 205
Brintwood, NH. *See* Brentwood, NH
Bristol, CT, 31, 54, 71
Bristol, MA, 171, 224. *See also*
    Bristol, RI
Bristol, ME, 105, 129
Bristol, NH, 249, 265. *See also*
    Dover, NH
Bristol, RI, 293, 302, 308. *See also*
    Bristol, MA
Bristol,VT, 323, 356, 385
Bristol Co., MA, 165, **170,** 171, 195,
    198. *See also* Bristol Co., RI
Bristol Co., RI., 291, **292,** 293
Brockton, MA, 189, 205
Bromley,VT. *See* Peru,VT
Brookfield, CT, 29, 54, 71
Brookfield, MA, 193, 205
Brookfield, NH, 243, 265
Brookfield,VT, 339, 356, 385
Brooklin, ME, 99, 129
Brookline, MA, 187, 205
Brookline, NH, 251, 265
Brookline,VT, 347, 356, 385
Brooklyn, CT, 43, 54, 71
Brooks, ME, 117, 129
Brooksville, ME, 99, 129
Brookton, ME, 119, 152
Brownfield, ME, 107, 130
Brownington,VT, 341, 356, 385
Brownville, ME, 111, 130
Brunswick, ME, 95, 130
Brunswick,VT, 331, 356, 385
Buckfield, ME, 107, 130
Buckingham, NH. *See* Unity, NH
Buckland, MA, 177, 205
Bucksport, ME, 99, 130
Buckstown, ME. *See* Bucksport, ME
Buels Gore,VT, 329, 394
Burke,VT, 327, 357, 385
Burlington, CT, 31, 54, 71
Burlington, MA, 183, 205
Burlington, ME, 109, 130
Burlington,VT, 329, 357, 385
Burnham, ME, 117, 130
Burrillville, RI, 299, 302, 308
Burton, NH. *See* Albany, NH
Buxton, ME, 121, 130
Byron, ME, 107, 130

C
Cabot,VT, 345, 357, 385
Calais, ME, 119, 130

Calais,VT, 345, 357, 385
Caldersburgh,VT. *See* Morgan,VT
Caledonia Co.,VT, 321, **326,** 327, 351
Cambridge, MA, 183, 205
Cambridge, ME, 115, 130
Cambridge, NH, 247, 278
Cambridge,VT/NY, 337, 357, 385,
    396
Cambridge Village, MA. *See*
    Newton, MA
Camden, ME, 103, 130
Camden, NH. *See* Washington, NH
Campbell's Gore, NH. *See* Windsor,
    NH
Campton, NH, 249, 265
Canaan, CT, 33, 54, 71
Canaan, ME, 115, 130
Canaan, NH, 249, 263, 265
Canaan,VT, 331, 357, 385, 396.
    See also Canaan, NH
Candia, NH, 255, 265
Canterbury, CT, 43, 54, 71
Canterbury, NH, 253, 265
Canton, CT, 31, 55, 71
Canton, MA, 187, 205
Canton, ME, 107, 130
Cape Ann to Gloucester. *See*
    Gloucester, MA
Cape Elizabeth, ME, 95, 130
Cape Porpoise/Porpus, ME. *See*
    Kennebunkport, ME
Caratunk Plantation, ME, 115, 130
Cardigan, NH, 263. *See also* Orange,
    NH
Cardigan,VT, 396. *See also* Orange,
    NH
Caribou, ME, 93, 130
Carlisle, MA, 183, 205
Carmel, ME, 109, 130
Carrabassett Valley, ME, 97, 130
Carroll, NH, 247, 265
Carroll Co., NH, 239, **242,** 243,
    260, 261
Carroll Plantation, ME, 109, 131
Carthage, ME, 97, 131
Carver, MA, 189, 205
Cary Plantation, ME, 93, 131
Casco, ME, 95, 131
Castine, ME, 99, 131
Castle Hill, ME, 93, 131
Castleton,VT, 343, 357, 385
Caswell, ME, 93, 131
Cavendish,VT, 349, 357, 386
Center Harbor, NH, 241, 265
Centerville, ME, 119, 131
Central Falls, RI, 299, 302, 308
Central Somerset, ME, 115, 152
Chandlers Purchase, NH, 247, 278
Chandlerville, ME. *See* Detroit, ME

Chaplin, CT, 43, 55, 72
Chapman, ME, 93, 131
Charlemont, MA, 177, 205
Charleston, ME, 109, 131
Charleston,VT, 341, 358, 386
Charlestown, MA, 183, 224
Charlestown, NH, 259, 263, 265
Charlestown, RI, 301, 303, 308
Charlestown,VT, 396. *See also*
    Charlestown, NH
Charlestown Village, MA. *See*
    Woburn, MA
Charlotte, ME, 119, 131
Charlotte,VT, 329, 358, 386
Charlotte Co., NY, 321
Charlotte Co.,VT. *See* Charlotte
    Co., NY
Charlton, MA, 193, 205
Charmingfare, NH. *See* Candia, NH
Chatham, CT, 72. *See also* East
    Hampton, CT
Chatham, MA, 167, 205
Chatham, NH, 243, 265
Chauncey, MA. *See* Westborough, MA
Chebeague Island, ME, 95, 131
Chelmsford, MA, 183, 205
Chelsea, MA, 191, 206
Chelsea, ME, 101, 131
Chelsea,VT, 339, 358, 386
Cherryfield, ME, 119, 131
Cheshire, CT, 37, 55, 72
Cheshire, MA, 169, 206
Cheshire, NH. *See* Chester, NH
Cheshire Co., NH, 239, **244,** 245,
    260, 261
Cheshire Mills, NH. *See* Harrisville,
    NH
Chester, CT, 35, 55, 72
Chester, MA, 179, 206
Chester, ME, 109, 131
Chester, NH, 255, 266
Chester,VT, 349, 358, 386
Chester Woods, NH. *See* Hooksett, NH
Chesterfield, MA, 181, 206
Chesterfield, NH, 245, 263, 266
Chesterfield,VT, 396. *See also*
    Chesterfield, NH
Chesterville, ME, 97, 131
Chichester, NH, 253, 266
Chicopee, MA, 179, 206
Chilmark, MA, 173, 206
China, ME, 101, 131
Chiswick, NH. *See* Dalton, NH;
    Lisbon, NH; Littleton, NH
Chittenden,VT, 343, 358, 386
Chittenden Co.,VT, 321, **328,** 329, 351
Claremont, NH, 259, 263, 266
Claremont,VT, 396. *See also*
    Claremont, NH

Gilford, NH, 241, 268
Gill, MA, 177, 209
Gilmanton, NH, 241, 268
Gilsum, NH, 245, 263, 268. *See also* Gilsum, VT
Gilsum, VT, 396. *See also* Gilsum, NH
Glastenbury, VT, 325, 394
Glastonbury, CT, 31, 58, 73
Glenburn, ME, 109, 135
Glenwood Plantation, ME, 93, 135
Glocester, RI, 299, 304, 308
Gloucester Co., NY, 321
Gloucester Co., VT. *See* Gloucester Co., NY
Gloucester, MA, 175, 209
Glover, VT, 341, 362, 387
Goffstown, NH, 251, 268
Gorham, ME, 95, 135
Gorham, NH, 247, 268
Gorham's-town, NH. *See* Dunbarton, NH
Goshen, CT, 33, 58, 73
Goshen, MA, 181, 209
Goshen, ME. *See* Vienna, ME
Goshen, NH, 259, 268
Goshen, VT, 323, 362, 387
Goshen Gore No. 1, VT. *See* Stannard, VT
Goshen Gore No. 2, VT, 323, 394
Gosnold, 173, 209
Gosport, NH, 255, 277
Gouldsboro, ME, 99, 135
Grafton, MA, 193, 209
Grafton, NH, 249, 263, 268. *See also Grafton, VT*
Grafton, VT, 347, 362, 387, 396. *See also* Grafton, NH
Grafton Co., NH, 239, **248,** 249, 260, 262.
Granby, CT, 31, 58, 73
Granby, MA, 181, 209
Granby, VT, 331, 362, 387
Grand Falls Plantation, ME, 109, 153
Grand Isle, ME, 93, 135
Grand Isle, VT, 335, 362, 387
Grand Isle Co., VT, 321, **334,** 335, 351
Grand Lake Stream Plantation, ME, 119, 135
Grant Isle, ME. *See* Grand Isle, ME
Grantham, NH, 259, 268
Grantham, VT, 396. *See also* Grantham, NH
Granville, MA, 179, 209
Granville, VT/NY, 323, 362, 387, 396
Gray, ME, 95, 135
Great Barrington, MA, 169, 209
Great Harbour, MA. *See* Edgartown, MA

Great Island, NH. *See* New Castle, NH
Great Meadows. *See* Westmoreland, NH
Great Pond, ME, 99, 135
Greenbush, ME, 109, 136
Greene, ME, 91, 136
Greenfield, MA, 177, 209
Greenfield, ME, 109, 153
Greenfield, NH, 251, 269
Greenfield, VT/NY, 396
Greenland, NH, 255, 269
Greens Grant, NH, 247, 278
Greensboro, VT, 341, 363, 387
Greenville, ME, 111, 136
Greenville, NH, 251, 269
Greenwich, CT, 29, 58, 73
Greenwich, MA, 181, 225
Greenwood, ME, 107, 136
Grenville, NH. *See* Newport, NH
Griswold, CT, 39, 58, 73
Groton, CT, 39, 58, 73
Groton, MA, 183, 209
Groton, MA, Second Precinct of. *See* Pepperell, MA
Groton, NH, 249, 269
Groton, VT, 327, 363, 387
Groveland, MA, 175, 209
Guildhall, VT, 331, 363, 387
Guilford, CT, 37, 59, 73
Guilford, ME, 111, 136
Guilford, VT, 347, 363, 387
Gunstock Parish, NH. *See* Gilford, NH
Gunthwaite, NH, 263. *See also* Lisbon, NH
Gunthwaite, VT, 396. *See also* Gunthwaite, NH; Lisbon, NH

H
Haddam, CT, 35, 59, 73
Hadley, MA, 181, 209
Hadleys Purchase, NH, 247, 278
Hales Location, NH, 243, 278
Halestown, NH. *See* Weare, NH
Halifax, MA, 189, 209
Halifax, VT, 347, 363, 387
Hallowell, ME, 101, 136
Hamden, CT, 37, 59, 73
Hamilton, MA, 175, 209
Hamlin, ME, 93, 136
Hammond, ME, 93, 136
Hampden, MA, 179, 209
Hampden, ME, 109, 136
Hampden Co., MA, 165, **178,** 179, 196, 199
Hampshire Co., MA, 165, **180,** 181, 196, 200
Hampstead, NH, 255, 269

Hampton, CT, 43, 59, 73
Hampton, ME. *See* Aurora, ME
Hampton, NH, 255, 269
Hampton Falls, NH, 255, 269
Ham's-town, NH. *See* Wakefield, NH
Hancock Co., ME, 89, **98,** 99, 122, 124
Hancock, MA, 169, 209
Hancock, ME, 99, 136
Hancock, NH, 251, 269
Hancock, VT, 323, 363, 387
Hanover, MA, 189, 210
Hanover, ME, 107, 136
Hanover, NH, 249, 263, 269. *See also* Hanover, VT
Hanover, VT, 396. *See also* Hanover, NH
Hanson, MA, 189, 210
Hardwick, MA, 193, 210
Hardwick, VT, 327, 363, 388
Harlem, ME, 101, 153
Harmony, ME, 115, 136
Harpswell, ME, 95, 136
Harrington, ME, 119, 136. *See also* Augusta, ME
Harris Gore, VT, 327, 394
Harrison, ME, 95, 136
Harrisville, NH, 245, 269
Harrytown, NH. *See* Manchester, NH
Hartford, CT, 31, 59, 73
Hartford, ME, 107, 136
Hartford, VT, 349, 363, 388
Hartford Co., CT, 27, *30,* 31
Hartland, CT, 31, 59, 73
Hartland, ME, 115, 136
Hartland, VT, 349, 364, 388
Hart's Location, NH, 243, 269
Hartwood Plantation. *See* Washington, MA
Harvard, MA, 193, 210
Harwich, MA, 167, 210
Harwick, VT. *See* Mount Tabor, VT
Harwinton, CT, 33, 59, 73
Haskell, ME. *See* Greenville, ME
Hatfield, MA, 181, 210
Haverhill, MA, 175, 210
Haverhill, NH, 249, 269. *See also* Haverhill, VT
Haverhill, VT, 396. *See also* Haverhill, NH
Haverhill District. *See* Plaistow, NH
Haversham, RI. *See* Westerly, RI
Hawke, NH. *See* Danville, NH
Hawley, MA, 177, 210
Haynesville, ME, 93, 136
Heath, MA, 177, 210
Hebron, CT, 41, 59, 73
Hebron, ME, 107, 136
Hebron, NH, 249, 269

Sturbridge, MA, 193, 220
Success, NH, 247, 278
Suckanesset. *See* Falmouth, MA
Sudbury, MA, 183, 220
Sudbury, VT, 343, 377, 392
Suffield, CT, 31, 67, 76. *See also*
    Suffield, MA
Suffield, MA, 193, 226. *See also*
    Suffield, CT
Suffield Equivalent Lands. *See*
    Blandford, MA
Suffolk Co., MA, 165, **190,** 191,
    197, 200
Sugar Hill, NH, 249, 275
Sullivan, ME, 99, 147
Sullivan, NH, 245, 275
Sullivan Co., NH, 239, **258,** 259,
    261, 262
Summersworth, NH. *See*
    Somersworth, NH
Sumner, ME, 107, 147
Sunapee, NH, 259, 275
Suncook. *See* Pembroke, NH
Sunderland, MA, 177, 220
Sunderland, VT, 325, 377, 392
Surry, ME, 99, 147
Surry, NH, 245, 263, 275. *See also*
    Surry, VT
Surry, VT, 396. *See also* Surry, NH
Sutton, MA, 193, 220
Sutton, NH, 253, 275
Sutton, VT, 327, 377, 392
Swampfield, MA. *See* Sunderland, MA
Swampscott, MA, 175, 220
Swan Island, ME. *See* Perkins, ME
Swan's Island, ME, 99, 147
Swansea, MA, 171, 220
Swanton, VT, 333, 377, 392
Swanville, ME, 117, 148
Swanzey, NH, 245, 275
Sweden, ME, 107, 148
Sylvester-Canada. *See* Richmond,
    NH

T

Talmadge, ME, 119, 148
Tamworth, NH, 243, 275
Tauconnuck Mountain Plantation.
    See Mount Washington, MA
Taunton, MA, 171, 220
Taunton North Purchase. *See* Easton,
    MA
Taylortown, ME. *See* Union, ME
Temple, ME, 97, 148
Temple, NH, 251, 276
Templeton, MA, 193, 220
Tewksbury, MA, 183, 220
Thetford, VT, 339, 377, 392
Thomaston, CT, 33, 67, 76

Thomaston, ME, 103, 148
Thomlinson, VT. *See* Grafton, VT
Thompson, CT, 43, 67, 76
Thompson and Meserves Purchase,
    NH, 247, 278
Thompsonborough, ME. *See* Lisbon,
    ME
Thorndike, ME, 117, 148
Thornton, NH, 249, 275
Three Ponds, NH. *See* Milton, NH
Tilton, NH, 241, 276
Timberlane, NH. *See* Hampstead, NH
Tinmouth, VT, 343, 378, 392
Tisbury, 173, 220
Tisbury, Manor of. *See* Chilmark, MA
Tiverton, MA, 171, 226. *See also*
    Tiverton, RI
Tiverton, RI, 297, 306, 309. *See also*
    Tiverton, MA
Todd's-town, NH. *See* Henniker, NH
Tolland, CT, 41, 67, 76
Tolland, MA, 179, 220
Tolland Co., CT, 27, CT, **40,** 41
Tomlinson, VT. *See* Grafton, VT
Topsfield, MA, 175, 220
Topsfield, ME, 119, 148
Topsham, ME, 113, 148
Topsham, VT, 339, 378, 392
Torrington, CT, 33, 67, 76
Townsend, MA, 183, 221
Townsend, ME. *See* Southport, ME
Townshend, VT, 347, 378, 392
Trecothick, NH. *See* Ellsworth, NH
Tremont, ME, 99, 148
Trenton, ME, 99, 148
Trescott, ME, 119, 154
Troy, MA. *See* Fall River, MA
Troy, ME, 117, 148
Troy, NH, 245, 276
Troy, VT, 341, 378, 392
Trumbull, CT, 29, 67, 76
Truro, MA, 167, 221
Tuftonboro, NH, 243, 276
Tunbridge, VT, 339, 378, 392
Turner, ME, 91, 148
Turnersburg, VT. *See* Chelsea, VT
Twenty-fivemile Pond Plantation.
    See Burnham, ME
Twitcheville, NH. *See* Harrisville,
    NH
Two Heroes, VT, 335, 394. *See also*
    North Hero, VT; South Hero,
    VT; Middle Hero, VT; Grand
    Isle, VT
Twombly, ME, 109, 154
Tyng's Town, NH. *See* Manchester,
    NH
Tyngsborough, MA, 183, 221
Tyringham, MA, 169, 221

U

Uncataguisset, MA. *See* Milton, MA
Underhill, VT, 329, 378, 392
Union, CT, 41, 67, 76
Union, ME, 103, 148
Unity, Kennebec Co., ME, 101, 154
Unity, Waldo Co., ME, 117, 148
Unity, NH, 259, 276
Upper Ashuelot. *See* Keene, NH
Upper Gilmanton, NH. *See*
    Belmont, NH
Upton, MA, 193, 221
Upton, ME, 107, 148
Usher, ME. *See* Stoneham, ME
Uxbridge, MA, 193, 221

V

Van Buren, ME, 93, 148
Vanceboro, ME, 119, 148
Vassalboro, ME, 101, 148
Veazie, ME, 109, 148
Vergennes, VT, 323, 378, 392
Vernon, CT, 41, 68, 77
Vernon, VT, 347, 379, 392
Verona Island, ME, 99, 148
Vershire, VT, 339, 379, 392
Victory, VT, 331, 379, 392
Vienna, ME, 101, 149
Vinalhaven, ME, 103, 149
Vineyard, VT. *See* Isle La Motte, VT
Volunteers' Town, CT. *See*
    Voluntown, CT
Voluntown, CT, 39, 68, 77

W

Wade, ME, 93, 149
Waite, ME, 119, 149
Waitsfield, VT, 345, 379, 392
Wakefield, MA, 183, 221
Wakefield, NH, 243, 276
Walden, VT, 327, 379, 392
Walden Gore, VT, 339, 394
Waldo, ME, 117, 149
Waldo Co., ME, 89, **116,** 117, 123,
    125
Waldoboro, ME, 105, 149
Wales, MA, 179, 221
Wales, ME, 91, 149
Wallagrass, ME, 93, 149
Wallingford, CT, 37, 68, 77
Wallingford, VT, 343, 379, 392
Walpole, MA, 187, 221
Walpole, NH, 245, 263, 276. *See also*
    Walpole, VT
Walpole, VT, 396. *See also* Walpole,
    NH
Waltham, MA, 183, 221
Waltham, ME, 99, 149
Waltham, VT, 323, 379, 392